Praise for The Law, Then and Now: What About Grace?

"How should modern-day believers—Jewish or non-Jewish—relate to the Law of Moses? This is the question John Metzger attempts to answer in this well-written and interesting book. Solidly based in Scripture, both Old and New Testaments, he attempts to show us how we stand regarding the Mosaic law, and how we can "fulfill the Law of Messiah" (Galatians 6:2). This book nicely fills a lacuna in the literature on this specific question. I like Metzger's practical answers, and I suspect you will too."

> David L. Allen, Southwestern Baptist Theological Seminary
> Dean, School of Preaching and Distinguished Professor of Preaching
> George W. Truett Chair of Ministry

In a Messianic world that is becoming increasingly inundated with the false message of the Hebrew Roots Movement and efforts to entrap people in the concept that we (Jewish and Gentile believers) are obligated to live under some aspect of the post-Yavneh Rabbinic milieu, it is refreshing to know that there is a voice of reason out there. John Metzger's examination of the conditional Mosaic Covenant and the UNCONDITIONAL New Covenant of Jesus is such a voice of reason.

> Dr. Amy Downey, Director of Tzedakah Ministries

I've been following my friend John Metzger's ministry for many years. He is a premier Bible teacher whose thinking is firmly grounded in the Scriptures. In particular, I appreciate his unique way of analyzing complex topics and making them easy to understand. In this important book, that's what he has done with the controversial topic of Torah observance or Law-keeping. He masterfully and patiently explains that there are two Torahs (i.e., two sets of "Laws" or "Instructions") in the Bible. These two laws are complementary rather than contradictory, but one of them has been broken and is therefore no longer in force as binding law, whereas the other one remains fully applicable to all believers, whether Jewish or non-Jewish. The lists throughout the book and the extensive appendices near the end are especially useful. Believers in Yeshua (Jesus) from all denominational and nondenominational backgrounds will greatly benefit from reading this illuminating book.

Dr. Gary Hedrick, President of CJF Ministries

For all who struggle to know how, or if, the Law of Moses fits into living the Christian life, this book is written for you. For all those asking "If the Law of Moses is not the standard and guide for how believers should live today, what is?," this book is especially written for you. While explaining the purposes and the provisions of both the Law of Moses and the Law of Messiah, this book gives a clear and biblical and free grace understanding that believers are under the Law of Messiah today. John Metzger carefully explains how the Law of Messiah (basically the divinely inspired apostolic teaching recorded in the New Testament) gives believers guiding principles and specific instructions for victorious Christian living. Instruction is combined with practical application to help you as you seek to live the victorious Christian life. It is refreshing to read a book written about this topic that is thoroughly grounded not only in truth, but also in grace. Many believers are far from the abundant life that Christ talked about and wants all who believe on Him to experience, for many live shallow Christian lives filled with despair and discouragement. This book describes the liberating and empowering work of the

Holy Spirit in the life of the believer who seeks to walk in the truths contained in the Law of Messiah. I highly recommend this book to those who desire to grow in the grace and knowledge of our Savior the Lord Jesus Christ.

Pastor James D. Preslar, Grace Bible Church, Charlotte, NC

For more than 30 years it's been my privilege to be part of the Messianic Jewish movement of believers in Messiah Jesus, with 17 of those years spent in leadership of a Messianic congregation in a heavily Jewish suburb of New York City. While our congregation was very Jewish in its culture, we also fully embraced Grace. At the same time, it was easy to see that in many corners of the Messianic movement there was confusion over a central question: Are believers in Messiah obligated to keep Mosaic law? In my circles of Grace-embracing Jewish believers in Messiah Jesus, I have heard much discussion over whether the Law of Messiah is something that can be enumerated and written out, or if it is simply a phrase that reflects a heart that is yielded to the Lord, a heart of flesh on which God has written. However, about the Law of Moses there should be no such question, for the Scripture that instructs New Covenant believers tells us with complete certainty that we are no longer under Mosaic law, but are under Grace. So, why is there still confusion? In most cases the cause for uncertainty is unwillingness or failure to see the context in which Scripture is given. That is where John Metzger's book will be so helpful to sincere Bible students. His treatment of the Law of Moses is masterful; I highly recommend it as a guidebook to fully embracing the freedom for which Messiah has set us free.

Messianic Rabbi Mottel Baleston, Messengers Messianic Outreach, NJ

THE LAW,
Then and now

Other Works by This Author

The Tri-Unity of God Is Jewish

Discovering the Mystery of the Unity of God

God in Eclipse: God Has Not Always Been Silent

God in Eclipse [Russian Translation]

Israel's Only Hope: The New Covenant

Poking God's Eye: A Theological and Historical View of Anti-Semitism Based on the Blessings and Curses of Genesis 12:3

THE LAW,
THEN AND NOW:
WHAT ABOUT GRACE?

John B. Metzger

LARKSPUR, COLORADO

Grace Acres Press
PO Box 22
Larkspur, CO 80118
www.GraceAcresPress.com

© 2019
Printed in the United States of America
22 21 20   02 03 04 05 06

ISBN: 978-1-60265-056-5
Ebook ISBN: 978-1-60265-057-2

No part of this publication may be reproduced, stored in a retrieval system, or transmitted in any form or by any means, electronic, mechanical, photocopying, recording, scanning, or otherwise, except as permitted by law, without the prior written permission of the Publisher.

Grace Acres Press also publishes books in a variety of electronic formats. Some content that appears in print may not be available in electronic books.

Scripture in this book has been quoted from the King James Version (public domain), with modernization of the language by the author.

Library of Congress Control Number:2019942752

Cover design: Jesse Gonzales

Dedicated to
Lloyd Elias Scalyer

Lloyd is my brother in Messiah Yeshua. I am a Gentile and he is of the seed of Abraham. He is my friend and spiritual leader at our Messianic congregation that the LORD led him to develop, called The Seed of Abraham Messianic Congregation and located in Lititz, PA.

Lloyd was born in Brooklyn, New York, and as he says, "I was circumcised and had a Bar Mitzvah according to the laws and traditions of our people [Israel]." He remembers worshipping and attending Sabbath school in the synagogue every Sabbath. He also stated that although he read the Hebrew Scriptures and regularly did his morning and evening prayers, he "never had inner peace and assurance, nor did I know anyone who did."

He married a Jewish girl by the name of Judith, and they have spent 59 years together. He refers to himself and Judith as "transplants from Brooklyn" who settled in Ronks, PA, in the Pennsylvania Dutch country in the spring of 1969. It was there in Ronks that he developed the Cherry Lane Motor Inn.

It was also there that, through the witness of a chiropractor, he was confronted with the claims of Christ—and Lloyd's response was, "I couldn't believe it! This guy must be nuts! Can you imagine asking me, someone who is Jewish, if I ever gave adult consideration to the claims of Christ on my life? Because of Jesus, my people were persecuted, suffered, and died. He [Christ] could never be the long-awaited Messiah!" However, because of that question Lloyd began reading his Tanakh [Jewish Old Testament] "incessantly, fall asleep, wake up and read again."

In 1971, both he and Judith called on the name of the LORD for salvation in Messiah Yeshua. As a believer, Lloyd has stated: "I was born a Jew and I will die a Jew, but I have found the Messiah promised to us in the Old Testament and He is Jesus Christ [Yeshua ha Moshiach]." Lloyd became a believer in Messiah Yeshua after 35 years as a devout Jew, studying the Talmud and practicing its law. With that same energy Lloyd also felt the call of his Messiah to share his faith in the Jewish Messiah with the Jewish community in Lancaster, Pennsylvania.

He began a ministry called "Beth Emmanuel Mission" to reach out to the Jewish population, which "raised hackles in the Jewish community." One of those groups was Jews for Judaism, who were very offended by this new ministry in Lancaster targeting Jewish people. They tried to intimidate Lloyd with threatening calls, but to no avail. I remember attending a meeting with him at the Jewish Community Center in Lancaster that hosted an antimissionary to challenge the Jewish community not to be persuaded by these Jewish believers in Jesus Christ. When Lloyd walked in, you could have cut the air with a knife. The tension was very apparent, as was the animosity against Lloyd and all believers in Christ who were present.

Later, in 1993, Lloyd began the Messianic congregation called Seed of Abraham in Lititz. He never got caught up in the erroneous teaching in Messianic circles of Torah observance, because—being Jewish and loving his Jewish heritage—it has been more important to him to be like his Messiah, Jesus Christ. When asked what to call him, he very clearly stated not to call him a Messianic rabbi, but to call him pastor and refer to him as the spiritual leader. I appreciate Lloyd's heart, as he has always encouraged us in Jewish ministry never to take the applause of others but always to give the praise and credit to our LORD. His sensitive heart to his flock is always seen in his words and actions. He is a student of Scripture and his desire to be a witness to the

Jewish community of Lancaster has not abated. He and Judith have also been self-sacrificing financially in serving his LORD without adequate compensation for his labors, often having to dip into savings and retirement funds to live month to mouth. Now, as Lloyd approaches his 82nd year, he is still very active, yet slowing down a bit. I am sure he will one day receive those coveted words from his LORD and Messiah: "Well done, thou good and faithful servant."

Lloyd, thank you for being an example of the believers in Messiah Yeshua. May He give you and Judith continued strength and wisdom in your sunset years of this life. I know you eagerly anticipate the rapture of the body of Messiah. But even in the reality that physical death could come first, you are anticipating the fulfillments of your Messiah, the Son of David, and your King who inaugurated the New Covenant with the circumcision of Jewish and Gentile hearts. He will fulfill for you and all other believing sons and daughters of Abraham, Isaac, and Jacob the Abrahamic Covenant in the Land, with Messiah Himself sitting on the throne of David because of the reality of the New Covenant, our regeneration and our circumcised heart by the blood of Messiah on the "tree" at Calvary.

With love and a life well lived, your Gentile friend,

John B. Metzger

Missionary/Educator with Ariel Ministries

Table of Contents

Dedication ix

Preface xv

Introduction 1

1 The Scriptural Setting of the Law of Moses 9

2 Participants in the Covenant 11

3 The Unity of the Law of Moses 15

4 The Prologue to the Purpose of the Law of Moses 25

5 Purposes of the Law of Moses 35

6 Provisions of the Mosaic Covenant 49

7 The Law of Moses Rendered Inoperative 59

8 The Letter of the Law or the Spirit of Christ 83

9 Points of Clarification 121

10 Examining the Text of Galatians 6:2 135

11 Examining the Text of 1 Corinthians 9:21 187

12 Examining the Text of Romans 8:2 203

13 Participants in the Law of Messiah 233

14 What Is the Law of Messiah ? 241

15 Purpose of the Law of Messiah 247

16 Provisions of the Law of Messiah 251

    Three Key Concepts of the New Covenant 254

17 The Underlying Principle of Freedom for Believers under the Law of Messiah 259

18 Uniqueness of the Law of Messiah 263

19 The Law of Messiah 289

20 The Law of Messiah and Our Sanctification: What Does It Matter? 329

Appendix: Imperative Commands 345

Endnotes 389

Bibliography 403

Preface

My habit has been to write on subjects that are rarely (if ever) talked about, studied, or taught to our families or local churches. Almost every Christian in our sphere of reference is aware of the Mosaic law, whether that term is taken to refer to the Ten Commandments (also called the Decalogue) or the other 603 laws of Moses. What do we, as Christians, do with the Law of Moses? What do Jewish believers in Messiah do with the Law of Moses? How are we to relate to the Law of Moses in the present Church age? Do we obey the Mosaic law system? Do we observe parts of the Mosaic law? Do we relate to the Law of Moses at all?

There is an enormous amount of confusion in the lives of both Jewish and Gentile believers regarding our response to the Law of Moses. Christians, who are members of the body of Christ [Messiah], whether on an individual level, family level, or a church or Messianic congregational level: *what do we do with the law?* There is a biblical answer, but many people have been so programmed by parents, or their local church, or a Messianic synagogue or other religious body that they cannot accept a biblical answer. This is mainly because the biblical answer is so liberating and freeing that most of these people fear that, without the law, [to them] license to sin enters into the picture. This could not be more mistaken. Nowhere in the Scriptures does God issue a license to sin for Christians. The Scriptures teach that both Jewish and Gentile believers have been set apart for holy use by God: He has justified and sanctified us, not for the purpose of allowing us to sin and/or live for self, but to achieve God's purpose of *conforming us to the image of His Son*. So, how does our understanding of His law fit into our daily lives? Within the Messianic movement, the Law of Moses has become an intrinsic part of the belief system in Jesus Christ [Messiah], and for them it is inseparable from their Jewishness.

Even though in this book I am dealing with theology, I am writing for the average person. I am not going to bury you with scholarly theology, but instead help you to understand practical theology. In this book I hope to bring you to an understanding of the purposes and provisions of the Mosaic law and understand the God-intended purpose of it. What we need to understand is that God does not leave us in a lawless vacuum, because every member of the body of Christ [Messiah] is under a law. We further must understand *what* law we are under. One side teaches that the New Covenant is an extension or continuation of the Mosaic law, whereas the other states that Mosaic law has ended because of the outworking of the New Covenant into another law. This new law is called by three names in the writings of Paul: *The Law of Christ* [Messiah], *the Law to Christ* [Messiah] and *the Law of the Spirit of Life*.

You Gentiles who are walking in grace, do you comprehend the idea that you could still be under a law, the Law of Messiah? There is a two-pronged question for you to consider: If so, what is the Law of Messiah; and can I be living in grace and yet be under *any* law? For Jewish believers who abide under the Mosaic law, is it possible that there could be a different law than the Mosaic system? Or do you believe that the Law of Moses is eternal and cannot be replaced? For Jewish believers who long to be embraced by the larger unbelieving Jewish community: Could it be that being Jewish trumps new revelation in the New Testament? Here is a question for both Jewish and Gentile believers: How does the law from each perspective relate to us in the 21st century? Both sides are dug into their trenches, doing religious combat to prove and defend their positions. Churches today do not teach sound doctrine. They are more interested in entertaining people and making them feel good about themselves than in obeying the Law of Messiah, which is based on and enveloped in grace.

I personally have been on a spiritual journey for several years, and I believe that both sides need to look at His context. Come with me on this spiritual journey, during which I have fallen in love with my Savior, the Jewish Messiah. I am only beginning to grasp the riches of His grace as a believer, as Paul states that I have been blessed in heavenly places in Christ Jesus. I am learning what it means to walk in the Spirit and to have victory over my flesh and my sinful nature. It is my passion to bring glory to God in our bodies, and together, as Jew and Gentile, to find ways to live out our lives on a daily basis in this earthly place that is not our home. This is an emotional subject, and opinions and conviction run high for everyone, because no one likes to be wrong. As for me, I am concerned about what God has said.

I readily acknowledge that this is my first attempt to understand and categorize the Law of Messiah by dividing it into categories. It definitely is not a finished product and needs much more attention.

John B. Metzger

Introduction

As we embark on this spiritual journey, the first thing we need to understand is the purpose and the components of the Law. We need to see and grasp all that God has said in His word, which is the Scriptures. Without that understanding we are hopelessly lost in a maze of unbiblical Christian belief, tradition, and opinions. We need to have a proper biblical view of the whole law system that God gave to Moses and Israel at Mt. Sinai. We must recognize that this law was given to Jewish people as a conditional covenant and not to Gentiles.

Most Christians have divided the Mosaic law into three compartments: (1) the moral law; (2) the civil law, which is the legal or legislative aspect of the law; and (3) the ceremonial law, which includes all the temple and priestly functions. This is a convenient division of the law for the sake of study, but the Law of Moses is a unit; God never broke it down into compartments. In fact, the very structure of the law as given by God in the Law of Moses is singular—not the Laws of Moses, plural. God refers to the Law in the singular as a unit of one and not in the plural as many separate laws. The Law is a unit of one, made up of 613 statements of laws. James in his epistle says: *For whosoever shall keep the whole law* [singular, the unit], *and yet offend in one* [point of the law], *he is guilty of all* [the law, plural as a unit of one] (James 2:10).

When the Law of Moses was still in force, Jesus said (in Matthew 5:19) that whoever breaks even one of the more insignificant laws of Moses will be the least in the Messianic Kingdom. He was emphasizing the unity of the Law, of the 613 individual laws that make up the whole Law. The Law stands as a unit. So, he who ignores the Law as a unit, even o*ne of the least of the commandments* and teaches people so, he will be counted as the least in the Kingdom, but he who would obey and teach all the Law would be the greatest in the Kingdom.

Many Christians today have an unbiblical relationship to the Mosaic law and a complete lack of understanding of or knowledge of what replaced it; many do not want to believe it was replaced! The new relationship that believers have with God in Messiah is something called the *Law of Messiah* (Christ), which is a direct result of the New Covenant in His blood. Paul initiates the phrases *Law of Messiah*, the *Law to Messiah*, and the *Law of the Spirit of Life* in three of his epistles, which Christianity has paid little attention to or misunderstands what Paul states: *"For the law of the Spirit of life in Messiah Yeshua has made me free from the law of sin and death* [the Mosaic law system]" (Romans 8:2).

Now, look carefully at that verse. The Holy Spirit who regenerated us—made us alive in the spirit toward Messiah—has made us *free from the law of sin and death*. The law of sin and death is the Law of Moses: it is the ministry of *condemnation* and *death* (2 Corinthians 3:7, 9). That should be encouraging and freeing! So, why do so many people hold onto a system of sin, condemnation, and death as their standard of living when the Holy Spirit has given us life in Messiah?

Paul also uses the second term, "Law of Messiah": *To them that are without law, as without law (being not without law to God, but under the <u>law to Messiah</u>) that I might gain them that are without law* (1 Corinthians 9:21). *Bear you one another's burdens, and so fulfill the law of Messiah* (Galatians 6:2).

So, what is the Law of Messiah? Is the Law of Messiah a restatement of the Mosaic law? Are we as Christians under obligation to the Mosaic law? Many say we are not under law at all, but under grace. However, that verbal expression of belief is just as unbiblical as the statement that we are under the Law of Moses or parts of it. Being under grace does not negate law, but it does raise the question of *what* law we are currently subject to.

A good friend of mine, after being in the Jehovah's Witnesses for many years, said to me: "Now as a believer in Jesus Christ, what do I follow and obey? There is more to living the Christian life than loving one another as Christ loved us." Her question is profound, and reveals her recognition that there is more to the Christian life than what she had been told. There is so much confusion among believers as to the place of the law, the nature or identity of the law, and what we believe as Christians. Are you in that group? I was for many years. What is the Law of Messiah? I turned 73 this year, and have been a believer in Christ for 59 years. I have been in church regularly since my teenage years, and I remember nothing being taught about the Law of Messiah. I have been trained in Bible school and graduate school and have never heard or seen anything that even suggests this subject. Do we grasp the reality that man cannot, whether in a sinful or regenerated state, be without the Law of God?

What is the Law of Messiah? As Christians, what is our relationship to the Law of Moses, and does Mosaic law have any place in the life of a believer in Messiah? In the following chapters I examine the purpose and the unity of the Law of Moses as well as the end of Mosaic law. Legalism, the stepchild of the Mosaic law, has made life for believers a heavy and joyless life. Christ said that He came to give life more abundantly, not to make our lives burdensome, sad, or depressed, always being critical and judgmental. Jesus said: *I am come that they might have life, and that they might have it more abundantly* (John 10:10b).

An application can be drawn from Jesus' words in Matthew 11:29–30: *My yoke is easy and My burden is light.* What load are you under: the law of men, the Law of Moses, or the Law of Messiah? With an easy and light burden, our countenance ought to reflect joy. I have often seen people who have been living an artificial law system. That system has become a system called "legalism" which is not filled with joy, but rather is filled with strictness, sad faces, and sternness, with artificially made rules that to them have become a checklist designed to show Christian spirituality. This is not a picture of the abundant life that Jesus came to give. Paul spoke of joy in the life of a believer in all aspects of life's circumstances: not sadness, not a critical spirit because other believers do not match up to one's preset biases and lists of do's and do not's. Yet our contemporary and traditional religious churches today are filled with sinful, lawless attendees who are no different from the world outside the church doors. To emphasize this, let me share with you some verses from both the Hebrew Scriptures and the New Testament on the joy of a believer and the countenance that all of us are to emulate in all circumstances.

> *The joy of the LORD is your strength.* (Nehemiah 8:10)
>
> *The LORD is my strength and my shield; my heart trusted in Him, and I am helped: therefore my heart greatly rejoices; and with my song will I praise Him.* (Psalm 28:7)
>
> *Be glad in the LORD, and rejoice, you righteous: and shout for joy, all you that are upright in heart.* (Psalm 32:11)
>
> *My lips shall greatly rejoice when I sing unto You; and my soul, which You have redeemed.* (Psalm 71:23)
>
> *In Your Name shall they rejoice all the day: and in Your righteousness shall they be exalted.* (Psalm 89:16)
>
> *I have rejoiced in the way of Your testimonies, as much as in all riches.* (Psalm 119:14)

Your testimonies had I taken as an heritage forever: for they are the <u>rejoicing of my heart</u>. (Psalm 119:11)

<u>I rejoice</u> at Your word, as one that finds great spoil. (Psalm 119:162)

...<u>Your word was unto me the joy and rejoicing of mine heart</u>.... (Jeremiah 15:16)

<u>Rejoice, and be exceeding glad</u>: for great is your reward in heaven.... (Matthew 5:12)

These things have I spoken unto you, <u>that My joy might remain in you</u>, and that your joy might be full. (John 15:11)

And they departed from the presence of the council, <u>rejoicing</u> that they were counted worthy to suffer shame for His Name. (Acts 5:41)

And at midnight Paul and Silas prayed, and <u>sang praises</u> unto God.... (Acts 16:25)

<u>Rejoice</u> with them that do rejoice, and weep with them that weep. (Romans 12:15)

For the kingdom of God is not meat and drink; but righteousness, and peace, and <u>joy in the Holy Spirit</u>. (Romans 14:17)

As sorrowful, yet <u>always rejoicing</u>; as poor, yet making many rich; as having nothing, and yet possessing all things. (2 Corinthians 6:10)

Finally, my brethren, <u>rejoice in the Lord</u>. (Philippians 3:1)

Rejoice in the Lord always: and again I say, Rejoice. (Philippians 4:4)

> *Let the word of God dwell in you richly in all wisdom; teaching and admonishing one another in <u>psalms and hymns</u> and <u>spiritual songs, singing with grace in your hearts</u> to the Lord.* (Colossians 3:16)

> *Whom having not seen, you love; in Whom, though now you see Him not, yet believing, you <u>rejoice with joy unspeakable</u> and full of glory.* (1 Peter 1:8)

> *But <u>rejoice</u>, inasmuch as you are partakers of Christ's sufferings; that, when His glory shall be revealed, you may be <u>glad also with exceeding joy</u>.* (1 Peter 4:13)

From these (and many other) verses, it should be obvious that the Scriptures do not teach a sad or strict countenance, but rather a joy that bubbles up from the heart. Do you emulate that kind of joy in all of your life situations, or have you locked yourself in a shell to hide who you really are because you are afraid that people will think you are not "spiritual"? Is the law being forced upon you by others or even by yourself because you have a poor self-image spiritually? You are now a new creation in Christ. Learn of the grace of God at your disposal and what has been given to you in His grace. Joy is not because all things are good and wonderful and perfect; instead, joy is a state of heart and mind because we are loved by God, despite all our scars and warts and mistakes, and have a personal relationship with our Redeemer. This is not a detour from the subject of the law. Rather, this is what He in His grace has given us. We have the provisions of grace, but somehow we feel that we must also keep some law to merit God's favor.

Today, in the contemporary church, I see lots of praising and motivational speaking to make congregants feel good about themselves. Spiritual poverty is demonstrated by those churches and other pulpits, because they are not encouraging or challenging their flocks to live in obedience to the Law of Messiah. People go out from these churches as starving spiritual infants who are not being taught how to live with joy and lead a victorious Christian life according to the Law of Messiah.

So, what is the Law of Messiah? Are you hungry for the joy of the abundant life you can receive by obeying the Law of Messiah? The next chapters help us understand what the Mosaic law is (which we should *not* be keeping) and what the Law of Messiah is, which we should definitely be keeping and living by. The two systems are as different as day and night.

First one final matter. Two factions have developed, as expressed in the minds and teachings of many Christians, that have contributed to the creation of this problem. One is the practice of dividing the Law into ceremonial, legal, and moral commandments. On the basis of this division, many are led to think that the believer is free from the ceremonial and legal commandments but is still under the moral commandments. The second factor is the belief that the Ten Commandments are still valid today, but the other 603 commandments are not. When confronted by a Seventh Day Adventist, for example, an individual taking such an approach runs into problems concerning the fourth commandment about keeping the Sabbath. At that point, the believer begins fudging or hedging around the issue, and inconsistency results. Although many different groups—both Jewish and Gentile, Messianic and non-Messianic—claim that we are still under the Law of Moses, none who say so actually believe it in reality! Everyone who makes this claim then proceeds to make major adjustments—so many changes, in fact, that Moses himself would not recognize his own Law. No one who claims this today truly follows the Law of Moses *as it is written*. This book is intended to explain why trying to do so (or believing that one should try) is both unnecessary and unbiblical.

1
THE SCRIPTURAL SETTING OF THE LAW OF MOSES

The Scriptures concerning the Mosaic Covenant constitute the largest part of the whole of Old Testament revelation. The development of the law under Moses begins with Exodus 19 and does not end until Deuteronomy 32, a period that spans approximately 40 years. But that is only one aspect of the law that is contained in the Scriptures.

The Law of Moses was in effect for a much longer time period. After Deuteronomy 32 and the death of Moses, the period of the giving of the law was over. Nevertheless, those laws continue from Deuteronomy 32 through the death of the Messiah Yeshua in the Gospel accounts. This spans approximately 1,440 years, from the death of Moses to the death of the Messiah on the cross.

Thus, the total period of the law reaches from the giving of the law stated in Exodus 19 (1446 BC) to the beginning of the Church in Acts 2 (30 AD). When you put that together, the Law of Moses was valid for roughly 1,475 years, a period that includes the span of the four Gospels of Matthew, Mark, Luke, and John. For those 1,475 years, the law applied exclusively to the Jewish population of the earth and not to Gentiles; it simply was not for Gentiles to begin with. The Messiah came under the law to fulfill the law, which is exactly what He did. Again, the Church did not start until Acts 2, on the Jewish feast day of Shavuot, which we call Pentecost, when the Holy Spirit came and indwelt believers [a manifestation of the New Covenant (Ezek 36:26–27)]. The theological setting of the Gospels is Old Testament law theology and not New Testament grace theology of the Church. Do you understand the significant difference that this makes?

Chapter 1

David and Solomon wrote and spoke under the Law of Moses. David revealed the sweet psalmist of Israel, the Messiah, to the Jewish people (2 Samuel 23:1). Solomon wrote words of wisdom to instruct the young how to make godly decisions in life and how to live a good life before God and man using the principles of the law. The prophets challenged Israel to return to the Law of Moses; these prophets' primary goal as God spoke through them was to get Israel to repent and return unto Him so that He could bless Israel and not have to continue to curse Israel. Then the Gospels record the ministry of the Messiah as He came to fulfill the writings of Moses and the prophets and present the Kingdom to Israel. All of the conflicts between Jesus and the Scribes, Pharisees, Sadducees, and Herodians were over issues concerning the Law of Moses. To be precise, the tension centered on the reinterpretation of the Law of Moses made by the Pharisees, who had been adding thousands of man-made rules for more than four centuries.

With that setting in mind, we will proceed to study the participants, purpose, and provisions of the law so that we can understand what the law was to accomplish; why, when, and how it would end; and how it is not part of the Christian life today—though readers should note that I am *not* suggesting that Christians have free rein because of the abolition of the Law of Moses. I will also be presenting the Law of Messiah that we are living under today (a fact that most Christians do not understand). First, though, we must understand the Law of Moses.

2
PARTICIPANTS IN THE COVENANT

When examining any covenant with God, it is very important to know who the participants in the covenant are, as well as the other facts (covered in later chapters). The Mosaic Covenant was made between God and Israel, but it is *not* a unilateral covenant like the Abrahamic Covenant. Rather, it is a bilateral covenant (an agreement between two entities or persons). To understand the ramifications of both terms, it is best to define them up front:

Unilateral covenant: A sovereign act of God whereby He unconditionally obligates Himself to bring to pass specific blessings and conditions for the covenanted people(s). This covenant is characterized by the formula I will, which declares God's determination to do as He promises.[1]

Bilateral covenant: A covenant in which a proposal of God to man is characterized by the formula If you will do (blank), then I will..., whereby God promises to grant special blessings to man providing man fulfills certain conditions set out in the covenant. Man's failure to do so results in punishment.[2]

Here I examine the Mosaic Covenant, the Law of Moses that was made between God and the people of Israel. Moses acted as Israel's representative; that is, the law was introduced to Israel by God through His intermediary Moses. This is clearly shown in Exodus 19:3–8:

> 3 *And Moses went up unto God, and the LORD called unto him out of the mountain, saying, thus shall you say to the house of Jacob, and tell the children of Israel;* 4 *You have seen what I did unto the Egyptians, and how I bare you on*

> *eagle's wings, and brought you unto Myself. 5 Now therefore, if you will obey My voice indeed, and keep My covenants, then you shall be a peculiar treasure unto Me above all people: for all the earth is Mine: 6 And you shall be unto Me a kingdom of priests, and an holy nation. These are the words which you shall speak unto the children of Israel. 7 And Moses came and called for the elders of the people, and laid before their faces all these words which the LORD commanded him. 8 And all the people answered together, and said, all that the LORD has spoken we will do. And Moses returned the words of the people unto the LORD.*

Numerous passages spell out the conditional nature of the Mosaic Covenant. For example, in Exodus 15:26, God begins to lay out the conditional nature of this covenant to Israel: *And He said, if you will diligently hearken to the voice of the LORD your God, and will do that which is right in His eyes, and will give ear to His commandments, and all His statutes, I will put none of the diseases upon you, which I have put upon the Egyptians: for I am Yahweh [the LORD] that heals you.*

Forty years later, in Deuteronomy 28, God lays out the conditional nature of this covenant in clear and unquestionable terms. In verses 1 and 15 you can see that there is no room for misunderstanding the clear words of God: this is a conditional covenant.

> 1 *And it shall come to pass, if you shall hearken diligently unto the voice of the LORD your God, to observe and to do all His commandments which I command you this day, that the LORD your God will set you on high above all nations on the earth.*

> 15 *But it shall come to pass, if you will not hearken unto the voice of the LORD your God, to observe and to do all His commandments and His statutes which I command you this day, that all these curses shall come upon you and overtake you.*

The first passage, in Exodus, was spoken to the exodus generation (Exodus 19). The next passage, in Deuteronomy, was spoken to the children of that exodus generation, who at that point (40 years later) were poised to enter the Promised Land.

Notice as you read through the whole of the Hebrew Scriptures that the Church is never mentioned, contrary to those theological systems and scholars who want to include the Church in the Mosaic law system by reading it back into the Old Testament. The promises of the Mosaic Covenant, and of the Abrahamic, Land,[3] Davidic, and New Covenants, are given exclusively to Jewish people. The only difference is that the Mosaic Covenant is conditional, whereas the others are unconditional in nature. Many Christians today read a New Testament truth back into the Hebrew Scriptures that does not in fact appear in the Hebrew Scriptures, apparently because of their lack of understanding as to who the people of God are. All believers of all ages are the people of God, but God has made specific covenants with the Jewish people that He has not made with the Gentile nations or peoples. This is a foundational truth that must be recognized and understood.

The Church is believers from the nations. The Church is not a nation, nor is it a political force, nor is it an army, nor is it a government to rule over nations, nor is it a system to make the world better (contrary to popular Christian belief). The Body of Messiah is believers—both Jewish and Gentile believers—whose sole purpose is to spread the Gospel[4] of Messiah to all the peoples of the earth and to live in obedience to His Word. The Gentile aspect of the Church comes from all Gentile peoples or nations. God did not make any of the covenants just mentioned with anyone other than the Jewish people. The covenants and promises belong exclusively to Israel. This point is further emphasized by the following passages from the Hebrew Scriptures:

> 7 *For what nation is there so great, who has God so near unto them, as the LORD our God is in all things that we call upon him for?* 8 *And what nation is there so great, that has statutes and judgments so righteous as all this law, which I set before you this day.* (Deuteronomy 4:7–8)

> 19 *He showed His word unto Jacob, His statutes and His judgments unto Israel.* 20 *He hath not dealt so with any nation: and as for His judgments, they have not known them. Praise you the LORD.* (Psalms 147:19–20)

> 4 *Remember ye the law of Moses My servant, which I commanded unto him in Horeb for all Israel with the statutes and judgments.* (Malachi 4:4)

God, Who is the author of all the Scriptures as well as the author of language, has clearly set up a distinction between Jewish people and the Gentiles. The only participants in this Mosaic Covenant are (1) God and (2) Israel, the Jewish people.

3
THE UNITY OF THE LAW OF MOSES

There is a principle that people consistently misunderstand—and they live it out in their Christian lives on a daily basis as it relates to law keeping, whether inside or outside the Messianic community of Jewish believers in Messiah. As you go through your studies of Scripture, observe and note well that God never referred to *the* Law of Moses as being anything other than the singular *Law* of Moses.

Within the Law of Moses, there are 613 subunits (laws or rules) that make up the single, unitary Mosaic law. In Christianity, we have divided the Law of Moses up into three components:

1. The moral law—the Ten Commandments

2. Civil or legal law—governmental law, people dealing with people

3. Ceremonial law—relating to the function of the Temple and the priests that perform the sacrifices

In Judaism, the Law of Moses has been divided into 12 families of commandments (even though God did not divide them or dice them up into sections).

> The twelve families into which the law was categorized were according to the number of the twelve tribes of Israel. These were further subdivided into twelve families of affirmative and twelve of negative commands. The affirmative families concerned: (1) God and His worship, (2) the sanctuary and priesthood, (3) sacrifices, (4) cleanness and uncleanness,

(5) alms and tithes, (6) things to be eaten, (7) Passover and other feasts, (8) rule and judgment, (9) truth and doctrines, (10) women and matrimony, (11) criminal judgments and punishments, and (12) judgments in civil causes. The <u>negative</u> families concerned: (1) false worship, (2) separation from the heathen, (3) things sacred, (4) sacrifices and priests, (5) meats, (6) fields and harvest, (7) house of doctrines, (8) justice and judgment, (9) feasts, (10) chastity, affinity and purity, (11) marriages, and (12) the kingdom.[5]

Thus, both Christians and Jews have divided up the Law of Moses — but God has made no such divisions, for in His Word He clearly presented the law as a unit. Division may be useful for study and categorization of the 613 laws of Moses, but we always need to remember that God did not divide or separate them. James 2:10 captures the intent of the law being a unit: *For whosoever shall keep the whole law, and yet offend in one point, he is guilty of all.*

Then Moses and Paul also lay out the fact of the Law of Moses being a unit, thus creating the obligation to obey all of it and not selective parts of it:

26 *Cursed be he that confirms not <u>all the words of this law</u> to do them....* (Deuteronomy 27:26, emphasis added)

3 *For I testify again to every man that is circumcised, that he is a debtor to do the whole law.* (Galatians 5:3)

Read these verses again and notice that they speak of a plural law (meaning that there is more than one part in the unit), but place it into a singular context as a unit of one. The Law of Moses is a unit. Theologically speaking, it was not to be divided just for our convenience, nor is it referred to in Scriptures as a plurality of 613 items. Rather, it is a unit of one, as James, Paul, and Moses simply stated. The offense of breaking only one point of the Law of Moses before God makes you guilty of breaking the whole law.

Hence, you cannot say, "Well, I am following the moral law of the Mosaic law"; you must understand that there are more than ten moral statutes in the Law to be obeyed.

As we will see later in the discussion of the Law of Messiah, nine of the Ten Commandments were carried over to the age of grace, the Church age. The only one not carried over was Sabbath observance. As to moral laws, Satan was the first to break the moral law, and Adam was the second. The moral law was part of the Mosaic law. There is also a moral law incorporated in the Law of Messiah that Paul references three times (1 Corinthians 9:21, Galatians 6:2, and Romans 8:2). We are never without law! The Law of Messiah with His grace brings life and victory if we yield or submit to the Holy Spirit's control. We will investigate these verses later in this book.

In this description of the unity of Mosaic law, I am speaking to two groups of people: first to Christians who focus on keeping the law, and second to believers in the Messianic movement who are keeping the law so as to be better Jewish persons and because they believe that they are still under the Mosaic law. Remember that the Law is a unit as you read these points and say "I don't have to keep these." You would be right... but why do so many people want to keep their selected laws? It is because of unbiblical teaching, not understanding the Jewish background, and not recognizing the difference between the Mosaic law (which could not provide victory over sin or give eternal life) and the Law of Messiah. However, the Law of Messiah which replaced the Mosaic law does provide victory over sin and new life in Messiah. Some people also think that they have to *do* something to merit their salvation. But to offend in just one point before God makes us guilty of all, so it is important to grasp that all the points of the law are part of the unit as a whole. Messiah kept the law perfectly and paid the price by dying on the cross of Calvary for all our sins. For those who insist that one has to keep the law, let us look at some specific (though randomly selected) points of the Law and see what obedience entails:

- Men, if you do not have a beard and have it trimmed a specific way, you have violated the whole of the Law. (Leviticus 19:27)
- Men and women, the clothing you wear cannot have mixed threads (such as cotton, rayon, and acrylic), so if you wear such fabrics you are violating the whole of the Law. (Deuteronomy 22:11)
- If you have committed adultery, you are not only guilty under the law but you are also to be stoned to death. (Leviticus 20:10–12)
- If you work at all on the Sabbath day (the seventh day), you are to be stoned to death. (Numbers 15:32–36)
- If you have a completely rebellious child in your home, in your obedience to the Law you are to have that child stoned to death. (Deuteronomy 21:20)
- If you have any tattoos (so popular today!), you have violated the Law. (Leviticus 19:28)
- If your married brother died without children, did you marry his widow and raise up seed for your brother? If not, you have violated the Law. (Deuteronomy 25:5–6)
- If you have homosexual relations, you have violated the Law. (Leviticus 18:22; 20:13–14)
- Have you eaten unkosher foods like pork (Leviticus 11:4), shark or shrimp (Leviticus 11:11–12), or vulture or eagle (Leviticus 11:13–20)? If so, you have violated the Law.

- Have you eaten the meat of an animal that died without ritual slaughter? If so, you have violated the Law. (Deuteronomy 14:21)

- Have you given false witness or have sworn falsely in [God's] Name? If so, you have violated the Law. (Leviticus 19:12)

- If you have used God's Name in vain, you have violated the law. (Exodus 20:7; Leviticus 24:11–16)

- If you have made oaths or vows and not kept them, you have violated the Law. (Numbers 30:2)

- If you have fields of wheat and corn, do you leave the corners of your fields for the orphans and widows? If not, you have violated the Law. (Leviticus 19:9; Ruth 2:15–16)

- If you have a vineyard, do you leave gleanings for the poor? If not, you have violated the Law. (Leviticus 19:10)

- If you have cheated people with false measurement on your scales or weights, you have violated the Law. (Leviticus 19:35)

- If you covet your neighbor's belongings, you have violated the Law. (Deuteronomy 5:18)

- If you have loaned money at interest to another believer, you have violated the Law. (Leviticus 25:37)

- Have you borrowed money through a loan that bears interest? If so, you have violated the Law. (Deuteronomy 23:20)

- If your relative dies, you violate the Law if you do not bury that relative the same day. (Deuteronomy 21:23)

- If a court of law does not give a sorcerer the death sentence, it has violated the Law. (Exodus 22:17; Leviticus 20:6, 27)

- A judge who perverts justice violates the Law. (Leviticus 19:15)

- If a witness testifies falsely, he or she is to get the same punishment being sought for the defendant. (Deuteronomy 19:19)

- Have you cursed your father or mother? Have you violently struck them? These are violations of the Law. Do you respect your parents and revere them? If not, you violate the Law. (Exodus 21:17, 21:15, 20:12; Leviticus 19:3)

- Women: when you gave birth to your son or daughter, did you go and have a ritual cleansing 40 days or 80 days after the birth at the temple? If not, then you have violated the law. (Leviticus 12)

- Have you oppressed and taken advantage of the weak? If so, you have violated the Law. (Exodus 22:21)

- Do you or your children imitate the customs and clothing of the pagan world? Any who do so violate the Law. (Leviticus 20:23)

- If you have gone into a trance to foresee events (Deuteronomy 18:10) or engaged in astrology (Leviticus 19:26) or muttered incantations or attempted to talk to the dead (Deuteronomy 18:11), you have violated the Law.

- If you are a cross-dresser (men wearing women's clothing or vice versa), you have violated the Law. (Deuteronomy 22:5)

Now, I have not even touched upon what has been called the moral law, the Ten Commandments, which none of you have obeyed, let alone the ones just listed. None of you! You have violated all or most of the Ten Commandments. The preceding list samples only 30 of the 613 subunits of the Law of Moses. Have you made the appropriate sacrifice to cover your sin or sins before your Holy God? You say, "I do not have to observe the sacrificial and temple laws because Christ died for our sins." Correct, but why do you (a human) try to cancel out the ceremonial requirements of the Mosaic law when God did not cancel them or separate them from all the other points of moral and civil laws in the Mosaic law? Read carefully the statement by Fruchtenbaum:

> In other words, if one breaks a legal commandment, he is guilty of breaking the ceremonial and moral ones as well. The same is true of breaking a moral or ceremonial commandment. To bring the point closer to home, a person under the Law of Moses who eats ham is guilty of breaking the Ten Commandments, although none of the Ten says anything about ham.[6]

All the law stands as a unit. If you violate any of the humanly divided parts, whether moral, civil, or ceremonial aspects of the law, you are guilty of violating the whole. Do you really want to submit to something that God Himself has canceled? Why would you want to go back to a system of condemnation and death (2 Corinthians 3:7, 9)? Does the law give life? Paul without hesitation says no! What does the Mosaic law do? It condemns you so that you cannot stand before God. So, if you want to be Torah observant, go right ahead with your selective, unbiblical law-keeping, which condemns you and through that condemnation asks for death:

> 7 *But if the <u>ministration of death</u> written and engraven in stones was glorious, so that the children of Israel could not steadfastly behold the face of Moses for the glory of his countenance; which glory was to be done away:*

> 9 *For if the <u>ministration of condemnation</u> be glory, much more doth the ministry of righteousness exceed in glory.* (2 Corinthians 3:7, 9)

The Mosaic law was intended to point out your sin, as we will see in chapter 4. There was no power in that law to help you avoid violating the law by sinning against God. Today, though, God has placed at your disposal the power and victory over sin and the law through the blood of the New Covenant and the ministry of the Holy Spirit in all believers' lives, if they want to appropriate it to their lives and walk as He walked (1 John 2:6).

There has been much confusion concerning the application of Mosaic law to people in general. There is no biblical precedent for dividing that law into ceremonial, legal, and moral commandments. There is also no biblical precedent for believers to believe that they are free from the ceremonial and legal commandments, but are still subject to the moral commandments. The Ten Commandments do not stand alone: they are part of the unit that is the Law of Moses. The Law of Moses does not have the power to help you live the godly life that comes as a result of the blood of the New Covenant in Messiah and through the indwelling ministry of the Holy Spirit. Paul asked the Galatians if they received new life from the Law or from the Holy Spirit:

> 2 *This only would I learn of you, received you the Spirit by the works of the law, or by the hearing of faith?* 3 *Are you so foolish? Having begun in the Spirit, are you now made perfect by the flesh [works of the law]?* (Galatians 3:2–3).

As recommended earlier in this chapter, take a good look at the words of Moses in Deuteronomy 27:26, Paul in Galatians 5:3, and James in James 2:10: all these point out the unity of the Law of Moses as a whole. If you want to obey the Law, brace yourself, because you are thus obligated to obey *all* of that Law. Ryrie makes a good point concerning the unity of the Law:

James's use of the law is based on this same concept of the unitary nature of the law. When dealing with the problem of partiality in the synagogues, James decries it on the basis that it is in contradiction to the law of loving one's neighbor as one's self (Lev 19:18; James 2:8). The single violation, he says, makes them guilty of [violating] the whole law (James 2:10). He could not make such a drastic statement if the law were not considered as a unity.[7]

Paul refers to James's point in Galatians 5:14, which we analyze in chapter 9. Notice the point that Yeshua gives in His response to the lawyer who asks Him what is the greatest commandment (Matthew 22:37–40). All these verses refer back to one point of law in Leviticus 19:18, but to be guilty of violation of that one point made them guilty of violating the whole law.

As a passing thought, Adam and Eve in the Garden of Eden, who had only two laws to obey, did not obey them—and look where that got the human race!

4
THE PROLOGUE TO THE PURPOSE OF THE LAW OF MOSES

This chapter shows that the purpose of the Law of Moses has absolutely nothing to do with salvation. Salvation is and always has been *by faith* in the knowledge of the revelation of God to man that had been made in whatever period of biblical history one was born into. This book deals with the dispensation of the law, and the first major covenant during this dispensation was the Law of Moses. This was a covenant made to the Jewish people only, specifying how they were to live out their faith; it was not a means of salvation. It was designed to guide believing Jewish people who were under the law on how to express their faith to their God. Although the content has changed from age to age depending on progressive revelation, the means of salvation has never changed: it is attained *by faith*.

Covenants

As mentioned in chapter 2, there are two distinct types of covenants, and these are not subject to vague ideas or words being imposed by a third unrelated party. First, there are unconditional unilateral covenants, which are formed by God saying I *will* do for an individual or for the nation of Israel what He declared in the covenant irrespective of what humanity does. There are six of theses covenants (see the following list).

The second type of covenant is a conditional bilateral covenant, which uses a formula expressing an agreement between two parties (God and individuals; God and the nation of Israel). That formula is "If you will obey" then "I will" carry out blessing upon you and "if you will not obey" then " I will" carry out My curses

Chapter 4

upon you. Thus, the blessing promised in the Mosaic Covenant is conditioned on Israel's obedience. Table 4.1 is a listing of all the covenants, with the references and parties involved; two are conditional and six are unconditional covenants.[8]

Table 4.1   Covenants

Covenant	Type	With Whom	Source
Edenic Covenant	Conditional Covenant	Adam	Genesis 1:28–30; 2:15–17
Adamic Covenant	Unconditional Covenant	Adam	Genesis 3:14–19
Noahic Covenant	Unconditional Covenant	Noah	Genesis 9:1–17
Abrahamic Covenant	Unconditional Covenant	Abraham	Genesis 12:1–3, 7; 13:14–17; 15; 17; 22:15–18
Mosaic Covenant	Conditional Covenant	Israel	Exodus 19 through Deuteronomy 34
Land Covenant	Unconditional Covenant	Israel	Deuteronomy 29:1–30; 30:1–20
Davidic Covenant	Unconditional Covenant	David	2 Samuel 7:11–16; 1 Chronicles 17:10–14
New Covenant	Unconditional Covenant	Israel	Jeremiah 31:31–34; Ezekiel 36:27–28

These covenants were also made with two different groups of peoples: The first three covenants were given to humanity in general; the other five covenants were given specifically to Israel. These foundational covenants lay down God's development of His plan and purpose for humankind and Israel.

Dispensations

The term *dispensation* comes from two Greek words: *oikonimia* and *aion*. The first means to manage, to regulate, to administer, or to plan; the second word simply means "for an age."

A key to understanding the economies of God, which are also called dispensations, derives from the fact that God progressively revealed Himself and His plan to humankind. To illustrate: Noah did not know what Abraham knew, nor did Abraham know what Moses knew, and so on through biblical history. The Bible was revealed to humanity in a progressive manner, and humanity was responsible to respond to God *by faith* in the then-known will of God: specifically, what God had revealed at that time.

Dispensationalism is at odds with three other forms of theology (replacement theology, amillennial theology, and covenant/reform theology). In this book I use the literal method of interpretation of Scripture, as opposed to the allegorical or spiritualizing methods. We recognize that God is not yet finished with Israel, for He has covenants to fulfill to them. We do not believe that the New Testament Church is Old Testament Israel because we consistently use the literal grammatical method of interpretation. Table 4.2 lists the dispensations and their connection to the covenants, with the *by faith* principle always in effect. The *by faith* principle is expressed in Hebrews 11 which is the third column, with only one name being mentioned for a whole grouping.

Table 4.2 Dispensations

Dispensation	Covenant	With Whom
Innocence	Edenic Covenant	Adam
Conscience	Adamic Covenant	Abel
Human Government	Noahic Covenant	Noah
Promise	Abrahamic Covenant	Abraham
Law	Mosaic, Land, Davidic Covenants	Moses
Grace	New Covenant	Church Believers
Kingdom	(all unconditional covenants fulfilled)	

If you want to see this in more detail, I recommend Renald Showers's book,[9] which will help you to grasp the distinctions of each of these covenants and dispensations in the plan of God. These are key in grasping the unity of the plan of God as He wrote in the Scriptures.

Prologue to the Law of Moses

Look with me at certain passages found in Romans and Galatians, where the point is clearly made that the law cannot justify the person under the law. Pay close attention to what Paul said: *Therefore by the deeds of the law there shall no flesh be justified in His sight: for by the law is the knowledge of sin* (Romans 3:20).

Notice how clearly Paul states his position: *no flesh*—no member of the human race—can *be justified in His sight* by the deeds or works of the law. The law is incapable of justifying man before a Holy God. However, there is a way to be justified, and it goes beyond the scope of the Law of Moses to the New Covenant where we are justified by Messiah's blood (Romans 3:24–25), which is stated in the Hebrew Scriptures as a coming future event. The prophesies of the New Covenant by Moses, Isaiah, Jeremiah, Ezekiel, and Joel were given and would be inaugurated by Messiah with His blood on the cross of Calvary.[10] The law lays out the problem, which is sin. But the law has no power to redeem and justify; that power comes only through the blood of Messiah, not through the Law of Moses or the blood of bulls or goats (Hebrews 9:12–15). Now look again at the words of Paul as to what justifies man and what does not justify man: *Therefore we conclude that a man is justified by faith without the deeds of the law* (Romans 3:28).

Paul is simply saying, as he gives the logical conclusion, that the *deeds of the law* cannot justify humanity. As Paul moves through his teaching in Romans 3, he clearly states that the righteousness of God is without the law. It was manifested and witnessed to by Moses and the prophets (in particular Jeremiah and Ezekiel, but not exclusively by them):

> 21 *But now the righteousness of God without the law is manifested, being witnessed by the law and the prophets;* 22 *Even the righteousness of God which is by faith of Jesus Christ unto all and upon all them that believe: for there is no difference:* 23 *For all have sinned, and come short of the glory of God.* (Romans 3:21–23)

As Paul said, the law had a purpose, and that purpose was not to bring salvation by redemption or justification. Given all this, why try to build your life around the Mosaic Covenant and its law? It is futile to build your spiritual walk in Messiah around a system that has been displaced by the blood of the New Covenant.

Now let us continue with the book of Galatians, in which Paul wrote to Gentile Christians who were being persuaded by Judaizes

Chapter 4

to be law (Torah) observant. Again, look at Paul's clarity as he speaks to the Galatian Church:

> 16 *Knowing that a man is <u>not</u> justified by the works of the law, but by the faith of Yeshua ha Moshiach* [Jesus Christ], *even we have believed in Yeshua ha Moshiach, that we might be justified by the faith of Messiah, and not by the words of the law: for by the works of the law shall no flesh be justified* (Galatians 2:16).

Here Paul reiterates that there is no justification by the works of the law. That justification comes only through Yeshua ha Moshiach (Jesus Christ). We are justified through and by Him, not through keeping a system of law that He has fulfilled and displaced or rendered inoperative. Look at Galatians 3:11, where Paul illustrates, with reference to the dispensation of law and the dispensation of grace, *that no man is justified by the law in the sight of God, it is evident: for the just shall live by faith.* Can we ask for anything clearer?[11]

The promise of salvation is purely and simply stated in Habakkuk 2:4, which Paul references in Galatians. Paul's statement in Galatians 3:21 is a clincher:

> *Is the law then against the promises of God? God forbid: for if there had been a law given which could have given life verily righteousness should have been by the law.*

Question: What produces life, the law or the Spirit (Galatians 3:2)? Did the law provide salvation, or were you saved by faith in Messiah through the ministry of the Holy Spirit? The law cannot provide life; new life is in Messiah. Law will produce *death* and *condemnation* (2 Corinthians 3:7, 9).

Why do people insist on keeping something and living under a system that give nothing but a false spirituality? Also, there is a curse for not keeping the Mosaic law, as Jeremiah clearly states.

So if you want to place yourself under the Law, you are also placing yourself under a curse. See what Jeremiah said:

> 1 *The word that came to Jeremiah from the LORD, saying,* 2 *Hear you the words of this covenant* [Mosaic Covenant], *and speak unto the men of Judah, and to the inhabitants of Jerusalem;* 3 *And say you unto them, thus says the LORD God of Israel; cursed be the man that obeys not the words of this covenant.* (Jeremiah 11:1–3)

Do you want to try and obey part of the law? You have violated all of it. Do you want to be Torah observant? You have violated all of it. You violated it because you *cannot* keep it. The law has come to an *end*. It has been rendered inoperative because God has offered a better law, the Law of Messiah, which through the New Covenant gives regeneration, removal of sin, and the indwelling presence of the Holy Spirit. It gives a life of victory instead of condemnation and death.

There are always some who object to the whole idea of *the end of the law* in Romans 10:4, voiced mainly by people who believe that we are still under the Law of Moses. We are under law, but it is the Law of Messiah, and that is completely different from the Mosaic law.

Some believe—and teach—that the end of the law meant that the Messiah was the "goal" of the law. This distorts the context and the clear words of Paul in Romans and Galatians. The context of the passage as well as the context of Scripture must be observed to see how the Greek word *telos* is to be interpreted. Although "goal" is a possible use or meaning of *telos*, it is not the primary usage. "End of law" is the primary usage. In addition, one must also consider the context of how God worked with man between the systems of law and grace. If your emphasis is keeping the law, you interpret *telos* as being the "goal" of the law. If you understand that we are now under the New Covenant and grace, you can clearly see that the context emphasizes *telos* as the end of the law. To illustrate this, read Matthew 5:17–18, where Christ says that He came to fulfill the law: it was true in that day, because the law was in effect until the death, burial, and resurrection of Messiah.

When He inaugurated the New Covenant, the Law of Messiah replaced the Law of Moses. The Law of Messiah is a new system (and covenant) of law. Some things are repeated or reused, such as nine of the Ten Commandments. Other things are intensified, but other things, such as most of the Mosaic law, are left out. Go back to the previous citations, review some of the Law of Moses, and ask yourself: Are these applicable to me as a believer in Jesus who freed us from the burden of the law?

Others argue that only the ceremonial law was done away with. How can that be, if the law is a unit? Remember: if you offend God in one point of law, you are guilty of breaking the whole law. This extends to the civil or legal aspects of the law as well, and one aspect of the Ten Commandments has also been done away with (the Sabbath).

Another argument that is often made for continued adherence to the law is that "the Hebrew Scriptures say that the Mosaic law observance is eternal." The Hebrew word for "eternal" and "everlasting" is *Olam*. *Olam* in the Hebrew does not mean eternal. The translators of the Scriptures have done believers in both testaments a disservice in translating the Hebrew *Olam* as "forever" or "eternal." In fact, there is no Hebrew word for "everlasting" or "infinite" in the sense of the New Testament Greek words. The word *Olam* in the Hebrew means a specific period of time, because man is limited by and subject to time: It could mean a generation of time, a lifetime, or a long duration of time.[12] Only when used of God, who is not limited by time, does it connote the idea of forever or eternity. This clear distinction must be recognized, because when we understand the contextually bound meaning of the Hebrew *Olam*, it offers a whole new perspective as to its God-given meaning.

The final argument that Jewish believers often make is that "without the Law of Moses, we can no longer be Jews." Since when does God define Jewishness by the law? God defined Jewishness by being a descendant of Abraham, Isaac, and Jacob (Exodus 6:3–4), and identified the sign of Jewishness as circumcision (Genesis 17:9–14). Jewish believers are focusing on a law system that produces death and condemnation (2 Corinthians 3:7, 9). It cannot give life and cannot give us power over sin. The most Jewish thing that Jewish believers in Messiah can do now is to place themselves under the Law of their Messiah.

By maintaining that one must observe the Mosaic law, you belittle the work of Messiah on the cross of Calvary. You thereby regard the Blood of the New Covenant, the Blood of the Lamb of God, as being inadequate to bring life; you make the Law of Moses (a conditional covenant) superior to the New Covenant (an eternal covenant) and consider the Blood of that New Covenant inadequate. You supplant the finished work of Messiah by placing the Law of Moses over the New Covenant—which Jeremiah specifically states *replaces* the broken law system of Moses.

5

Purposes of the Law of Moses

This chapter investigates nine purposes of the Law of Moses, which will help us understand the reasons why God gave the Law of Moses to begin with. It too is an overview rather than a theological treatise. Previous chapters have already made the point that the covenant imposing Mosaic law was made between God and Israel, and that it was a bilateral (conditional) covenant made between two parties: God, being the king of Israel, making this a monarchical rule as the sovereign God over His subjects; and Israel, which agreed to keep His law, statutes, ordinances, and commandments (Exodus 24:3–8). The Mosaic covenant was not made with Gentiles. As Gentiles, we are completely separated from this covenant and its promises (Ephesians 2:11–13), which were given to Israel alone.

Purpose number 1: The Law of Moses was given to reveal the holiness of God and the standard of righteousness that God demanded for a proper relationship with Him; (1 Peter 1:15–16). Paul also states that the Law itself was holy, righteous, and good:
> 1 *And the LORD spoke unto Moses, saying,* 2 *Speak unto all the congregation of the children of Israel, and say unto them, You shall be holy: for I the LORD your God am holy.*
>
> 37 *Therefore shall you observe all My statutes, and all My judgments, and do them: I am the LORD.*
> (Leviticus 19:1–2, 37)

> 15 *But as he which has called you is holy, so be you holy in all manner of living;* 16 *because it is written, Be you holy for I am holy.* (1 Peter 1:15–16)

Chapter 5

> 12 *Wherefore the law is holy, and the commandment holy, and just, and good.* (Romans 7:12)

Let me emphasize that at no time is it taught in Scripture that the Mosaic law was the means of salvation; rather, it was given to reveal the holiness of God to a sinful group of people, chosen by God to be His instrument to reveal His holiness to the Gentile nations. If Israel could have acquired holiness by the works of the Law (which they could not do), it would have constituted teaching the concept of salvation by means of works. We know, instead, that salvation was *always* by grace through faith. The content of faith has changed from age to age, as was reflected in the chapter 4 discussion of dispensations and covenants. The conditional Mosaic law was different from the unconditional Abrahamic Covenant that was instituted before it. The Law of Moses was also different from the New Covenant that Messiah inaugurated with His blood on the cross, which would set in motion the Age of Grace, the Church Age (Acts 2), and the Law of Messiah (discussed later). Again, whether in the dispensation of promise, law, or Grace, what one had to believe in order to be saved differed from age to age, depending on progressive revelation (that which God has revealed over time). However, the means of salvation—*by faith*—never changes: the Mosaic law was never intended to give the Jewish people a way of salvation. It was given to a people already redeemed from Egypt, not in order to redeem them.

Purpose number 2: The Law of Moses <u>provided the rule of conduct</u> for Old Testament Jewish saints. As we saw in chapter 4, the Jewish people were never justified by the works of the law:

> 20 *Therefore by the deeds of the law there shall no flesh be justified in His sight: for by the law is the knowledge of sin.* (Romans 3:20)

28 *Therefore we conclude that a man is justified by faith without the deeds of the law.* (Romans 3:28)

The purposes of the Mosaic law did not include salvation, as Paul clearly states. What that law did do was provide a rule of life for Old Testament Jewish people, dictating how they were to live before God and their fellow men. The law was to be the center, the focus of their spiritual life, and Israel's delight was to be in it, as stated in the Psalms:

2 *But his delight is in the law of the LORD; and in His law does he mediate day and night.* (Psalms 1:2)

77 *Let your tender mercies come unto me, that I may live: for your law is my delight.* (Psalms 119:77)

97 *O how I love your law! It is my meditation all the day.* (Psalms 119:97)

103 *How sweet are your words unto my taste! Yea, sweeter than honey to my mouth.* 104 *Through your precepts I get understanding: therefore I hate every false way.* (Psalms 119:103–104)

159 *Consider how I love your precepts: quicken me, O LORD, according to your lovingkindness.* (Psalms 119:159)

As a reminder, Paul makes clear that no man was justified by the works of the Law (see Romans 3:20 and 3:28, quoted earlier). The law was never, ever a means of salvation. Rather, the law had other purposes: in this case, it provided the rule of life for the Old Testament believer. We must also understand that the more recent Law of Messiah provides the rule of life for New Testament Church saints, who are made up of both Jewish and Gentile believers. The New Testament presented the Law of Messiah, which would also be the rule of life for Church saints (see chapter 8).

Chapter 5

Purpose number 3: This purpose is not generally understood by believers today, because it is so different from what we regularly practice in the Church. The Law of Moses provided <u>occasions for individual and corporate worship</u> for the Jewish people.

According to Exodus 23:14–17 and 34:18–23, Israel was to have three times of corporate worship each year: the Feast of Unleavened Bread, Shavuot (Pentecost), and Succoth (Tabernacles). The first two were in the spring and the third was in the fall:

14 Three times you shall keep a feast unto Me in the year. 15 You shall keep the feast of unleavened bread: You shall eat unleavened bread seven days, as I commanded you, in the time appointed of the month Abib [now Nisan]; *for in it you came out from Egypt: and none shall appear before Me empty: 16 And the feast of harvest* [Shavuot or Pentecost], *the Firstfruits of your labors, which you have sown in the field: and the feast of ingathering* [Succoth, Tabernacles, or Booths], *which is in the end of the year, when you have gathered in your labors out of the field. 17 Three times in the year all your males shall appear before the Lord GOD. 18 The feast of unleavened bread shall you keep. Seven days you shall eat unleavened bread, as I commanded you, in the time of the month Abib* [now Nisan]: *for in the month Abib you came out from Egypt. 19 All that opens the matrix is mine; and every firstling among your cattle, whether ox or sheep, that is male. 20 But the firstling of an ass you shall redeem with a lamb: and if you redeem him not, then shall you break his neck. All the firstborn of your sons you shall redeem. And none shall appear before me empty.*

21 Six days you shall work, but on the seventh day you shall rest: in earing [plowing] *time and in harvest you shall rest. 22 And you shall observe the feast of weeks, of the Firstfruits of wheat harvest* [Shavuot/Pentecost], *and the feast of ingathering* [Succoth/Tabernacles/Booths] *at the year's end.*

23 *Three times in the year shall all your men children appear before the Lord GOD, the God of Israel.*

These were the only days of prescribed worship before God. To the surprise of many people, the Sabbath was never prescribed by God in Scripture to be a day of corporate worship: only a day of rest, not worship.[13] The Sabbath is always the seventh day of the week, it is never the first day of the week. Not only was it never a day of worship, the seventh day was not observed even as a day of rest until the Law of Moses was given.

Some people like to cite Genesis 2:2, which says:
And on the seventh day God ended His work which He had made; and He rested on the seventh day from all His work which He had made.

However, this is a statement of fact, not a command. It simply states what God did after six days of creation. Note too that there is no mention of Sabbath observance through the days of Adam, Noah, Abraham, Isaac, Jacob, and Joseph, or the first eighty years of Moses' life. A day of rest is not mentioned again until the Exodus from Egypt. That is a span of more than 2,000 years in which the Sabbath was not practiced or even mentioned. People might say Sabbath observance is a principle, but a principle is entirely different from a *Thus says the LORD* command.

Purpose number 4: The Mosaic law was to keep the Jewish people a distinct and separate people from the Gentile world around them (Leviticus 11:44–45; Deuteronomy 7:6, 14:1–2). This purpose was to make Israel unique and separate in all their customs and culture; they were not to absorb the customs and culture of the pagan nations around them. Here is a brief sampling of the laws that separated the Jewish people from the Gentiles:

- Dietary laws, involving their eating habits (Leviticus 11:1–47)

- Clothing habits and laws, again to make them different in dress from the nations around them (Leviticus 19:19)

- Worship habits, to separate them from all the heathen idolatry practice of the nations around them (Leviticus 1, 7, 16, 23)

- Sexual habits (Leviticus 12)

- Beard cutting (Leviticus 19:27)

These laws were not intended to make Israel and Jews appear weird, but to differentiate them from the common pagan practices of the heathen nations around them. They were to be a kingdom of priests by how they lived before the Gentile world.

Purpose number 5: The Law of Moses was to serve as a <u>wall of partition to separate the Jewish people and the Gentiles</u>, as stated in Ephesians 2:11–16. These laws were to keep Gentiles, as Gentiles, from enjoying the Jewish spiritual blessing of the unconditional covenants. Because of this purpose, Gentiles were both alienated from the commonwealth of Israel, and made strangers to the covenants of the promises. Observe how clearly Paul makes the distinction in Ephesians:

11 Wherefore remember, that you being in time past Gentiles in the flesh, who are called uncircumcision by that which is called the circumcision in the flesh made by hands. 12 That at that time you were without Messiah, being aliens from the commonwealth of Israel, and strangers from the covenants and promise, having no hope, and without God in the world: 13 But now in Messiah Yeshua you who sometimes were far off are made nigh by the blood of Messiah. 14 For He is our peace, who has made both one, and has broken down the middle wall of partition between us; 15 *Having abolished in His flesh the enmity, even the law of commandments contained in ordinances; for to make in Himself of two, one new man, so making peace.* 16 *And that He might reconcile both unto God in one body by the cross, having slain the enmity thereby.* (Ephesians 2:11–16)

19 *Now therefore you are no more strangers and foreigners, but fellow citizens with the saints, and of the household of God;* 20 And are built upon the foundation of the apostles and prophets, Yeshua Messiah Himself being the chief cornerstone. (Ephesians 2:19–20)

Along with these verses, consider the event that happened in the Temple at the death of Messiah, when the veil of the temple was rent in two from the top to the bottom. It was torn by God to indicate that now man will have access to God without the Aaronic high priest and the sacrificial blood (Matthew 27:51; Mark 15:38). Now Messiah's blood is the sacrificial blood, the blood of the New Covenant. Look also at Hebrews 10:19–21 and see again the ramifications of the veil, His flesh:

19 *Having therefore, brethren, boldness to enter into the holiest by the blood of Yeshua,* 20 *By a new and living way, which He has consecrated for us, through the veil, that is to say, His flesh;* 21 *and having an high priest over the house of God.* (Hebrews 10:19–21)

What power is in these words! We can now with boldness enter before the presence of God in the most holy place of all places in the whole universe: before the very throne of God, because of the blood of Yeshua (Jesus). In the past, it would be death for anyone, even the high priest, to enter the holy of holies except with blood on the Day of Atonement; now, through the blood of Messiah, we can enter His presence, coming before His throne without fear of death and bringing our praise, requests, and worship before

God in a *new and living way*. There is another great benefit of the New Covenant that was not present in the Mosaic law. Hebrews continues to say that the veil, His incarnation, was His flesh. Meditate on what the writer of Hebrews just said. It is breathtaking! Yes, we now have a new high priest, one who is of the order of Melchizedek.

This Mosaic law and the commandments were given to keep the Gentiles separate from Israel. Israel received the Abrahamic, Land, Davidic, and New Covenants. This Mosaic covenant kept the Gentile as a Gentile and the Jew as a Jew, but with the change in covenants both Jew and Gentile are brought together: the *middle wall* was broken down and with *His flesh*, the veil, God has made the two one body in Messiah.

Purpose number 6: The Mosaic law was <u>to reveal sin</u>, as stated in Romans:

19 *Now we know that what things so ever the law says, it says to them who are under the law: that every mouth may be stopped, and all the world may become guilty before God.* 20 *Therefore by the deeds of the Law there shall no flesh be justified in His sight: for by the law is the knowledge of sin.* (Romans 3:19–20)

5:20 *Moreover the law entered, that the office might abound, but where sin abounded, grace did much more abound.* (Romans 5:20)

7:7 What shall we say then? Is the law sin? God forbid. No, I had not known sin, but by the law: for I had not known lust, except the law had said, You shall not covet. (Romans 7:7)

The Mosaic law both revealed sin and condemned sin, calling for sinners to be put to death. Israel was subject to the 613 individual rules that made up the Law of Moses and also revealed their sin.

The purpose of revealing sin can be used even today to show unsaved individuals that they are sinners and in need of salvation.

Purpose number 7: The Law of Moses would make one sin more as Romans 4:15 and 5:20 states:

> 15 *for the law works wrath; but where there is no law, neither is there transgression.* 20 *And the law came in besides, that the trespass might abound; but where sin abounded, grace did abound more exceedingly.*

Paul continued to lay out the law in Romans 7 as he tried to help people understand that the Law brings not life, but rather condemnation and death. Without the law, humankind would not have known sin; that is, they would not have known they were sinners. It does not mean that they did not sin before the law was issued; it means that sin was thereafter identified and clarified in their lives, and they were more guilty with the law than without it. Ken Ham makes an interesting observation:

> The Bible clearly teaches [as in Romans 7:7] that each human being is a sinner, in a state of rebellion against God. Initially, the Law was given, as Paul states, to explain sin. But knowing about sin was not a solution to the problem of sin.[14]

Knowing about sin does not solve man's dilemma, nor does the Law of Moses have the solution. In Romans, 7 where Paul helps the believer see that law made man sin more:

> 7 *What shall we say then? Is the law sin? God forbid. No, I had not known sin, but by the law: for I had not known lust, except the law had said, "You shall not covet."* 8 *But sin, taking occasion by the commandment, wrought in me all manner of evil desire. For without the law sin was dead.* 9 *For I was alive without the law once: but when the commandment came, sin revived, and I died.* 10 *And the commandment, which was ordained to life, I found to be unto death.* 11 *For*

Chapter 5

> sin, taking occasion by the commandment, deceived me, and by it slew me. 12 Wherefore the law is holy, and the commandment holy, and just, and good. 13 Was then that which is good made death unto me? God forbid. But sin, that it might appear sin, working death in me by that which is good; that sin by the commandment might become exceeding sinful. (Romans 7:7–13)

Paul then summarized the situation in 1 Corinthians 15:56: *The sting of death is sin; and the strength of sin is the law.*

Why do believers want to put themselves under a system whose epitaph is death?

Purpose number 8: Paul points out that this would <u>show sinners that there was absolutely nothing they could do on their own to please God</u>; man has no ability to keep the law perfectly or to attain the righteousness of the law:

> 14 *For we know that the law is spiritual: but I am carnal, sold under sin. 15 For that which I do I allow not: for what I would, that do I not; but what I hate, that do I. 16 If then I do that which I would not, I consent unto the law that it is good. 17 Now then it is no more I that do it, but sin that dwells in me. 18 For I know that in me, that is, in my flesh, dwells no good thing: for to will is present with me; but how to perform that which is good I find not. 19 For the good that I would I do not but the evil which I would not, that I do. 20 Now if I do that I would not, it is no more I that do it, but sin that dwells in me. 21 I find then a law, that, when I would do good, evil is present with me. 22 For I delight in the law of God after the inward man: 23 But I see another law in my members, warring against the law of my mind, and bringing me into captivity to the law of sin which is in my members. 24 O wretched man that I am! Who shall deliver me from the body of this death? 25 I thank God through Yeshua Messiah our Lord. So then with the mind I myself serve the law of God;*

but with the flesh the law of sin. (Romans 7:14–25)

This passage shows that the Apostle Paul struggled with the flesh and sin just as you and I do! Although the law sealed our fate before Messiah's death on the Cross, we can now have victory over sin and death because of the blood of the New Covenant and the indwelling of the Holy Spirit. Also Romans 7 is not dealing with Paul before his salvation. He was writing to the church that was struggling as he did with this reality.

Purpose number 9: The law was intended to drive one to faith, according to Romans 8:1–4 and Galatians 3:24–25.

All of these purposes point to the fact that the law was inadequate for salvation. The law has been impossible to escape, and the reality of the law makes us sin more. In itself the law has absolutely no merit, instead having been designed by God to show us our sin, reveal that we are indeed sinners separated from God, and drive us toward saving faith in Messiah.[15]

These purposes of the law can be generally categorized in four aspects:

- The first aspect is in relation to God, as it reveals His holiness and His righteous standards.

- The second aspect is in relation to Israel, to keep them a distinct people, to provide a rule of life for them, and to guide individual and corporate worship.

- The third aspect is in relation to Gentiles; for them it serves as the middle wall of partition keeping them separated from the covenants and promises given to Israel.

- The fourth aspect is in relation to sin, to reveal and show what sin is, and to make it clear that humans cannot attain the righteousness of the law on their own, thus driving them to faith.

The law manifested by the flesh produced death, but by Messiah's blood, all condemnation is removed: we can now walk in the spirit and not suffer the condemnation of the law because of our carnal flesh. Another very important fact is that the law was abolished and nullified at the death, burial, and resurrection of Messiah. He rendered the law inoperative by the blood of the New Covenant. Both Paul and the writer of Hebrews make four points that clearly show the law to be temporary and finished:

For Messiah is the end of the law unto righteousness to everyone that believes. (Romans 10:4)

Knowing that a man is not justified by the works of the law, but by the faith of Yeshua [Jesus] Messiah [Christ], even we have believed in Yeshua Messiah, that we might be justified by the faith of Messiah, and not by the works of the law: for by the works of the law shall no flesh be justified. (Galatians 2:16)

For the law made nothing perfect, but the bringing in of a better hope did; by the which we draw night unto God. (Hebrews 7:19)

Wherefore then served the law? It was added because of transgressions, till the Seed should come to whom the promise was made. (Galatians 3:19)

All nine purposes of the law show that the law was temporary, intended to lead us to Messiah, who would not only fulfill the law, but also, in His death, burial, and resurrection with His blood of the New Covenant, finish the law and institute something that was promised in the Hebrew Scriptures. All this He inaugurated at the cross of Calvary.

Though the law has been rendered inoperative, we are certainly free to keep portions of it if desired, as long as the individual doing so understands that it merits him or her nothing before God. It also means that a person who has the freedom in Messiah to practice an aspect of the law (or any other personal conviction) does not have the right to force his conviction upon another believer; this is legalism and bondage of one's conviction placed on others. I know several Jewish believers who keep certain aspects of the law (such as the feasts, Sabbath meal, and so on) as a means to stay connected with and to their unsaved Jewish family and friends. They have the freedom to "keep" portions of the law if desired, and others have the freedom not to. The Apostle Paul teaches in Romans 14:13–21 and 1 Corinthians 8:1–13 that both Jewish and Gentile believers have that right unless their exercise thereof causes a weaker brother to stumble.

Basically, Paul is saying that a sin nature needs a base of operations; furthermore, our sin nature uses the law as such a base. Paul notes that where there is no law, there is no transgression; the term *transgression* refers to a specific type of sin that violates a specific commandment. He did not mean, of course, that there was no sin before the law was given. Men have always been sinners, but they were not transgressors of the law until the law was given. Once the law was established, the sin nature of humankind had something to transgress, causing individuals to violate the commandments and sin all the more.

The overall purpose of the law was to lead Jews (and Gentiles) to faith: specifically, faith in Jesus the Messiah (Galatians 3:24). As hard as we may try to keep the law perfectly, our sin nature prevents us from doing so, as Paul describes in the seventh chapter of Romans. God in His grace sent the Messiah to establish the New Covenant; He thereby rendered the law null and void and clarified that salvation is attainable *by faith alone*.

6
Provisions of the Mosaic Covenant

Chapter 5 dealt with the purposes of the Mosaic Covenant, and in this chapter we will look at the actual provisions of that covenant.[16] A *provision* is a clause within a covenant or document that sets out the details of the document or law. Thus, going through these provisions that the Scriptures make concerning the law allows us to define the boundaries of the law. In short, the Mosaic Covenant is God's rules for governing His people Israel in His theocracy.

Limitations

The Mosaic law had limitations. It was limited in that it was given only to the Jewish world, it was limited in its scope of time, and it was limited in what it could do regarding sin.

The Mosaic law was given only to Israel, whereas God gave the first three covenants to the Gentile population at large. With the fourth covenant, God dealt with one of the many families on the earth, making His covenant with the father of the Jewish people, Abraham. The Mosaic law, the fifth covenant, was not unconditional: it was a bilateral covenant between God and Israel, and it was limited in both time and coverage, in that the covenant would apply only until the New Covenant was inaugurated by Messiah when He died on the cross—not just for Jewish sin, but for Gentile sin as well. So, the time period of this covenant went from the giving of the law through Moses to the death, burial, and resurrection of Messiah. Also, the Mosaic law only covered the sin of an individual or the nation on a limited basis, and had to be repeated annually. When a man sinned, he had to make the appropriate sacrifice to cover his sin, though this did not remove the sin. It was a temporary and inadequate measure for dealing with sin, which stopped the gap until sin was finally and ultimately conquered by Messiah.

Bilaterality and Conditionality

The Mosaic law was a conditional covenant, a bilateral covenant between their King/Redeemer and Israel as the vassal nation. Exodus 15:26 records God's giving of the conditional terms and Exodus 24:3–8 relates the agreement of Israel to abide by the treaty (covenant) that their Sovereign made with them.

26 And said, if you will diligently listen to the voice of the LORD your God, and will do that which is right in His sight, and will give ear to His commandments, and keep all His statutes, I will put none of these diseases upon you, which I have brought upon the Egyptians: for I am the LORD that healeth you. (Exodus 15:26)

3 And Moses came and told the people all the words of the LORD and all the judgments: and all the people answered with one voice, and said all the words which the LORD has said will we do. 4 And Moses wrote all the words of the LORD, and rose up early in the morning and built an altar under the hill, and 12 pillars, according to the 12 tribes of Israel. 5 And he sent young men of the children of Israel, which offered burnt-offerings, and sacrificed peace-offerings of oxen unto the LORD. 6 And Moses took half of the blood, and put it in a basin; and half of the blood he sprinkled on the altar. 7 And he took the book of the covenant, and read in the audience of the people: and they said, all that the LORD has said will we do, and be obedient. 8 And Moses took the blood, and sprinkled it on the people, and said, Behold the blood of the covenant, which the LORD has made with you concerning all these words. (Exodus 24:3–8)

In Deuteronomy 28, the stark reality of the conditional nature of the covenant is clearly seen. In chapter 28:1–15, Israel's Sovereign King lays out the blessings that will be given to them if they will obey His law, statutes, and commandments. In verses 16–68, God lays out how He will curse them if they do not obey His law, statutes, and commandments. This type of covenant was called a suzerain/vassal treaty.

Blood Sacrifices

Before this covenant, the patriarchs or an individual of a family was obligated to make blood sacrifices for sin. God set up a system whereby the Levitical priests (the children of Levi, the son of Jacob) would officiate between the sinner and God. The Mosaic law demanded several types of sacrificial offerings. In Leviticus 1–7 God laid out five sacrificial offerings that must be given by an individual sinner: (1) burnt offering, (2) trespass offering, (3) sin offering, (4) peace offering, and (5) meal offering. There was also one other offering, made annually, to atone for the sins of the nation (Leviticus 16). The Day of Atonement did not remove sin, but it did cover sin until the blood of Messiah was given on the cross of Calvary. Many people do not understand the need or necessity that God has placed on the blood of animals to be given in the place of the sinner. The following verses help to show why God has emphasized blood.

For the life of the flesh is in the blood: and I have given it to you upon the altar to make an atonement for your souls: for it is the blood that makes an atonement for the soul. (Leviticus 17:11)

1 For the law having a shadow of good things to come, and not the very image of the things, can never with those sacrifices which they offered year by year continually make the comers thereunto perfect. 2 For then would they not have ceased to be offered? Because that the worshippers once purged should have had no more conscience of sins. 3 But in those sacrifices there is a remembrance again made of sins every year. 4 *For it is not possible that the blood of bulls and of goats should take away sins.* (Hebrews 10:1–4)

10 *By the which we are sanctified through the offering of the body of Yeshua ha Moshiach* [Christ] *once for all.* 11 *And every priest stands daily ministering and offering oftentimes the same sacrifices, which can never take away sins:* 12 *But this Man, after He had offered one sacrifice for sin forever, sat down on the right hand of God.* 13 *From henceforth expecting to His enemies to be made His foot-stool.* 14 *For by one offering He has perfected forever them that are sanctified.* (Hebrews 10:10–14)

Diet

Under the Noahic Covenant, humans ceased being vegetarians only and were permitted to eat meat. The Mosaic Covenant still allows both vegetarian and meat diets, but God imposed restrictions on Israel, which were for Israel only. God put in place the kosher dietary laws, which made the following provisions about animals:

- Beasts had to be both cloven-hoofed and cud-chewing
- Fish had to have both fins and scales
- Concerning fowls, no birds of prey were allowed
- Concerning insects, only one type of locust was permitted

Kosher law can be confusing, because there are actually two kosher laws: one given by God from Mt. Sinai and the other consisting of rabbinic man-made kosher rules. One is from God; the other was created by man and was not authorized by God.

Death Sentences

The Noahic Covenant established capital punishment for murder. Under the Mosaic law—which relates to Israel only!—this death penalty was expanded, to be carried out for the sins of "premeditated murder, kidnapping, adultery, homosexuality, incest, bestiality, incorrigible delinquency in a child, striking or cursing parents, offering a human sacrifice, false prophecy, blasphemy, profaning the Sabbath, sacrificing to false gods, magic and divination, unchastity (adultery), rape of a betrothed virgin,"[17] and cursing God. Under the Noahic unconditional covenant, the death sentence was still to be carried out, but in the Age of Grace the multiple death sentences are not applicable, because the law itself has been rendered inoperative.

Circumcision

Under the Mosaic law, all Jewish males were to be circumcised, as a sign of the covenant. Circumcision was first instituted under the Abrahamic Covenant (Genesis 17), to show Jewishness. Under the Mosaic law, circumcision was a sign to the Jewish male that he was a son of the covenant, meaning that he was obligated to obey the Law of Moses. Thus, circumcision is mandated in two covenants, though to serve two different purposes. Moses and the Apostle Paul clearly give the purpose of circumcision in Leviticus 12:3 and Galatians 5:3:

> And in the eighth day the flesh of his foreskin shall be circumcised. For I testify again to every man that is circumcised, that he is a debtor to do the whole law.

Many people become confused as to these two reasons for circumcision. Under the Abrahamic Covenant, it was a sign of the covenant—a sign of Jewishness—and it was mandatory for Jews only. Under the Mosaic Covenant, circumcision was the means of indicating submission to the Law of Moses; it was mandatory for all Jews. Circumcision under the Mosaic law denoted a male's becoming a son of the commandments. It was also mandatory for any Gentiles who wished to become part of the Commonwealth of Israel.

Thus, the reasons for circumcision are completely different and separate. Jewish believers in Messiah circumcise their sons because of the Abrahamic Covenant, not the Mosaic Covenant, for they are no longer under the Law of Moses but under the Law of Messiah.

In the New Testament, under the New Covenant, Paul warned the Galatian believers that if they submitted to circumcision, they would be obliged to keep the whole Mosaic law, not just this one commandment (Galatians 5:3). They were not Jewish to begin with, nor were they proselytes to Judaism, which means they were not under the law in any way. But by getting circumcised, a man would become subject to the whole law, not just one point of the law. James said to Jewish believers in Messiah that to offend in one point of the law is to become guilty of all. In Galatians 5:3, Paul is saying the same thing as James (though from a different angle): *"I testify again to every man that is circumcised, that he is a debtor to do the whole law."*

Sabbath Observance

Israel was given Sabbath observance as the token of the Mosaic Covenant. Five observations are important in understanding God's provision for Israel regarding their observance of Sabbath.[18]

First, the token of the Mosaic Covenant was a sign between God and Israel. It was a sign that Israel had been set apart by God (Exodus 31:12–17); it was a sign of the Exodus (Deuteronomy 5:12–15; Ezekiel 20:10–12); and it was a sign that Yahweh was Israel's God (Ezekiel 20:20). Every reason given for observance of the Sabbath has relevance only to Israel, not to Gentiles or the Church.

12 *And the LORD spoke unto Moses, saying,* 13 *Speak you also unto the children of Israel, saying, Verily My Sabbaths you shall keep: for it is a sign between Me and you throughout your generations; that you may know that I am the LORD that does sanctify you.* 14 *You shall keep the Sabbath therefore; for it is holy unto you: every one that defiles it shall surely be put to death: for whosoever does any work thereon, that soul shall be cut off from among his people.* 15 *Six days may work be done; but in the seventh is the Sabbath of rest, holy to the LORD: whosoever does any work on the Sabbath day, he shall surely be put to death.* 16 *Wherefore the children of Israel shall keep the Sabbath, to observe the Sabbath throughout their generations, for a perpetual covenant.* 17 *It is a sign between Me and the children of Israel forever: for in six days the LORD made heaven and earth, and on the seventh day He rested, and was refreshed.* (Exodus 31:12–17)

12 *Keep the Sabbath day to sanctify it, as the LORD your God has commanded you.* 13 *Six days you shall labor, and do all your work:* 14 *But the seventh is the Sabbath of the LORD your God: in it you shall not do any work, you, nor your son, nor your daughter, nor your manservant, nor your maidservant, nor your ox, nor your ass, nor any of your cattle, nor your stranger that is within your gates; that your manservant and your maidservant may rest as well as you.* 15 *And remember that you were a servant in the land of Egypt, and that the LORD your God brought you out from there through a mighty hand and by a stretched out arm: therefore the LORD your God commanded you to keep the Sabbath day.* (Deuteronomy 5:12–15)

10 *Wherefore I caused them to go forth out of the land of Egypt, and brought them into the wilderness.* 11 *And I gave them My statutes, and showed them My judgments, which if a man do, he shall even live in them.* 12 *Moreover also I gave*

> *them My Sabbaths, to be a sign between Me and them, that they might know that I am the LORD that sanctifies them.* (Ezekiel 20:10–12)
>
> *And hallow My Sabbaths; and they shall be a sign between me and you, that you may know that I am the LORD your God.* (Ezekiel 20:20)

Second, the Sabbath was not a creation ordinance; it began only with Moses. Genesis 2:1–3 only states what God did on that day; there is no command to observe that day in any way. The word *Sabbath* is not even used in the Genesis account, in which that day of the week is just called the seventh day.

> 2 *And on the seventh day God ended His work which He had made; and He rested on the seventh day from all His work which He had made.* 3 *And God blessed the seventh day, and sanctified it: because that in it He had rested from all His work which God created and made.* (Genesis 2:2–3)

From Adam to Moses, there is no record of anyone keeping the Sabbath. Although God imposed a number of obligations upon humanity in the previous covenants, keeping the Sabbath was not one of them.

Third, the Sabbath was a day of rest, not a day of corporate worship (another common misconception). As the Sabbath commandment was further developed in other parts of the Law of Moses, what was meant by "resting" on the Sabbath was largely a matter of prohibitions in the Law of Torah:

- No gathering of manna (Exodus 16:23–30)
- No kindling of fire (Exodus 35:3)
- No gathering of wood (Numbers 15:32)

Outside the Law or Torah, other prohibitions for the Sabbath included:

- No burden bearing (Jeremiah 17:21)
- No trading (Amos 8:5)
- No marketing (Nehemiah 10:31; 13:15, 19)

Nothing was said of corporate worship in the Law of Moses; the Sabbath was simply a day of rest and cessation of labor, and [physical] refreshment before the Lord. The Sabbath synagogue services found in the New Testament originated with the Babylonian captivity, not with the Law of Moses. Note: Some confusion might be caused by the fact that the phrases *the Sabbath* and *a holy convocation* are often used together. There were three times of corporate worship, called the Pilgrim Feasts: Unleavened Bread, Shavuot (Pentecost), and Succoth (tabernacles). These are different from the Sabbath.

Fourth, the Sabbath was a token sign of the Mosaic Covenant and it was intended only for Israel and not the Church.

Fifth, as a sign, the Sabbath was in force only as long as the Mosaic Covenant was in force. Mandatory Sabbath keeping thus came to an end when the Mosaic Covenant came to an end.

Some clarification and distinction should be made concerning the Sabbath mandated in the Mosaic law and the Christian Sunday worship which many people call the Sabbath Day. Although the other nine commandments of the Ten Commandments were carried over into the Church Age, the Sabbath commandment in the Ten Commandments of the Mosaic law was not. There is no statement in Scriptures identifying Sunday as the Sabbath or commanding the Church to have a worship day.

Chapter 6

The Sabbath was a Jewish token given to Jewish people in the Mosaic Covenant. The Law of Moses has been rendered inoperative, and Gentiles were never bound by or to it.

Also, Sabbath is always the seventh day of the week, never the first day. Biblically there is no such thing as a Christian Sunday Sabbath. In the New Testament, you will find that the Church consistently met on the first day of the week because the Lord Jesus rose from the grave on the first day of the week. Nowhere in the New Testament is the Church told or commanded to meet either on the Sabbath or on the first day of the week. The New Testament church has the freedom to meet on any day of the week. That goes against Christian culture, but then "Christian culture" is a man-made thing anyway.

7

THE LAW OF MOSES RENDERED INOPERATIVE

This chapter will be a challenge to some people, especially those who believe that the Law of Moses is central in their walk with Messiah. Others in the Gentile Christian community will also struggle with the biblical fact that the Law of Moses is history and the Law of Messiah is now reality. These two systems of law are as different as night and day. My aim is to be biblical, because the reality of the Law of Messiah transcends any other laws and beliefs.

The Gospels reveal an undercurrent of an upcoming change, which started at the beginning of Yeshua's ministry. As a Jew, Yeshua came under the Law of Moses. But Yeshua states that the law and the Prophets were unto John, and that since then the kingdom has been preached by him (Matthew 11:13; Luke 16:16). Throughout the Gospels you find change, something entirely new and different from the old law. Messiah challenges people to "come to Him, learn of Him, listen to Him, obey Him as if all other authority was at an end."[20] He spoke as having authority, not as the scribes. He spoke of His coming death and glorification knowing that something very different, something strange and uniquely important in God's dealing with men, was about to happen. He spoke of not putting new cloth on old wine skins, and he stated that His yoke is easy in contrast to the yoke of the Mosaic law [and in particular the rabbinic laws]. He referenced a ministry change ahead, the putting aside of the Law of Moses because in the immediate future there would be the indwelling of the Holy Spirit and the initiation of the New Covenant in His blood.

The Mosaic Covenant was the basis for the dispensation of law. It was a Jewish, conditional, bilateral covenant that ended with its fulfillment in the Messiah who kept it perfectly. So, the status of the Mosaic law today is that it is rendered inoperative;[21] it has ceased to be an active covenant (Romans 10:4; 2 Corinthians 3:3–11; Galatians 3:19–29; Ephesians 2:11–18; Hebrews 7:11–12, 18–20), because it has been fulfilled in the blood of Messiah, the blood of the New Covenant. This is the basis for the Law of Messiah in the New Covenant that we are under in the dispensation of grace today. To Jewish believers, Messiah died on the cross, shed His sacrificial blood to free them from the penalty of the law which had been constantly broken (Jeremiah 31:32; Deuteronomy 31:16–20; Ezekiel 36:16–35). The Law of Moses is not a believer's focus now; it cannot be kept and its epitaph is condemnation and death (2 Corinthians 3:7, 9).

The clear teaching of the New Testament is that the Law of Moses has been rendered inoperative with the death of Messiah. In other words, that law in its totality no longer has any authority over individuals or the Jewish people. Here I lay out nine points from Scripture conclusively showing that the Law of Moses was rendered inoperative, and thus should not be of concern today.

1. End of the Law, Not the Goal

This is evident first of all from Romans 10:4, with Paul telling us that *Christ is the end of the law*. Galatians 2:16 concurs, stating that there is no justification through the law. Furthermore, there is no sanctification or perfection through the law (Hebrews 7:19). Look with me at those verses, with the critical wording underlined:

> *For Messiah is the <u>end of the law</u> for righteousness to everyone that believes.* (Romans 10:4)

> *Knowing that a man is <u>not justified by the works of the law</u>, but by faith in Yeshua [Jesus] Messiah [Christ], even we have*

believed in Yeshua Messiah that we might be justified by the faith of Messiah, and not <u>by the works of the law: for by the works of the law shall no flesh be justified</u>. (Galatians 2:16)

19 For <u>the law made nothing perfect</u>, but the bringing in of a better hope did: by the which we draw nigh unto God.

In Messianic circles, there is disagreement concerning Romans 10:4 and the word end, which some translate as "goal" and thus claim that the verse says that the goal of the law is the Messiah. However, the Greek word *telos* has a range of meanings in the biblical context. So, how do we correctly translate *telos* in the context of Romans 10:4 and the broader context of the same issue elsewhere? The primary meaning of *telos* in the Greek is "termination," not "goal." Context also favors "termination" here because that fits the immediate context and the context of related verses. In many other places, Paul speaks to the point that the law has been rendered inoperative. The word "goal" that is suggested by Torah-observant believers is a less common translation[22] that does not fit the context of this passage, nor does it agree with the rest of Paul's writings or the author of Hebrews. To emphasize the "termination" of the Law of Moses, read Romans 7:5–6. Paul further explained law observance to the Galatians, who were considering placing themselves under the Mosaic law as Gentile believers:

5 For when we were in the flesh, the motions of sins, which were by the law, did work in our members to bring forth fruit unto death. 6 But now we are delivered from the law, that being dead wherein we were held; that we should serve in newness of spirit, and not in the oldness of the letter. (Romans 7:5–6)

19 Wherefore then serve the law? It was added because of transgressions, till the seed should come to whom the promise was made;.... (Galatians 3:19)

Chapter 7

The context of all of Paul's writing indicates the "termination" of the law (a temporary bilateral conditional covenant); it cannot readily be taken to mean Messiah as a "goal." [Another observation on the term "goal", once the Messiah reached the goal it is over and the purpose of the law is completed!]

The work that Messiah completed on the cross inaugurated the New Covenant that Moses, Isaiah, Jeremiah, Ezekiel, and Joel had all prophesied would come in the future. Some Messianic believers hold that the word "new" in Jeremiah 31:33 indicates the renewal of the old Mosaic system and making it an appendix to the Law of Moses. Again, though, the context indicates otherwise: the results are that the New Covenant brings something absolutely new, the Law of Messiah. The New Covenant and the Law of Messiah are nothing like the Mosaic law, which fulfilled its purpose with the death of Messiah on the cross as the ultimate sacrificial offering for sin.

2. Righteous Provided in Messiah

Was righteousness obtained by the Mosaic law or by Messiah? In Romans 10:4 there are several words that are largely neglected: *unto the righteousness of God*. From our study we have seen that the Law of Moses provided condemnation and death, not righteousness (2 Corinthians 3:7, 9). Yet because of the New Covenant (Jeremiah 31:31–34; Ezekiel 36:26–27) and Messiah's sacrifice (Isaiah 53) on the cross as the Lamb of God, and the regenerating ministry of the Holy Spirit (Titus 3:5), Messiah's righteousness is imputed to us (Romans 5:17–18). The Law of Moses had many purposes, but nothing therein gave the sinner righteous standing before a holy God. Two of Paul's statements in Romans specifically mention righteousness, although it can be hard to understand all the ramifications of his words.

> 21 *But now the righteousness of God <u>without the law</u> is manifested being witnessed by the law and the prophets.* (Romans 3:21)

26 *To declare, I say, at this time His righteousness: that He might be just, and the justifier of him which believes in Yeshua.* (Romans 3:26)

This much is clear: the righteousness of God is witnessed by the law and prophets in the coming of the Messiah to deal with sin because we *have all sinned and come short of the glory of God* (Romans 3:23) — and this applies to both Jews and Gentiles (Romans 1:18–3:20). Thus, the Law of Moses is now of no benefit spiritually before God; it does not produce righteousness. Only Yeshua can produce righteousness in us, because righteousness is His and not ours. Longenecker makes the following statement showing the emphasis of Paul (not only in Romans, but also in Galatians) and the author of Hebrews that the Law of Moses ended:

> Paul makes much of the change that has taken place in the purpose of the Law with the coming of Christ in such contrasts as "before" [Romans 3:21] and "but now" [Romans 3:21; 7:6; Colossians 1:26]. Before, Israel had been "kept under" [Galatians 3:23] the contractual obligation of the Law; "but now" we are discharged from that contractual obligation which held us captive. Righteousness is "no longer" [Romans 6:14; 7:1–14; Galatians 3:10–13] to be associated with works in that God has done something new in manifesting His righteousness "apart from the law" [Romans 3:21–24]. Formerly such righteousness had been kept hidden, "but now" it has been disclosed to His saints. The Apostle pictures what was preparatory as completed by what was anticipated, what was meant to be temporary being set aside for what is lasting, what was mediated as resolved into what is immediate. The Law in its contractual obligation — i.e., "in its connection with righteousness" — has been abrogated. It has died, been "torn down." Not because it has evolved into something new, but because God has established a new covenant wherein

"commandments" and "ordinances" [Ephesians 2:15] are ended and the distinction between Israel under contract and the Gentiles outside the covenant is abrogated. It is because Christ in His Person and work has terminated the contractual purpose of the Law that Paul expected his placarding of Christ Jesus to settle once and for all this question of whether righteousness in the New Covenant is "through the Law" or "in Christ." "It is finished" is just as much a cry of Paul as of Christ.[23]

Paul's writings clearly show what the Law of Moses was before, in the old economy — but now we are under grace, under Messiah, which is better than and superior to the Law of Moses. Our righteousness comes from Messiah and not the law, so why obligate yourself to the old, dead law? We Gentiles who were outside the covenants and promises are now brought near. The Jerusalem Council clearly stated that the Gentiles were not to be burdened by a law that could not be kept and could not provide righteousness.

3. The Mosaic Law Is Sterile, with No Life in It

In Romans 2:29, Paul develops his argument for Jewish unbelievers, pointing out that the Law of Moses could not produce life, could not change an uncircumcised heart which the New Covenant promises:

> *But he is a Jew, which is one inwardly, and circumcision is that of the heart, in the spirit, and not in the letter; whose praise is not of men, but of God.*

The New Covenant is a promise of life given by the Holy Spirit, who is the activator of the New Covenant and the Law of Messiah, which stands in contrast to humanity's frustration with and inability to keep the former law which did not give life. The Mosaic law could do nothing more than show us that we cannot keep God's holy law. It was the New Covenant that established new life, by the ministry of the Holy Spirit in regeneration, the "circumcision of the heart," rather than the law of condemnation and death. Ezekiel 36:26–27 reveals the promise of the indwelling ministry of the Holy Spirit, which has a direct connection with Yeshua's words in John 14:17 and 16:7–11. The Holy Spirit's ministry to Israel in the future (Isaiah 59:21) is connected with Joel 2:28–32 and Zechariah 12:10, where Israel is promised a national new birth: the Holy Spirit will empower them with dreams and visions and they will all be regenerated (gaining a circumcised heart) in one day (Zechariah 3:9; Romans 11:26). As we move into the New Testament, the ministry of the Holy Spirit jumps off the pages, for He regenerates Jew and Gentile with the circumcision of Christ (Colossians 2:11). I discuss the Holy Spirit's ministry further in chapter 10.

4. Old Covenant Temporary, New Covenant Eternal

A fourth important point is that the Mosaic law was never meant to be permanent. In the context of Galatians 3:19, Paul describes the Law of Moses as an addition to the Abrahamic Covenant, created in order to make sin and humanity's sin nature very clear so that all would know they have fallen woefully short of God's standard for righteousness. It was a temporary addition until Messiah arrived (*till the seed should come*); now that He has come, the law ceased to be an operating system. Look again at Galatians 3:19:

> *Wherefore then served the law? It was added because of transgressions, till the Seed should come to whom the promise was made....*

The Law of Moses was normative for Israel; it was given to them as a temporary means to lead them to Messiah. The Law of Moses was binding on Israel until it was fulfilled by Christ, and rendered inoperative by the work of Messiah on the cross, which inaugurated the New Covenant and the Law of Messiah. The Law of Messiah is now binding for both Jewish and Gentiles believers after the establishment of the Church by God at Pentecost.[24] As Strickland notes:

> This law of Christ is discussed both by Paul and by James. It is no mere rephrasing of the Mosaic law, for it consists not of a concrete corpus of demands, but rather of basic principles, for each believer is promised permanent indwelling by the Holy Spirit. Since the Holy Spirit ministers in the life of the New Testament believer on behalf of Jesus Christ, there is no need for any lengthy, detailed, codified, <u>external means of restraint as in the Mosaic law</u>.[25]

I would go further than Strickland's characterization of the Law of Messiah as "not of a concrete corpus of demands, but rather of basic principles." In my view, the Law of Messiah does consist of laws to be obeyed: they are imperative commands rather than "basic principles." The Law of Moses was a means of restraint, but restraint is now an internal byproduct of the ministry of the Holy Spirit indwelling in us.

5. Order of Melchizedek Requires a New Law System: the New Covenant

With Messiah there is a new priesthood, according to the order of Melchizedek, instead of the former order of the Aaronic priesthood. Whereas the Law of Moses provided the basis for Levitical and Aaronic priesthoods, this new priesthood required a new law under which it could operate. Hebrews 7:11–12 explains that only one type of priesthood was permitted in the Hebrew Scriptures. The Levitical priesthood officiated in the Temple. But the Levitical priesthood, and its sacrificial system of animal blood, could not bring perfection; only the Messiah's blood could do that (Hebrews 9:11–10:18). For the Levitical priesthood to be replaced by a new priesthood (the priesthood of Melchizedek), a change of the law was required.

> 11 *If therefore perfection were by the Levitical priesthood (for under it the people received the law), what further need was there that another priest should rise after the order of Melchizedek, and not be called after the order of Aaron?* 12 *For the priesthood being changed, there is made of necessity a change also of the law.* (Hebrews 9:11–12)

Was there a change of law? Hebrews 7:18 states that the Mosaic law was *disannulled*. Because it is no longer in effect, we can now have a new priesthood after the order of Melchizedek. If the Mosaic law were still in effect, Yeshua could not function as a High Priest, for He was of the tribe of Judah and not Levi. Now, though, with the Mosaic law no longer in effect, Yeshua can be a priest after the order of Melchizedek. Douglas Moo argues that Jeremiah's New Covenant prediction about the law being "written on the heart" need not mean that the Mosaic law as such was to become the internal moral guide for the Christian.[26] That which was written on the heart is the Law of Messiah, which is superior to and replaces the Mosaic law.

6. New Covenant: Better Covenant and Promises

Hebrews 8 indicates that the New Covenant is a better covenant with better promises. If the Mosaic Covenant had been faultless, there would not have been a need for a second covenant to be sought or established. But, because the old covenant was weak due to the flesh, it became obsolete and was superseded.

> 6 *But now has He obtained a more excellent ministry, by how much also He is the mediator of a <u>better covenant</u>, which was established upon <u>better promises</u>. 7 For if that first covenant [Mosaic law] had been faultless, then should no place have been sought for the second* [New Covenant]. (Hebrews 8:6–7)

> 13 *In that he says a New Covenant, He has made the first old. Now that which decays and waxes old is ready to vanish away.* (Hebrews 8:13)

Verse 6 uses the Greek word—*mesites*, which means a mediator, arbitrator or go-between.[27] Messiah is our "go-between," the One who stands between God and man. The picture laid out for us in the Hebrew Scriptures shows Moses as the mediator between God and Israel. In the Messianic psalm of Solomon (Psalms 72:2), he says, *He shall judge your people with righteousness, and your poor with judgement.* The New Testament Scripture paints the same picture of a mediator—a go-between—but this time the parties are different (1 Timothy 2:5).[28] This time it is the Prophet like Moses (Deuteronomy 18:18–19) who is superior to Moses. *For there is one God, and one Mediator between God and men, the man Messiah Yeshua* [Christ Jesus].

Yeshua the Prophet like unto Moses (Deuteronomy 18:18–19; Numbers 12:5–8) supersedes Moses, who was the mediator of the Mosaic law. Yeshua the God-Man is now our mediator, given the New Covenant and the Law of Messiah that proceeds from that covenant. That is the same thing that the author of Hebrews said in 8:6.

Now, of what is Yeshua a mediator? He is a *mediator* of a *better covenant* (the New Covenant) that has *better promises*: the promise of life, promise of a regenerated heart instead of condemnation and death, and a promise of victory over sin through the ministry of the Holy Spirit, which the old covenant could not provide. If the Mosaic law could have provided regeneration and victorious living, there would have been no need for a New Covenant: *then should no place have been sought for a second.* God established a New Covenant, in the fullness of time, when Yeshua gave Himself as the ultimate sacrifice for sin. Hebrews 8:13 uses the word *old* (Greek *palaios*), meaning that because the old was inadequate, a new covenant was needed, as stated by Wuest: "The Greek word for 'old' here is not *archaios*, namely, that which is old in point of time, but *palaios*, that which is old in point of use, worn-out, antiquated, useless, outmoded. Even in Jeremiah's time, the insufficiency of the First Testament was recognized, and the need of a new one proclaimed."

The words "made old" are a translation of the Greek *palaioo*, a verb that has the same root as the noun *palaios*. It is in the perfect tense, which indicates an action completed in past time having present results. Thus, we could translate it as "In saying new, He has permanently antiquated the first [covenant]." The word "decayeth" is a translation of the same verb, and we have "that which is being antiquated." The words "waxeth old" are a translation of *gerasko*, which means "to grow old" and implies the waning strength and decay that come with old age. It also has the connotation of being obsolescent, failing from age.[29]

Moses Maimonides understood the ramifications of Jeremiah 31 and the teachings of believers in the church when he said, in the ninth of his Thirteen Principles of Faith, "I believe with a complete faith that this Torah will not be exchanged and there will be no other Torah from the creator."[30] Maimonides acknowledged—but rejected—a line of Jewish thought that a "New Torah" would be given by the Messiah, as some of the sages (rabbis) both before and after Maimonides claimed.[31] Yet the prophet Jeremiah said a New Torah would be given: the New Covenant with the Law of Messiah. Maimonides refused to see the clear intent and teachings of Moses and the Prophets. In 2 Corinthians 3:14–15, Paul says that a particular blindness is upon the Jewish people:

> 14 *But their minds were blinded: for until this day remains the same veil, not taken away in the reading of the old testament; which veil is done away in Messiah. 15 But even unto this day, when Moses is read, the veil is upon their heart.*

Steve Ger, a fourth generation Jewish believer, focuses on a very important principle that should not be missed, which is that we are dealing not with law as the focus, but with a change in covenants:

The point of Hebrews 8 does not involve specific areas of Mosaic legislation or even the Torah itself. The issue is not one of law but of the covenant from which they are derived. Hebrews 8 argues that the whole Mosaic covenant, as an entire contractual, constitutional system of relationship between God and His people, has been replaced. While there may be some areas of overlap between old and the new constitutional systems, only one contract is capable of yielding dividends.[32]

7. New Covenant: Regenerating Ministry of the Holy Spirit

The seventh point of evidence is that the Law of Moses did not promise the coming indwelling of the Holy Spirit. The Holy Spirit is the pledge of God to believing Jewish people and to Gentiles. In Ezekiel 36:26–27 and 37:14, the LORD states three times that the Holy Spirit will come and indwell Jewish believers in the New Covenant and give life to them and restore them to the land. Later He (the Holy Spirit) includes all Gentile believers in the Jewish Messiah who inaugurated the New Covenant with His blood at the cross. In 2 Corinthians and Ephesians, Paul points to the promise of the indwelling and sealing presence of the Holy Spirit:

> 22 *Who has also sealed us, and given the earnest [guarantee] of the Spirit in our hearts.* (2 Corinthians 1:22)

> 13 *In whom you also trusted, after that you heard the word of truth, the gospel of your salvation: in whom also after that you believed, you were sealed with that Holy Spirit of promise,* 14 *Which is the earnest of our inheritance until the redemption of the purchased possession, unto the praise of His glory.* (Ephesians 1:13–14)

Peter also refers to the ministry of the Holy Spirit in his Acts 2 message where he quotes from Joel 2:28. The Holy Spirit is God's pledge to us that the New Covenant is a reality in the hearts and lives of believers. The Holy Spirit is the activator of the New Covenant: He is the one who guides and teaches us in the Word (John 14:27; 16:13), and He is the one who enables us to live a victorious life over sin as we surrender or yield to Him.

8. Subject Centrality Is on Covenant, Not Law

The eighth line of evidence for the annulment of the Mosaic law focuses on the part of the law that most people want to retain: the Ten Commandments. 2 Corinthians 3:2–11 is very significant here, especially verse 6 onward:

> 6 *Who also has made us able ministers of the new covenant: not of the letter, but of the spirit: for the letter kills, but the spirit gives life. 7 But if the <u>ministration of death</u> written and engraven in stones was glorious, so that the children of Israel could not steadfastly behold the face of Moses for the glory of his countenance; which glory was to be done away:* 8 *How shall not the ministration of the spirit be rather glorious?* 9 *For if the <u>ministration of condemnation</u> be glory; much more does the ministration of righteousness exceed in glory.* 10 *For even that which was made glorious had no glory in this respect, by reason of the glory that excelled.* 11 *For if that which is done away was glorious, much more that which remains is glorious.* (2 Corinthians 3:6–11)

We need to examine what Paul is saying in this passage concerning the Law of Moses. He calls that law both the *ministration of condemnation* and the *ministration of death* (vv. 7, 9)—both without question negative but valid descriptions. In addition, in these verses Paul is clearly emphasizing the Ten Commandments, which are *engraven on stones*. The point is that the Law of Moses, especially as represented by the Ten Commandments *engraven in stones*, is a ministration of *death* and of *condemnation*. This would remain true if the Ten Commandments were still in force today in the Mosaic system.

Chapter 7

In 2 Corinthians 3:7–11 (ESV), notice how clearly Paul states the superiority of the Holy Spirit's ministry, which superseded that which was graven on stone:

> 7 *Nor if the ministry of death carved in letters on stone, came with such glory that the Israelites could not gaze at Moses' face because of its glory, which was being brought to an end.* 8 *Will not the ministry of the Spirit have even more glory?* 9 *For if there was glory in the ministry of condemnation, the ministry of righteousness must far exceed it in glory.* 10 *Indeed, in this case, what once had glory has come to have no glory at all, because of the glory that surpasses it.* 11 *For if what was being brought to an end came with glory, much more will what is <u>permanent</u> have glory.*

In all of chapter 3, Paul contrasts that which was engraved on stone and the ministry of the Holy Spirit Who activated the New Covenant. Verse 7 states that the Law of Moses (that which was engraved on stone) was rendered inoperative, was done away, was brought to an *end*. That is the same thing Paul said in Romans 10:4: the Law of Moses was brought to an end by Messiah. Now, the Law of Moses had much glory, for Moses had to veil his face, but the regenerating ministry of the Holy Spirit has far more glory, as stated in verse 8. The Holy Spirit gave new life—regenerated life—rather than the legacy of *death* and *condemnation* under the Law of Moses. In verse 9, Paul again points out that although there was *glory in the ministry of condemnation, the ministry of righteousness* by the Holy Spirit must far exceed the Law of Moses *in glory*. Verse 10 says the old law now has *no glory,* because of the permanent glory of the Holy Spirit's ministry which superseded it. In verse 11 Paul acknowledges that the Law of Moses, engraved on stone, had glory, but clearly says that was brought to an *end*, overtaken by the greater and permanent glory of the *ministry of the Holy Spirit.*

Nevertheless, some who wish to preserve law-keeping as under Moses use some form of religious gymnastics to reinterpret the clear words of Paul here, as well as in Romans and Galatians, and the words of the author of book of Hebrews. However, the Mosaic law is no longer in force: that law has passed away or been *done away* with (vv. 7, 11). The Greek word used is *katargeo*, meaning "to render inoperative." Because the emphasis in this passage is on the Ten Commandments, this means that the Ten Commandments have passed away. Paul's point is very clear: the Law of Moses, including the Ten Commandments, is no longer in effect. Also notice, in Hebrews, the description that the writer of Hebrews gave around 66 AD, just a couple of years before the destruction of the city and sanctuary (Daniel 9:26), saying that the Mosaic law is *old* and *ready to vanish away:*

> In that he saith, a New Covenant, he has made the first old. Now that which decays and waxes old is ready to vanish away (Hebrews 8:13).

This *"old"* covenant that was about to *vanish* had actually already been replaced with the New Covenant. The Holy Spirit replaced the Mosaic law with the blood of Messiah. God gave 40-some years of grace to Israel to respond to the message of Messiah through the apostles before the physical system of the Law of Moses and the Temple compound were completely destroyed. The superiority of the Law of Messiah is underscored by the fact that it will never be rendered inoperative.

Paul sheds more light on this in his letter to the Ephesians, explaining that God made certain covenants with the Jewish people. In fact, God made four unilateral, unconditional eternal covenants with Israel: the Abrahamic, the Land, the Davidic, and New Covenants. All of God's blessings to Israel, both material and spiritual, are mediated by means of these four Jewish covenants, which are eternal as well as unconditional.

11 Wherefore remember, that you being in time past Gentiles in the flesh, who are called Uncircumcision by that which is called the Circumcision in the flesh made by hands; 12 That at that time you were without Messiah, being aliens from the commonwealth of Israel, and strangers from the covenants of promise, having no hope, and without God in the world: 13 But now in Messiah Yeshua you who sometimes were far off are made nigh by the blood of Messiah. 14 For He is our peace, who has made both one, and has broken down the middle wall of partition between us; 15 Having abolished in His flesh the enmity, even the law of commandments contained in ordinances; for to make in Himself of two, one new man, so making peace; 16 And that He might reconcile both unto God in one body by the cross, having slain the enmity thereby: (Ephesians 2:11–16)

6 That the Gentiles should be fellow heirs, and of the same body, and partakers of His promise in Messiah by the gospel. (Ephesians 3:6)

Notice that Paul describes Gentiles (before the New Covenant) as a people being *without Messiah, aliens, strangers, without God, far off,* and having *no hope.* At the same time, Paul points out God's fifth covenant—the Mosaic Covenant containing the Mosaic law—which was temporary and conditional. According to Paul, the Mosaic law served as a wall of partition (Ephesians 2:15) to keep Gentiles from enjoying Jewish spiritual blessings. In the Old Testament, if a Gentile wished to become a recipient of Jewish spiritual blessings, he had to take upon himself the entire obligation of the law, from circumcision to living as every other Jew lived. Only a Gentile who converted to Judaism could enjoy the blessings of the Jewish covenants. If the Mosaic law were still in effect, there would still be a *wall of partition* to maintain this distinction between Jews and Gentiles. But the *wall of partition* was broken down with the death of Christ; the wall of partition was the Mosaic law, so the Law of Moses was rendered inoperative. Now, on the basis of faith, Gentiles can and do enjoy Jewish spiritual (though not physical) blessings by becoming fellow partakers of the promise in Christ Jesus.

Paul used another analogy in Galatians that should to be restated concerning the temporary aspect of the Law of Moses:

> 23 *But before faith came, we were kept under the law, shut up unto the faith which should afterwards be revealed. 24 Wherefore the <u>law was our schoolmaster</u> to bring us unto Messiah, that we might be justified by faith. 25 <u>But after that faith is come, we are no longer under a schoolmaster</u>* [guardian]. *26 For you are all the children of God by faith in Messiah Yeshua. 27 For as many of you as have been baptized into Messiah have put on Messiah. 28 There is neither Jew nor Greek, there is neither bond nor free, there is neither male nor female: for you are all one in Messiah Yeshua. 29 And if you be Messiah's, then are you Abraham's seed, and heirs according to the promise.* (Galatians 3:23–29)

> 1 *Now I say, that the heir, as long as he is a child, differs nothing from a servant, though he be lord of all. 2 But is under tutors and governors <u>until the time appointed of the father</u>. 3 Even so we, when we were children, were in bondage under the elements of the world. 4 But when the <u>fullness of the time</u> was come, God sent forth His Son, made of a woman, made under the law. 5 To redeem them that were <u>under the law</u>, that we might receive the adoption of sons. 6 And because you are sons, God has sent forth the Spirit of His Son into your hearts, crying* Abba Father. *7 Wherefore you are no more a servant, but a son; and if a son, then an heir of God through Messiah.* (Galatians 4:1–7)

Observe the underlined sections: the law was the *schoolmaster* until the *appointed time*. Once the appointed time arrived, *God sent forth His Son under the law*; the schoolmaster (the law) was no longer needed.

However, the words "schoolmaster" and "tutor" that the King James Version (KJV) and the New American Standard Bible (NASB) respectively use do not present the whole idea behind the original Greek word *pedagogue*, which connotes a guardian more than a teacher or schoolmaster. The law was our guardian or *pedagogue* until Christ came (Galatians 3:24). The word "guardian" used here is important. Neither the KJV's rendering of this word as "schoolmaster," nor the NASB's "tutor" are helpful for, as Longenecker has pointed out, "[w]hile today we think of pedagogues as teachers, in antiquity a *paidagogos* was distinguished from a *didaskalos* (teacher) and had <u>custodial and disciplinary functions rather than education or instructional ones</u>."[33] In ancient Greco-Roman society, the *paidagogos* was a domestic slave who was responsible for supervising the children from infancy to late adolescence. *Paidagogos* is probably best translated "babysitter" or "nanny" in this context, as Paul clearly uses the term to refer to the law-covenants' temporal nature. Nannies are only needed until maturity is reached, then they become unnecessary.[34]

The word "schoolmaster" could more aptly be the translation of *didaskalos*, meaning "a teacher." The English word "pedagogue," which refers to a schoolmaster, is only derived from the Greek *paidagogos*: the Greek word did not have that meaning. *Paidagogos* designated a slave of a Greek or Roman family who had general charge over a boy from the age of about 6 until about age 16. The *paidagogos* watched over the boy's outward behavior, and took charge over him whenever he went away from home (for instance, to school). This slave was entrusted with the moral supervision of the child. His duties were therefore quite different and distinct from those of a schoolmaster. Furthermore, the metaphor of a paidagogos seems to have grown out of the word *kept (phroureo)* of verse 23, which means "to guard." Thus, the word actually refers to a guardian of a minor child rather than to a teacher or schoolmaster.

By describing the law as a *paidagogos*, Paul emphasizes both the inferiority of the law to grace, and the temporary character of the law. Properly read, the law was the guardian of Israel, keeping watch over those committed to its care, accompanying them with its commands and prohibitions, keeping them in a condition of dependence and restraint, and continually revealing to them sin as a positive transgression.[35]

> The second purpose of the law was that it was designed to act as a "custodian" until the incarnation of Christ. ... In the Greek world, a paidagogos was generally a slave who functioned in both a custodial and an educative fashion as a tutor. His responsibility was to supervise the entire lifestyle of the child, giving constant attention to the academic, social, and spiritual nourishment of the child until maturity. In a similar manner, therefore, the Old Testament Jew was a child supervised by the law. The redeemed Jew needed this constant supervision in order to know how to please and worship God. The law had this function until Christ arrived and led believers to himself to be justified by faith in him. Thus the law is regarded by Paul as clearly inferior, in the sense of being preparatory to the gospel of Jesus Christ. With the advent of faith in Jesus Christ, however, the law as a pedagogue is no longer necessary. In other words, the law is temporary with regard to this regulatory purpose. The context makes it clear that the apostle is speaking ... of the historic succession of one period of revelation upon another and the displacement of the law [of Moses] by Christ.[36]

Both the *Manual Greek Lexicon of the New Testament*[37] and *Vines Expository Dictionary of Old and New Testament Words*[38] give the same definitions and context as the ones already quoted. The point regarding use of the word *pedagogue* is that the law was intended to function for time-limited guidance and instruction of the master's children, giving them parameters for their behavior.

Chapter 7

The definition does not lend itself to the Law of Moses being anything other than temporary.

9. New Covenant: God's Circumcision Made Without Hands

The ninth line of evidence: Moses was very clear on the circumcision of the heart. What he stated in Deuteronomy 10:16 is impossible for a human heart. Showing the inadequacy of the Mosaic law, Jewish hearts could not circumcise themselves (nor could Gentiles', for that matter). Notice as well that the prophet Jeremiah picks up Moses' theme to state that all Israel is uncircumcised in heart (9:26). Thereafter, Moses in Deuteronomy 30:6 states that God will do what a human heart and hands are incapable of doing: He will circumcise Jewish hearts! That is accomplished by the New Covenant, which replaces the old Mosaic covenant of *condemnation* and *death* with regenerated new life. This is what Moses was talking about in Deuteronomy 30:6. Look what Paul said to the Church at Colosse (Colossians 2:11): Messiah will circumcise the heart *without hands*; this is a God thing, something completely out of humans' hands, control, and ability. Look at these verses in Deuteronomy, Jeremiah 9, and Colossians 2:

> 16 *Circumcise therefore the foreskin of your heart, and be no more stiff-necked.* (Deuteronomy 10:16)

> 25 *Behold, the days come, saith the LORD, that I will punish all them which are circumcised with the uncircumcised:* 26 *Egypt, and Judah, and Edom, and the children of Ammon, and Moab, and all that are in the utmost corners, that dwell in the wilderness: for all these nations are uncircumcised, and all the house of <u>Israel are uncircumcised in heart</u>.*
> (Jeremiah 9:25–26))

> 6 <u>*And the LORD your God will circumcise thine heart*</u>, *and the heart of your seed, to love the LORD your God with all your heart and with all your soul, that you may live.*
> (Deuteronomy 30:6)

11 *In whom also <u>you are circumcised with the circumcision made without hands</u>, in putting off the body of the sins of the flesh by the <u>circumcision of Messiah</u>.* (Colossians 2:11)

To summarize, the Mosaic law is a unit comprising 613 commandments, and all of it has been invalidated. No Mosaic commandment (not even the Ten Commandments) has continued beyond the cross of Yeshua, although that law can be used as a teaching tool to show God's standard of righteousness and our sinfulness and need of substitutionary sacrifice for our sin. It can be used to point people to Christ (Galatians 3:23–25). The Mosaic law has, however, completely ceased to function as an authority over individuals. Hebrews 8:1–13 draws a parallel between the Mosaic law and the New Covenant. The writer, quoting Jeremiah 31:31–34, states that as soon as a "new" covenant is enacted, it renders the Mosaic Covenant the "old" one—and that which is old is *vanishing away* (Hebrews 8:13). The Mosaic law grew old under Jeremiah and disappeared when Messiah died.

7 For if that first covenant had been faultless, then should no place have been sought for the second. 8 For finding fault with them, he said, behold, the days come, says the LORD, when I will make a new covenant with the house of Israel and with the house of Judah: 9 Not according to the covenant that I made with their fathers in the day when I took them by the hand to lead them out of the land of Egypt; because they continued not in My covenant, and I regarded them not, says the LORD. 10 For this is the covenant that I will make with the house of Israel after those days, says the LORD; I will put My laws into their mind, and write them in their hearts; and I will be to them a God, and they shall be to me a people. 11 And they shall not teach every man his neighbor, and every man his brother saying, know the LORD: for all shall know Me, from the least to the greatest. 12 For I will be merciful to their unrighteousness, and their sins and their iniquities will I remember no more. 13 In that he said a new covenant,

Chapter 7

> *He has made the first old. Now that which decays and waxes old is ready to vanish away.* (Hebrews 8:7–13)

Here the author of Hebrews repeats Jeremiah 31:31–34, reminding us that this New Covenant would be made for the Jewish people because they had broken the old covenant. God will regenerate and "circumcise" the hearts of the Jewish people and write His Law—the Law of Messiah—on their hearts, and the old, broken covenant would disappear, made obsolete and rendered inoperative by the new.

Before I close this chapter, I want to share one additional point that is very sobering concerning the Law of Moses (the system of law that has been replaced by the Law of Messiah under the New Covenant). Doug Friedman has done a spreadsheet on each of the 613 commands in the Mosaic law, in the course of a study on the commandments in that law, and divided the commands into five very revealing categories.

Well over half of the 613 commandments cannot be observed by anyone today, even if they wanted to. Therefore, whoever claims to be Torah observant is not telling the truth.

Most believers—even church attendees who are not striving to observe the Mosaic law—actually observe 28% of them anyway.

Most Messianic believers only observe about 5% more than the non-Messianic church attendees.

Even those who are serious Messianic Torah Positive (MTP) fail to observe 8% of the commandments that they could observe.

The difference between the number of commandments that most MTPs observe and those that most Messiah Believers (MBs) observe is only about 1%. In other words, MTPs observe only about five more commandments than MBs.

There is precious little difference between the MTPs and the MBs! So, why the division?[39]

Here is the astounding fact: Of the 613 total commandments in the Mosaic law, about 355 of them (58%) *cannot* be kept today. That is a sobering statistic in and of itself. On top of that, Friedman finds that serious Torah-observant believers do not keep another 8% of the commands that they could keep. That is roughly another 50 commands on top of the initial 355, making it more than 400 commands that are not kept. He raised an interesting question under his first point: "Therefore, whoever claims to be Torah observant is not telling the truth" about his religious practices and belief. They have deceived themselves. For Torah-observant believers, this stands as a powerful condemnation of their own beliefs and practices.

Another useful reference is Mal Couch's *The New Covenant Blessings for the Church*.[40] This book is very useful in any study of the New Covenant as it relates to New Testament believers, for out of this New Covenant came the Law of Messiah.

8

THE LETTER OF THE LAW OR THE SPIRIT OF CHRIST

The believer today must be careful not to be so zealous in obeying laws that do not apply to him that he ends up living in a state of disobedience to the laws that do apply to him.

—Arnold G. Fruchtenbaum

So far in this book we have observed the boundaries of the Law of Moses, and have seen not only the tremendous contrasts between that law and the Law of Messiah, but also the superiority of the Law of Messiah. Here is a quick summary of the most important points:

The Law of Moses was a covenant with Israel—a physical, national, ethnic people we call the Jewish people today—and that law was given to eventually lead the Jewish people to Messiah (Galatians 3:22–25).

The purpose of the Mosaic law was to reveal the holiness of God and to reveal to Israel the standard of living for the faithful Jewish Old Testament saints; it was *not* a means of salvation.

The law was a schoolmaster/guardian to lead the Jewish people to Messiah; once Messiah came, the purpose and fulfillment of the Mosaic law became apparent biblically. After Messiah, there was no longer a need for the Law of Moses to continue and it was rendered inoperative.

The law set out three times in the year when Israel was to come before God in corporate worship of Him at the Tabernacle/Temple.

The law was intended to keep the Jewish people distinct from the Gentiles.

The law was designed to exclude Gentiles from its covenants and promises (Ephesians 2:12); it was a wall between the two groupings (Ephesians 2:14–15): Jewish people and Gentiles.

The law revealed sin and also made Jewish people sin more, so as to drive Jewish people to faith in Yahweh and in His time to faith in Messiah as their God and Redeemer. In the time leading up to Jesus' day, the Jewish Pharisees had complicated the Mosaic law by adding a large number of rabbinic, man-made laws (the traditions of the Elders) that superseded and obscured the original God-given Mosaic law. When they disregarded the Mosaic law, the Pharisees became focused on their man-made law of prohibitions, which did not drive them to Messiah Yeshua.[41]

Comparison of the Law of Death and Condemnation with the Law of Life in Messiah

The Law of Moses was hard, rough, burdensome, and impossible to keep (Acts 15:10), yet it was holy (Romans 7:12). It was a standard of holiness for Israel which set Jews apart from all the other nations. However, this law was sterile (1 Corinthians 15:56); it could not produce life, but it did produce *death* and *condemnation* (2 Corinthians 3:7, 9). Andrew Murray states:

The Old [Law] was carved in stone [Exodus 31:19; 2 Corinthians 3:1–18], the New [Covenant Law] in the heart. The Old could be written in ink and was in the letter that kills; the New is of the Spirit that makes alive [Romans 8:2; Titus 3:5]. The Old was a ministration of *condemnation* and *death*; the New, of righteousness and life. The Old indeed had its glory, for it came from God, and brought its Divine blessing, but it was a glory that passed away, and had no glory by reason of the glory that surpasses, the exceeding glory of that which endures. With the

Old there was the veil on the heart; in the New, the veil is taken away from the face and the heart. The Spirit of the Lord gives liberty, and, reflecting with unveiled face the glory of the Lord, we are changed from glory to glory, into the same image, by the Spirit of the Lord [2 Corinthians 3:16 18]. The glory that surpasses proved its power in this, that it not only manifested on its Divine side, but so exerted its power in the heart and life of its subjects, that it was seen in them too, as they were changed by the Spirit into Christ's image, from glory to glory.[42]

The Law of Messiah is easy and smooth, but it could not be kept perfectly because of our *old man*, our sinful nature (Romans 6:6). Confession of sin before God through our advocate is ever present in Messiah (1 John 1:9 2:1), and we now have, through the Holy Spirit, the power to keep His law most of the time because of our new nature, the *new man* that we are in Christ (2 Corinthians 5:17). We thus have a battle of hearts (natures) that seek to control us:

In the promises of the New Covenant, as we find them in Jeremiah and Ezekiel, and also in many other passages of Scripture, it is clear that God's great aim in salvation is to get possession of the heart. The heart is the real life: with the heart a man loves, and wills, and acts. The heart makes the man. God made man's heart for His own dwelling place, that in it He might reveal His love and His glory, God sent Christ to accomplish a redemption by which man's heart could be won back to Him—nothing but that could satisfy God. And this is achieved when the Holy Spirit makes the heart of God's child what it should be.[43]

The heart of man is God's aim: it is His desire to control our hearts for His glory. Yet man on his own cannot merit anything before such a holy God. Even believers struggle to walk as He walked (1 John 2:6), because of believers' divided hearts. Even believers have two natures: First, the *old man* is at enmity with

Chapter 8

God and cannot produce anything that resembles righteousness before a holy God (Genesis 6:5; Isaiah 64:6; Jeremiah 17:9; Romans 3:23; 6:23). Believers also have the new nature; we are a *new creation* in Christ (2 Corinthians 5:17), remade by the regenerating ministry of the Holy Spirit based on the finished work of Messiah on the cross of Calvary in shedding His blood, the blood of the New Covenant.

So we have to deal with two natures. We are walking schizophrenics, for if we follow the old man (sin nature) we are carnal, fleshly, walking in darkness, and not doing the things of God. Now, if you truly walk according to the regenerated new man, you will walk in the Spirit, walking in the light and not sin ... although you will not walk in sinless perfection (more on this later).

In 1 Corinthians 2:14–3:4 Paul spiritually identifies three kinds of people. In verses 14–16, there is the <u>natural man</u>, who is dead in his sins. In verse 1 there is the <u>spiritual believer</u>, who walks under the power and control of the Holy Spirit, being submitted to Him. In the rest of verses 1 through 4, we find <u>carnal believers</u>, ones who are walking in the flesh with *envying, strife, and divisions*. Many Holiness Pentecost believers have a huge problem accepting the reality of these two natures in every believer, even though they themselves are often walking after the flesh in carnality and not in the spirit. They do not understand or acknowledge the depths of depravity and sin of the human heart that afflicts us on a daily basis. This denial will ultimately bring discouragement and disillusionment because they are not walking in the Spirit. All believers still have to deal with two natures: they do not (and cannot) shed the old carnal fleshly nature, as Paul clearly documents in his epistle.

This New Covenant, through the regenerative work of the Holy Spirit in us, is the foundation of not only the New Covenant of Jeremiah but also of the Law of Messiah, which is superior to the Law of Moses. Without the blood of the New Covenant, there would be no Law of Messiah! Jesus spoke of the fact that His *yoke is easy* and His *burden is light* (Matthew 11:30), in a passage that contrasts the Law of Messiah with the Mosaic law and rabbinic laws. However, that truth is applicable here because His Law—the Law of Messiah—which He provided through the blood of the New Covenant is *easy* and *light* compared to the Mosaic law.

The Law of Moses could not provide salvation, justification, sanctification, reconciliation, or imputation of Messiah's righteousness to our account, as the indwelling of the Holy Spirit does. All of that was contingent on the blood of the New Covenant in Messiah Yeshua on the cross of Calvary and in the ministry of the Holy Spirit. Covenant/Reform theology is simply misguided in its teaching that God permanently cast Israel aside when they condemned Yeshua to death and handed Him over to the Romans to be crucified. Noah was counted as righteous (Genesis 6:8–9), and Abram was justified (Genesis 15:6), but all that rested on a future work of Messiah to be accomplished. He would take on flesh and dwell among us (John 1:14 through Romans 8:3) for the explicit purpose of shedding His blood on the cross of Calvary, after being rejected by Israel. It was all part of God's eternal plan, made before the foundations of the earth.

Look at some of the contrasts that the Scriptures make between these two law systems: the Law of Moses versus the Law of Messiah. Table 8.1 is incomplete, but it gives us a stark contrast of the important differences between these two law systems.

Andrew Murray also grasped the chasm between these two systems:

> The Old Covenant man had failed in what he had to do. In the New [Covenant], God is to do everything in him.

Table 8.1 Mosaic and Messiah Laws Contrasted

Law of Moses	Law of Messiah
Repetitious offering of a sacrifice	One sacrifice, offered once
Holy	Holy
OT Saints standard of living	NT Saints standard of living
Death and condemnation	Walking in the newness of life
Priest never had rest	Our Priest made one sacrifice and sat down at the right hand of the Father
Salvation was by faith in the known	Salvation is by faith in the finished will of God and the promise of a work of Messiah on the cross
Uncircumcised heart—no regeneration	Heart circumcised by Messiah—regeneration
No power over sin	Freedom from the power and penalty of sin
Physically blessed if obeyed	Spiritual blessing in heavenly places
Redemption contingent on the future work	Redemption complete in, of, and by Messiah
Conditional on obedience	Reconciliation is permanent
Animal blood was sprinkled on the Mercy Seat in propitiation once a year, on Day of Atonement, and repeated annually to satisfy God's holy righteous demands	Blood of Messiah was shed on the cross <u>only</u> <u>once</u>, thereby satisfying God's holy righteous demands
Inability to act on Israel's behalf	Enabling Him to act on our behalf

The Letter of the Law or the Spirit of Christ

(no comparison)	Imputed righteousness of Messiah
Covering of sin	Forgiveness and removal of sin
Justification based on future work of Messiah	Justification because of the finished work of Messiah on the cross
Unfulfilled reality	Sactification because of the finished work of Messiah on the cross
(no comparison)	Future glorification
Son of Abraham, Isaac, and Jacob	Adoption, both Jew and Gentile
Contigent on the future work of Messiah	Transferred from the kingdom of darkness to the kingdom of light
Holy Spirit only came upon individuals for a limited time to achieve a particular purposes	Permanent indwelling of the Holy Spirit in every believer
Filling only for designated period of time	Filling of the Holy Spirit only when believers are walking in the Spirit
(no comparison)	Sealing of the Holy Spirit
(no comparison)	Baptism of the Holy Spirit
(no comparison)	Partakers of teh divine nature
(no comparison)	We are God's Temple
Physical temporal blessings with obedience	Spiritual blessings in heavenly places

Chapter 8

> The Old [Covenant] could only convict of sin. The New [Covenant] is to put it away and cleanse the heart from its filthiness.
>
> In the Old [Covenant], it was the heart that was wrong; for the New [Covenant] a new heart is provided, into which God put His fear and His law and His love.
>
> The Old [Covenant] demanded, but failed to secure obedience; in the New [Covenant], God causes us to walk in His judgments.
>
> The Old [Covenant] gave no power; in the New [Covenant] all is by the Spirit, the mighty power of God.
>
> The New [Covenant] is to fit man for a true holiness, a true fulfillment of the law of our loving God with the whole heart, and our neighbors as ourselves, a walk truly well-pleasing to God.
>
> The New Covenant has no power to save and to bless except as it is a ministration of the Spirit. That Spirit works in lesser or greater degree, as He is neglected and grieved, or yielded to and trusted. Let us honour Him, and give Him His place as the Spirit of the New Covenant, by expecting and accepting all He waits to do for us. He is the great gift of the [New] Covenant.[44]

In any comparison of the two law systems, the work of the Holy Spirit in activating the New Covenant that Messiah completed on the cross is truly breathtaking. The old one falls short, the other is glorious.

Comparison Between the Two Law Systems

The Law of Messiah coincides in only a few aspects with the Law of Moses. The law set before the true Body of Christ (Christians) is quite different from what was set before the Jewish people.

Although there is some small overlap and a few similarities between the Law of Messiah and the Law of Moses (e.g., nine of the Ten Commandments are in both systems), this does not mean that both laws are still functioning. To illustrate, I live in North Carolina. The laws of North Carolina are not all the same as the laws of Pennsylvania (where I lived before), although there are similarities. In moving from Pennsylvania, I am no longer bound by Pennsylvania laws, but I am bound by the laws of North Carolina. So, living in North Carolina I am not bound by the laws of Pennsylvania, and though they are similar, they are also distinct.

The Law of Moses is a unit of 613 laws. If you break one, you become guilty of breaking all. That concept is not present in the Law of Messiah.

The Mosaic law was conditionally based on Israel's response as to whether they would receive blessing from the hand of the LORD or curses from the hand of the LORD (Deuteronomy 28). In the Law of Messiah, no physical blessings or curses are spelled out, except in Galatians 1:8 to Judaizers and Acts 5 for lying to the Holy Spirit, as well as 1 Corinthians 5 (for immorality) and 11 (improper use of the Lord's Table). Under the Law of Messiah, there are provisions for chastening or discipline of a believer (Hebrews 12:5–11), but not a cursing as is provided so distinctly in the Law of Moses.

The Law of Moses established many different kinds of blood sacrifices to deal with Israel's sin and renew fellowship with God, and those sacrifices only provided a covering for sin (not forgiveness or removal). In the Law of Messiah, there is and was only one blood sacrifice: the voluntary sacrifice of Messiah, with His blood being the basis for our salvation by the removal of our sin. When sin occurs and breaks our fellowship, we simply confess our sin to the Father through our advocate, Yeshua the Messiah (1 John 1:9–2:2).

Chapter 8

Israel had kosher diet restrictions imposed on them. In the Law of Messiah, there are no restrictions, except that Gentile Christians were not to eat blood, a statute which is based on the Noahic Covenant (Acts 15:20).

In the Law of Moses, the death penalty was expanded from murder to idolatry, cursing God, cursing parents, breaking the Sabbath, and practicing witchcraft. None of this appears the Law of Messiah.

The token of the Mosaic law was the practice of Sabbath, which was a day of rest and not worship. It was given to Israel and it was not repeated to the Gentiles or the Church.

The Law of Moses could not provide salvation; rather, it provided *condemnation* and *death* (2 Corinthians 3:7, 9). The Law of Messiah, which is an outgrowth of the New Covenant, provided a *circumcised heart* (Colossians 2:11) and set out how believers in Messiah were to live before God, other believers, and the unsaved world.

The Law of Moses curses anyone who does not keep the whole law. The Law of Messiah has no such curse associated with it. Look at the words of Moses in Deuteronomy 27:26: *Cursed be he that confirms not all the words of this law to do them.*

A practical and logical examination of this verse reveals several problems for those who were under Mosaic law or who would keep it now. Firstly, today you cannot possibly keep *all the words of this law*: approximately 58% of the law cannot be kept because the Temple and sacrificial system no longer exist. Secondly, don't try to excuse yourself and make exceptions. There are no exceptions in that verse: if you want to live without the curse of God upon you, you must keep the whole law, because it is a unity. It is not to be broken down into groups of rules to be kept and groups of laws to be ignored. You can deceive and trick men, but you cannot trick God: He will hold you accountable. This is His word.

Now look at the words of Paul in Galatians 3:10:
For as many as are of the works of the law are under the curse: for it is written, cursed is every one that continues not in all things which are written in the book of the Law to do them.

Paul wrote this to the church in Galatia who were being deceived into keeping the Law of Moses by Judaizers (Torah-observant folks of the first century). He pointed out that placing oneself under the Mosaic law means placing yourself under the curse of God, because no human can keep all the provisions of that law. (If you want to keep Torah, try and keep Deuteronomy 27:26!)

Now, in the Law of Messiah, none of these problems arise. We live under grace, and we are not deemed to break all the law with an infraction of one point of the Messiah's Law. Because of the New Covenant and the blood of Messiah, when we sin we are told to *confess our sin* to God, who will *forgive us* for our violations of His standards (1 John 1:9), which will restore our fellowship with our God. God promises us blessings, but the blessings are spiritual blessings and not physical blessings, regarding which only Israel received any promises. However, because of the Abrahamic Covenant Jewish believers are promised both physical and now spiritual blessings in Messiah. Today in the Church we make no blood offerings; rather, we are told by Paul to make ourselves living sacrifices to God (Romans 12:1). Israel was subject to kosher laws with diet restrictions, which we as believers (whether Jewish or Gentile) are not obligated to keep (Acts 10:9–16). Today in the Church there is no death sentence for any violation of God's standards. God may choose to take a life because of the continual violation of His Word, but the carrying out of that death penalty is not in the hands of Christians or the Church, and never has been—even though the Church has, over the centuries, done so repeatedly. The punishment for murder still rests in the hands of government based on the Noahic Covenant (Genesis 9:6). A good illustration and contrast between the law systems is the case of a son who commits fornication with his stepmother. Under the Law of Moses, he was to be stoned to death (Leviticus 18:6–8). However, in 1 Corinthians 5:1–5, which describes such a case happening within the Church: the Law of Messiah prescribed excommunication from the Church and turning over the offending individual to Satan for the destruction of his flesh. Lastly, the Sabbath is not a law to be kept by Christians today; it was specifically given to Israel as a token by God in the Mosaic Covenant.

The Law of Messiah is completely different from the Law of Moses. As we compare the fruits of these laws, we discover that we are not comparing apples with apples; rather, we are dealing with apples and oranges: that is, totally and completely different laws and instructions as to how to live out our lives before God and our fellow men.

Nevertheless, this continues to be a controversial issue for some. Two other related passages and three other points may shed more light on it. First, James and then Paul gave clear and precise answers to this age-old issue of the place of the Law of Moses in the life of Christians. Look at the issue in the Jerusalem Counsel described in Acts 15 and see the argument of the believing Pharisees in the Church contrasted by Peter and Paul and the decision by James and the counsel. The issue was first raised by the Pharisees and then resolved by the decision of James and the counsel:

> 5 *But there rose up certain of the sect of the Pharisees which believed, saying, that it was needful to circumcise them* [Gentiles], *and to command them* [Gentiles] *to keep the law of Moses.*

8 *And God, which knows the hearts, bare them* [Gentiles] *witness, giving them* [the Gentiles] *the Holy Spirit, even as He did unto us* [Jewish believers]; 9 *And put no difference between us* [Jews] *and them* [Gentiles], *purifying their hearts by faith.* 10 *Now therefore why tempt your God, to put a yoke upon the neck of the disciples* [Gentiles], *which neither our fathers nor we were able to bear?* 11 *But we believe that through the grace of the Lord Yeshua Messiah we* [Jewish believers] *shall be saved, even as they* [Gentile believers]. 19 *Where my* [James's] *sentence is, that we trouble them not, which from among the Gentiles are turned to God.*

24 *Forasmuch as we have heard, that certain which went out from us have troubled you with words, subverting your souls, saying, You must be circumcised, and keep the law; to whom we gave no such commandment.* (Acts 15:5, 8–11, 19, 24)

If you read the whole section dealing with the Jerusalem Council (Acts 15:1–35), you will discover a clear decision by the Church that the new Gentile believers were not to be forced to hold to the Law of Moses. Notice as well that the council clearly references the Law of Moses as a unit, and that circumcision is the key to placing oneself under obedience to all the law. There is a clear understanding that to violate one law is to violate the whole law, which is what James said later in James 2:10, referencing Leviticus 19:18, which was the law that Yeshua referenced in Matthew 22:39 and Paul referenced in Galatians 5:14. Notice as well that James asks why would we want to put a yoke (the Mosaic law) on the necks of these Gentile believers when even *our fathers were not able bear it?* In short, why trouble these new Gentile believers who have turned to God? Today, because the Law of Messiah has not been properly taught, Jewish believers and some Gentile believers are still trying to keep the law even though the Jerusalem Council clearly said not to, and noted that those representing themselves as speaking for the council, who had been trying to get Gentile believers in Messiah to keep the Mosaic law, had been given *no such commandment* (Acts 15:24).

Secondly, Paul puts a question to the Galatian believers to get them to understand that the Mosaic law is not for the Gentiles, and that if they undergo circumcision it obligates them to all of that law, not just part of it. Paul understood the decision of the Jerusalem Council, for he was personally present as they all listened to what God had done by means of Peter and what God had done through the ministry of Paul and Barnabas. Here is the question that Paul asked of the Galatian believers that today no one seems to consider or understand: How did you become a believer in Jesus? How did you receive new life? Were you regenerated by means of law [of Moses] observance or by faith in the finished work of Messiah on the cross of Calvary? Many Christians want to continue to tack the Law of Moses onto their faith walk, despite Paul's statement that there is a new law, the Law of Messiah, which was a direct result of the blood of the New Covenant. Look at these verses:

> 1 *O foolish Galatians, who has bewitched you that you should not obey the truth, before whose eyes Yeshua Messiah has been evidently set forth, crucified among you? 2 This only would I learn of you, received you the Spirit by the works of the law, or by the hearing of faith? 3 Are you so foolish? Having begun in the Spirit, are you now made perfect by the flesh?* (Galatians 3:1–3)

The Mosaic law cannot make the flesh perfect. In fact, it actually accomplishes the opposite; it makes you sin more! It condemns you; it requires death, not new life. A life regenerated by the indwelling, sealing, and baptism of the Holy Spirit in a believer did not even exist under the Law of Moses.

A book by Lancaster, which promotes Judaizing, reveals that the author's logic is flawed by his bias toward Torah observance.

Regarding Galatians 3:1–3, he diverts the reader from the issue by giving the traditional Christian view and then saying, "That explanation does not work for us in Messianic [Torah-observant] Judaism because we maintain the gospel does not abrogate the Torah, that Christianity does not replace Judaism, and that Christians do not replace the Jewish people." [45]

This statement is a mixture of falsehood and truth. Christianity does not replace "biblical" Judaism, but it does fulfill it. Rabbinic Judaism in Yeshua's day and our day is a counterfeit law system, which was never authorized by God but became a pharisaic instrument to hinder the Jewish people from believing (Luke 13:22–30) in Yeshua their Messiah.[46] Having said that, biblical Judaism is incomplete and unfulfilled. It stands in anticipation of the Messiah Who did fulfill biblical Judaism and brought the Mosaic law system to an end, rendering it inoperative. Nor do Christians replace the Jewish people. However, if by the generic term "Christianity" the author meant the theologies of replacement, amillennial, and covenant/reform theologies, then perhaps he would be correct.

The Scriptures as reflected in dispensational theology do teach that the Law of Moses ended with the inauguration of the New Covenant by the blood of Messiah on the cross at Calvary. Dispensationalism teaches that the New Covenant is the fulfillment of biblical Judaism. In that process, the New Covenant and the work of Messiah and the Holy Spirit have rendered the Law of Moses inoperative, thus laying it aside in favor of the Law of Messiah. Both Judaism and dispensational theology vehemently maintain that the Church (Christianity) does not and never will replace the Jewish people.

Lancaster goes on to promote the Torah-observance belief that there was no history at that time to point toward Judaizers as being the ones who *bewitched* or were the "influencers" at the Galatian church. The believers whom he calls Christians were part of Judaism already, so this is a distortion of historical fact. The Roman government looked at Christians as part of Judaism, though this was not the message that Paul or the other apostles preached! Was there a precedent for Paul to teach concerning the Judaizers' false gospel of works? Yes, absolutely. Again, look at Acts 15 and Galatians 1–2. The word "Judaizer" is not mentioned in the Greek text of either Acts or Galatians—but who else would be teaching circumcision? For the answer, read Acts 15:5, which gives the context for the Jerusalem Council and the question of Gentiles' circumcision that the apostles needed to answer:

> *But there rose up certain of the sect of the Pharisees which believed, saying that it was needful to circumcise them, and to command them to keep the law of Moses.*

Consider the confrontation that Paul had with Peter over the issue of law observance and the freedom that believers have in the Law of Messiah:

> *11 But when Peter was come to Antioch, I withstood him to the face, because he was to be blamed. 12 For before that certain came from James* [from the Jerusalem assembly], *he did eat with the Gentiles: but when they were come, he withdrew and separated himself, fearing them which were of the circumcision. 13 And other Jews dissembled* [acted hypocritically] *likewise with him; insomuch that Barnabas also was carried away with their dissimulation* [hypocrisy]. *14 But when I saw that they walked not uprightly according to the truth of the gospel, I said unto Peter before them all, if you, being a Jew, live after the manner of Gentiles, and not as do the Jews, why compel you the Gentiles to live as do the Jews?* (Galatians 2:11–14)

So again, was there a precedent for Paul's message to the Galatians about circumcised believers? Yes. Many times Lancaster avoids condemnation of Torah observance to promote his flawed and biased theology of Torah observance today for both Jews and

Gentiles. He teaches that the ones who were *bewitched* or "influencers" in the Galatian church were Gentiles who were "irked" by the fact that Paul did not teach the *God fearers* to be circumcised like they themselves were before Paul came on the scene. He then takes another illogical leap by making the assumption that these, either new Gentile believers or former *God fearers*, were the problem. However, Scripture shows who the culprits were in the community of believers:

> *For as much as we* [Apostles] *have heard, that certain which went out from us* [sect of the Pharisees (Judaizers)] *have troubled you with words, subverting your souls, saying, you must be circumcised, and keep the law; to whom we gave no such commandment.* (Acts 15:24).

There is a principle that runs throughout the Bible: Scripture interacts with Scripture. Luke, who was recording the history of the Church, was a companion of Paul, and he fully recorded the issue and the participants in the discussion. Also, remember our principle of interpretation of Scripture, as well as the crucial need to understand Scripture <u>within its context</u>. For Lancaster, who promotes Torah observance, it is not convenient or profitable to reference verses like Acts 15:5, or verse 24; instead, he deflects the reader to secondary verses that do not give a biblical answer to the reality of the immediate context of the book of Galatians.

Paul's words are harsh and severe against fellow believers of the pharisaic persuasion who are violating the Jerusalem Council. Galatians 1 gives a dogmatic statement:

> 6 *I marvel that you are so soon removed from Him that called you into the grace of Messiah to another* [heteros] *gospel.* 7 *Which is not another* [allos]; *but there be some that trouble you, and would pervert the gospel of Messiah.* 8 *But though we, or an angel from heaven, preach any other gospel unto you than that which we have preached unto you, let him be accursed.* 9 *As we said before, so say I now again, If any man*

preach any other gospel unto you than that you have received, <u>let him be accursed</u>. (Galatians 1:6–9)

In verse 6 the first word used for "another" is the Greek word *heteros*; a different word (used elsewhere in verse 6) for "another" is *allos*. The Greek word *heteros* means "another of a different kind," whereas *allos* means "another of the same kind."[47] Now read that again: another of a different kind! This other gospel taught that belief in Jesus was necessary, and also taught the necessity of being circumcised and becoming obedient to the Law of Moses, which boils down to faith <u>plus</u> the works of the law. What the Judaizers were saying is that to have all of what God wants you to have, you must be circumcised and obey the Mosaic law. Those Judaizers were supplanting and rebelling against all that God had done in giving them and us something superior to the Law of Moses through the New Covenant and the blood of the Lamb of God. That message of the law in turn judges you, condemns you, and gives you death because it has absolutely no life in it. Paul refers to them as ones who *trouble you*, who pervert *the gospel*; they are *accursed*. That is very strong language. Here is its meaning: "The word accursed is from *anathema*. It is a word used in the [Septuagint, Greek translation of the Hebrew Scriptures], of a person or thing set apart and devoted to destruction, because [it is] hateful to God. Hence in a spiritual sense it denotes one who is alienated from God by sin."[48]

There is an active ingredient in Paul's statement of a curse, *anathema*, being placed on the believing Jews of pharisaic belief, called Judaizers, who would make the Good News (word of gospel) a different kind of gospel. Again, they were doing this in direct violation of the Jerusalem Council (see Acts 15). That alone should be a wake-up call to the Torah-observant believers within the Messianic movement today. They too are actively violating the Jerusalem Council, and also violating the terms of the New Covenant. In reality, they were and still are perverting the Good News of salvation *by faith alone*, by touting salvation by and through the works of the law. Many Mosaic law observers today who use the term "Torah observance" have forfeited the Law of Messiah for the default system of the old law that is *decaying and ... ready to vanish away* (Hebrews 8:13). They are perverting the pure, clear Good News of salvation by grace alone, and Paul says they are cursed. This does not affect the Judaizers' salvation, which was secured by the initiation of the New Covenant by Yeshua on the cross of Calvary by His blood, but it will result in their lack of rewards at the Bema Seat of Messiah (2 Corinthians 5:10). I stand amazed today that in the more than 2,000 years since Pentecost (the birthday of the Church), people have not studied the Law of Messiah, instead forfeiting it for something that God has rendered inoperative, something completely inadequate and (according to Galatians 1:6) accursed!

The third aspect to consider is that there are eight covenants in the Bible (see chapter 4). Often when a new covenant (not the New Covenant of Jeremiah) is given, it contains some of the same commandments as the previous covenant(s). For instance, some aspects of the conditional Edenic Covenant were carried over to the Adamic unconditional Covenant, but the Edenic Covenant ceased to function because of the fall of man. Likewise, aspects of the Mosaic law, also a conditional covenant, were carried over to the Law of Messiah, which came from the unconditional New Covenant. However, the maintenance of some similar commandments in the Law of Messiah does not mean that the Mosaic law is still in force. As Fruchtenbaum puts it:

> A simple comparison of the details will show that it is not and cannot be the same as the Law of Moses. Four observations are worth noting:

- First, many commandments are the same as those of the Law of Moses. For example, nine of the Ten Commandments are also in the Law of Christ.

- Second, many are different from the Law of Moses. For example, there is no Sabbath law now (Romans 14:5; Colossians 2:16) and no dietary code (Mark 7:19; Romans 14:20).

- Third, some commandments in the Law of Moses are intensified by the Law of Christ. The Law of Moses said: *love your neighbour as yourself* (Leviticus 19:18). This made man the standard. The Law of Christ said: *love one another, even as I have loved you* (John 15:12). This makes the Messiah the standard and He loved us enough to die for us.

- Fourth, the Law of Messiah provides a new motivation. The Law of Moses was based on the conditional Mosaic Covenant and so the motivation was: do, in order to be blessed. The Law of Christ is based on the unconditional New Covenant and so the motivation is: you have been and are blessed, therefore, do.[49]

The fourth point comes from Hebrews. There are many contrasts between the inability of the Law of Moses to deal ultimately with sin and the completeness that the Law of Messiah offers. Here is only one of many passages that could be used to illustrate the point. Hebrews 10:1–18 states that the Law of Moses was but a shadow of things to come, whereas the Law of Messiah in the New Covenant is complete. It also references Leviticus 16 in noting that the yearly Day of Atonement was completely incapable of dealing permanently with sin, whereas the blood of Messiah's offering was once and for all, forever. Then the author of Hebrews references Psalms 40:7–8 and connects it to Messiah, which is an astounding statement.

Now notice verse 9:
> *Then said He, Lo, I come to do your will, O God. He taketh away the firs*t [Law of Moses], *that He may establish the second* [the Law of Messiah by the New Covenant].

Take a moment to meditate on that thought that the writer of Hebrews attributes to Messiah. The Hebrews author is saying the same thing as Paul did in Romans 10:4, the same thing as Yeshua did in Matthew 5:17.

In verses 10–18, the Hebrews author again contrasts the two law systems, showing the inability of the Mosaic law to permanently deal with sin and the ability of the Law of Messiah in the New Covenant to completely remedy the problem and totally remove all sin forever. The author makes a stark contrast between the two law systems and shows throughout the book of Hebrews that what Messiah did through the New Covenant and the Law of Messiah that proceeds from it is infinitely superior to the old law system, which at that point (66 AD) *was waxing old and ready to vanish away.*

So the Law of Moses was nullified, rendered inoperative, and now we are under a new law, the Law of Messiah. Today the rule of law is the Law of Messiah and not the Law of Moses. These two law systems are completely distinct from each other. They are as different as night and day. However, many Christians fall back on the Mosaic law because they have never been properly instructed in the Law of Messiah.

Most important for any believer to recognize and comprehend is that the foundation of the Law of Messiah is laid down in the New Covenant. Most Christians do not understand the nature and purpose of the New Covenant that Yeshua inaugurated with His blood on the cross of Calvary and with what He said: *do this in remembrance of Me.* Instead of studying and investigating the Law of Messiah, they go into a default mode, back to the Mosaic law or to legalistic checklists. I encourage you to read my book, *Israel's Only Hope: The New Covenant*,⁵⁰ which should help you grasp the significance of the New Covenant and the ramifications of the New Covenant in the lives of Jewish people, as well as the blessing that flows over to us Gentile believers in Messiah as partakers with our Jewish brothers and sisters in Messiah.

Provisions of the Law of Messiah

Very simply, three main promises or provisions come out of the Jewish New Covenant of Jeremiah 31:31–34 and Ezekiel 36:26–27 that we as Gentiles in the Church today are allowed to partake of along with Jewish believers in Messiah.

- Jeremiah and Ezekiel are in complete agreement with Moses' promise concerning the regeneration [of uncircumcised] hearts (Deuteronomy 10:16; 30:6). There was never a provision for regeneration in the Law of Moses.

- Jeremiah and the prophets speak of the removal of sin rather than just a "covering" of sin, which is all the Mosaic law provided. Under the Law of Moses sin was only covered, whereas under the New Covenant it is completely forgiven and removed.

- Ezekiel, Isaiah, and Joel speak of the indwelling of the Holy Spirit. This indwelling is completely different from the ministry of the Holy Spirit in the Old Testament. In the Hebrew Scriptures, the Holy Spirit only came upon an [selected] individual[s] to fulfill a task, and upon completion of the task the Holy Spirit would leave. That temporary indwelling had nothing to do with salvation, as indwelling does in the New Covenant's dispensation of grace.

These three provisions all deal with our new relationship with God and His Messiah Who is God incarnate. Our <u>hearts</u> are changed, regenerated and circumcised; our <u>sin</u> is removed, not merely covered; and the ministry of the Holy Spirit now <u>indwells</u> us, not just using [I prefer the words "coming upon" because that is the biblical expression used in the Hebrew Scriptures as it relates to the ministry of the Holy Spirit in the OT.] a believer to fulfill a particular task that God wants accomplished. These provisions deal with being born again, *being born from above, being born of the spirit* (John 3:3–7); we are now a *new creation* (2 Corinthians 5:17) in Messiah. These new laws of Messiah largely deal with our spiritual walk in Messiah; unlike the Mosaic law, there is no list of restrictions on food, clothing, feast days, sacrifices, and daily laws that make you different from those around you. Today we are to be different, but the difference appears in the inner quality of the heart, rather than by subjection to external laws that make us look different or that we cannot keep.

Focus of the Law of Messiah

Here are some of the most important areas that the Law of Messiah focuses on:

- Our relationship to our government
- Our relationship to other believers in Messiah
- Our spiritual walk in Messiah
- How to be a testimony to the unsaved
- The inner man that would control all our outward expressions
- Marriage and family relationships

- The job that God has given us to do and the spiritual gifts He grants to help in accomplishing His will for a believer's life

- Positive instruction on how to live before God

- How we are to imitate Messiah in our daily walk

- An intimate relationship with God (unknown in the Law of Moses)

- Warnings about false teachers who would lead us astray from our walk in Messiah

Of course, there are many more things that the Law of Messiah does, but these suffice to make the point that this new system of law has very little in common with the old, dead Mosaic system. The Law of Messiah has a different basis or foundation, operating from the believer's new, regenerated, circumcised heart. The Law of Messiah is based on the finished work of Messiah on the cross, which never need be repeated, in contrast to the blood sacrifices of the Mosaic law that had to be repeated over and over again. The Law of Messiah encourages our daily conduct to *walk worthy of our calling* in Messiah (Ephesians 4:1) with all the blessings that God has poured out upon us. In the Mosaic law, if you wanted God's blessing, you were to be obedient—period. In the Law of Messiah, we are blessed because of Him, not because we are obedient or because we have done anything meritorious. Being blessed, we, out of a new motivation of love for how He has blessed us, are morally obligated to live and walk in obedience to His will and His new law, the Law of Messiah (1 John 2:6). We are to be in love with Him.

The Blessings

In the Law of Messiah we are blessed by God, and we are to walk in Him because our hearts are full of thanksgiving for all of those blessings. Here is a partial list of His blessings (Ephesian 1:3) which neither Jew or Gentile deserves: they are granted strictly by His grace.

- We have been <u>regenerated</u> (Ephesians 2:5; Titus 2:5), made alive spiritually to once again walk and commune with our holy God. It is the Holy Spirit that imparts life and it is the Word of God that the Holy Spirit uses as His instrument in regeneration (1 Peter 1:23).

- We have been <u>justified</u> (Romans 5:8; 1 Corinthians 6:11); He has declared us righteous because the <u>righteousness</u> (Romans 3:26) of Messiah has been <u>imputed</u> (Romans 4:22–25) to our account.

- He has <u>reconciled</u> us (2 Corinthians 5:18; Ephesians 2:16–18, 22) because whereas we were the enemies of God, now we are <u>joint heirs</u> (Romans 8:17) with Messiah. He has also given us the <u>Ministry of Reconciliation</u> (2 Corinthians 5:17 20) through which we ourselves are to live reconciled lives on a daily basis, and He has given us the power to do so by the ministry of the Holy Spirit in our lives.

- He is our <u>propitiation</u> (Romans 3:25), which means that because of His blood sacrifice on the cross He has satisfied all of God's holy and righteous demands, enabling Him to act on our behalf.

- We have been <u>sanctified</u> (1 Corinthians 6:11; 2 Thessalonians 2:13; 1 Peter 1:2), set apart for holy use because we have been cleansed by His blood. We are now the very temple of God where He personally dwells (1 Corinthians 3:16; 6:19–20).

- He has <u>redeemed</u> (Romans 3:24) us out of the slave market of sin; we have <u>redemption</u> (Ephesians 1:7) because of

His blood sacrifice.

- We have been given the Holy Spirit of God to <u>indwell</u> us (1 Corinthians 3:16), <u>fill us</u> (Ephesians 5:18), <u>seal us</u> (Ephesians 1:13–14) and <u>baptize us</u> (1 Corinthians 12:13) into the body of Messiah.

- He has <u>circumcised our hearts</u> (Romans 3:30; Colossians 2:11–13).

- He has made us <u>partakers</u> with Him in God's divine nature (2 Peter 1:4).

- He has literally blessed us with all <u>spiritual blessings in heavenly places</u> in Messiah (Ephesians 1:3).

- He has transferred us from the kingdom of darkness into the Kingdom of Light (Acts 26:18; Colossians 1:13; 1 Peter 2:9).

Could the Law of Moses do any of this? The answer is a resounding NO! The relationship that we now have with God, because of the blood of the *New Covenant*, is completely different from what the Law of Moses presented.

Contemplate the ramifications of the Law of Messiah in contrast to the Law of Moses. When Jeremiah introduced the term New Covenant in Jeremiah 31:31, his words would carry power and change beyond Judaism's (and in particular rabbinic Judaism's) wildest imagination. The provisions of this New Covenant, as it would be unpacked after the death, burial, and resurrection of Messiah and coupled with the coming of the Holy Spirit on the day of Pentecost, are simply breathtaking. Many within the Messianic Movement argue that the New Covenant is a renewal of the Mosaic Covenant. They have done a great disservice thereby both to the work of their Messiah and to the work of the Holy Spirit in what was accomplished, for both Jew and Gentile, through the unfathomable riches of His grace (Ephesians 3:8, 16–21).

The final point that I want to bring to your attention is the difference between law and grace. First of all, law and grace are mutually destructive of one other. It is impossible for them to coexist. In the very nature of the law system there is no grace, because a holy God is completely offended by our sin and our depraved hearts. The Mosaic law became a system of works instead of a lifestyle to live by in Old Testament times. The Law of Moses guarantees failure: that is an undeniable historical fact. The law cannot provide spiritual life for spiritually dead men. Law cannot remove sin. Law cannot regenerate the uncircumcised heart of man. Law is the prosecuting attorney with no one to defend us as we stand before a holy God while the law (correctly) accuses man as a sinner: unholy, impure, and unclean before a holy God. Man stands before a holy God and a holy law, convicted and judged. There is not even the slightest hint of any grace coming from the throne of God under the law system, because of the unresolved issue of our sin. The law purports to offer salvation by works (observance of the law), but because no human can keep the law, all men are doomed.

The merit of Messiah's work on the cross of Calvary is the foundation of grace. Grace comes from the New Covenant of Grace that will regenerate walking dead men. The blood of Messiah satisfies all the holy righteous demands of God and thereby gives us, the walking dead men, new life and eternal fellowship with Him. The grace of God cancels out the law of the Mosaic system. The Law of Messiah is completely different: It gives us power to walk a godly life because the price of spiritual and physical death has been paid by God Himself when He came and dwelt among us and died for us, taking our place. Because of what His grace did on the cross, we no longer experience the ministry of *condemnation and death*; instead, His grace provides everlasting life.

The Law of Messiah Changes It All

A passage that has a direct relationship to the controversy between the Law of Moses and the Law of Messiah is Ephesians 2:1–10. These verses make it obvious that Paul clearly understood that the Law of Moses had been rendered obsolete and inoperative and that the Law of Messiah had become the system by which humanity was to abide.

> 1 *And you have He quickened* [made alive], *who were dead in trespasses and sins;* 2 *Wherein in time past you walked according to the course of this world, according to the prince of the power of the air, the spirit that now works in the children of disobedience:* 3 *Among whom also we all had our conversation* [manner of living] *in times past in the lusts* [desires] *of our flesh, fulfilling the desires of the flesh and of the mind; and were by nature the children of wrath, even as others.* 4 *But God, who is rich in mercy, for His great love wherewith He loved us,* 5 *Even when we were dead in sins have quickened* [made alive] *us together with Messiah,* [by grace you are saved] 6 *And have raised us up together, and made us sit together in heavenly places in Messiah Yeshua:* 7 *That in the ages to come He might show the exceeding riches of His grace in His kindness toward us through Messiah Yeshua.* 8 *For by grace are you saved through faith; and that not of yourselves: it is the gift of God:* 9 *Not of works, lest any man should boast.* 10 *For we are His workmanship, created in Messiah Yeshua unto good works, which God has before ordained that we should walk in them.*

Now let us look at the biblical conviction of Paul in relationship to these two law systems. Which one does he see as superior?

Beginning with verse 1 he describes the character of the unsaved, unregenerate individual. First we were dead in trespasses and sins (Romans 3:23, 6:23). Did the Law of Moses change that fact? No! Did the Law of Moses *quicken* you, make you alive spiritually? No! However, that which was dead because of trespasses and sin was quickened by God (not Moses' law): we were quickened, made alive, and regenerated by the *circumcision of Christ* (Colossians 2:11–13). This verse clearly states that the Law of Moses is helpless to remove our trespasses and sin. The blood of bulls, goats, or lambs could not remove our trespasses and sins; they could only cover them (Hebrews 9:11–15). It was the ministry of the Holy Spirit in the New Covenant that activated us and made us alive.

Verse 2 specifies that the Law of Moses could not deal with our *walk according to the course of this world*, which is satanically controlled by *the prince of the power of the air*. It is his spirit with our old nature in us working out disobedience. So, these first two verses confirm that the Law of Moses had absolutely no power to change the plight of man. He is dead, he has trespassed, he has missed the righteousness of God, he has walked according to the satanic system of the world which is the power of the air: we are *children of disobedience*. The Mosaic law could not and did not change anything—but the New Covenant did.

Verse 3 emphasizes that our negative position created by our living for our fleshly desires and the desires of our carnal minds was a product of our sinful nature, which the Law of Moses was powerless to change. So, we were not only *children of disobedience*, but also *children of wrath*, just like every other person, Jewish or not. The Law of Moses was impotent: It was unable to change our sinful nature and the fact that we were spiritually dead, separated from a holy God. Mosaic law observance is utterly unable to make us acceptable before a holy God.

Chapter 8

Verse 4 has two of the most precious words in Scripture: but God. It does not say "but Moses" or "but the Mosaic law"; rather, *God in His rich mercy* with great and unspeakable love loved us, even when we were dead in sins (verse 5). The Mosaic law does not love, it condemns (Romans 7:23–24; 2 Corinthians 3:7–9; Galatians 3:13)—but God loves (John 3:16–18), and He restored the spiritual connection that was lost in the Garden of Eden. He did something that the Law of Moses could never do: He made us alive, He regenerated us. The Law of Moses is incapable of regenerating our hearts; it is a ministry of *condemnation* and *death*. The result and outworking of the New Covenant is that the Holy Spirit regenerates our hearts as promised (Titus 3:5), which the Law of Moses could not do.

Verse six says that when He regenerated our hearts and made us new creations in Christ (2 Corinthians 5:17), He raised us up from being dead, from being prisoners in the control of the world system and the prince of darkness, and made us to sit in heavenly places in Messiah. When, in all of the Hebrew Scriptures, was the Law of Moses capable of doing such a thing? Never.

Verse 7 informs us that He will present us as trophies of His grace, as examples of the exceeding riches of His grace to us who were dead. He will continue to do that as the ages pile themselves one upon another. Despite the passage of time, through the finished work of Messiah Yeshua our eternity is secure in His grace. Can law plus works do that? No!

Paul reiterates in verse eight we are saved from death and the clutches of the evil one—not by the works of the law, not by our own merit and works, but by grace through faith in Jesus Christ. To combine grace and the works of the law is to say that salvation can be achieved by works rather than by grace alone. To add the law to grace is another kind of gospel (Galatians 1:6–9) and not the gospel that the New Testament teaches. The Mosaic law and the holiness of God cannot be reconciled by grace under the law even though grace was demonstrated by God. You could perhaps say that in God's mercy, grace was given, but it was not salvific. However, because of the finished work of Messiah on the cross, with God's holiness satisfied by Messiah's volunteer substitutional vicarious sacrifice, God in His grace then saved us; the Law of Moses has been rendered inoperative because of the blood of Messiah, with the New Covenant and the Law of Messiah becoming operative thereby.

Verse nine reminds us again that salvation is not gained by the works of the law; thus, we cannot boast of our own merit. The Law of Moses is not even on the radar screen as to what it takes to remove us from death, to regenerate our uncircumcised hearts and raise us up as His trophies of His grace in the ages to come. Messiah does it all, without law observance, but rather by His grace through faith alone.

Finally, in verse 10 works are mentioned positively for the first time—but not the works of the Law of Moses done by Torah observance: Instead, this verse extols Messiah's workmanship, not Moses'. We are now created in Messiah unto good works based on the Law of Messiah through the New Covenant.

This portion of Ephesians confirms the truth of the New Covenant and the Law of Messiah in one's own heart. God's focus today is on grace, not on the Law of Moses. His focus is on the finished work, the final sacrifice, and not on law observance.

Teachings That the Law of Messiah Would Be Superior

It was an eye-opening experience to see that even some rabbis of the past ages acknowledged that the Law of Messiah would be superior to Moses and the Law of Moses, and that the Messiah would be divine as well as human. The following quotes come from a book written by Rabbi Itzhak Shapira,[51] a Sephardic Jew in Israel who came to faith as he studied and read rabbinic writings such as the Talmud,[52] Midrash,[53] Targum,[54] and Zohar.[55] His book, which is intended to show the deity of the Messiah from within rabbinic Judaism, was derived from his study of many references from the Sages[56] before Rashi[57] and Maimonides.[58] Here I have reproduced selected comments from Shapira's study (throughout, underlining/emphasis is mine).

Comments by Rabbi Shimon Bar Zavdi:

In Ecclesiastes Rabbah, Rabbi Hezekiah in the name of Rabbi Shimon Bar Zavdi explains that the <u>Torah of men</u> is called *hevel*, "foolishness," <u>because it is not eternal</u>. However, in the future the Torah will be <u>in the hearts of Israel</u> [Jer 31:33; Ezek 36:26] and they will never forget it [Jer 31:32]. There will be no *hevel* because the <u>"new" Torah will be eternal</u>, as Ecclesiastes Rabbah explains in connection with Jeremiah 31. The sages go on to declare that any tranquility that a man experiences in this world is *hevel* in compassion to the tranquility of the world to come, [and] <u>all the Torah that a man learns in this world is foolishness compared to the Torah of the world to come</u>, because in this world a man studies and forgets, but the <u>Torah of Mashiach [Messiah] will be remembered forever</u>.[59]

Here David Stern and the Haftorah conflict with the rabbis before them. They say that Law of Moses is eternal, however Rabbi Zavdi says it is foolishness, for the New Torah is eternal, the Torah of Messiah.

Comments by Rabbi Shapira:

We read these words in the Talmud about the ownership of the Messiah over the Torah and his divine presence:

It is written, then the moon shall be confounded, and the sun ashamed, when the LORD of Hosts shall reign; whilst [elsewhere] it is written, moreover the light of the moon shall be as the light of the sun, and the light of the sun shall be sevenfold, as the light of seven days. It is not difficult: the latter refers to the Messianic era, and the former to the world to come.

It is striking to see that the sages of the Talmud interchange the term "Messiah's reign" (in other areas of the text) with the term "the LORD of Hosts shall reign." It is also interesting to note that the sages understood that Messiah will bring a new reality and a new Torah as Ba'al Torah [Owner of Torah].

If we were to ask the question, "Who is the Ba'al Torah?" the answer would be clear to everybody; it is the God of Israel and his name is ADONAI. However, as we will learn…, it is the Messiah who is the true Ba'al Torah and he was given the authority to change (as shocking as it sounds) and to even nullify the Torah! One cannot argue that any human can change the eternal Torah and the written Torah of God unless he has the full authority of God himself and he is in essence part of God.[61]…

I could not help but wonder about the nature of the "fence" that the Messiah will break by his authority to redefine the Torah and our servanthood toward God. … The great Hebraic scholar Franz Delitzsch… translated the word *phragmos*, meaning "fence" into Hebrew as *mechitzat hagader*, or "the fence of partition." According to the text, Yeshua is the breaker who broke the barrier of Judaism to include the Gentiles in God's promises by writing his Torah on their hearts and grafting them into Israel.[62]

Comments by Rabbi Yalkut Shimoni:

Most scholars believe that some of these midrashim in the Yalkut dated back to the 1st and 2nd century or even earlier. In this remez [clue], according to the Yalkut, the Messiah will be greater than the patriarchs, higher than Abraham, lifted up above Moses, and higher than the ministering angels.[63]

Chapter 8

Comments by Rabbi Schneerson:

Rabbi Menachem Mendel Schneerson in his book said concerning Messiah ("Torat Hamemachem — Hitvadhut" pgs. 272–273), "The words 'Behold, My servant shall prosper, he shall be exalted and lifted up, and shall be very high' are referring to King Messiah.... The scripture mentions <u>five attributes of the Messiah</u>; prosper, exalted, lifted up, raised up, greatly because <u>the Messiah is from above and he is greater than the three fathers</u> (Abraham, Isaac, Jacob), Moses, and Adam-Kadmon.... <u>Moses is the first and last redeemer, but king Messiah is greater.</u>"[64]

Comments by Rabbi Yalkut Shimoni:

HaShem will sit in the garden of Eden and give a new Torah to Israel that will be given by the Messiah.[65]

Comments by Rabbi Shapira:

The Rambam himself claimed that the Torah is eternal and cannot be changed or modified, yet the sages of the Talmud thought otherwise.[66] ...

Summary point: The sages of the Talmud understood and agreed that the Messiah's Torah is superior to the Torah that we study today.[67]

Comments by Rabbi Shapira:

We read in Jeremiah that only God can bring stillness to nature and to people, and God alone controls the forces of nature (see Proverbs 30). Yet, it was Yeshua who manifested the same attributes as Nehorah, the light of the world, just as Isaiah and Jeremiah prophesied.

Lastly, let us examine one more important detail from Isaiah 51:4: The phrase "give ear unto me," *Elai Ha'azinu*, describes the obedience that we are to give to the Torah. <u>Many of the main</u>

Jewish commentators related this verse to the new Torah that will be given to us by the Messiah. In Metudat David we read that it will be King Messiah who will give new instruction to Israel first and also to the nations on how to walk in the ways of the LORD. This text applies the term Davar Adonai (the word of the LORD) to King Messiah.

The Malbim explains that the words "give ear unto me" are important because the Messiah of Israel declares that we are to listen "only to him" and not to the voice of any other prophet, as Messiah equates himself in Authority with God.[68] [See Deuteronomy 18:18–19]

Comments by Rabbi Shapira:

When the LORD says "instruction or Torah shall go forth from Me," we must wonder which Torah Isaiah 51:4 refers to. Does it refer to rabbinic Torah as is thought today? Notice that in the words, the Torah will "go forth from me," the possessive term in the Hebrew language should not be changed if we are to stay true to the scriptures. The word *meti* (from me) refers to the fact that the new Torah will be given by the Messiah because he is the Ba'al [Master] of the new Torah and he is the giver of the New Torah![69]

In an earlier chapter, we saw that the Messiah is to be the Ba'al [Master] Torah and a greater prophet than even Moses himself, based on early rabbinic interpretations of Isaiah 52:13.[70] [See Deuteronomy 18:18–19; 34: 10]

Comments by Rabbi Carmiel Cohen on Deuteronomy 34:10

The Ralbag finds three differences between the prophecies of Moshe [Moses] and the other prophets. (1) He knew God face to face ... also by the (2) quality and (3) quantity of the miracles that Moses did in front of the eyes of the Children of Israel. The Ralbag continues: "However, the words 'arisen a prophet since

Chapter 8

in Israel like unto Moses,' raise an interesting question; do we have a Prophet like him outside the land of Israel?... The truth is that there is no Prophet in Israel as great as Moses, who was a Prophet in Israel, but there <u>will be a Prophet to the nations (greater than Israel) and he will be King Messiah</u>. As it is stated in the Midrashim, "Behold, my Servant shall prosper." <u>He will be greater than Moses; his miracles will be greater than Moses because Moses anointed Israel alone to serve HaShem, but the Messiah will anoint all the nations to serve HaShem</u>.[71]

Comments by Rabbi Shapira:

The reason that the Torah is to be remembered during the Messianic age is that Moses represents the shadow of the Messiah to come, who will give Israel a greater Torah than the Torah of Moses!... The point is clear: the first redeemer brought a Torah that redeemed Israel; the last redeemer will bring an even greater Torah that will redeem <u>Israel and all the nations of the earth</u>.[72]

I personally found the contents of Shapira's book very enlightening and helpful, with many points of agreement. In some places it is easy to get a little lost in rabbinic logic, but most of it was very insightful and helpful in understanding the place of Messiah (Christ) and His authority to give a new Torah or instruction—not just to Israel but to the Gentiles and the world at large. In discussing the words of the sages, Shapira sees the presentation of the Law of Messiah by the apostles as relating the Law of Messiah to both the Jewish world and those in the Gentile world who have placed their faith and trust in Messiah (Christ) as their Savior, for He is the LORD, or HaShem (The Name). He is the one who revealed the will of the Father and the one who consistently interacted with men from Genesis to Revelation.

Throughout his book, Shapira quotes and references rabbis of the past as recognizing that the Messiah is divine and that the new Torah He gives is superior to and greater than Moses and the law of Moses given to Israel. He also clearly states that the Scriptures (Old and New Testaments) are the final authority, following that line of thought consistently in relation to the divinity of the Messiah. However, Shapira does not follow that same authority in relation to the New Torah (Instruction) given by the Messiah. He calls the New Torah eternal, superior, greater even than the Law of Moses, yet he follows rabbinic and Messianic theology in holding that the Law of Messiah is an appendix to the Law of Moses. He continually notes that the Law of Moses "will be renewed" in the Law of Messiah, and in this I disagree and find him inconsistent.

What I attempt to show, here and throughout this book, is that Messiah's finished work on the cross fulfilled the requirements of the law. The Mosaic law as a unit thus ended; it was rendered inoperative by Messiah with His finished work. The law was Israel's guardian or schoolmaster until that finished work of Messiah was accomplished with His blood, the blood of the New Covenant. So, as Jeremiah said, there will be a New Covenant (Jeremiah 31:31) or a New Torah (new instruction), replacing the Mosaic Covenant (Jeremiah 31:32). A new heart is placed internally (Jeremiah 31:33; Ezekiel 36:26) by God in the heart of Jew and Gentile alike, in a circumcision of the heart (Colossians 2:11).

9

POINTS OF CLARIFICATION

This chapter attempts to clarify a couple of points so that I am not misunderstood. Throughout this book I use the terms "Torah," "grace" and "Christian liberty." I do not have varying meanings for these words; rather, I use them uniformly whether speaking of Jewish people, Messianic Jewish believers, or Gentile believers. (In all quotations and extracts, underlining is added by this author.)

Torah

Torah can be interpreted in several different ways. First, let us see how Robinson uses this word:

> The word *torah* comes from the Hebrew root yorah/<u>teach</u>. Although it is often translated as "laws" and includes a lot of material that could be called legal in nature, it would be more accurate to call the Torah "<u>Instruction</u>" or "<u>Teachings</u>." Jews often refer to "the torah" when they are discussing a specific section of the Pentateuch covering a single topic, as in the "Torah of the Nazirite."[73]

Neusner and Green have a slightly expanded definition:

> Torah (Heb., <u>instruction</u>) referring especially to divine law, a fundamental concept in Jewish texts beginning with the Tanakh (Old Testament). The term is used in several senses, ranging from an individual commandment to the whole Tanakh. It often designates the first five books, Genesis through Deuteronomy, called the "Law of Moses" and regarded as the heart of Tanakh.... Torah, Oral: The orally revealed and transmitted part of the Torah. At Sinai, God gave

the Torah to Moses in two media, oral and written; the oral part was formulated for memorization and handed on from master to disciple, in the model of God to Moses: "Moses received Torah at Sinai and handed it on to Joshua, Joshua to elders, and elders to prophets. And prophets handed it on to the men of the great assembly."[74]

In Judaism the term *Torah* is a very elastic word involving the written (Law of Moses) and oral laws (rabbinic laws) from the books of Moses (also called the Pentateuch). It can also include the book of Deuteronomy, and may include teaching from one point of Torah to rabbinic literature like the Mishnah or Talmud (which is nonbiblical instruction or teaching). Thus, the simpest definition of *Torah* is "instruction" or "teaching." Therefore, the "Law" of Moses or the "Law" of Messiah simply means instruction and teaching to Israel in the Old Testament context, and to the believers in Christ (Messiah) in a New Testament context which is based on the Jewish New Covenant from Jeremiah 31. The term "Torah observance," which I frequently use in this book, refers to the selective law observance. Now remember, *Torah* means "instruction" or "teaching," so "Torah observance" (Mosaic law observance) refers to instruction or teaching of a group of Jewish and/or Gentile believers in Messiah who have incorporated or combined the gospel message of salvation and the believer's walk with added instruction and teaching from the Mosaic law. When one speaks of teaching Torah, one must know what Torah is being taught in a biblical context.

The controversy concerning Torah observance arises among people who are believers in Messiah and have the same salvation that I have; we are brothers and sisters in Christ. However, some of those believers think that we are still subject to and bound by the instruction and teaching that was given only to Israel (in the Law of Moses), although that Torah was never given to the Church or the body of Messiah (Christ). In essence, this book is intended to help believers understand what Torah we are to obey! Do we obey the Law of Moses, or a combination of the Laws of Moses and Christ, or the instruction and teaching from Christ and His apostles called the Law of Messiah?

With this understanding of the word *Torah*, it is true that we all are to be Torah observant. However, I propose in this book that God has rendered Mosaic Torah observance inoperative, because the Law of Moses has been fulfilled in the death, burial, and resurrection of Christ and thus has come to an end. The Torah (instruction and teaching) of the author of Hebrews, who was writing to Jewish believers who were contemplating going back to Judaism and the law because of persecution, is that Messiah is superior to and better than the old covenant, which is *vanishing away*. Likewise, the teaching and instruction of Paul are also directed to believers who only obey the Law of Messiah.

Free Grace

A number of years ago I came across the term "free grace." That means different things to people with different theological orientations. Here is a definition of "free grace" taken from a magazine called *Grace Focus*:

> Free Grace theology is the view that (1) everlasting life is a free gift (which the Lord Jesus fully paid for by His death on the cross for our sins) which is received by faith alone in Christ alone, apart from works of any kind; (2) that assurance of one's eternal destiny is based solely on believing Jesus' promise to the believer and not at all on our works or on our feelings; and (3) that all people, believers and unbelievers, are accountable for their works, receive recompense for what they do in this life, and will be judged at the end of the age (in two separate judgments) to determine degrees of reward (believers) or degrees of torment (unbelievers) in the life to come, but not to determine their eternal destinies.[75]

Chapter 9

As presented here, I can say that I have believed in "free grace" all my life. Salvation in Christ the Messiah of Israel is achieved by faith in Him ... plus nothing. He paid it all, thereby providing my regeneration. There are no works in a believer's life that give that believer any merit in God's eyes; all the work was done by Messiah. Works have absolutely nothing to do with being saved, but for the believer they have everything to do with how we live out our lives after becoming believers. When we stand before the Bema Seat of Messiah in heaven, our salvation is never in question, but the quality of our works is, as it relates to our position in the eternal order.

Free grace is not a license to sin, as Paul clearly states in Romans 6:1–2:

> 1 *What shall we say then? Shall we continue in sin, that grace may abound?* 2 *God forbid. How shall we, that are dead to sin live any longer therein?*

In fact, free grace theology vehemently opposes sin, despite some who say that we believe in license or leave the door open for sin. We do <u>not</u> teach that, nor do we encourage it in any way.

I also disagree with the *Grace in Focus* statement that: "[w]hile Free Grace people believe in and proclaim the cross and the resurrection, <u>we do not say that all those who believe Jesus died for our sins and rose again have eternal life</u>. Why not? Because someone can believe those things about Jesus and also believe in salvation by works. That is not a saving message."[76] I simply believe that God's grace is bigger than us, and God knows the hearts of believers, even if they try to add to God's grace through works. God's grace, which is given to all believers at the point of their believing by faith in the work of Messiah on the cross for our salvation, cannot be brought into question. They have believed by faith, and the fact that they have been taught mistaken or wrong doctrine does not negate their salvation. As an example, look at Acts 15:5:

But there rose up certain of the sect of the Pharisees which believed, saying, that it was needful to circumcise them, and to command them to keep the Law of Moses.

Apparently, men who believed nevertheless wanted to add circumcision and the Law of Moses to the faith of the Gentiles. That whole discussion was soundly renounced by the apostles and the First Jerusalem Council. Notice that nowhere in Acts 15 were the Pharisees of this sect told to repent because they had lost their salvation or they did not believe by faith alone. They did believe by faith alone, but they were also carrying a lot of rabbinic baggage and thought it necessary to add that baggage to the Gentiles' faith. Notice that they were not told by the apostles at the Jerusalem Council that they were not saved by faith in Messiah. The men and women in the Torah observance movement today are saved by faith in Messiah alone, but like their forerunners they add works, a mistake that is the subject of this book. In summary, whether a believer is torah observant, Calvinist, or Arminian who believes in Jesus as his personal saviour is saved. However, the addition of works to keep his salvation or enhance his salvation minimizes the understanding and ramifications of the grace of God. He has dwarfed God's grace and has lowered it to a human level adding works. It has nothing to do with eternal life given by God. That is secure.

Another man who believed in free grace, and preached it many years ago, was Dwight L. Moody,[77] an evangelist during the late 19th and early 20th centuries. He said that some people linger at Sinai, when we should be lingering at the cross to grasp the grace of God given to us. He made numerous statements contrasting the work of the law and the work of grace in our hearts. Remember, without the New Covenant which led to the Law of Messiah, the age of Grace would not have happened (John 1:17). Here are some of Moody's comments:

- "What the law of God does to the sinner; it brings him right to death, and leaves him there" but by His free grace picks us up and gives us life.

- "Life never came through the law. As has been observed: when the law was given, 3000 men lost their lives; but when grace and truth came at Pentecost, 3000 obtained life." [Exodus 32:28; Acts 2:41]

- "The law says, stone him! — Grace says embrace him."

- "The law says Smite him! — Grace says kiss him."

- "The law went after him, and bound him; grace said, loose him and let him go!"

- "Law tells me how crooked I am [Amos 7:8–9]; grace comes and make me straight."

- "The law cannot give life; all it can do is to bring us to Him who is the life." [John 14:6]

- "He takes us out from under the law, and puts us under grace."

Throughout this book I have been making contrasts between the Mosaic law and the Law of Messiah through which His grace is given. Moody did that same more than 125 years ago, compiling a list of contrasts between the law which is *death* and *condemnation* and the grace of God which gives life:

- The Law was given by Moses [Deuteronomy 33:4]; Grace and truth came by Jesus Christ [John 1:17].

- The Law says This do, and you shall live [Deuteronomy 4:1; 5:33; 8:1]; Grace says Live, and then you shall do [Ephesians 1:3; Colossians 3:1–3].

- The Law says Pay me that which you owe [Romans 1:32; 5:12, 21; 6:16, 23]; Grace says I frankly forgive you all [Ephesians 4:32].

- The Law says The wages of sin is death [Romans 6:23]; Grace says The gift of God is eternal life [Ephesians 2:8].

- The Law says The soul that sins, it shall die [Romans 3:23]; Grace says Whosoever believes in Jesus, though he were dead, yet shall he live: and whosoever lives and believes in Him shall never die [John 11:25–26].

- The Law pronounces Condemnation and death [2 Corinthians 3:7, 9]; Grace proclaims Justification and life [John 3:16; Romans 3:24; 6:1 4; 1 John 5:20].

- The Law says make you a new heart and a new spirit [Deuteronomy 10:16]; Grace says a new heart will I give you, and a new spirit will I put within you [Ezekiel 36:26–27].

- The Law says Cursed is every one that continues not in all things which are written in the book of the law to do them [Deuteronomy 28:15 68]; Grace says Blessed is the man whose iniquities are forgiven, whose sin is covered; blessed is the man to whom the Lord will not impute iniquity [Romans 4:7 8].

- The Law says Thou shalt love the Lord your God with all your heart, and with all your mind, and with all thy strength [Deuteronomy 6:5]; Grace says Herein is love: not that we love God, but that He loved us, and sent His Son to be the propitiation for our sins [John 3:16–18; Romans 5:8; 1 John 2:2; 4:10].

- The Law speaks of what man must do for God [Deuteronomy 5:31]; Grace tells of what Christ has done for man [Ephesians 2:8–10].

- The Law addresses man as part of the old creation [Genesis 3:19; Isaiah 64:6; Romans 7:23–24]; Grace makes a man a member of the new creation [Romans 6:10–14; 2 Corinthians 5:17].

- The Law bears on a nature prone to disobedience [Genesis 6:5, 8:21; Job 5:7; Ecclesiastes 7:20; Jeremiah 17:9]; Grace creates a nature inclined to obedience [Romans 5:19, 6:16; 2 Corinthians 10:5; 1 John 3:6, 5:18].

- The Law demands obedience by the terror of the Lord [Exodus 19:16; Deuteronomy 6:22–26; 18:16]; Grace beseeches men by the mercies of God [Romans 12:1–2].

- The Law demands holiness [Leviticus 11:44, 19:2; Isaiah 6:3]; Grace gives holiness [1 Corinthians 1:2; 1 Peter 1:15–16, 2:9].

- The Law says Condemn him [2 Corinthians 3:7, 9]; Grace says Embrace him [Luke 15:11–24].

- The Law speaks of priestly sacrifices offered year by year continually, which could never make the comers thereunto perfect [Leviticus 16]; Grace says But this Man, after he had offered one sacrifice for sins forever... by one offering has perfected forever them that are sanctified [Hebrews 9:11–15].

- The Law declares that as many as have sinned in the Law, shall be judged by the Law [Galatians 5:3; James 2:10]; Grace brings eternal peace to the troubled soul of every child of God, and proclaims God's salvation in defiance of the accusations of the adversary. "He that hears My word, and believeth on Him that sent Me, has everlasting life, and shall not come into judgment (condemnation), but is passed from death unto life." [1 Chronicles 21:1; Job 1:6–8; Psalm 109:6; Zechariah 3:1–2; 1 John 2:1; John 3:16, 36; 5:24; Romans 8:1].

Law inserts a consideration of work into grace. No works of the law merit any favor before God, for favor is achieved by His grace and His grace alone: it is *free grace*.

Why Use Bold on the Word *Blood*?

In this section I have bolded the word *blood* as it relates to the blood of Messiah and His sacrifice for our sins. Very simply, I want to emphasize the supremacy and centrality of the **blood** of Christ in the Scriptures. Without the **blood** of Messiah we have absolutely nothing. We have no regeneration; no redemption; no sanctification; no reconciliation; no propitiation; no indwelling, sealing, and baptism of the Holy Spirit; and no imputation of the righteousness of Messiah to our accounts. On top of that, we without the **blood** do not experience being transferred from the kingdom of darkness into the kingdom of light — that occurs solely by His **blood**. The Scriptures state in Leviticus 17:11 *that without the shedding of blood there is not remission of sin.* The **blood** of Messiah is central; it is the key to all that we as believers enjoy in heavenly places. His **blood** is the focus of the New Covenant even as Yeshua said, lifting up the cup: "This is the New Covenant in my **blood**." Please notice, as you read each of the following verses, the emphasis that the word of God places on the **blood**. This is the **blood** of the Messiah: He is the one of whom the Father said in Isaiah 42:6 that the Servant of the Lord, the Messiah of Israel, would be the covenant. It is His **blood**, the **blood** of the New Covenant that was inaugurated by the Messiah on the cross of Calvary and that activated the regeneration ministry of the Holy Spirit. Without His **blood** we have absolutely no salvation, no deliverance from sin, no adoption into the household of God. Life would be meaningless without hope: that is, without the **blood** of Messiah.

> 27 *And He took the cup, and gave thanks, and gave it to them, saying drink you all of it;* 28 *For this is My **blood** of the new covenant, which is shed for many for the remission of sins.* (Matthew 26:27–28)

> *Take heed therefore unto yourselves, and to all the flock, over the which the Holy Spirit has made you overseers, to feed the church of God, which he has purchased with His own **blood**.* (Acts 20:28)

> *Much more then, being now justified by His blood, we shall be saved from wrath through Him.* (Romans 5:9)

> *The cup of blessing which we bless, is it not the communion of the **blood** of Messiah? The bread which we break, is it not the communion of the body of Messiah?* (1 Corinthians 10:16)

> *After the same manner also He took the cup, which He had supped, saying, this cup is the New Covenant in My **blood**: this do, as oft as you drink it, in remembrance of Me.* (1 Corinthians 11:25)

> *In whom we have redemption through His **blood**, the forgiveness of sins, according to the riches of His grace.* (Ephesians 1:7)

> *But now in Messiah Yeshua you who sometimes were far off are made nigh by the **blood** of Messiah.* (Ephesians 2:13)

> *In whom we have redemption through His **blood**, even the forgiveness of sins.* (Colossians 1:14)

*And, having made peace through the **blood** of His cross, by Him to reconcile all things unto Himself; by Him, I say, whether they be things in earth, or things in heaven.* (Colossians 1:20)

*How much more shall the **blood** of Messiah, who through the eternal Spirit offered Himself without spot to God, purge your conscience from dead works to serve the living God.* (Hebrews 9:14)

*20 Saying, this is the **blood** of the testament which God has enjoined unto you. 21 Moreover He sprinkled with **blood** both the tabernacle, and all the vessels of the ministry. 22 And almost all things are by the law purged with blood; and without shedding of blood is no remission.* (Hebrews 9:20 22)

*Having therefore, brethren, boldness to enter into the holiest by the **blood** of Yeshua.* (Hebrews 10:19 20)

Wherefore Yeshua also, that He might sanctify the people with His own blood, suffered without the gate [Jerusalem]. (Hebrews 13:12)

*Now the God of peace, that brought again from the dead our Lord Yeshua, that great shepherd of the sheep, through the **blood** of the everlasting covenant.* (Hebrews 13:20)

*Elect according to the foreknowledge of God the Father, through sanctification of the Spirit, unto obedience and sprinkling of the **blood** of Yeshua Messiah: Grace unto you, and peace, be multiplied.* (1 Peter 1:2)

*But with the precious **blood** of Messiah, as of a lamb without blemish and without spot.* (1 Peter 1:19)

*But if we walk in the light, as He is in the light, we have fellowship one with another, and the **blood** of Yeshua Messiah His Son cleanses us from all sin.* (1 John 1:7)

Chapter 9

> *And from Yeshua Messiah, who is the faithful witness, and the first begotten of the dead, and the prince of the kings of the earth. Unto Him that loved us, and washed us from sins in His own **blood**.* (Revelation 1:5)

> *9 And they sang a new song, saying, You are worthy to take the book, and to open the seals thereof: for you were slain, and have redeemed us to God by your **blood** out of every kindred, and tongue, and people, and nation....*
> (Revelation 5:9)

Law Observance in Connection with Christian Liberty

I have strongly implied that we are not to be like Jews but like Christ. What does that mean? It can be misconstrued as saying that Jewish believers in Messiah are to lay aside their Jewishness, with all its culture and heritage, and become like other Gentile believers in Messiah. That is incorrect: so, what do I mean?

Biblically, there are two different groups of peoples in the Scriptures: Jews and Gentiles. The Law of Moses was given to the Jewish people, for it was they who made the bilateral covenant with the LORD called the Mosaic Covenant. Because they were not parties to that covenant, the Gentiles biblically are not told to adhere to the Law of Moses; rather, they are told to adhere to the Law of Messiah, because of the New Covenant. This book stresses the fact that Gentiles are to be Gentiles and the Law of Moses is not for them. That should be a moot issue, but it is not because even today Gentiles are being sucked into observance of the wrong law system. Their focus should be completely and only on the Law of Messiah and all the commands in the epistles directed to them.

A more difficult distinction is made regarding Jewish believers in Messiah, called Messianic Jews or Hebrew Christians. In this context, the Christian liberty that Paul taught to believers is very pertinent to both Jew and Gentile. However, the issue at hand is the statement that I have made, in the context of Jewish believers, to be Christ-like and not Jewish-like.

Many Jewish believers in Messiah have become very legalistic, teaching that the law given to them is to be obeyed both by Gentiles and by themselves as a necessary component of faith. The New Testament simply does not teach this concept. Jewish believers in the Messiah have every right to practice and observe any of the Laws of Moses that they want to keep; they have that freedom in Messiah to do so. That is the teaching of Paul in Romans and 1 Corinthians. However, they are not to export or demand this practice of others because the Law of Moses is not the active law system now—the Law of Messiah has overtaken and nullified the Mosaic law. Thus, to teach other Jewish and Gentile believers to keep the Torah of Moses is simply unbiblical: it is legalism and out of step with God. At the same time, it is equally unbiblical for other Gentile Christians to teach that Jewish people should be like other Gentile believers and lay aside their culture and heritage. I have personal friends who are Jewish believers but still keep kosher, and observe other parts of the law, because they are Jewish and want to identify with their Jewish roots and community. They have also told me that they know that it does not give them any extra "righteousness merit points" with God, and they do not try to obligate others to practice as they do. A friend of mine who is in Jewish ministries (as I am) used as an illustration the story of a Jewish believer co-worker:

> Sometimes Christians criticized him for keeping kosher. They'd say: You're a Christian now! You're not under the Law anymore! Go ahead and have some pork or lobster.
>
> But for this believer it wasn't about Law-keeping. It was more about culture and his Jewish heritage. In his way of thinking, he was Jewish, and Jewish people don't eat pork.

> He was well aware that he could eat pork and it wouldn't affect his standing before God one iota. But he chose not to eat pork. In fact, he told us many times that he had no desire whatsoever to eat anything unclean.
>
> He had no problem with his Messianic Jewish brethren who didn't keep kosher. He could take Moishe Rosen out for dinner, for example, and buy him a big, two-pound lobster—and they'd sit and talk for hours and have a great time. He didn't care what anyone else did. But for him, he didn't want to eat anything that was biblically unclean.[78]

That is a great illustration of the exercise of Christian liberty on the parts of both Jewish believers. Neither one reprimanded the other: they respected each other and the biblical principle of the liberty that a believer has in Messiah.

However, in the Torah observance movement such is not the case, for they encourage other Jewish believers to wear the Jewish religious garb and urge Gentiles to do the same. Thus, their focus is more on being Jewish by selectively keeping Mosaic law than on adhering to the Law of Messiah, which calls believers to be like Christ, the Messiah.

10

EXAMINING THE TEXT OF GALATIANS 6:2

Before we transition from studying the Law of Moses to studying the Law of Messiah, we need to look at three sets of verses and their context. One thing that we in dispensational circles value is consistent literal interpretation of biblical verses in their context, as opposed to allegorical or spiritualized interpretations of the text. We do not look merely at the verse, but also at the context of the verses that surround a particular text in relationship to the larger context of the passage. In chapters 10, 11, and 12 we will be examining the context and background of three passages: Galatians 6:2, 1 Corinthians 9:21, and Romans 8:2.[79] We will take these in the order that Paul wrote them, beginning with Galatians.

Galatians 6:2 Law of Messiah

Bear you one another's burdens, and so fulfill the Law of Christ. (Galatians 6:2)

After checking some forty-plus commentaries on Galatians, Hong's comment on the concept of the Law of Christ (Messiah) seems to ring true: "The question then remains: What about the Law of Christ in 6:2? This has been an extremely baffling phrase to many interpreters. It is not therefore surprising that a variety of opinions about the meaning of the phrase have been proposed."[80]

I think that this phrase has been inadequately understood because would-be interpreters do not consider the Jewishness of Paul, the Jewish context of the book of Galatians, and the Jewishness of the Scriptures as a whole. First, let us look very briefly at the book of Galatians to see what Paul is trying to correct in giving these instructions to the Galatian believers.

Chapter 10

The Problem

The problem was that Messianic, pharisaic Torah-observant believers came in after Paul and preached to the new babes in Messiah a different kind of gospel: one of faith plus works in order to be a genuine believer in the Jewish Messiah. This teaching continues to plague the Messianic believers in Messiah even today, because of modern-day Judaizers. Paul preached the same gospel in Galatia as he did in Ephesus:

> 8 *For by grace are you saved through faith; and that not of yourselves: it is the gift of God:* 9 *Not of works, lest any man should boast* (Ephesians 2:8–9).

Earlier in this book, in chapter 8, I referenced Ephesians 2 to show Paul does not even acknowledge the Mosaic law as he speaks of our past in sin and our present salvation (our being *His workmanship, created in Messiah Yeshua unto good works*). After Paul, the Judaizers preached another gospel. The Greek word for *another* (*heteros*) means another of a different kind rather than another of the same kind (*allos*). In fact, according to Wuest, *heteros* sometimes not only refers to difference in kind, but also carries the connotation that the character of the thing is evil or bad.[81] Paul names the Judaizers as ones who are perverting the gospel (Galatians 1:7) that he preached with the authority of Yeshua the Messiah (Galatians 1:12), Who is the Prophet like Moses (Deuteronomy 18:15–19; Leviticus 12:5–8), and of the Jerusalem Council (Acts 15), although this fact is usually not considered when people try to understand the meaning of Galatians 6:2. Because those Judaizers were violating the letter put out by the Jerusalem Council (Acts 15:23–24) to all the churches of *the Gentiles in Antioch and Syria and Cilicia*, Paul calls the Judaizers anathema of God (Galatians 1:7, 9), cursed of God. Fruchtenbaum wrote on the meaning of and the concept that comes from the word *anathema* or curse: "The word *anathema* comes from the Hebrew concept of the *cherem*,[82] which means 'something that is untouchable,' 'something that is to be devoted to destruction.' Anyone teaching a different gospel is to be devoted to destruction."[83]

It is amazing how clear the Scriptures can be, and yet believers in Messiah, whether Jewish or Gentile, avoid or completely neglect such verses. Next Paul uses the word *pervert*. In the Greek, *metastrepho* means to "twist something around" or "to reverse it."[84] Wuest picks up the same idea and presses it home to make the same point.[85] Wuest also points out that in Galatians 1:7, the Judaizers *trouble you*, which means "to disturb mentally." Notice that Paul says in verse 12 that he preaches the gospel that he received directly *by the revelation of Jesus Christ, the Prophet like Moses*, and that Jewish people are accountable for every word that He gives (Deuteronomy 18:18–19). Paul gives a little history lesson in the rest of chapters 1 and 2 during his confrontation with Peter, who was being inconsistent. Paul concludes, in 2:16:

> *Knowing that a man is not justified by the works of the law, but by the faith of Jesus Christ, even we have believed in Jesus Christ, that we might be justified by the faith of Messiah, and <u>not by the works of the law: for by the works of the law shall no flesh be justified</u>"* (emphasis added).

Notice the underlined words. Salvation is only through the finished work of Christ on the cross, which He completed by shedding His blood, the blood of the New Covenant; no flesh shall be justified by the law. We are <u>not</u> saved or completely saved by returning to the works of the law. To repeat, <u>no</u> flesh is justified before God through the works of the law. In chapter 3 of Galatians Paul presses the issue again by asking a question:

> *2 Received you the Spirit by the works of the law, or by the hearing of faith? 3 Are you so foolish? Having begun in the Spirit, are you now made perfect by the flesh?*

The answer is no! You received the Holy Spirit by faith and faith alone in the finished work of Messiah on the cross of Calvary.

Chapter 10

Paul also is equating the flesh as the enemy of God with the works of the law. In Romans 7–8, as well as in chapter 5 of Galatians, Paul focuses on the whole spirit-and-flesh issue. Then, in Galatians 3, he continues by using Abraham as an illustration contrasting law and faith: again, salvation comes by faith alone. Remember, Abraham lived 400 years before the Law of Moses. Now look at some verses of Galatians in which Paul shows just how completely inadequate the Mosaic law is:

3:11: *no man is justified by the law in the sight of God*

3:13: *Messiah has redeemed us from the curse of the law*

3:19: *Wherefore then serve the law? It was added because of transgressions, till the Seed should come to whom the promise was made.*

3:24 25: *Wherefore the law was our schoolmaster to bring us unto Messiah, that we might be justified by faith. But after that faith is come, we are no longer under a schoolmaster* [*guardian* (see chapter 7 for a discussion of this translation)].

4:4–5: *But when the fullness of time was come, God sent forth His Son, made of a woman, made under the law, to redeem them that were under the law, that we might receive the adoption of sons.*

4:9: *But now, after that you have known God, or rather are known of God, how turn you again to the weak and beggarly elements* [the Mosaic law], *whereunto you desire again to be in bondage?*

5:1: *Stand fast therefore in the liberty wherewith Messiah has made us free, and be not entangled again with the yoke of bondage* [the Mosaic law].

> 5:3: *For I testify again to every man that is circumcised, that he is a debtor to do the whole law.*
>
> 5:4: *You are fallen from Grace.*

It is with astonishment that I read authors who want to teach aspects of the Law of Moses that have absolutely no spiritual power or benefit. They also want to dice up the Law of Moses into three parts. and, even though the moral aspects of the Law of Moses are still invalid, they try to say that we are simultaneously under the moral aspects of the Law of Moses and under Grace. If that is true, what do you do with the commandment *you shall keep the Sabbath day*? That is also part of the moral law that was written on stone (2 Corinthians 3)! You can see from these chapters in Galatians that Paul is making the point, time and time again, that the law is not to be added to our faith. The one thing that rabbinic law has done for unbelieving Israel is hold them together and preserve them as a people over the centuries.

The law is not our controller, our code of conduct. Rather, it is the ministry of the Holy Spirit in our lives which guides us and directs us through the New Covenant into the Law of Messiah. Since Messiah died on the cross, the believer's whole motivation is to place himself *in Christ* and develop a Christ-like character. Thus, we should not place ourselves into Judaism and strive vainly to obey the external Law of Moses, but rather accept and follow the internal Law of Messiah. To return to the Law of Moses is to return to *the weak and beggarly* elements and thus renounce and nullify the works of the Messiah and the New Covenant, and make useless all the agony that He endured to free us from the deeds of the Law of Moses to give us righteousness by His act of justification. We now operate in His grace that He has bestowed upon us, because the Mosaic law has been rendered inoperative. Even though nine of the Ten Commandments originally given on *stone* were carried over into the Law of Messiah, this new Law emphasizes His grace. Grace has been given by God throughout the Scriptures but it was the sole focus of God in the dispensation of grace. Don't misunderstand: There was grace during the time of the law and there is also law in the time of grace, but the motivating factor has changed, as Olander expressed:

> This may at first sound as if we are under law as Christians after all. Paul contrasted law with grace because the <u>primary characteristic of the Mosaic law was its legal character</u> whereas the <u>primary characteristic of the Law of Christ is its grace character</u>. He did not mean that there is no law under grace any more than he meant that there was no grace under the Mosaic law. <u>The motivation for keeping the Mosaic law was external for the Old Testament believer, but the motivation for keeping the law of Christ is internal</u>.[86]

Paul moves on to a great discourse on the conflict of the law and the flesh that holds the law captive and contrasts that with living in freedom and being liberated by the ministry of the Holy Spirit in the lives of believers (Galatians 5:13–26). So let us spend a little time here with Galatians 5.

Law and the Flesh in Contrast to the Spirit: Galatians 5:13–26

Let us focus on Galatians 5:13–26 to reinforce what Paul said in Galatians 6, as well as his other epistles: that the works of the Law of Moses have no place in the believer's life in the Law of Messiah, in the New Covenant, or in grace. "Works" is a foreign object to be rejected. I worked for six weeks in a county prison as a guard, and our practice was not to allow contraband to get to the prison inmates. The Law of Moses to the believer is as contraband: it should be rejected, as Paul clearly teaches in Galatians and his other epistles. That contraband will do spiritual harm to believers. How? Let's look at the ministry of the Holy Spirit in our lives versus the law of the flesh.

In this section I often quote Edgar Andrews, who has presented some very helpful insights. His commentary is one of the few that I believe correctly delineates the ramifications to believers in their spiritual journey, as we are being conformed to the image of Messiah and not to the image of the Mosaic law.[87]

Galatians 5:13–15
13 For, brethren, you have been called unto liberty: only use not liberty for an occasion to the flesh, but by love serve one another. 14 For all the law [toward man] *is fulfilled in one word, even in this; you shall love your neighbor as yourself* [Leviticus 19:18].

15 But if you bite and devour one another, take heed that you be not consumed one of another.

In Romans 8:2, Paul says very clearly that we are free! We are liberated from the law! The law which used the flesh as its base of operation could not and cannot give us power over the flesh. In Romans 8:2 Paul depicts law as embracing *sin and death*. He states that we are now called by God unto liberty, *freedom from the law of sin and death*. Still, we need to be careful not to allow our freedom to be used by the flesh to work in tandem with the law. Paul says that the law can be fulfilled by love, but does the law give us power to love as God loved? No! That love is self-sacrificial love, *agape* love, the kind the Father demonstrated in sending Messiah, and the kind of love that Messiah demonstrated on the cross of Calvary. It is the kind of love that the Holy Spirit demonstrated in regenerating and indwelling us.

Freedom from the law, however, can be misused and abused by believers. Andrews states: "Without the external compulsion and restraint of rules and regulations, the old nature (the flesh) can, in principle, run riot.... How does Paul deal with this danger? He does not reimpose the law, or some substitute for it, but simply instructs the Galatians to make a better choice."[88]

Chapter 10

One does have to make a choice (Romans 6:11–14; Ephesians 4:22, 24; Colossians 3:5, 8, 10, 12). These are choices that we make and can fulfill as we *walk in the Spirit*. Paul also speaks to the issue in a parallel passage (Romans 6:15–19), which reminds us that not being under the Law of Moses is <u>not</u> throwing the door open to sin.

> Shall we sin because we are not under law but under grace? Certainly not!... For just as you [once] presented your members as slaves of uncleanness... so now present your members as slaves of righteousness for holiness.... We are now free to obey righteousness.[89]

> Freedom from the law, he declares, does not mean freedom to indulge the old nature, but rather the opportunity to bear the fruit of the Spirit in righteous living.[90]

That righteousness is not an outward righteousness of the law, but rather inward qualities and principles placed in the heart by the New Covenant, which gave us our new birth by the regenerating work of the Holy Spirit. The motivation of love cannot "remain a mere attitude or inner experience; it will reveal itself in action."[91] This righteousness is a direct result of our filling, sealing, baptism, and indwelling of the Holy Spirit, which Paul discusses in the next verses. So use *agape* love, the love that is the foundation for the Law of Messiah. This is the kind of love that Paul references in quoting Leviticus 19:18—love that puts others first and self second—but the flesh rejects that understanding. The neighborly kind of love is a horizontal love among humankind, whereas man's vertical love to God is expressed in the Shema in Deuteronomy 6:5. Love has two components, to God and to man, and you cannot fulfill one without the other (Matthew 22:36–40). However, in Galatians 5 Paul is dealing with the lives of believers and humankind in general. In this regard Andrews makes a sobering observation:

Those who embrace the law are in danger of neglecting the Spirit. One of the problems with living by law is that once the explicit duties of the law have been fulfilled, the person feels that nothing more is required. By contrast, those who cultivate the fruit of the Spirit seek to imitate Christ, whose Spirit inhabits their hearts and minds (Gal. 2:20). They run life's race looking to Jesus, the author and perfecter of their faith (Heb. 12:2). Their actions and attitudes are dictated by the Spirit within, rather than by external rules.[92]

Believers are to live by the Spirit because we are empowered by the Spirit, regenerated by the Spirit, and indwelt by the same Spirit. The Law of Moses focused on the exterior expressions of law obedience, but the law also made the Jewish people powerless to obey. The Law of Messiah centers on our empowerment by the Holy Spirit, who enables us to *walk in the Spirit* and produce the *fruits of the Spirit*.

In dealing with external law-keeping versus internal law-keeping, Paul picks up on the principles and teachings of Yeshua's Sermon on the Mount. To illustrate: If you hate in your heart, you have broken the spirit of the law even if you never did the act of murder or actually broke the letter of the law. The same is true of two more examples from Yeshua: If you lust after a woman in your heart, you have broken the intent or spirit of the Law even if you never committed the act of adultery. If you do your alms before men to receive public praise, you may receive your earthly reward, but will not be rewarded by God. Again, the inward heart motivation is key. Yeshua reveals the heart intention of the individual, whether an act be done under the Law of Moses or the Law of Messiah. Remember Hebrews 4:12:

> *For the word of God is quick, and powerful, and sharper than any two-edged sword, piercing even to the dividing asunder of soul and spirit, and of the joints and marrow, <u>and is a discerner of the thoughts and intents of the heart.</u>*

Chapter 10

You can even externally fulfill the Law of Messiah, in the flesh, but as Hebrews 4:12 reveals, you do not fool God, only yourself. Notice the distinction that Paul is making concerning the fulfillment of the Law (the letter of the Law). Paul's proposition is not that believers do the law, but that the righteous requirement of the law is fulfilled in us (intent of the law).[93] Longenecker makes another important distinction about law-keeping and walking in the Spirit and fulfilling the Law of Messiah:

> Paul in v. 14 carefully distinguishes between the "doing" and the "fulfilling" of the Torah—the "doing" of the Jewish Torah is not required for Christians, but the "fulfilling" is. ... Paul in his own mind drew a deliberate distinction between "doing" the Mosaic law (as in 3:10, 12; 5:3; *cf.* Romans 10:5) and "fulfilling" the Mosaic law (as here; *cf.* Romans 8:4; 13:8, 10), never saying that Christians "do" the law. ...Galatians 5:14 is not itself a command to fulfill the law but a statement that, when one loves one's neighbour, the whole law is fully satisfied in the process.[94]

> The difference between them, however, was in the manner in which that obligation is to be fulfilled. For the Judaizers, Christian obligation is to be understood in terms of subjection to the Mosaic law as the expressed will of God, with the prescriptions of Torah given guidance for ethical living. For Paul, the obligation of the Christian is love that expresses itself in service to others, with that obligation being grounded in and guided by the Christian's new existence [walking] in "the Spirit."[95]

We as believers are <u>to fulfill</u> the Law of Moses, <u>not do</u> the Mosaic law: there is a huge distinction between these. Paul is saying that in the Law of Messiah, you love your neighbor as yourself and serve others. Paul is pressing the fact to the Galatians that the external expression of "doing" the law, which is hopelessly entangled with the flesh, sin, and death, should not be the focus of believers. The problem of the flesh is constantly with us, and we must turn away to *walk in the Spirit* that empowers us to *fulfill the Law*. The *works of the flesh* are depicted in verse 15 as biting and devouring one another as wild beasts attack their prey, which is the opposite of loving your neighbor as yourself and thereby fulfilling the Law.

Note well that the words are an imperative command: **Love** your neighbor. Believers do not consume or destroy each other. The desire of Judaizers, whether in Paul's day or our own, is to make us focus on the old law, which is inferior to the superior New Covenant law, which is *walking in the Spirit*. The Judaizers become hopeless victims of sin and death, again as Longenecker states: "Paul speaks of 'the flesh' not as itself the culprit, but as a captive of sin. Nevertheless, 'flesh' as a captive also acts in behalf of its captor, and so produces 'desires and passions' that are at work against the Spirit."[96]

The next grouping of verses shows that the Spirit and the flesh are contrary to each other, and they are not compatible for the believer and his new life in Messiah. This law issue is a serious one for a follower of Messiah as he lives out his life before the great audience of One. Next, Paul discusses the *works of the flesh*, the exterior, and shows that the Law of Moses cannot possibly give victory over the base nature of the flesh.

Galatians 5:16–21
> 16 *This I say then, walk in the Spirit, and you shall not fulfill the lust of the flesh. 17 For the flesh lusts against the Spirit, and the Spirit against the flesh: and these are contrary the one to the other: so that you cannot do the things that you would. 18 But if you be led of the Spirit, you are not under the law* [of Moses]. *19 Now the works of the flesh are manifest, which are these; adultery, fornication, uncleanness, lasciviousness,*

> 20 *Idolatry, witchcraft, hatred, variance, emulations, wrath, strife, seditions, heresies,* 21 *Envying's, murder, drunkenness, revellings, and such like: of the which I tell you before, as I have also told you in time past, that they which do such things shall not inherit the kingdom of God.*

In the last passage and the beginning of this passage Paul gave two exhortations: (1) through love serve one another (v. 13) and (2) live by the Spirit (v. 16). Paul is purposefully making a connection with the word "walk," as Witherington notes: "The expression 'walk by (or according to) the Spirit' is a Jewish way of describing a manner of living, and is a deliberate echo of the O[ld] T[estament] phrase 'walk according to the statutes of the Law' (Ex 16:4; Lev 18:4; Jer 44:23; Ezek 5:6–7)."[97]

The references given concerning Israel walking in the law also connect with or echo the way we as believers in Messiah are connected to God through the Law of Messiah. We will be judged at the Bema Seat of Messiah according to how we have walked in the Spirit by demonstrating the Law of Messiah.

- These verses reveal the set pattern of the flesh as it shows its clear nature: Not fulfill the lust (desires) of the flesh.

- The flesh lusts (or desires) against the work of the Holy Spirit.

- The flesh and the Spirit are <u>not</u> compatible.

- The flesh will not allow you to do what you know to be right (this harks back to Paul's frustration in Romans 7:15–25).

- [The c]haracter of the flesh is given under five categories: (1) sexual sins; (2) idolatry and sorcery, (3) the hatred of man for man; (4) heresies; (5) and public works of the flesh, the visible fruit of unrighteousness.[98]

Verse 18 tells us that if we are led and guided by the Holy Spirit, we are not under the Law of Moses. "The apostle Paul tells us very simply that, for the believer, the indwelling Spirit has supplanted the external law as the controlling principle that guides his conduct."[99] In short, life in the Spirit, not life lived under the Mosaic law, should mark the Christian's life.[100]

The command to walk in or by the Spirit indicates that effort and resolve are required on the part of the Christian to proceed on the right course. It doesn't happen by accident or chance. At the same time, the discussion about allowing oneself to be led by the Spirit makes equally clear that the Spirit must take the lead and must provide the power for "walking."[101]

Our walk in Messiah and His law is not an accident or a chance happening. It is a deliberate choice, a deliberate yielding on our part to walk in and be led by the Holy Spirit. He is the same One who regenerated us, filled us, sealed us, baptized us, and indwells us. He is the One Who can and will empower us over the flesh which holds the Law of Moses captive.

This part of Galatians is a very negative regarding the flesh and its relationship to the Spirit, stating that the flesh desires against the Spirit and the Spirit desires against the flesh. This raises a very pertinent question: Why live (or try to live) under the law which cannot help us and is in complete conflict with the Holy Spirit? Of the link between these verses and what Paul said to the Galatians in verse 16, Andrews states, "The outward conduct of the believer is to be dictated and controlled by an inward, spiritual principle."[102]

He is completely correct. The Law of Moses cannot give us any access to or control over the inward man who is *walking in the Spirit*. But the Holy Spirit can, by empowering and guiding us when we yield to Him to live in obedience to the Law of Messiah. As Andrews said: "It is not to be dictated by external laws, social conventions, herd instinct, peer pressure, the expectations of others, or the fear of what people will think. Nor will it be controlled by the sinful desires of the old Adamic nature."[103]

The law and the flesh are in tandem because the flesh and the law are in conflict with the Holy Spirit, Who desires to lead all believers into truth. Paul lays out an imperative command to <u>walk in the Spirit, and you shall not fulfill the lust</u> [desires] <u>of the flesh</u>. Notice that Paul again equates flesh and law in verse 18. If we *walk in the Spirit* we <u>are not</u> under the Law of Moses. Meditate on that verse if you are a Mosaic law keeper.

Here is another point made by Andrews about being alive in Christ:

> Paul has already defined this in unforgettable terms in Galatians 2:20: "It is no longer I who live, but Messiah lives in me; and the life which I now live in the flesh [my day-to-day practical life] I live by faith in the Son of God who loved me and gave Himself for me." The Holy Spirit indwells believers and guides them in their thinking, their attitudes and their behavior. He pours out God's love in their hearts, so that they are motivated by love rather than selfishness and covetousness.[104]

Can the Law of Moses give us what Messiah gave to us, or supplement the Holy Spirit's guiding and directing as we yield to Him to live out the Law of Messiah from our inner being, our new regenerated heart? No; the Mosaic law is a law of flesh. Remember Paul's statement that he would not have known sin without the Law of Moses (Romans 7:7–11). Let me show you what is guaranteed in our lives if we live according to the flesh,:

- Sexual sins: adultery, fornication, uncleanness, licentiousness

- Idolatry and sorcery: religious sins, things we made as gods, witchcraft and the like

- Hatred of man for man: hatred, contention, jealousy, outbursts of wrath, selfish ambitions, dissension

- Public demonstration of the flesh (the visible fruit of unrighteousness): envy, murder, drunkenness, revels and the like

These can be restrained [or limited] by human laws and punishment; but only grace can deal with their root cause. The Law of Moses labels the cause, but gives no power for victory over it. In contrast, the New Covenant under the regenerating power of the Holy Spirit deals with the root cause, making us a new creation in Messiah Yeshua.

Galatians 5:22–26
   22 <u>*But*</u> *the fruit of the Spirit is love, joy, peace, longsuffering, gentleness, goodness, faith,* 23 *Meekness, temperance: against such there is no law.* 24 *And they that are Messiah's have crucified the flesh with the affections and lusts.* 25 *If we live in the Spirit, let us also walk in the Spirit.* 26 *Let us not be desirous of vain glory, provoking one another, envying one another.*

The word used to introduce these verses is a word of contrast, *but*. Paul is contrasting apples and oranges, so to speak. The obvious contrast here is the complete opposites of verses 19–21 with verses 22–23. One is dealing with the *works of the flesh* and the other with the *fruit of the Spirit*. "The flesh produces 'works', but the Spirit bears 'fruit.'"[105]

Look again at the teaching of Yeshua in John 15:4–5:
   4 *Abide in Me, and I in you. As the branch cannot bear fruit of itself, except it abide in the vine; no more can you except*

> *you abide in Me. 5 I am the vine, you are the branches: He that abides in Me, and I in him, the same brings forth much fruit: for without Me you can do nothing.*

Did you notice that Yeshua did not say abide in the Law of Moses? The Law of Moses in the flesh produces works, whereas if you abide in Yeshua as a branch to the vine you will bring forth much fruit. This is the same thing that Paul speaks of in Galatians 5. The Law of Moses is captive to the flesh and produces the *works of the flesh*. Paul said that the Law of Moses is holy (Romans 7:12); the problem is with us and our old nature, the flesh and not the Law of Moses. The Law of Moses is held hostage by the flesh. However, the Law of Messiah produces the *fruit of the Spirit* that we have when we are yielded to His Holy Spirit. The two are opposites. As Longenecker puts it:

> "The phrase the fruit of the Spirit may be used here in conscious opposition to the works of the flesh that heads the catalogue of vices earlier, and so was meant to suggest (1) the spontaneous quality of a life directed by the Spirit as opposed to human efforts to live according to the directives of the law [of Moses] or the flesh, (2) ... in the Spirit-directed life as opposed to 'outbursts of undisciplined passion' when guided by fleshly concerns."[106]

What is the first fruit of the Spirit listed by Paul? *Love*. Connect that to verse 14 where love is called the fulfillment of the Law. The love we express is not us doing the Law, but being in submission to the Holy Spirit, and it is He who fulfills the Law in love by His fruit. As Yeshua said, we should abide in the vine, for He is the vine (John 15:1)! You can easily define or identify all the *fruit of the Spirit*. Notice as you investigate the *fruits of the Spirit* that they all express the inner quality that, when yielded to Him, the Holy Spirit produces in our hearts (in contrast to the works of the Law of Moses, which are external only from the flesh, the old nature). Observe that the fruit of the Spirit operates out of

Examining the Text of Galatians 6:2

one's new regenerated heart, an outworking of the New Covenant expressed as well in the Law of Messiah. Observe also that the works of the flesh come out of a heart of flesh, the unregenerate old man.

If we, as Gentile and Jewish believers in Messiah, are really walking in the Spirit, that comes as a result of the fact that we have, <u>by choice</u>, *crucified the flesh*. Since we *live in the Spirit, let us also walk in the Spirit*. Notice that Paul proceeds to list the fruits of the Spirit. In doing so, he does not write about specific acts such as alms-giving, hospitality, forgiveness and the like but rather about the basic attitudes from which such actions flow.[107]

The fruits of the Spirit are attitudes that control and dictate actions, rather than the actions themselves. Thus the believer's manner of life flows from a genuine inner principle, not from adherence to an external law. It is the believer himself who is responsible for translating these attitudes into good deeds.[108] ... Spirit-led behavior transcends the requirements of any law. Spiritual fruitfulness supersedes external law as the spring and basis of moral action.[109]

Problem Examined More Closely

The problem within Messianic circles is the question of Torah and its application to the body of Messiah. In Stern's *Jewish New Testament Commentary*,[110] the author presents some troubling views concerning the Law of Moses, which he rightfully calls Torah. However, he also parses the New Covenant of Jeremiah, as well as Jesus' Sermon on the Mount (in Matthew 5) and passages in the Book of Acts, to argue against and discredit Christians who say that Christ fulfilled the Mosaic law and has fulfilled it and replaced it with the Law of Messiah. Stern's intent is to prove that the Law of Moses did not end, although it was modified by the Law of Messiah, and that the Law of Moses must be observed today by Jew and Gentile alike. Stern lays out the fundamental

Chapter 10

problem and difference: "Here the question is whether Yeshua instituted a new Torah different from the Torah given at Mount Sinai. In other words, is fulfilling "the law of the Messiah" different from fulfilling the Law of Moshe [Moses]?"[111]

That is the crux of the matter. What is the difference or interchange between these two laws? First of all, Stern declares that the new law given in the New Covenant is the "same Torah that Moshe [Moses] received and promulgated."[112] However, in Jeremiah 31:31–34, the Law of Moses is specifically contrasted with the New Covenant, showing that the New is not merely a restatement or renewing of the old system, which was broken (Leviticus 26:14–15; Deuteronomy 31:16, 20; Jeremiah 11:10; Ezekiel 16:59). Stern reads this text with a predetermined bias, because he and many within the Messianic movement view the Law of Moses as being an unconditional covenant. However, the Hebrew Scriptures clearly relate that it was broken, abhorred, and violated by the people of Israel, for the Mosaic Covenant was a <u>bilateral</u> (not a unilateral) covenant. (Read my book, *Israel's Only Hope: The New Covenant,* to get a full grasp of its Old Testament context and the foundation that is laid down by the New Covenant for the Law of Messiah.)

Stern acknowledges Yeshua's statement in Matthew 5:17 that He did not come to "abolish the Torah." In the very next sentence he states, "However, the eternity of the Torah does allow for changes in its historical manifestation and application to society." This claim rests on exceedingly shaky ground. Perhaps it does in Orthodox Rabbinic Judaism and Messianic Judaism, which "search for common ground with non-Messianic Judaism"—but this is Messianic Judaism's fatal flaw.[113] Before I go on, please observe Stern's choice of words: "eternity of the Torah." Contrary to common teaching, the Hebrew word *olam* that is often translated into English as "forever," "everlasting," or "eternity" is misunderstood, and this translation presents an unbiblical concept. *Olam* in Hebrew refers to a designated period of time (albeit possibly a very long time), but not eternity. Read in Deuteronomy 15:17 of the servant who wished to be a servant to his master "forever," *olam*. Did the master live forever? Did the servant live forever? You say those are absurd questions. Are they? Understand that both the master and the servant died within a generation, which is certainly not forever! Another incorrect use of olam appears in regard to the Sabbath, which was to be observed forever—but only by Jewish people, not by Gentile believers in Messiah. This is why, in the New Testament epistles, which are the teachings for the body of Messiah in the Church, no Sabbath worship is commanded or observed. The Hebrew word *olam* indicates a designated period of time, not eternity.

Another fact weighing against Stern's interpretation is the Jewish context of Yeshua in Matthew 5–7, where He contrasts the righteousness of the Mosaic law with the rabbinic, man-made law; the latter is also called the Oral Law, the fence around the Law, the Mishnah, or the *tradition of the elders* (a biblical term). First Yeshua was being accused of going against the Law of Moses, which in fact He completely obeyed. He went against the rabbinic law, tearing down the "fence around the law" because of the spiritual hypocrisy and double standard of the Pharisees (noted throughout the Gospel accounts) that often held the *tradition of the elders* greater than the Mosaic law itself, subverting even that law. Of course, Messiah upheld the Law of Moses, of which He was the author, until His own death, burial, and resurrection. He had to be obedient to the Mosaic law in order to fulfill it. Context is crucial in any study of Scripture. Stern conveniently ignores 5:18, which says: *For verily I say unto you, till heaven and earth pass, one jot or one tittle shall in no wise pass from the law, till all be fulfilled.*[114]

Yeshua fulfilled the Law of Moses to the letter. Understand that the centrality of the Scriptures is not the law; rather, it is what the law pointed to: the promise of and the coming of the Messiah that Moses, David, and the Prophets wrote about. When Yeshua rose from the grave and the Holy Spirit came upon the believers at Pentecost (Feast of Shavuot), the need for the old law ceased because it was replaced—superseded—by another Law, far superior to that of Moses: the Law of Messiah. His Law, intended for the Church and the multitude of believers who would come from every culture and language on the earth, supersedes the Mosaic law. The Law of Moses was for Israel alone. It was not given to Gentiles, nor was it appropriate for Gentile believers in Messiah. Paul states that the Law of Moses was holy—and indeed it was, but our flesh was incapable of keeping it. The problem was not the holy law of God given through Moses; the problem lies solely at our sinful feet, our carnal sinful flesh. The Law of Moses could only offer *death* and *condemnation*, because of our sin nature. In complete contrast, the Law of Messiah offers life.

Stern describes Romans 10:4, which says that Yeshua brought the Torah to an end, as a "Christian erroneous" view and compares the Christian view to that of an apostate Jew who claimed to be the Messiah in the 1600s.[115] This is a very weak attempt to discredit the Christian view of Romans 10:4. In the context of Romans, Paul destroys the concept that the law could give righteousness, or eternal life, or victory over sin and death. Only by removing verses from their immediate and extended context within the Bible can you teach an erroneous Messianic view that does not accept to the teaching of God through Paul. Another Messianic Jewish believer, Dr. Arnold Fruchtenbaum, states the following concerning Romans 10:4 and the meaning of *Christ is the end of the law*. Here I quote a passage from Fruchtenbaum in which he makes a case against Dan Juster (a Messianic Jewish believer who holds to Torah observance for all believers in Messiah):

As for Romans 10:4, Juster resorts to dogmatism while ignoring the lexicons in the process, lexicons which do not have a dispensational bias. He states that the Greek word for "end" is *telos*, not *finis*. It is hard to believe that Juster is serious here. His statement implies that if Paul wanted to say that the law has come to an end, Paul would not have said *telos*, but *finis*. However, the word *finis* is Latin and not Greek and the epistle was written in Greek and not Latin. If Paul wanted to say that the Law of Moses has come to an end, *telos* would be the right word to use. Yet Juster claims that *telos* does not mean "the finish of something" but "goal" or "purpose." That *telos* can mean "goal" is not the issue. To claim it does not mean "finish" is dogmatism and ignores what every Greek lexicon teaches. For example, Thayer gives the primary meaning of *telos* as: End, i.e. termination, the limit at which a thing ceases to be, ... in the Scriptures also of a temporal end; ... Christ has brought the law to an end ... .

Not only does Thayer give "termination" as the primary meaning of *telos*, but he includes Romans 10:4 as belonging to that category of usage. Nor is "goal" listed as a secondary or even a third in priority of usage; it is fourth down the list. Arndt and Gingrich give the primary meaning of the verbal form as "bring to an end, finish, complete." The nominal *telos* is given the primary meaning of: "end ... in the sense [of] termination, cessation." They, too, list Romans 10:4 in this category and list the meaning of "goal" as being third down the list.

Is there any good or contextual reason to ignore the primary usage of *telos* in favor of a third or fourth usage? Only if one's theology requires it for Romans 10:4 does not demand it and the primary meaning makes good sense.[116]

Stern also attempts to use Acts 6:13–14 to confirm that Stephen recognized the Law of Moses as being valid in the Church or New Testament period. Stern points out a passage "where Stephen was accused of saying 'that Yeshua from Natzeret [Nazareth] will … change the customs Moshe handed down to us.'"[117] During his defense, Stephen did <u>not</u> say that the Torah had been abrogated, but instead upheld its sanctity and countercharged his accusers with disobeying it (Acts 7:1–53).

Of course, Stephen in his message to the Sanhedrin upheld the law because the entirety of his message up to verses 51–52 was from a law context. When he condemned them as being *stiffnecked and uncircumcised in heart and ears*, they lost it and stoned him to death. Stephen did not even get the opportunity to speak about the law itself, so Stephen did not uphold the law before the Sanhedrin as Stern implies. The charges levied against Stephen were made as a purposeful *set-up* by *false witnesses*. So much for using Acts 6:13–14 to confirm Torah observance.

Some of Stern's points are very subjective and he makes unbiblical assumptions to uphold the Law of Moses. He uses the U.S. Constitution in a comparison with the Law of Moses, stating that just as the Constitution has been amended, so had the Mosaic law:

> One considers the United States constitution to be "the same" as when it was promulgated, although it has been amended many times, and specific provisions have even had their meaning reversed by court interpretation. Similar processes — normal legal processes — have taken place within Judaism. One can say, for example, that the Torah was "amended" in the Tanakh itself when Purim was made a required festival centuries after Moshe. … If there is anything in the existing Oral Torah not consistent with the New Testament, it will have to be modified or discarded.[118]

Stern is saying that if the Oral Law does not agree with the New Testament, the Torah must be modified or discarded. This is partly true, because the Oral Torah, also called Oral Law, is not Scripture! However, one cannot modify Oral Law to fit the New Testament; one must completely discard the Oral Torah or law as the singular unit that it is. At the least, Stern's statements are disturbing, and actually biblically incorrect. The Oral Law is not Scripture, and it carries no weight or authority on how to live out Scripture. The Oral Law is a man-made rabbinic construct, created by humans who can and do err. That which came from Sinai came from a perfect God and cannot be amended by Judaism (flawed human men). Stern also goes off track in referring to Purim, because the Festival of Lots was never sanctioned by Yahweh in the Old Testament, nor is Purim listed by God in Leviticus 23 as a God-given feast. Purim was instituted by Mordecai (see Esther 9:26–32), not the LORD. It is an added feast and not commanded by the LORD. There is nothing wrong with celebrating Purim, but to say that the Torah was amended by Mordecai is a stretch beyond limits. Purim, the Feast of Esther, was established after all the Hebrew Scriptures were written except Malachi, and he says absolutely nothing about it. Judaism cannot amend *thus says the LORD!* Judaism today, as in the days of Yeshua, is apostate Judaism.

Fasts on the Fifth and Seventh Months

Let's look at God's attitude toward feast or fast days accepted by Judaism. As we saw earlier, Purim was not a feast day commanded by the LORD, and the LORD did not amend the Law of Moses for its use. Here is another point concerning man-made fasts that Stern failed to study, which is clearly presented by Zechariah the prophet after the captivity, when Sherezer and Regem-melech came down (probably from Bethel to Jerusalem) to consult with the priests and prophets (Haggai and Zechariah) and ask the religious leadership a question. In Zechariah 7:3, they ask if they

Chapter 10

should continue to *weep in the fifth month*. The LORD responds to the priests in verse 5, saying, *when you fasted and mourned in the fifth and seventh months, even those 70 years, did you all fast unto me?* In verses 8–14 the LORD states that had they obeyed the former prophets this would not even be a question, for they would never have been dispersed as a *whirlwind among all the nations*. Today the fast during the fifth month is called the ninth of Av, commemorating when the Temple was destroyed by Nebuchadnezzar in 586 BC. The seventh month is the fast of Gedaliah when he was assassinated (Jeremiah 41:1–3; 2 Kings 25:25). These were made fasting days by Judaism, especially the fifth month, on the ninth of Av, which is still a fasting day in Judaism. In 8:19 God mentions four fasts that Jews were observing at that time and what He will do with them:

1. The fast of the fourth month commemorates the time when Jerusalem was taken. This is recorded in 2 Kings 25:3–7; Jeremiah 39:2–9 and 52:6–11.

2. The fast of the fifth month recalls the time the city was destroyed, detailed in 2 Kings 25:8–9 and Jeremiah 52:12–14.

3. The fast of the seventh month was when they commemorated the killing of Gedaliah, mentioned in 2 Kings 25:25 and Jeremiah 41:1 3.

4. The fast of the tenth month was when Jerusalem was actually first besieged, as spelled out in 2 Kings 25:1; Jeremiah 39:1 and 52:4.

He says that all of these four presently observed fasts shall be turned into three things:

a. They shall be to the house of Judah joy.
   (Fasting is a time of mourning.)

b. They shall turn to <u>gladness</u>.
   (Usually fasting expresses sadness.)

c. They shall turn to <u>cheerful feasts</u>.
   (The exact opposite of fasting.)[119]

The point that God makes in verses 20–23 is this: If you want to fast on your man-made fast days, go right ahead; that's fine. But if you choose not to fast on these days, that is also fine. God is really saying it is unimportant, because in the future Messianic kingdom I will turn all of these days into feasting with joy, gladness, and cheerfulness. So whether it is the feast of Purim or the fast of ninth of Av, the LORD does not sanction them. He has not amended the Law of Moses to add these feasts or fasts. So Stern's idea of amending the allegedly "eternal" Law of Moses is simply a futile human effort to build a case that the Law of Moses could or can be amended. New feasts or fast days were never sanctioned by God. The Law of Messiah does not amend the Law of Moses, nor is it an appendix to the Mosaic law. The Law of Messiah supersedes the Mosaic law, for, as it says in the book of Hebrews, *it is better*.

Stern's logic resembles what the Pharisees did with the Oral Torah in Messiah's day: they amended the Law of Moses by their "legal processes" with rabbinic man-made laws. It became one of the two reasons why the Pharisees loathed Messiah, Who taught against them and their Oral Torah, and why they hated Him and crucified Him. If you study the writings of Paul in Romans and Galatians and of the author of Hebrews, you will see that they destroy the whole concept of Torah observance, and abrogate the necessity of doing so for all believers. In short, continued Torah observance is unbiblical.

Stern's teaching grieves my heart, because he says that as a Christian Gentile I am biased, and that Jewish believers need to ignore Christians who teach a biblical theology. That means

Chapter 10

ignoring not only Gentile believers like myself, but also Jewish believers such as Arnold Fruchtenbaum, Barry Leventhal, Sam Nadler, Mottel Baleston, Steven Ger, Jacques Gabizon, Robert Morris, Mark Robinson, Mitch Treistman, Steve Herzig, Jay Bockisch, Michael Rydelnik, and my own Messianic pastor Lloyd Scalyer. There are many more Jewish believers in Jesus Christ who could be added to that list. Whether the Messianic Movement wants to acknowledge it or not, when they embraced Yeshua as their Savior, they were baptized into the body of Christ and became members of the universal Church, not a fourth branch of Judaism called Messianic Judaism. Their Messianic congregations are churches, not synagogues. Here is Stern's statement:

> The time has come for Jews to ignore anti-Torah Christian theology developed by people with an anti-Jewish bias, and to acknowledge instead that Yeshua the Messiah and the New Testament have not abolished, abrogated or "exchanged" the Torah of truth "for another" Law.[120]

In his use of the words "'for another' Law," he is twisting Paul's words in Galatians 1:6, where Paul speaks of the Judaizers promoting *another gospel*, a gospel of a different kind.

Stern and many other Messianic Jewish believers are in violation of the Jerusalem Council in Acts 15 which clearly — and I do mean clearly — stated that the Law of Moses was not to be laid on the shoulders of Gentile believers in Messiah. Coupled with that is Paul's repudiation of Torah observance by the Galatians, which extends to Gentile believers who get sucked into Torah observance today by Judaizers of the 21st century. Paul said that this is a different gospel, and he called a curse upon the Judaizers of the 1st century (repeating it twice for emphasis in Galatians 1:8–9), which falls equally on the heads of 21st-century Judaizers.

The central focus of many within the Messianic Movement is being Jewish and observing the Law of Moses. They are not focused on being Christlike, but on being like Moses. All believers, whether Jewish or Gentile, need to focus on the Law of Messiah, the foundation of which is love, evidenced by all the imperative commands issued by God as He inspired the Scriptures through Paul, Luke, James, Peter, and John.

Other Torah-observant Jewish believers, besides David Stern, attempt to persuade or circumvent the meaning of the Scriptures to promote their unbiblical perspective. In Thomas Lancaster's book on Galatians,[121] he completely avoids any real exegesis of the text, instead diverting his readers to illustrations from Josephus, misapplying who the Galatians were, making the "God Fearers" in his context different from those in Paul's context and totally distorting the usage of the term "gospel."

It is Stern's (and others') desire to promote Torah observance among both Jewish and Gentile believers. This is completely against the arguments and statements of Paul in his epistles, and the author of Hebrews. Stern is very smooth in avoiding the clear teachings of Paul as he presses for adherence to the old law. As has been seen, and we will continue to see in the biblical text, the Law of Moses, as holy as it was, could not give life or victory over sin.

I am sorry if I come across as being hard-nosed. I am not interested in political correctness and biases, nor am I interested in religious "correctness" and unbiblical biases, which are both cut from the same cloth. My view of those in the Torah observance movement is that they have a personal bias against the New Covenant, against Yeshua who initiated it, and against the New Covenant ministry of the Holy Spirit in the lives of Jewish and Gentile believers today. I challenge both my Christian and my Hebrew brothers in Messiah to think from a biblical Jewish perspective and not adopt a doctrine that the New Covenant and the Law of Messiah do not promote or teach.

Jesus and the Father

Yeshua was on the Mount of Transfiguration (Mt. Hermon) with three disciples, Peter, James, and John. While Yeshua was discussing His death, Moses and Elijah appeared (Luke 9:31), and the Father stated audibly (Matthew 17:5): *this is My beloved Son in whom I am well pleased, hear ye Him.* The appearance of Moses represents the law and the appearance of Elijah represents the prophets: together, the whole of the Old Testament period. Moses also represents all saints who have died and Elijah represents all saints in the future who will be translated (raptured out of this earth) without seeing death.

The words of the Father are clear and unquestionable: *this is My beloved Son in whom I am well pleased.* After His resurrection, Peter, James, and John passed on, through their writing of Scripture, what had happened on the Mount of Transfiguration to all believers. Thus, Yeshua takes preeminence over Moses and Elijah; His words and work are superior to those of Moses and Elijah. The Father did not put Moses or Elijah on the same level; He placed Yeshua on a superior level. He did not address the law, for Yeshua would fulfill all the law and prophets. Again, recall the words of Moses himself and the LORD in Deuteronomy 18:18–19, where the LORD required every Jewish person to adhere to the words of *the Prophet like Moses*, Yeshua ha Moshiach.

> 15 *The LORD your God will raise up unto you a Prophet from the midst of you, of your brethren, like unto me; unto Him you shall hearken;* 16 *According to all that you desired of the LORD your God in Horeb* [Mt. Sinai] *in the day of the assembly, saying, let me not hear again the voice of the LORD my God, neither let me see this great fire any more, that I die*

> *not.* 17 *And the LORD said unto me, they have well-spoken that which they have spoken.* 18 *I will raise them up a <u>Prophet</u> from among their brethren, like unto you* [Moses], *and will put My words in <u>His mouth</u>; and <u>He</u> shall speak unto them all that I shall command <u>Him</u>.* 19 *And it shall come to pass, that whosoever will not hearken unto My words which <u>He shall speak in My Name</u>, I will require it of him.*

Again, who is preeminent in these verses? Moses? No, the Prophet to come like Moses, whom the LORD wrote about in Genesis 3:15, 49:10; Exodus 23:20 23; Numbers 24:9, 17; Deuteronomy 18:15–19, and John 6:46. The Law of Moses focuses on the Prophet like Moses who will fulfill that law (Matthew 5:17–18), because we in the flesh cannot keep it; it condemns us as unholy. Also notice that the LORD put "Prophet" in the singular: not prophet<u>s</u>, but Prophet! Notice, too, the singular pronouns in verses 18–19, again referring to the Prophet in the singular. How would He be like Moses? Numbers 12:5–8 lays out the context that must not be missed:

> 5 *And the LORD came down in the pillar of the cloud, and stood in the door of the tabernacle, and called Aaron and Miriam: and they both came forth.* 6 *And He said, hear now My words: if there be a prophet among you, I the LORD will make Myself known unto him in a vision and will speak unto him in a dream.* 7 *My servant Moses is not so, who is faithful in all mine house.* 8 <u>*With him will I speak mouth to mouth*</u> [face to face], *even apparently, and not in dark speeches; <u>and the similitude</u>* [form] <u>*of the LORD shall he behold*</u>: *wherefore then were you not afraid to speak against My servant Moses?*

Verse 8 sets out the credentials of Moses that made him unique, unlike any other of the prophets. The LORD states that Moses talked with Him face to face (Deuteronomy 34:10), which no other prophet would experience (according to verse 8), and Moses beheld the very form of God, which no other prophet of

Chapter 10

Israel did. This *Prophet like Moses* would speak to God *face to face* because He would be God, He would behold the *form of God* because He was God who became flesh and dwelt among us (John 1:14, 18; 5:37). The Prophet and His law, the Law of Messiah, are superior to the Law of Moses, for His Law replaced Moses' law because He is greater than Moses. Now let us turn to the book of Hebrews and see what the author of Hebrews had to say about Messiah, the Prophet, and Moses:

> 1 *God, who at sundry* [many] *and in divers* [different] *manners spoke <u>in time past unto the fathers by the prophets</u>,* 2 *Hath <u>in these last days spoken unto us by His Son</u> whom He has <u>appointed heir of all things</u>, by <u>whom also He made the worlds</u>.* 3 *Who being the brightness of His glory, and the express image of His person, and <u>upholding all things by the word of His power</u>, when He had by Himself purged our sins, sat down on the right hand of the Majesty on high;* 4 *Being made so <u>much better than the angels</u>* ... (Hebrews 1:1–4a)

Notice God in the first century spoke by His Son, not by prophets and not by Moses, for His Son the Messiah was the *Prophet like Moses*. He is heir; He made the worlds; He upholds all things by the word of His power. He the Prophet is superior to any of the prophets before Him because they all spoke of Him and Yeshua will hold the Pharisees accountable for His rejection which led to the rejection of the people, which then led to the destruction of Jerusalem in 70 AD.[122] He is the focus of Scripture: not Moses and not the Law of Moses, but He and His Law, the Law of Messiah which is based on the New Covenant and is superior to all other laws today. By His Law, the Law of Moses has been rendered inoperative. In Hebrews, He is counted worthy of more glory than Moses.

> 1 *Wherefore, holy brethren, partakers of the heavenly calling, consider the Apostle and High Priest of our profession, Messiah Yeshua;* 2 *Who was faithful to Him that appointed Him, as also Moses was faithful in all his house.* 3 *<u>For this Man was counted worthy of more glory than Moses</u>, inasmuch*

as He who had built the house has more honor than the house. 4 For every house is built by some man; but He that built all things is God. 5 And Moses verily was faithful in all his house, as a servant, for a testimony of those things which were to be spoken after; 6 <u>But Messiah as a son over His own house; whose house are we</u> [1 Peter 2:5], *if we hold fast the confidence and the rejoicing of the hope firm unto the end.* (Hebrews 3:1–6)

Why do Jewish and Gentile believers still try to observe and use the Law of Moses as their default system, when He who is superior to Moses and the prophets has given us a law that is compatible with all peoples, all cultures and customs and languages, not just Jewish culture and customs? The Law of Moses was for Israel <u>only</u>, not for Gentiles. Consider the emphasis that God places on Messiah at the transfiguration of Messiah borne out by the Father. The Law of Messiah was uniquely crafted by Messiah to give believers life and victory over sin.

Messiah Is Superior to the Law of Moses

In this section I give several examples of how Yeshua the Messiah is superior to Moses and to the Law of Moses. Before I do, let's examine and understand the words of the writer of Hebrews in chapter 1:

1 *God who at many times and in different ways spoke in times past unto the fathers by the prophets,* 2 *Has in these last days spoken unto us by His Son whom He had appointed heir of all things, by whom also He made the worlds;* 3 *Who being the brightness of His glory, and the express image of His person, and upholding all things by the word of His power, when He had by Himself purged our sins, sat down on the right hand of the Majesty on high* ... (Hebrews 1:1–3)

God has spoken through the Son, whom He has appointed His heir, rather than through Moses, who was a servant. Through the

Chapter 10

Son, God made the world; Moses was only a sinful man in the world. The Son was the expressed image of the Father having the brightness of His glory — the glory that reflected off of Moses at Sinai. The Son upholds all things, not Moses. The Son purged us of our sins; Moses was judged for his sin and disobedience and punished by not being allowed to enter the Land. The Son sat down at the right hand of the Father on high, whereas Moses died. The Son is superior to Moses, and also superior to the angels, as the writer of Hebrews proceeds to reference in the rest of chapter 1; in addition, Psalms 2:7; 2 Samuel 7:14; Deuteronomy 32:43; Psalms 104:4, 45:6–7, 102:25–27, and 110:1 refer to the Son's superiority over the angels.

Messiah is also superior to the Law of Moses, as reflected in the following examples. Christ is superior to the Law of Moses, for it says in Leviticus 15:25–27 that anyone who touches a woman with a discharge of blood, they will become unclean themselves. But in Mark 5:24–34 Yeshua is touched by a woman who has been menstruating (with the issue of blood) for 12 years. Instead of being deemed unclean under the Mosaic law, He remains clean and cleanses her in turn. He thus overrides the principle expressed in Haggai 2:11–13. Sin and uncleanness are contagious and make that which was holy unholy (Leviticus 6:27). Messiah, Who is holy, was not made unclean as the law states: He is the exception, obviously greater than Moses and greater than the Law of Moses!

The same type of occurrence is recorded in Luke 5:12–14: a leper who was condemned as unclean by the priests and whose uncleanness was recorded in the temple is touched by Yeshua. Yeshua is not contaminated or made unclean; instead, He Who is superior immediately healed the leper and told him to report to the temple to be declared clean by the religious authorities. Again, here He shows himself greater than the Mosaic law.

Leviticus 11:3–23 and Deuteronomy 14:3–21 set out the kosher food laws, but the Lord (Yeshua), in Acts 10:9–16, clearly tells

Peter that the Mosaic kosher laws he formerly adhered to are no longer relevant. Yet again, Messiah greater-than-Moses supersedes the old law.

Circumcision under the Law of Moses is no longer necessary, although circumcision under the Abrahamic Covenant is necessary for Jewish believers. Circumcision places a person under the authority of the Mosaic law. But, because of the finished work of Yeshua on the cross and the regenerating ministry of the Holy Spirit, we now have the circumcision of Messiah *made without hands* (Colossians 2:11–13). Circumcision under the Mosaic law placed them into bondage under a law they could not keep (Galatians 5:1; Acts 15:10); this was the ministry *of death* and *condemnation* (2 Corinthians 3:7, 9). However, the circumcision of Messiah, which was done by the ministry of the Holy Spirit for our regeneration, produced life. There is a greater-than-Moses here!

In Exodus 20:8–10 and 35:3, Israel was instructed to keep the Sabbath by resting and not making a fire on that day. No work was permitted on that day, and violators could be punished by death (Numbers 15:32–36). Yet Yeshua clearly violated rabbinic law by performing healing on the Sabbath; as He said, He is the Lord of the Sabbath (Matthew 12:1–8; Mark 2:23–28; Luke 6:1–11). The New Testament shows that Sabbath law was not passed on to the Age of Grace: greater than Moses.

In the book of Hebrews, Yeshua is called better than angels, Moses, and the sacrificial system; in short, He is greater than all things, and certainly greater than Moses.

In Matthew 17:24–27, Peter is asked why Yeshua did not pay His temple tax, which was based on the Law of Moses from Exodus 30:13–16. Yeshua asked Peter: Who under Roman law pays taxes, sons or strangers (foreigners and slaves)? Citizens of Roman did not pay taxes, only the subjugated peoples paid taxes. If you are a son, then you are free! Yeshua did not have to pay the tax because He was also lord of the temple.[123] It is clear: He was greater than the law; He fulfilled the law, for He was the author of that law; and He was superior to that law, as He replaced that law with the Law of Messiah based on the blood of the New Covenant.

In Romans 7, where Paul deals with marriage, he says that a wife is bound to her husband as long as he lives, but at his death she is loosed from the bonds of marriage and can be married to another. Paul then says to the believers in Rome:

> 4 *Wherefore, my brethren, you also are become dead to the law by the body of Christ; that you should be married to another, even to Him who is raised from the dead, that we should bring forth fruit unto God. 5 For when we were in the flesh, the motions of sins, which were by the law, did work in our members to bring forth fruit unto death. 6 But now we are delivered from the law, that being dead wherein we were held; that we should serve in newness of spirit, and not in the oldness of the letter.* (Romans 7:4–6)

Israel was married, so to speak, to the Law of Moses and was bound by it until the Law was rendered inoperative by Messiah Himself. Now that the law was dead, they can be married to another law, the Law of Messiah, and not be an adulterer according to Paul's illustration.

Messiah is greater than the law, for we will all be His bride at the marriage supper of the Lamb. Yes, there is a greater-than-Moses here!

The unclean principles of the law did not contaminate Yeshua; He is the only one who has overridden (or could override) those principles, for He is holy. He is the Lord of the Sabbath, and He Who is God cancelled the kosher laws, and circumcised all believing human hearts—not by human hands, but by the Holy Spirit through His finished work on Calvary.

Work of the Spirit

Paul continues through Galatians: look again at the ministry of the Holy Spirit in our lives and what it produces, what the Law could not produce. Here I use a different format to help emphasize the work of the Holy Spirit in a believer's life. In this case the context begins with the parenthetical that extends from Galatians 5:13–6:10, where Paul stresses life in the Spirit.

Believers are to *walk in the Spirit* (Galatians 5:16),

be led by the Spirit (Galatians 5:18),

manifest the *fruit of the Spirit* (Galatians 5:22 23),

live by the Spirit (Galatians 5:25),

keep in step with the Spirit (Galatians 5:25),

and *sow to the Spirit* (Galatians 6:8).

Thus, we can conclude that the believer can fulfill the Law of Christ only by the power of the Spirit. Indeed, this exhortation is addressed (Galatians 6:1) to *the spiritual*, who live in the strength provided in the Spirit.[124]

New life in Messiah is focused on the ministry of the Holy Spirit, which is one of the key aspects that the New Covenant presents in Ezekiel: the indwelling ministry of the Holy Spirit which Yeshua references in John 14:17 virtually explodes off the pages of the New Testament. The ministry of the Holy Spirit, rather than the law, takes over the driver's seat, and the Mosaic law is rendered inoperative with respect to New Testament believers. The Law of Moses now has no part in the life of the believer; the Holy Spirit directs all. Note the points from Galatians 5: to *walk in the Spirit* includes each and every aspect of a believer's life on earth; being *led by the Holy Spirit* is only possible when we submit to the Holy Spirit. The *fruit of the Spirit* is the product, the results of a life submitted to the Holy Spirit. *Keeping in step* is a military term referencing marching in unison, in this instance with the Holy Spirit and with other believers; we *sow to the Spirit* and expect an abundance of fruit. The negative counterpart of this exhortation is the saying "what you sow you will reap," which is applicable in the context of sin (2 Corinthians 9:6). Here, though, it is used positively in the context of sowing and reaping the *fruit of the Spirit* as we walk or are led, and exhibiting spiritual fruit which comes only by living by the Spirit. As we march in step with the Holy Spirit, we will sow and reap to the Holy Spirit. The commandments of the law, written on *stone* as Paul says in 2 Corinthians 3, are an instrument of *condemnation* and *death*. Here are ten things that the law on stone (let alone the other 603 rules within the Mosaic Code) cannot do:

- They cannot justify man before God (Galatians 2:16; 3:11).

- They cannot make man righteous (Galatians 2:21).

- They cannot liberate or set man free; rather, they keep him in bondage (Galatians 5:1).

- They cannot give the Holy Spirit to man (Galatians 3:2, 14, 17).

- They cannot make man perfect in God's sight (Galatians 3:3; Hebrews 7:19).

- They cannot give man eternal life or sonship (Galatians 3:21, 26).

- They cannot make man an heir of God, nor give him the inheritance of the Spirit (Romans 8:17).

- They cannot redeem; rather, they curse (Galatians 3:13; 1 Peter 1:18–19).

- They cannot empower or give strength to live a godly life (Galatians 4:9; Romans 8:3).

- They cannot offer forgiveness from heaven to the sinner (Colossians 1:14).[125]

The Mosaic law has absolutely no eternal benefit, as these points clearly show. The Christian life cannot be lived by the law or any other legal system that is unbiblical and spiritually carnal, for that is the flesh, walking in darkness, as John says in his first epistle (1 John 1:5–7; 2:8–11). A Christian life is to be strictly and completely lived in the ministry of the Holy Spirit Who will guide us into all truth (John 16:13) and teach us (John 14:26) and lead us as we walk in submission to Him (Romans 8).

The Text at Hand

We have been on a necessary detour, but now let us move to Galatians 6:1–2 and investigate the phrase *the Law of Christ*. Here Paul refers to the Galatian Church as *brethren*. This is a very friendly term, not confrontational or instructional as is the rest of the epistle. Paul speaks of a man *overtaken in a fault*. Two things are important here. The word *overtaken* means someone who has fallen out of step with the Messiah's pure doctrine and has committed a fault. Something came upon him, deceiving him so that he fell into fault. Wuest states the following about the word "fault":

> The word fault is from *paraptoma*. The word means "a fall beside, a false step, a blunder, a failure to achieve." It is the antithesis to walk in [Galatians] 5:25, which later the word (*stoicheo*) means "to walk in a straight line." The word in the papyri means "a slip or lapse," rather than "a willful sin."[126]

It was interesting to note, as I read through numerous commentaries, that some wanted to make this a hypothetical case.[127] It is not hypothetical; the whole book of Galatians deals with one particular fault! Namely, the Galatians were considering accepting the teaching of the Judaizers who taught faith in Messiah <u>plus</u> the works of the law, which was not only against Paul's teaching (which he received personally from Yeshua), but was also against the Jerusalem Council's teaching on salvation by faith alone and not faith plus works.

In verse 1 Paul states that the spiritual ones in the congregation are to restore (*katartizo*), meaning to "to repair, to restore to a former good condition, to prepare, to fit out, to equip."[128] These believers, who were in the process of accepting the Judaizers' teaching of faith in Messiah plus the works of the law for salvation, needed to be repaired spiritually. Wuest notes that "[t]he Galatian saints who have not been enticed away from grace by the wiles of the Judaizers and who therefore are still living Spirit-controlled lives, are exhorted to restore their brethren who have been led astray, back to the life under grace."[129]

The ones who are walking in the Spirit are also the ones who fulfill verse 2. My observation is that only the spiritual ones can fulfill the Law of Messiah, because they are walking with, or being led by, the Spirit to fulfill the Law of Messiah.

Bearing One Another's Burdens

Galatians 6:2—*Bear you one another's burdens, and so fulfill the Law of Messiah*—has two parts (two phrases) that must be understood. First, what does bearing *one another's burdens* refer to in the context of this verse; second, what is fulfilling the *Law of Messiah*? Paul is speaking to the spiritual ones, telling them that they are to help bear the heavily weighted burdens of their Galatian brethren who have been overtaken in a fault by adding law observance to faith in Messiah. The specific fault here is being deceived by the Judaizers. That principle can be applied in a much broader context as a practical reference to believers in general. In my research, I found a multitude of explanations in commentaries, but it seems to me that they all miss the point. Some want to tie bearing one another's burdens into Galatians 5:14, which states: *For all the law is fulfilled in one word, even this: You shall love your neighbor as yourself.*

They say that the Law of Messiah is love as expressed in the Law and by Yeshua Himself. However, this verse only speaks of the human response to fellow men; Deuteronomy 6:5 is the other half of the equation, which emphasizes the human response to God. In Galatians Paul does not even mention that verse, which deals with the relationship of man to God. Why? As we saw back in the section titled "Law and the Flesh in Contrast to the Spirit," in 5:14 Paul did not say to do the law in love, but rather to fulfill the Law in love. The key word in understanding the relationship of 5:14 to 6:2 is the word *fulfill*. By the Spirit, we are to fulfill the law of loving our neighbor as ourselves (5:14) and we are to fulfill the Law of Messiah because of the transformation that has taken place in our new, regenerated hearts. In Matthew 22:37–39, Yeshua couples these together and states that on these two commandments *hang all the law and prophets*, meaning "vertical love and horizontal love are inextricably bound together."[130] Without doubt, love is foundational to the Law of Messiah, but there is far more to fulfilling the Law of Messiah than love. Some authors then jump to John 13:34–35, 15:12 and 1 John 3:23, which state:

> 34 *A new commandment I give unto you, that you love one another; as I have loved you, that you also love one another.*
> 35 *By this shall all men know that you are My disciples, if you have love one to another.*

> 12 *A new Commandment I give unto you, that you love one another; as I have loved you, that you also love one another.*

> 23 *This is my commandment, that you love one another, as I have loved you.*

These verses relate only to the foundation of the Law of Messiah, not the superstructure built on that foundation. Other commentators want to go further and say that the ethics of the Sermon on the Mount and all of Yeshua's character and teachings constitute the Law of Messiah. The command of our Lord instructs us, as true believers, to interact with other believers in love in the same way He interacted with us. Some say that in place of the Old Testament law, Christians are to obey the Law of Christ. Rather than trying to remember and observe the 613 commandments in the Old Testament law, Christians are simply to focus on loving God and loving others ... but what does that look like? If Christians would truly and wholeheartedly obey those two commands, we would be fulfilling everything that God requires of us. But is that the Law of Messiah? No, although the Law of Messiah encompasses them and helps to define them. Those commands lay down the foundation for the Law of Messiah, but love is only the core that is surrounded by the Law of Messiah. Love does not completely explain the Law of Messiah.

In 59 years of being in Christ, I have learned that love, as critical as it is, is not what gives me the power to walk the Christian life, although love is at the core of that life. Others have implied that the Law of Messiah is expressed in the Sermon on the Mount in Matthew 5–7. Granted, there is much we can learn from the Sermon on the Mount, and there is much we need to learn concerning the self-sacrificial love that Yeshua displayed in His earthly ministry. But is that the Law of Messiah? Although this expresses aspects of the Law of Messiah, it is not the entire Law of Messiah in its fullness.

One must remember that much of Yeshua's teaching was in the dispensation of law and not the dispensation of grace. Of course, His statements are true, but their thrust is misplaced by men. The New Commandment of love, the Sermon on the Mount, and all the words of Yeshua are true. But remember that one always must consider the <u>context</u> of Yeshua's words. Love is the core element of the Law of Messiah. Yeshua teaches this in His upper-room discourse (John 13–16), which largely refers to the Church Age and the dispensation of grace, not to the dispensation of law which was shortly to be rendered inoperative by the death, burial, and resurrection of Yeshua. The Sermon on the Mount does not tell Christians how to walk the Christian walk. That Sermon is Yeshua's statements on the righteousness of the Law versus man-made rabbinic righteousness; in our Christian culture of man-made rules and "grocery lists" of false spirituality, that is the context of Matthew 5–7 in the dispensation of law.

Others want to tie in the law by saying that the ceremonial and civic laws are fulfilled in Christ. Paul, in referencing the moral law of the Mosaic code as being in play with the Law of Messiah by quoting Galatians 5:14, goes completely against what Timothy George says:

> However, as Paul has shown already in Gal[atians] 5–6, the moral law of God has never been abrogated or annulled, although the civil and ceremonial aspects of the Mosaic legislation have been made obsolete by the coming of Christ. The moral law epitomized in the Ten Commandments and summarized in Jesus' restatement of the "new commandment" given to his disciples (John 13:34; 15:12; 1 John 3:23) continues to play an important role in the life of the justified believer. In sum, the "law of Christ" is for Paul "the whole tradition of Jesus' ethical teaching, confirmed by his character and conduct and reproduced within his people by the power of the Spirit (cf. Rom 8:2).[131]

I remind you that the Mosaic law is a unit, not a series of statutes to be divided up or sectioned out, as Paul clearly states in Galatians 5:3. All of the law has been rendered inoperative by the finished work of Messiah on the cross. It is always interesting to me how believers want to sweep under the rug passages that destroy their position, a practice which we investigated in preceding chapters. Charles Ryrie brings it back into perspective:

> James's use of the law is based on this same concept of the unitary nature of the law. When dealing with the problem of partiality in the synagogue, James decries it on the basis that it is in contradiction to the law of loving one's neighbor as one's self (Lev 19:18; James 2:8). The single violation, he says, makes them guilty of the whole law (James 2:10). He could not make such a drastic statement if the law were not considered as a unit. All of this, of course, has a very important bearing on the doing away of the law; for it seems to point to the fact that, unless the New Testament expressly says so, part of the law cannot be ended without doing away with all of it.[132]

George attempts to incorporate part of the Law of Moses into the Law of Messiah, which is not possible because the Law of Moses is a unit. One thing is true of the Law of Messiah: it is for us as believers to love each other as Messiah loved us. However, that is not all of the Law of Messiah, and as good and perfect as the character and teachings of Yeshua are, most of that was given under a different dispensation and not to the Church. Love is the foundation for the Law of Messiah, but it is not the entire structure. In John 13:34–35, 15:12–14, and 1 John 3:23, Yeshua is referring to a self-sacrificial love. Love is essential: it was God who loved us first by sending His Son for us, and it was the Son's self-sacrificial love for us on the cross that saved us, but even that love is not all of the Law of Messiah. There is more, which most believers have never been systematically taught. Let me reorganize White's statement to show this:

- Love is central to the law of Christ.

- Christians are called to seek the good of our neighbor, not ourselves (1 Corinthians 10:24).

- Above all, we are to put on love, which binds everything together in perfect harmony (Colossians 3:14).

- Paul tells Timothy, "The aim of our charge is love that issues from a pure heart and a good conscience and a sincere faith" (1 Timothy 1:5).

- We are to "love one another with brotherly affection" (Romans 12:10).

- Paul prays that the Lord would make us increase and abound in love for one another and for all (1 Thessalonians 3:12).

- Everything we do is to be done in love (1 Corinthians 16:24).

- Peter writes, "Having purified your souls by your obedience to the truth for a sincere brotherly love, love one another earnestly from a pure heart" (1 Peter 1:22).

- All we do is for the glory of God (1 Corinthians 10:31).

- The immediate context of this verse is all about the other: giving no offense to Jews or Greeks or the church, trying to please everyone in everything we do, not seeking my own advantage but that of many (1 Corinthians 10:32–33).[133]

Love is the foundation, but the Apostle John continues to emphasize the centrality of love in his first epistle. This again is noted by White:

> John also emphasizes the centrality of love. Whoever loves his brother abides in the light (1 John 2:10). The one who does not love his brother is not a child of God, but of the devil (1 John 3:10). "For this is the message that you have heard from the beginning, that we should love one another"

(1 John 3:11, cf. 2 John 5 6). "We know that we have passed out of death into life, because we love the brothers. Whoever does not love abides in death" (1 John 3:14). "By this we know love, that he laid down his life for us, and we ought to lay down our lives for the brothers" (1 John 3:16). "And this is his commandment, that we believe in the name of his Son Jesus Christ and love one another, just as he has commanded us" (1 John 3:23).[134]

The Abrahamic Covenant is enveloped in God's love for both Jewish people and Gentiles (Genesis 3:15; 12:3). The New Covenant, a byproduct of the blessing aspect of the Abrahamic Covenant, is enveloped in God's love for humankind (John 3:16–18). The Law of Messiah is the byproduct of the New Covenant, as here again God has enveloped us in His love to show us how (and give us the power) to live a life of victory over sin if we learn to yield to and submit to the Holy Spirit.

Apostles Spoke the Words of Yeshua

Some scholars recognize the Law of Messiah only as Yeshua's New Commandment and His other teachings from His earthly ministry. However, the Law of Messiah includes more than the teachings of Yeshua; it also includes the teachings of the apostles. At the time of His upper-room discourse in John 13–17, what we call the Church was not yet a reality, and all that was to be taught in the Church was simply too much for the apostles to handle just then. At that time the apostles did not even understand the two coming programs of Messiah. Of course, the words of Yeshua help clarify that what the apostles would be teaching in the future would be from Him through the ministry of the Holy Spirit. Read what Yeshua said in John 16:12–14, as He gave the apostles a glimpse of something they could not understand at that point:

12 *I have yet many things to say unto you, but you cannot bear them now.* 13 *Howbeit when He, the Spirit of Truth, is*

come, He will guide you into all truth: for He shall not speak of Himself; but whatsoever He shall hear, that shall He speak: and He will shew you things to come. 14 He shall glorify Me: for He shall receive of Mine, and shall shew it unto you.

Look at these verses closely, especially verse 12, and meditate on what He said to them. *I have yet many things to say unto you, but you cannot bear them now.* After the resurrection Yeshua began to teach the apostles what they could not bear before the cross: things concerning the future Church and its new standard of living, the Law of Messiah. This was all completely new to and unexpected by the apostles. Major changes were about to take place theologically, and He would instruct the apostles through the teaching ministry of the Holy Spirit. The Spirit's teaching ministry gave the apostles the words of the Messiah through the new teacher, the Comforter, concerning the nature, theology, and practical living of believers as it would be altered from the Mosaic law that had been their and Israel's focus since Moses.

Here I set out materials that express the Law of Messiah. These are the building blocks that are placed on the foundation of His love, and show us how to express that love to God, to the unsaved, and to the body of Messiah of which we are part. Please read them carefully and slowly and let them sink in; the schoolmaster, the guardian, is no longer needed (Galatians 3:24–25) because the Seed (Genesis 22:18; Galatians 3:16, 19) has come and has bestowed on us blessing and the power through the Holy Spirit to walk the kind of life that enables Him to conform us to His image (Romans 8:29).

- The "law of Christ" encompasses the whole of Jesus' teaching in person, while He was on earth, and <u>through His apostles and prophets</u> from heaven following His ascension (Acts 1:1 2).[135]

- Here Paul uses the word *law* (*nomos*) in a positive way.

The law of Christ alludes specifically in this case to Christ's command to love one another. More broadly, it includes all of which He commanded. <u>Even the New Testament commands of the apostles that He sent are definitely part of the law of Christ.</u>[136]

- Living in the Spirit is the means by which believers fulfill the law of Christ.[137]

- Christians no longer live under the Mosaic Law; we live under a new code, the law of Christ (cf. Galatians 5:1).[138]

- The Law of Messiah is far more difficult to systematize in that it deals not only with actions and behavior, but with the intent of the heart and attitudes. Consider the Law of Messiah to be every propositional directive contained within the New Testament. In other words, <u>the Law of Messiah is quite simply defined as divinely revealed apostolic teaching.</u>[139]

- Christian behavior ... is now guided directly by the "law of Christ." This "law" does not consist of legal prescriptions and ordinances [like the Mosaic law], <u>but of the teaching and example of Jesus and the apostles,</u> the central demand of life, and the guiding influence of the indwelling Holy Spirit.[140]

- The law of Christ is not an exhaustive list of rules [like the Mosaic law] but principles centered on love, guided by the Spirit, and <u>drawn from the example and teachings of Christ and his apostles,</u> and ultimately drawn from the entire canon viewed through the lens of Jesus Christ [not Moses].[141]

- <u>Law of Messiah are all the commandments either given directly by Yeshua or through His apostles in the epistles which are directly given to the believers of the New age</u>

of Grace. Not all commandments given by Yeshua are applicable such as the commandments not to go to the Samaritans or the Gentiles but only to the lost sheep of the house of Israel. In the Gospels, the turning point is Matthew 12–13.[142]

As God spoke through Moses, David, Isaiah, and Zechariah in the Hebrew Scriptures under the Mosaic law, God spoke through the apostles in the economy of grace to the Church. Look at the unique words of Paul concerning Christ and the Ephesians:

15 By abolishing the law of commandments [Law of Moses] *expressed in ordinances, that He might create in Himself one new man in place of the two, so making peace, 16 and might reconcile us both to God in one body through the cross, thereby killing the hostility. 17 And <u>He came and preached peace to you</u> who were far off and preached to those who were near. 18 For through Him we both have access in one Spirit to the Father.* (Ephesians 2:15–18, ESV)

According to Paul, who spoke to the Ephesians? Who came and preached to the Ephesians? Jesus Christ! Christ came and preached through Paul: He did not come to them personally. The words of Paul were Yeshua's words, just as Moses' words were Yahweh's words. The authority of Yeshua was passed on through the apostles. Now look at 2 Corinthians 5:20: *Now then we are ambassadors for Christ, as though God did beseech you by us: we pray you in Christ's stead, be ye reconciled to God.*

We are the ambassadors of Christ; we are "an authorized representative or messenger." Paul was an ambassador of Christ; he spoke the words of Christ in his epistles. We are also ambassadors for Christ, and we relay the words already spoken to the Church and a lost humanity. I like how Lenski illustrates the word *ambassador*:

"An ambassador speaks wholly for his ruler; he is his ruler's mouthpiece. He never utters his own thoughts, offers, promises, demands, but only those of his ruler. An ambassador's person lends no weight to what he says. They to whom he is sent see and hear in him only the king who sent him."[144]

We can add one other dimension to the authority of the apostles. The Hebrew word *shaliach*, which Wikipedia defines as a Jewish legal emissary or agent, also reflects the authority of the apostles. A *shaliach* performs an act of legal significance for the benefit of the sender (rather than for his or her own benefit). This Hebrew term is comparable to the Greek word ἀπόστολος (*apostolos*, whence the English "apostle"). This is illustrated in Scripture when Abraham sent his servant Eliezer to find a wife for Isaac in Genesis 24:1–61. White makes the following connection:

> The Lord gave them [the apostles] their authority. This was similar to the *shaliach* in Judaism. In the Jewish legal system, the *shaliach* was given legal power to represent another person, and "so unique was his relationship to the one he represented that the *shaliach* was regarded as that person himself." So Jesus can say to them, "The one who hears you hears me, and the one who rejects you rejects me, and the one who rejects me rejects him who sent me" (Luke 10:16, Matt 10:40, Mark 9:37, John 13:20; 17:8). John 14–16 are crucial chapters in this regard. Therefore, the authority of the apostles, now found in the New Testament, is bound up with the authority of the risen Messiah Himself. Their teaching is His teaching. The prophets and apostles are the foundation of the church (Eph 2:20).[145]

Now do you realize that in the New Testament epistles of Paul, James, Peter, and John, and the book of Hebrews, the authors speak with the authority of Yeshua, and have thereunder given us hundreds of commands (imperatives) in the Law of Christ? (This does not apply to most of the four Gospels, for the events and teachings therein are still under the Mosaic law, and so reflect the dispensation of law, not grace.) In the Greek, these words are in the imperative form, meaning they are commands, laws given by the apostles to the Church so that we can live with victory in our walk with Yeshua. These imperative commands have replaced the old law system which could only give *condemnation* and *death*. The new system, the Law of Messiah, now gives life and the power to live it. If we submit to the Holy Spirit and allow Him to empower us so that we *walk in the spirit* (Galatians 5:16), we can then be *led by the Spirit* (Galatians 5:18) in four areas. First, He can manifest the *fruit of the Spirit* in our lives (Galatians 5:22–23); second, we can daily *live by the Spirit* (Galatians 5:25); third, we can stay in step with the Spirit in our daily walk; and fourth, we can *sow to the Spirit*, and in the Spirit reap life eternal (Galatians 6:8).

The Law of Christ stands in contrast to the Law of Moses. It is an inner principle rather than an external precept, and is fulfilled as we bear spiritual fruit.[146] It is this law that God said through Jeremiah *I will put My law in their inward parts, and write it in their hearts* (Jeremiah 31:33). This is part of the New Covenant that we as Gentiles enjoy with our Jewish brethren in Messiah Yeshua because of His finished work on the cross of Calvary to which it pointed. The theme of Galatians is so very important that if not corrected immediately it would have changed the course of the Church perhaps for all time. It was important for Paul to make a frontal assault on this false teaching: "Galatians, which in attacking Jewish legalism proclaims the true freedom based on Christ, consequently contains more exhortation, admonition, and summons to obey the law of Christ... than any other letter, and to quite a remarkable degree — a third of the whole letter."[147]

According to this author, we have a summons to obey the Law of Messiah in all of its commandments throughout the epistles. Ryrie also emphasizes the importance of the Law of Messiah:

Chapter 10

> The laws through Moses were codified formally and fearfully by being handed down from Mount Sinai. The New Testament speaks of the "law of Christ" (Gal 6:2) and the "law of the Spirit of life" (Rom 8:2). In the law of Christ are the hundreds of commandments of the New Testament epistles, and together these form a new and distinct code of ethics.[148]
>
> The Mosaic Law has been done away in its entirety as a code. God is no longer guiding the life of man by this particular code. In its place He has introduced the law of Messiah. Many of the individual commands within that law are new, but some are not. Some of the ones which are old were also found in the Mosaic Law and they are now incorporated into the law of Messiah. As a part of the Mosaic Law they are completely and forever done away [with]. As part of the law of Christ they are binding on the believer today. There are also in the law of Christ commandments from pre-Mosaic codes [Noahic], as, for instance, the permission to eat meat (1 Tim 4:3).[149]

The book of Hebrews does not use the term "Law of Messiah," but it does echo the sentiment of Paul. The author of the book of Hebrews clearly teaches that the Mosaic law has been superseded (Hebrews 7:11–12). Messiah is a High Priest—not after the order of Aaron, but of the order of Melchizedek, because the priesthood of Aaron could not bring perfection to the people. So, why keep using Mosaic law as a default or fall-back system when there is something better, superior to it? The Law of Moses could not do the job, so there was a critical need for another priesthood. The fact that Messiah is our high priest necessitates the conclusion that the Mosaic law has ceased and the Law of Messiah is our new code of living (Hebrew 7:12).

Here is a concise summary of the ministry of Paul in the place of his Lord and Saviour Yeshua. Gordon Fee says of Paul's ethics:

"God's glory is their <u>purpose</u>,

the Spirit is their <u>power</u>,

love is the <u>principle</u>,

and Christ is the <u>pattern</u>."[150]

Chapter 10

11
EXAMINING THE TEXT OF 1 CORINTHIANS 9:21: THE LAW OF THE MESSIAH

To them that are without law [Gentiles], a*s without law, (being not without law to God, but under the law to Messiah) that I might gain them that are without law* [the Gentiles].

In chapter 10 on Galatians, we laid some foundations as to the Law of Messiah, which I will not repeat here. In 1 Corinthians Paul uses the term *under the Law to Christ*, which is similar to the phrase that appears in Galatians. However, here Paul gives a personal attachment and accountability to the Law of Messiah as it relates to him, saying *Law to Messiah* instead of the *law of Christ* [Messiah]. Notice the difference from Galatians: in Galatians it is the *Law of Christ* and in Corinthians it is the *Law to Christ*. In choosing these words, Paul clearly and distinctly indicates that he is *under the Law to Christ* and not under the Law of Moses. Paul has made a change of commitment from the Law of Moses to the Law of Messiah. Notice the key words: one is descriptive (Galatians) and the other is more personal (Corinthians).

Before we investigate further, let's gain some background on 1 Corinthians.[151] Paul established this church in a real center of paganism. You can read about the biblical background of Paul establishing the church in Corinth in Acts 18:1–18.[152] Paul had written to the church at Corinth because of the divisions among its members that had to be corrected.

Chapter 11

Chapters 1–4	Divisions in the church body
Chapters 5–6	Problems of immorality among the believers and taking each other to court
Chapters 7–8	Problems and counsel concerning marriage
Chapters 9–10	Problems with meals offered to idols (Christian liberty)
Chapter 11–14	Abuses of worship and the spiritual gifts
Chapter 15	Teaching on the resurrection and rapture of the Church
Chapter 16	Greetings to believers

Chapters 1–8 are a unit wherein Paul deals with the carnality and sin that was reported among the brethren in the preceding chapters. In chapters 11–14 he teaches them about spiritual things, for again he had to deal with the abuses of spiritual gifts in the church. Nestled in between these two sections are chapters 9–10, in which Paul deals with the use of Christian liberty and instructs believers how to care for and build up their weaker brothers in Messiah (along with defending his apostleship, in chapter 9).

Our main focus here is the phrase *under the law to Christ*. Let's look at the immediate context of this phrase, verses 19–21:

19 *For though I be free from all men, yet have I made myself servant unto all that I might gain the more.* 20 *And unto the Jews I became as a Jew, that I might gain the Jews; to them that are under the law* [of Moses], *as under the law, that I might gain them that are under the law* [of Moses]; 21 *To them that are without law* [Gentiles], *as without law, being* [Paul] *not without law to God, but under the law to Christ* [Messiah], *that I might gain them that are without law.*

In chapter 8 Paul teaches concerning Christian liberty. In 9:19, we see that this law of Christian liberty has made Paul *free from all men*; he is not under constraints to satisfy any group of people. Yet, in being *free from all men* he has made himself, through a voluntary action, a *servant unto all* men. He is free, but he has willingly placed himself under Messiah for a distinct purpose. He says twice *that I might gain the more*, indicating his hope to win over more men so that Jewish people and all ethnicities of Gentiles might put their faith in Messiah Yeshua.

In verse 20 Paul states that *unto the Jews, I became a Jew*. Because Paul was Jewish, of the tribe of Benjamin, concerning the law a Pharisee (Philippians 3:5), he understood what was accepted by the Jewish people according to the Law of Moses as well as rabbinically. It was not his intention to use his Christian liberty to offend his Jewish brethren, because he would thereby forfeit any opportunity to present the gospel of Messiah to his Jewish brethren. He was being very sensitive to all the cultural and religious beliefs of the Jews, so that he might *gain* some of the Jewish people unto Messiah Yeshua. Paul's main concern in these verses is how he ministers to Jewish people and Gentiles. He is willing to minister to Jewish people as a Jew and he is also willing to live as a Gentile among the Gentiles. But he clarifies it: he is not without law as are the Gentiles; rather, he is under the *law of God* which he calls the *Law to Christ* [Messiah]. Then he moves into the main thrust of this section by saying that whether he is ministering to Jewish people who are under the Mosaic law or to Gentiles who have no law, he is as a runner in a race and he wants to receive the prize. He wants to receive the rewards given to every believer at the Bema Seat of Messiah (Christ). In Philippians Paul expresses his loss and his gain:

> 2 <u>Look out for the dogs</u>, <u>look out for the evildoers</u>, *look out for those who mutilate the flesh.* 3 *For <u>we are the circumcision</u>, who worship by the Spirit of God and glory in Christ Jesus and put no confidence in the flesh,* 4 *though <u>I myself have</u>*

reason for confidence in the flesh also. *If anyone else thinks he has reason for confidence in the flesh. I have more:* 5 *circumcised on the eighth day, of the people of Israel, of the tribe of Benjamin, a Hebrew of Hebrews; as to the law, a Pharisee;* 6 *as to zeal, a persecutor of the church; as to righteousness under the law, blameless.* 7 *But whatever gain I had, I counted as loss for the sake of Christ.* 8 *Indeed, I count everything as loss because of the surpassing worth of knowing Christ Jesus my Lord. For His sake I have suffered the loss of all things and count them as rubbish, in order that I may gain Christ,* 9 *and be found in Him, not having a righteousness of my own that comes from the law, but that which comes through faith in Christ, the righteousness from God that depends on faith,* 10 *that I may know Him and the power of His resurrection, and may share His sufferings, becoming like Him in His death,* 11 *that by any means possible I may attain the resurrection from the dead.* 12 *Not that I have already obtained this or am already perfect, but I press on to make it my own, because Christ Jesus has made me His own.* 13 *Brothers, I do not consider that I have made it my own. But one thing I do: forgetting what lies behind and straining forward to what lies ahead,* 14 *I press on toward the goal for the prize of the upward call of God in Christ Jesus.* (Philippians 3:2–14 ESV)

Let me review some of my emphasis in the preceding passage. Three times he tells the Philippian church to *look out*, and this warning is in reference to Judaizers (verse 2) who *mutilate the flesh* (that is, undergo circumcision). He does not go into detail as he does in Galatians; he simply mentions it. In verse 3 he references the fact that he and the Philippian believers are circumcised, even as he told the Colossian believers, but again with more detail in Colossians: *In Him also you were circumcised with a circumcision made without hands, but putting off the body of the flesh, by the circumcision of Christ.* (Colossians 2:11 ESV).

Paul was of good pedigree, circumcised in accordance with the Abrahamic Covenant (Genesis 17:10–12), of the tribe of Benjamin. He was a Hebrew and a Pharisee and in his zeal he persecuted the church, *as to the* [Mosaic] *law blameless*. It is the same terminology used in Luke 1:5–6 for Zacharias, who was a believer and blameless. Before his Damascus Road conversion, Paul was an unbeliever, but blameless because he made the appropriate sacrifices. Paul states that all he had counted as gain—his Jewish pedigree—he counted as loss after knowing his Messiah, the Christ. In fact, in verse 8 he refers to all that as *rubbish* because being in Christ was much greater gain. This is not the attitude of the Torah-observant believers within the Messianic Movement.

Paul presses on, not in his Jewishness and not in Torah observance. He presses on leaving all his Jewish pedigree behind for the goal, the prize of his upward calling in Messiah. Do not misunderstand: Paul was a Jew and did not shy away from that fact, but to him there was much more to gain by being in Christ. This was his focus, not his Jewishness or Torah observance or the Law of Moses.

Today in the Olympics men and women strive, work, practice, and labor to receive the gold, silver, or bronze medals as their reward. But as true believers in Messiah we (and notice that Paul says we) all are running to receive an incorruptible crown (1 Corinthians 9:25; 1 Peter 1:4), and rewards of gold, silver, and precious stones in proportion to the quality of our labor for Him. What is your goal: to run unto Moses or to run unto Messiah?

Commentators are divided on the use of the word "law" (*nomos*); As I discussed earlier, some want to dice up the law into the three Christian divisions (moral, ceremonial, and civil), although neither God nor Paul does so. In looking over many commentaries,

Chapter 11

I found only two which recognized that the Law of Moses is a unit and not to be divided.[153] Hunt captures the thinking of Paul as he presented the gospel to his brethren, the Jewish people, and then to the Gentiles:

> Though he himself was not bound to the Law of Moses, he acted as under the law, that [he] might win those who are under the law. Those under the law is simply a reference to the Jews. Nevertheless in Paul's freedom he conformed to practices that allowed him to present an opportunity for Jews to respond to the Gospel He also shared with Gentiles—those who are without law. However, he was not … without law toward [men] (he was not lawless) and he was motivated because he was under law toward Christ, which governs Christian behavior.[154]

In contrast, Hodge tries to link the two laws by connecting the moral Law of Moses to the moral Law of Messiah, while excluding the ceremonial and civil: "Paul is careful to explain in what sense he acted as without law. When among the Gentiles he did not conform to the Jewish law; in that sense, he was without law; but he did not act as without law to God, i.e. without regard to the obligation of the moral law."[155]

Hodge inserts a foreign subject that is not in the immediate context when he says "without regard to the obligation of the moral law." All law systems contain moral law. What he is coupling together is the moral law of the Mosaic law with the moral law of the Law of Messiah. That concept is neither present in or nor derivable from Paul's words. Hodge is extracting the moral law from the Mosaic law and applying it to the Law of Messiah. The moral law of the Mosaic law is part of the unit of the whole of the Mosaic law; God does not divide it, nor should we.

In verse 2, Paul states where he will conclude his teaching in relation to the Jewish people and transitions to the subject of the Gentiles, whom he categorizes as ones *without the Law* [of Moses] in verse 21. The Gentiles did not have the Law of Moses, nor were they under that law. It was given to the Jewish people (Exodus 19:9–20:1–26) but not to Gentiles, as Paul points out clearly in Ephesians 2:11–13. Paul then says that he was as one *not without law*, meaning that he as a Jew was no longer bound to the Law of Moses because of the finished work of Messiah on the cross of Calvary. The blood of the New Covenant laid aside the Old Covenant of the Law of Moses in favor of a new law (a new code to live by) called the Law of Messiah and *under the Law to Messiah*. The Apostle Paul, as a Jew, clearly states that he is no longer under the Law of Moses, even though he abides by it when among the Jews: not because he is under it, but because it is his desire not to offend his physical brethren so that he can present to them the gospel of Messiah. Paul's own words also indicate that he was not Torah-observant as a Jew! Further, it means that Gentiles are not under the Law of Moses and are not to be Torah-observant, despite what modern-day Judaizers argue. Now, none of this says or even implies that the Gentiles do not have a law or abide under a law. Their law is the law of conscience, which is reflective of the unconditional covenant given to Adam in the Adamic Covenant. All men have a conscience, which God still uses to exercise limited control over man. I say "limited" because man can choose to ignore his conscience and move into sin of the heart and sin in action. Paul deals with this subject in Romans 2:14–15 where he says:

> 14 *For when the Gentiles, which have not the law* [of Moses], *do by nature the things contained in the law, these, having not the law, are a law unto themselves.* 15 *Which shew the work of the law written in their hearts, their conscience also bearing witness....*

In addition, the Gentiles were also under the Noahic Covenant, and they were to obey the law of the country or empire in which they lived. So, in this context you have Gentiles who

Chapter 11

did righteous things or good things toward men. This does not relate to or bear on salvation: here Paul is speaking of Gentiles listening to their consciences. Modern-day Judaism calls them "righteous Gentiles."[156]

Now look closer at verse 21: *as without law being under the Law to Messiah* that he might win some of the Gentiles for Messiah. Paul is very sensitive to the cultural and religious norms of the Gentiles. Paul did not do pagan ritual things, for that would have been sinning against God by violating his conscience and the law of God. Paul was not lawless and he did not open the door to license or sin; he was under the law of God, which he describes as being *under the law to Christ*. We want to focus on what Paul was targeting in this verse.

The genitive construction of the *Law of Messiah* in Galatians 6:2 and the *Law to Messiah* in 1 Corinthians 9:21 indicates that this law has its source in Christ, not the Law of Moses. This "law" from Christ dictates the way a believer's life in Christ should be lived. It is a new lifestyle in Christ and the new law for the New Covenant participants.[157]

Adeyemi clearly catches Paul's vision and understands that believers today have a new lifestyle, a Law to Messiah. The Mosaic law, as a system, has been laid aside because it could not produce life; it could only produce *condemnation* and *death*. Let's have Paul explain this change. 2 Corinthians 3:6–11 clearly lays out the fact that the Law of Moses has been done away with because it was ineffective:

> 6 *Who also has <u>made us able ministers of the New Covenant;</u> <u>not</u> of the letter* [Mosaic], <u>but</u> *of the spirit* [New Covenant]*: for the <u>letter kills</u>, but the <u>spirit gives life</u>. 7 But if the <u>ministration of death</u>, written and engraven in stones* [Decalogue; the Ten Commandments], *was glorious, so that the children of Israel could not steadfastly behold the face of Moses for the glory of*

his countenance; which glory was to be done away [dissipate]: *8 How shall not the ministration of the spirit fail to be even more with glory? 9 For if the <u>ministration of condemnation</u> be glory, much more does the <u>ministration of righteousness exceed in glory</u>. 10 For indeed what had glory, in this case has not glory on account of the glory that surpasses it. 11 For if that which fades away was with glory, much more that which remains is in glory.*

Notice in particular the underlined phrases and understand clearly what Paul is saying to the Corinthian church.

First, the believers in Corinth are to be ministers with Paul of the New Covenant, not the old one, which the writer of Hebrews said was *vanishing away* (Hebrews 8:13).

Second, to those who want to cling to the moral law (meaning the Ten Commandments), as many do today, Paul says that the *letter kills*, and clarifies the "letter" as the law engraven on stone that is a <u>*ministration of death*</u>. Remember, being in Christ makes you *a new creation* in Christ (2 Corinthians 5:17), and you are to be walking *in the newness of Life* (Romans 6:4). Death and life are poles apart and will never come together; the one repeals the other.

Third, Paul further discusses the glory that was expressed at Mount Sinai: Moses had to cover his face, because his skin radiated the glory of the presence of God. Knowing that Moses' glory would fade, Paul called this the *ministration of death*. Compare the ministration of *condemnation* and *death* with the ministration of righteousness that supersedes the Mosaic law.

Fourth, Paul states that the law given at Sinai was a ministry of condemnation: no one (other than Messiah), could keep the Mosaic law, and thus it was identified as a *ministration of condemnation* and *death*.

Those are serious and unsettling words for believers who want to cling to the moral law (the Ten Commandments and Torah observance) as being applicable today in the Church as part of the Mosaic law. Another author states the following:

> There is one other passage in the writings of Paul which, because it is more particular, is even more emphatic concerning the ending of the law. In 2 Corinthians 3:7–11 Paul makes the comparison between what is ministered through Moses and what is ministered through Christ. That which Moses ministered is called a ministration of death and it is specifically said to have been written and engraved in stones. The only part of the Mosaic Law which was written in stone was the Ten Commandments—that category which some designate as the moral part of the law. Thus, this passage says that the Ten Commandments are a ministration of death; and furthermore, the same passage declares in no uncertain terms that they are done away (vs. 11). Language could not be clearer, and yet there are fewer truths of which it is harder to convince people. All kinds of exegetical maneuvering goes on in the attempt to make this passage say something else.[158]

Paul categorically stated that the Decalogue—the moral law—kills and that the Mosaic Covenant is a covenant of death (2 Corinthians 3:6–7). As Ryrie notes, Paul is crystal clear about the end of the Mosaic law system, and yet this is one of the hardest concepts to get most Christians to accept.

Here are two more verses that restate the end of the Mosaic law and its inferiority of that Law:

> *For sin shall not have dominion over you: for you are not under the law, but under grace.* (Romans 6:14)

> *For Messiah is the end of the law for righteousness to everyone that believes.* (Romans 10:4)

Jewish and Gentile believers in Messiah should focus on the New Code of life for Christians, the *Law of Messiah*. This new law is completely different from the Mosaic code or any previous code of conduct or living. This Law of Messiah is superior to anything before it because of the one who initiated it by His blood once and for all. The book of Hebrew presents this as a believer's first priority, yet people still cling to that which is inferior. The Law of Messiah is not Moses' Law; His law was initiated by the Prophet like unto Moses that Israel was commanded to obey (Deuteronomy 18:15–19)—yet they would not because of an unbiblical bias that they maintained. Ryrie and Burtchaell explain it thus:

> The Mosaic law was one of several codes of ethics which God has given throughout history. That particular code contained ... 613 specific commandments. But there have been other God-given codes. The laws under which Adam's life was governed combine to form what might be called a code for the Garden of Eden. There were at least two commandments in that code—dress the Garden and avoid eating the fruit of one tree. Noah was given commandments which included, after the Flood, the permission to eat meat (Gen 9:3). God revealed many commandments, statutes, and laws to Abraham which guided his life; together these may be called the Abrahamic code of conduct. The laws through Moses were codified formally and fearfully by being handed down from Mount Sinai. The New Testament speaks of the "law of Christ" (Gal 6:2) and the "law of the Spirit of life" (Rom 8:2). In the law of Christ there are the hundreds of commandments in the New Testament epistles, and together these form a new and distinct code of ethics.[159]

Burtchaell argues that the law of Christ is a new kind of law, the "law of faith" (Romans 3:27) or "the law of the Spirit" (Romans 8:2). It is the inner working of the Holy Spirit, not a legal code.[160]

Just as Paul was not without the *Law to God*, we are not without the Law of God. Just as with that *Law to God* which Paul described as the *Law to Messiah*, we as believers in Messiah are responsible to the *Law to Messiah* just as much as Paul was. Wilkin emphasizes this:

> "He shared with Gentiles—those who are without law (cf. Rom 2:12). However, he was not ... without law toward God (he was not lawless) and he was motivated because he was under <u>law toward Christ,</u> which governs Christian behavior (Galatians 5:13–14)."[161]
>
> *For, brethren, you have been called unto liberty; only use not liberty for an occasion to the flesh, but by love serve one another. For all the law is fulfilled in one word, even this; You shall love your neighbour as yourself.* (Galatians 5:13–14)

Believers are to walk in the grace of God. That grace of God is <u>not</u> license: as Paul says, Should I sin that grace may abound? Absolutely not! Look at Romans 6:1–2:

> *What shall we say then? Shall we continue in sin, that grace may abound? God forbid. How shall we, that are dead to sin, live any longer therein?*

Paul does not mince words; he is clear and to the point.

Yet today Christians play the church game and live just like the world at home and at work. We in the Grace Movement have been accused time and time again of preaching license, by people who do not recognize that we are under a law and we are to live according to that law: a *Law to Christ*. When people understand their salvation and all the spiritual blessings that we have been given because of the blood of Christ, they should be standing in awe of our Savior. Understanding all this, we should be motivated to live and walk in the power of the Holy Spirit by submitting to Him, as Paul directs in Romans 8 and John writes in his first epistle to believers. In the warm-fuzzy, entertainment-oriented, seeker-friendly church of today, we have raised a whole generation of Bible-illiterate, naïve, and uncommitted believers who do not know the basis of their faith. In light of that I would like to make a strong and direct application to many believers today from Hebrews 6 and 10:

6:6b *Seeing they crucify to themselves the Son of God afresh, and put Him to an open shame.*

10:26 *For if we sin willfully after that we have received the knowledge of the truth, there remains no more sacrifice for sins. 27 But a certain fearful expectation of judgment and fiery indignation, which shall devour the adversaries. 28 <u>He that despised Moses' law died without mercy under two of three witnesses:</u> 29 Of how much more punishment, suppose you, shall he be thought worthy, <u>who have trodden underfoot the Son of God</u>, and have <u>counted the Blood of the</u> [New] <u>Covenant, where with he was sanctified</u>, an <u>unholy thing</u>, and have done insult unto the Spirit of Grace. 30 For we know him that has said, Vengeance belongs unto Me, I will recompense, said the LORD. And again, the Lord shall judge His people.*

I am not going to say much about these verses (which many people struggle with), except that they apply directly to Hebrew Christians whom God will discipline for their open and secret sins. In Hebrews, their sin would have been done openly before all and done in the face of God by returning to Judaism. For us, physical discipline and judgment could come while we live on (Hebrews 12:5–11; 1 Corinthians 3:16–17), but most likely it will occur at the Bema Seat of Christ when our works are judged and our rewards are issued... or not (2 Corinthians 5:10; 1 Corinthians 3:13–17). Too many believers in Messiah will stand empty-handed on that day because they did not obey the Law of Messiah. Many pastors, the undershepherds of the Good Shepherd, will bear great accountability for being delinquent with the Scriptures and the God of their own salvation. Is that strong enough? Let me be even stronger:

- To put the Son of God to open shame before the whole world by not being obedient to the Law of Messiah, but to mock Him as He was mocked and shamed on the cross in your return to Judaism, the *weak and beggarly elements*.

- You have received the knowledge of the truth and the Holy Spirit to aid you in your walk, but you allowed self to reign supreme instead of the Messiah.

- In abiding under the Law of Moses, at the word of two or three witnesses you would be judged. Now that the *Prophet like Moses* has come, do you think your punishment or judgment will be less? Think again!

- In violation of the Law of Messiah, believers have trodden underfoot the Son of God by their living; they have counted Him as unworthy, worthless to them.

- Believers have disregarded the blood of Messiah and have counted it as an unholy thing.

- Understand that the LORD of Glory says, *Vengeance is Mine; I will repay*—and He will (Romans 12:19).

Oh, you say "That cannot happen to me as a believer in Christ"? Are you sure about that? You say "Jesus died for my sins"; yes, He did. But what about after your salvation? After that, did God give you a blank check to live as you please? NO! He gave you a <u>new motivation</u> that we would walk and live for Him out of our love for Him; for all that He has done for us. Don't forget that God is holy: He does not wink at our sin or grade on a curve. We as believers have a law to obey: It is the Law of Messiah and there are hundreds of them in the epistles, which are written specifically to the body of Messiah, on how to live and walk. In all of this we have also been empowered by the Holy Spirit if we choose to submit to Him and let Him led us.

It is not my intent to be heavy or condemning. I only wish someone had explained all this to me and told me these things when I was younger. I had to learn these things in the school of hard knocks. I spent most of my life doing good things in the flesh, in carnality. I knew absolutely nothing of the meaning of the New Covenant and the Law of the Messiah that comes from it. *Because the carnal mind is enmity against God: for it is not subject to the law of God, neither indeed can be.* (Romans 8:7). Nevertheless, the Holy Spirit of God will lead us and guide us in our walk, for He indwells us, He fills us, He seals us, and He baptizes us, placing us in the body of Messiah.

All of this is helpful information, but the primary question still remains: What is the Law of Messiah? To answer this, look at what we have in the context to help us. This much we can say: Paul is operating under the *Law to Christ*... but again, what is that law? Paul is not operating under the Mosaic law, nor is he operating with license in lawlessness. John MacArthur weighs in by emphasizing love, which is correct, but as we will see is an inadequate answer: "Every believer is under complete legal obligation to Jesus Christ—even through love, rather than the externalities of the law, is to be the guiding force."[162] He alludes to more but gives nothing concrete that would flesh out the Law of Messiah. MacArthur in his commentary did not explain what the Law of Messiah is in context. Although his commentary (and those by others) make many good points, they leave an understanding of the Law of Messiah just as elusive as before.

12

EXAMINING THE TEXT OF ROMANS 8:2: LAW OF THE SPIRIT OF LIFE

For the law of the Spirit of life in Messiah Yeshua has made me free from the law of sin and death. (Romans 8:2)

What I see each of these three phrases is a growing climax in expressing to Christians the New Covenant lifestyle in the Law of Messiah. It is a steady progression and intensification of the meaning of the term *Law of Messiah*. Let me break it down:

- *Law of Messiah* in Galatians, as it is first used in the expression of the Christian's new lifestyle because of the New Covenant.

- *Law to Messiah* in Corinthians, as it denotes a more personal and then general expression, for we as Paul are to live unto the Law to Messiah.

- *Law of the Spirit of life in Messiah* is the victory that Christ, through the ministry of the Holy Spirit, can give over the old man (the flesh) to the new man who submits to the Holy Spirit.

A straightforward answer as to the meaning of Romans 8:2 also proves to be elusive. In researching this passage I again referenced about 30 commentaries on Romans, but found none that relate this ministry of the Holy Spirit to the New Covenant and the outgrowth of the New Covenant in the lives of believers as they walk in the Spirit, being in submission to the Law of Messiah issued by Yeshua and His apostles.

Chapter 12

Let's begin with a very brief survey of the book of Romans and what Paul lays out in this great doctrinal thesis addressed to the Church in Rome, which had twisted and disfigured it in their own man-made religious hypocrisy. I break it down as follows:

- Romans 1 — The depravity of man.[163]
- Romans 2 — The Gentile moralizers are also depraved.
- Romans 3 — The Jewish people who have received covenants and promises are also depraved.
- Romans 3:23 — Summary of all peoples: *For all have sinned, and come short of the glory of God.*
- Romans 3–4 — The Justification[164] of God for sinful man.

Paul also uses the terms *grace,*[165] *redemption,*[166] *propitiation,*[167] and *through faith in His blood.*[168] In verse 28 Paul states: *therefore we conclude that a man is justified by faith without the deeds of the law.* Justification includes the Gentiles: 29 *Is he the God of the Jews only? Is He not also of the Gentiles? Yes, of the Gentiles also:* 30 *Seeing it is one God, which shall justify the circumcision by faith, and uncircumcision through faith.* (Romans 3:29–30).

Paul uses Abraham as his illustration of the Promise of God, which came 400 years before the Law. Abraham had faith in the Promise of God and He acted upon it in faith and was justified. Paul gives a summary verses 22–25:

> 22 *and therefore it was imputed to him [Abraham] for righteousness.* 23 *Now it was not written for his [Abraham's] sake alone, that it was imputed to him;* 24 *but for us also [Jews and Gentiles], to whom it shall be imputed, if we believe on Him that raised up Yeshua our Lord from the dead;* 25 *Who was delivered for our offences, and was raised again for our justification.*

- Romans 5–8 — This justification[169] brings sanctification, and Paul lays out a clear argument that our sanctification stands because of the New Covenant and the blood of that covenant as Messiah reconciled[170] us to God. Through Adam we had sin imputed to us, but now through faith in Messiah, His righteousness is imputed[171] to us. This is summed up by Paul in Romans 5:12, 17–18:

12 Wherefore, as by one man sin entered into the world, and death by sin; and so death passed upon all men, for that all have sinned: 17 For if by one man's [Adam's] offence death reigned by one; much more they which receive abundance of grace and the gift of righteousness shall reign in life by one, Yeshua the Messiah. 18 Therefore as by the offence of one judgment came upon all men to condemnation, even so by the righteousness of one the free gift came upon all men unto justification of life.

Chapters 6 through 8 contain some of the hardest material to understand. But it is also the richest teaching on the sin nature that is always with us and the new nature given to us by the Holy Spirit: it teaches that we can have victory over sin, the old man, the flesh, and the law. We will pay particular attention to Romans 8:2

- Romans 8:18–39 — Glorification[172] of sinful believers because of the work of Messiah on the cross and the work of the Holy Spirit giving us new birth, for we and nature groan as we *wait for the adoption, the redemption of our body* (8:23).

- Romans 9–11 — God's faithfulness to Israel, showing God's commitment to His covenants and promises to Israel.

- Romans 12–15—Based on all Yeshua has done, Paul here instructs us on how to live out the Christian life by making ourselves *living sacrifices to God* (12:1) by not being conformed to this world, which now we can achieve because of the Holy Spirit's work in our lives, being *transformed by the renewing of your mind* (12:2).

Now let us look again at Romans 8:1–2 as we discuss the ministry of the Holy Spirit who works in us because of the finished work of Messiah on the cross, and the reality of us placing our faith and trust in Yeshua as our Saviour and God.

1 T*here is therefore now no condemnation to them which are in Christ Jesus, who walk not after the flesh, but after the Spirit.* 2 *For the law of the Spirit of life in Messiah Yeshua has made me free from the law of sin and death.*

There are several points that we need to grasp to get the full scope of Paul's words. In Romans, as well as in Galatians, Paul states that the Law of Moses is not the answer, and that it is not the standard of living for the believer in this dispensation or economy of God. The answer comes when we submit to the Holy Spirit, not unto the law that cannot lead us into godly living. The Mosaic law cannot help us in this respect, as we saw in the book of Galatians dealing with the subject of the law being taught by the Judaizers. Paul completely negates Torah observance for the Christian or the Messianic Jewish believer in Messiah, the true believers in Messiah:

Romans 2:23—*You that makes your boast of the law, through breaking the law dishonors God.*

Romans 2:25–29—*For circumcision verily profits, if you keep the law: but if you be a breaker of the law, your circumcision is made uncircumcision. Therefore if the uncircumcision keep the righteousness of the law, shall not his uncircumcision be counted for circumcision? And shall not uncircumcision which* is by nature, if it fulfill the law judge you, who by the letter and circumcision does transgress the law? For he is not a Jew, which is one outwardly; neither is circumcision, which is outward in the flesh: But he is a Jew, which is one inwardly; and circumcision is that of the heart, in the spirit, and not in the letter; whose praise is not of men, but of God.

Romans 3:20—*Therefore by the deeds of the law there shall no flesh be justified in His sight: for by the law is the knowledge of sin.*

Romans 3:28—*Therefore we conclude that a man is justified by faith without the deeds of the law.*

Romans 4:14—*For if they which are of the law be heirs, faith is made void, and the promises made of no effect: Because the law works wrath: for where no law is, there is no transgression.*

Romans 6:14—*For sin shall not have dominion over you: for you are not under the law, but under grace.*

Romans 7:4 5—*Wherefore, my brethren, you also are become dead to the law by the body of Messiah; that you should be married to another, even to Him who is raised from the dead, that we should bring forth fruit unto God. For when we were in the flesh, the motions of sins, which were by the law, did work in our members to bring forth fruit unto death. But now we are delivered from the law, that being dead wherein we were held; that we should serve in newness of spirit, and not in the oldness of the letter.*

Romans 8:2–3—*For the law of the Spirit of life in Messiah Yeshua has made me free from the law of sin and death. For what the law could not do, in that it was weak through the flesh.*

Romans 6:14 is a very clear statement, given by Paul, that *you are not under the Law, but under grace.* Immediately before this, Paul gave four imperative commands to the Roman Gentile believers in Messiah:

> *Reckon you also yourselves to be dead indeed unto sin ...*
>
> *Let not sin therefore reign in your mortal body, ...*
>
> *Neither yield you your members as instruments of unrighteousness unto sin,*
>
> *But yield yourselves unto God.*

Then Paul refers to those that are alive from the dead as he contrasts death and life with Law and grace. The Mosaic law is incapable of producing life. In verse 14 Paul builds an argument that law does <u>not</u> make one holy, righteous, or just before God; instead, it reveals sin in the heart as well as in our lives and actions. He says we are not to let sin which is revealed by the law have dominion over us, for we are not under law, but under grace and the ministry of new life that He has given to us in Messiah; thus, we should be living in the Law of Messiah which gives life and power over sin through Messiah. Strickland puts it this way:

> Paul argues in Romans 6:14 that the authority of the law has been replaced by a different authority, grace. The two phrases "under law" (*hypo nomon*) and "under grace" (*hypo charin*) are set in contrast to each other. The phrase "under law" occurs several times in Pauline literature (1 Cor 9:20; Gal 3:23) and clearly refers to the Mosaic economy. In 1 Corinthians 9:20 (where the phrase occurs four times), it clearly designates the Mosaic law. Paul states in Galatians that Christ was born under the law (Gal 4:4); that is, he was born during the Mosaic or law dispensation, when the law was operative and authoritative. The same contrast between the present dispensation and the previous law period is presented in Galatians 5:18, where the work of the Holy Spirit, placing

believers into the body of Christ and guiding them, shows that the law period has been preempted.[173]

This must be taken at face value. We should not follow Messianic theology that tweaks or distorts this text to say that believers are still under the Law of Moses.

Paul often uses the term "law" in Romans, as he teaches that even though the law was holy, righteous, and good (7:12), we are sinful slaves to sin and our flesh is carnal and our sinful flesh is the enemy of God (Romans 5:10; Colossians 1:21). We are incapable of fulfilling the Mosaic law, for our sin has shackled us to that law and only Messiah could break those shackles of sin, by His finished work on the cross of Calvary. Paul notably uses the term "law" in his argument to show that the law establishes sin and that the only means of rescue is through the blood of the New Covenant which He shed on the cross of Calvary and by which He established the new Law of Messiah. Some people may argue with me concerning the law, but Paul is very clear, and the Word does not contradict itself:

20 *Therefore by the deeds of the law there shall no flesh be justified in His sight: for by the law is the knowledge of sin.*

28 *Therefore we conclude that a man is justified by faith without the deeds of the law.* (Romans 3:20, 28)

Jesus' Parable of the Wineskin

Yeshua makes an interesting statement that is pertinent to this investigation. In Matthew 9:16–17 (ESV) (and Mark 2:21–22; Luke 5:36–39), Yeshua states His case:

16 *No one puts a piece of unshrunk cloth on an old garment, for the patch tears away from the garment, and a worse tear is made.* 17 *Neither is new wine put into old wineskins. If it is, the skins burst and the wine is spilled and the skins are destroyed. But new wine is put into fresh wineskins, and so both are preserved.*

Chapter 12

You do not patch an old garment with new cloth. Likewise, you do not add the new wine of the Law of Messiah to the old wineskin that is the torn, *broken* Law of Moses, for if you do, you destroy both, in effect making the new (Law of Messiah) ineffective and of no value. The Messianic Movement is attempting to patch up the old, superseded Law of Moses with the new cloth of the Law of Messiah and thereby destroying both. You replace the old (Mosaic law) by putting the new wine in a new wineskin (Law of Messiah). The LORD said the same thing in Jeremiah 31:32 when He said that the old was *broken* and it would be replaced by the new. The author of Hebrews says the same thing (8:13). Paul and the author of Hebrews go to great lengths to show that the Law of Moses has been rendered inoperative by the making of a New Covenant. Nevertheless, many Jewish believers make extraordinary and futile efforts to patch up the old garment of Mosaic law with the new cloth of the Law of Messiah, thereby biblically making both useless.

Romans 7:1–7 — Principle of Death

We understand in life that physical death is the divider between the living and the dead. Messiah fulfilled the Law of Moses in His life and then in His death gave us *new life*. That which Jewish people were under in the Law of Moses died with Messiah in His death. However, Messiah did not stay dead; He rose from the grave to give us new life, something that the Law of Moses was incapable of doing. Liebi captures and expresses Paul's intent well, and then gives a startling statement from rabbinic literature:

> In Rom[ans] 7:17 the apostle Paul explains the principle that a Jewish person is under the Law so long as he lives. The bondage under the Law of Sinai is ended with death. Everyone who has converted, is identified with Christ through faith in Christ (Gal 1:20; Rom 6:5). This results in a powerful fact: the death and resurrection of Christ is seen legally as the

death and the resurrection of the believer in Christ. This has far-reaching consequences: In this way, it results in freedom from the bondage of the Sinai Covenant on the one hand, and the subjection to the "Law of Messiah" (Gal 6:2), on the other hand, which is at a higher level than the Law of Sinai. It has changed in the New Testament commandments of Jesus Christ. (The expression "Law of Messiah" is otherwise known from rabbinical literature. In the midrash qoheleth [in Barilan's Judaic Library] it reads [11.8/52a]: "The Torah which a person learns in this age is nothing compared to the Torah of Messiah."[174]

Did you see the last midrash statement on the superiority of the Law of Messiah? Messiah gave the Law from Sinai, fulfilled His own law, and then ended it by His own death on the cross. He who gave the Law of Moses died, freeing us from that impossible law so as to be related to Him and His New Torah or Law. He arose from the grave and gave us new life. In fact, Romans 6:2–4 clearly states that the umbilical cord of sin that the law revealed has been severed. Now both Jewish and Gentile believers are to *walk in the newness of life*. The midrash in this case is absolutely correct: Messiah initiated a new Torah called the Law of Messiah.

Romans 8:1 — No Condemnation

I want to investigate Romans 8:1 and the application of the word *condemnation* to believers in Messiah, *those who walk not after the flesh, but after the Spirit*. The word no in verse 1 is a translation of the Greek word *"ouketi,"* which is an emphatic negative adverb of time and carries the idea of complete cessation.[175] When you look at the word *condemnation*, you also see that Paul used an emphatic negative: *there is NO condemnation* to them who are in Christ Jesus. Many have made trenchant comments on the subject of condemnation.

"Condemnation" is the opposite of justification and justification implies the absence of condemnation. Since the justification which is the theme of this epistle is the complete and irreversible justification of the ungodly, it carries with it the annulment of all condemnation. ... "The law of the Spirit of life" is, therefore, the power of the Holy Spirit operative in us to make us free from the power of sin which is unto death.[176]

In Christ Jesus there remains not only no condemnation resting on the believer, but also no legal burden of any kind, no disability or handicap for living a life of righteousness.[177]

The reason believers are not under condemnation is because they have been freed from the tyranny of the law, for sin exercises dominion over those under the law.[178]

And why is there no condemnation? Because the law of the Spirit, that is, life in Christ Jesus, has set us free from the law of sin, which leads to death. ... The apostle was contrasting two different laws. The old law is the power of sin that inevitably results in death. The new law, which sets the believer free from the power of the old, is the law of the Spirit.[179]

[T]he Mosaic law was powerless to rescue human beings from the authority of sin and death. It was "weakened by the sinful nature"; that is, its demands could not be met because the people to whom the law was given were in the realm of "flesh" (*sarx*; NIV "sinful nature"). But God in Christ has intervened to do what the law could not.[180]

The answer to this great question and cry of distress with which the ... passage closes is given in a following verse (8:2): *For the law of the Spirit of life in Christ Jesus hath made me free from the law of sin and death.* This is more than a deliverance from the Law of Moses: it is the immediate deliverance from sin (the old) and death (its results; cf. Rom 6:23). The effect of this deliverance is indicated by the blessedness recorded in the eighth chapter, in contrast to the wretchedness recorded in the seventh chapter. It is all of the helpless and defeated "I," in the one case, and of the sufficient and victorious "I" by enablement of the Spirit, in the other. Christians, then, are to be delivered by the law or power of the Spirit. But attention must be called again to the fact, as stated in 7:25, that it is possible only "through Jesus Christ our Lord." Believers are delivered by the Spirit: but it is made righteously possible "through Jesus Christ our Lord" because of their union with Him in His crucifixion, death, and burial.[181]

"There is now no condemnation for those who are in Christ Jesus" takes us back to 5:12–21, where Paul showed how those who belong to Christ escape the "condemnation" (*katakrima*) that came to all people through Adam's sin.[182]

We, as true believers in Messiah, have *no condemnation* because... Yeshua as the vicarious voluntary sacrifice had all my sin laid on Him (Isaiah 53) on the cross. All that sin nature was on my account, Yeshua removed by His shedding of His blood on the cross, inaugurating the New Covenant and all the spiritual blessings we have because of His selfless love. The regeneration of the Holy Spirit, our new birth (John 3), our circumcision of the heart (Colossians 2:11, 13) and the full ministry of the Holy Spirit was because of Christ and not the Law of Moses. Nor was it the moral law that some try to tack onto the work of Messiah.

Believers are not under the moral law as a covenant of works, or as a means of sanctification. They are not under law but under grace. They are thus freed from the moral law by the law of the Spirit of life in Christ Jesus, that is by the gospel, of which the Spirit is the author—the gospel revealing a scheme of gratuitous justification.[183]

This law is neither the moral nor the Mosaic law; it is not the "law of the mind" (7:23), not the "law of faith" (3:27), but the operative force of the Holy Spirit, whose presence awakens spiritual life and sustains it. He that has the Son has life (1 John 5:12), because in the Son he finds the life-giving Spirit. By faith in Christ a man finds not only acquittal from sins, but also the power by which he no longer commits them; for this law of the Spirit sets him at liberty ("free") from the "law of sin and death," fully described in verse 23 ... as an enslaving force in his members.

We have been set free from sin and the law that condemns us.... The Spirit of Christ, the medium of that union with all its life-giving energies, enters and issues its laws from his heart, dispossessing the old usurper Sin, putting an end to its authority and to the fatal results which it brought with it. For where the old system failed, the new system has succeeded. The Law of Moses could not get rid of Sin.[185]

The means of our liberation Paul calls the law of the Spirit of life or the life-giving law of the Spirit. At first sight it seems strange that law should liberate us from law ....[186]

But the Law of the Spirit of Life does liberates us from the Mosaic law. It is amazing that the *old man* of my *old nature* has been put to death. It is even more amazing that we now have a *new man* which is created by the regeneration of our hearts by the Holy Spirit into new life in Messiah. That does not mean that now it is easy street. The old man though dead is still working in the flesh to produce the works of the flesh, but God in His grace has given me a *new nature* so that I can *walk in the Spirit* and not in the flesh. When I submit to Him I can bring glory and honor to Messiah. I have the Holy Spirit to guide me into all truth (John 16:13) and the power to live a Christ-like life. All truth does not mean in science, math or world history. It refers to all spiritual truth that the apostles and the Church needs for growth in godliness as 1 Corinthians 2:10–12 states....[187]

10 *But God has revealed them unto us by His Spirit: for the [Holy] Spirit searches all things, yes, the deep things of God.* 11 *For what man knows the things of a man save the spirit of man which is in him? Even so the things of God knows no man, but the Spirit of God.* 12 *Now we have received, not the spirit of the world, but the Spirit which is of God; that we might know the things that are freely given to us of God.*

The *all truth* that the Holy Spirit will guide us into is the same truth and Holy Spirit that will give us the power to live a Christ-like life. This can be very challenging, because we do battle with the old nature on a moment-by-moment basis, as Chafer notes:

It is further taught in the Scriptures that, since there are two natures in the believer, there is a conflict between the new nature, as operative through the Spirit, and the old nature, as operative through the flesh: "This I say then, Walk in the Spirit, and you shall not fulfil the lust of the flesh. For the flesh lusts against the Spirit, and the Spirit against the flesh: and these are contrary the one to the other: so that when walking by the Spirit you cannot do the things that you [otherwise] would" (Gal 5:16–17).[188]

Be warned: Our war with sin is not over! We can choose to be enslaved to sin, but we have the power given to us by the Holy Spirit to submit to Him, walking in the light and not in darkness. I do not have to be a slave to sin.

While believers are no longer slaves of sin in their position (5:16, 18; 6:18), only believers who do not live according to the flesh, but according to the Spirit will not experience slavery to sin.... The law of the Spirit of life refers to the power brought by the Holy Spirit that resides in believers.

> Paul has not mentioned the Spirit since Romans 5:5. In chapter 8 he mentions Him 21 times. This is appropriate since the Spirit brings life setting one free from the law of sin (resident in the Adamic nature; 7:18–23) which resulted in an experience of death.[189]

The frequent mentions of the Holy Spirit in Romans 8 should grab our attention. Paul completely understood what most Christians today either do not understand or have only a limited understanding of. The ministry of the Holy Spirit today was originally promised in the New Covenant to Israel, but now God has enlarged that promise to us Gentiles, thereby fulfilling another promise to the Gentiles through Abraham, Isaac, and Jacob that *in you shall ALL the families of the earth be blessed* (Genesis 26:3–4; 28:13–14). Today, this dispensation of grace transforms the life of every true believer in Messiah. Let us look at the Holy Spirit's current ministry to both Jewish people and Gentiles in the dispensation of grace:

Yeshua's Promises:

> *And I will pray the Father, and He shall give you another Comforter* [Holy Spirit], *that He may abide with you forever.* (John 14:16)

> *For He dwells with you and shall be in you.* (John 14:17)

> *The Spirit of truth is come, He will guide you into all truth: for He shall not speak of Himself; but whatsoever He shall hear, that shall He speak: and He will shew you things to come.* (John 16:13)

> *He shall glorify Me* [Yeshua]. (John 16:14)

> His Indwelling: *Know you not, that your body is the temple of the Holy Spirit which is in you, which you have of God, and you are not your own.* (1 Corinthians 6:19)

His Filling: *but be filled with the Holy Spirit.* (Ephesians 5:18b)

His Sealing: *... in whom also after that you believed, you were sealed with that Holy Spirit of promise, which is the guarantee of our inheritance until the redemption of the purchased possession ... .* (Ephesians 1:13 14)

His Baptism: *For by one Spirit are we all baptized into one body, whether we be Jews or Gentiles ... He has placed us into the body of Messiah.* (1 Corinthians 12:13)

He regenerates: *Not by works of righteousness which we have done, but according to His mercy He saved us, by the washing of regeneration, and renewing of the Holy Spirit.* (Titus 3:5; John 3:3, 5)

Gifts of the Holy Spirit: But all these [gifts] work that one and the same Spirit, dividing to every man severally as He will. (1 Corinthians 12:11)

Fruit of the Holy Spirit: But the fruit of the Spirit is love, joy, peace, longsuffering, gentleness, goodness, faith, meekness, self-control: against such there is no law. (Galatians 5:22 23)

Walk by the Spirit: Walk in the Spirit, and you shall not fulfill the lust of the flesh. (Galatians 5:16)

The Holy Spirit can be grieved by our sin: And grieve not the Holy Spirit of God whereby you are sealed unto the day of redemption. (Ephesians 4:30)

The Holy Spirit will guide us into all truth: 17 *Even the Spirit of Truth; whom the world cannot receive, because it sees Him not, neither knows Him: but you know Him; for He dwells with you and shall be in you. 26 But when the Comforter is come, whom I will send unto you from the Father, even*

> *the Spirit of truth, which proceeds from the Father, He shall testify of me. 6 We are of God: he that knows God hears us; he that is not of God hears us not. Hereby know we the Spirit of truth and the spirit of error.* (John 14:17; 15:26; 1 John 4:6)

Carnality and the Flesh Versus the Holy Spirit

In Romans 7, Paul identifies the flesh as carnality, the enemy of God. The flesh has completely polluted and defiled humanity, making our sin a stench in the nostrils of God. Why? Because the *old man* is incapable of righteousness because of the *law of sin*, the sin nature which is imputed to us through Adam's sin. Remember too what provides *condemnation* and *death*: the Law of Moses (2 Corinthians 3:7, 9) and our legalistic religious system that gives not life but death! "These 'many things' contain the truth of the holiness of the Law, which is pure and good, in contrast with man who is permeated with sin."[190]

Paul hammers this point home in Romans 7 as he lays the foundation for Romans 8. He speaks of our constant defeat at the hands of the flesh, and later he will speak to the reality of the Holy Spirit Who can give us victory and life over the flesh even in our earthly experience. Nevertheless, the flesh is a huge problem for believers until they learn that victory comes only through the ministering power of the Holy Spirit through Christ in our lives. Too many believers are caught in the web of the flesh and cannot break free.

> However, what has just been said cannot be true of a carnal Christian. A life given over to the sensual indulgences of the world is the extreme opposite of a godly life. A carnal Christian's life is filled with pit falls and inconsistencies. It lacks spiritual maturity and it does not make unbelievers desirous of becoming Christians. It does not ring true, since the observer cannot be sure what a carnal Christian actually believes, or whether his life is lived for God or for the flesh.

When a life is permeated with carnality it lacks all semblance of spiritual fervor, and is a stumbling-block to the sinner. It does not exemplify the Gospel or Christ; it does not bear fruit for Christ; it is not energized by the Holy Spirit; it is not interested in the Word of God. On the other hand, it is carnally motivated by the insatiable desires of the flesh and its gratification.[191]

Have you experienced this? I have, and I have repeated the words of Paul in Romans 7:24: *O wretched man that I am! Who shall deliver me from the body of this death?* The answer is to submit to the Holy Spirit, to walk in the light and not in darkness (1 John 1:5–7); it is to meditate on the Word (Joshua 1:8; Psalm 1; Romans 12:2). Do we really want victory, or are we content to live in sin, the flesh, and carnality?

Let me return very briefly to the first part of this book and the purpose of the law. That purpose was fulfilled in Messiah Yeshua. As Mills puts it:

> The contrast between the law of the "spirit of life" and the law of "sin and of death" is strikingly obvious. The old law brought with it the thunderous "Thou shalt nots" of Sinai. That law brought sin to the forefront, and vividly exhibited the evil nature in man.... In contrast to this, God provides a law that gives life (John 14:6).[192]

You can have victory, but do you want it? How badly do you want it? Would-be Olympians will spend years in practice to do the best humanly possible, because that is their focus in life. What is your focus in life? Does your position in Christ mean anything more to you than a fire escape out of hell? There is so much more to the Christian life than being saved from hell! He desires to reward you for the deeds done not in the flesh but in the Spirit. Your victory has already been supplied, promised by the Holy Spirit, because His focus is <u>you</u>. Is your focus on Christ and His life-giving power to be an *overcomer* in your regenerated life, to walk in Christ so that you can say, as Paul did who achieved this victory, *be imitators of me* (1 Corinthians 4:16; 11:1)?

Three Kinds of People

Our dual and ever-warring natures can lead to serious doctrinal mistakes. In a discussion with a man who espouses Holiness Pentecostal doctrine, he told me that his sect believes that when you become a believer you lose the old nature, meaning that as a believer you are operating only with and from the new nature. This Pentecostal doctrine is both erroneous and dangerous: the entirety of the New Testament shows that this doctrine is not of God. In examining specific points, I start with 1 Corinthians, which describes three types of people on the earth as they relate to God:

> 14 *But the <u>natural man</u> receives not the things of the Spirit of God: for they are foolishness unto him: neither can he know them, because they are spiritually discerned.* 15 *But he that is <u>spiritual</u> judges all things, yet he himself is judged of no man.* 16 *For who has known the mind of the Lord, that he may instruct him? But we have the mind of Messiah.* (3:)1 *And I, brethren, could not speak unto you as unto <u>spiritual</u>, but as unto <u>carnal</u>, even as unto babes in Messiah.* 2 *I have fed you with milk, and not with meat: for hitherto you were not able to bear it, neither yet now are you able.* 3 *For <u>you are yet carnal</u>: for whereas there is among you envying, and strife, and divisions, are you not carnal, and walk as men?* (1 Corinthians 2:14–3:3)

Verse 14 introduces the *natural man*. This is man in his lost, sinful condition, separated from and spiritually dead in his relationship to a holy God. Paul called the Ephesians, before they placed their faith in Yeshua, *dead in trespasses and sins* (2:1, 5).

Verse 15 introduces to the spiritual man, a person who has placed his faith and trust in Yeshua as his personal Savior from sin. He is also a person walking in the spirit of the Lord and in submission to the Holy Spirit, completely yielded to the guidance and direction of the Holy Spirit on a moment-by-moment basis [in] his life. He is not perfect in his walk, but if he sins he has *an advocate with the Father, Jesus Christ the righteous* (1 John 2:1). So *we confess our sins and He is faithful and just to forgive us our sins, and to cleanse us from all unrighteousness* (1 John 1:9).

The third kind of person is the *carnal man*. That person is one who has embraced Yeshua by faith as his personal Savior from sin, so he has been regenerated like the spiritual man and is no longer *dead in [his] trespasses and sins*. However, this man walks like a natural man and not like a spiritual man. This is the kind of person that the Calvinist and Holiness people have a problem with. The Calvinists say that such a person is not one of the "elect," meaning that the person was never really saved; the Holiness people claim that he lost his salvation. So the carnal person has a foot in each world (the world of the natural man and the world of the believer), but he mostly looks like and acts like the natural man. The Holiness individual with whom I spoke says there are only two kinds of people, the natural and the spiritual. If that is so, why does the New Testament epistles—written to believers—contain so much material on people who are called saints but are living and acting like the natural man? They are believers who are living in the flesh, in carnality; rather than walking in Christ on a moment-by-moment basis, they are actually living for self, the flesh.

Chapter 12

THE PARABLE OF THE SOWER

OR THE PARABLE OF THE FOUR TYPES OF SOIL

There are examples of such carnal people throughout the New Testament, starting with the Gospels using the words of Yeshua. In Matthew 13:1–23 (and Mark 4:1–20; Luke 8:1–15), Yeshua speaks of the sower who sowed four kinds of seeds. The first one fell on the ground and was eaten by the birds: this is the <u>natural man</u>, and there is no life in him. The next two seeds sprouted and produced life, but because the soil was not deep and because some fell among the thorns and weeds and were choked out, neither produced fruit: these are the <u>carnal man</u>. The fourth seed fell on good ground and it brought forth fruit, some 30-fold, some 60-fold, and some 100-fold: that is the <u>spiritual man</u>, regenerated by the Holy Spirit. Yeshua used this analogy as He spoke of the regeneration of believers, the types of people who are regenerated, and at what level each type would be living and serving Him.

In the Acts of the apostles, Ananias and Sapphira lied to the Holy Spirit, and God took their lives in judgment. If they had received the regeneration of God, then how is it that they sinned? It was because believers have two natures. The *old man*, the sinful nature, was not removed when we received our new nature, so believers live in constant daily combat with their old nature.

Some passages in 1 Corinthians 3:3–4 illustrate the carnal man. The carnal man produces *envying, strife,* and *divisions*. Were they believers? Yes! Look at 1:2: *Unto the church of God which is at Corinth, to them that are sanctified in Messiah Yeshua, called to be saints...* . These saints were involved in *envying, strife,* and *division*. They were involved in immorality in chapter 5, and were suing each other in court in chapter 6; they needed correction on marriage in chapter 7. In chapter 8 they were offending other believers, and in chapter 9 Paul even has to defend his apostleship before them. In chapter 10 he uses the example of Israel in the wilderness as a lesson to avoid provoking God by one's manner of living. In chapter 11 Paul has to straighten them out on their abuse of the Lord's Table: God had even taken some of them in death (1 Corinthians 11:30) because they had taken the cup *unworthily* and were *guilty of the body and blood of the Lord* (1 Corinthians 11:27). Lastly, in chapters 12–14 Paul has to correct them on their abuse of the spiritual gifts that they received as believers in Messiah. These are not spiritual believers but carnal believers, walking like the world around them and *not walking in the Spirit*. They have two natures, not just one.

Paul also has to deal with the Galatians again. These were believers who would have fallen from grace if they accepted circumcision from the Judaizers whom Paul curses: again, more carnal activity because of the Judaizers.

Now consider Ephesians: If everyone has only one nature and the old nature is gone, as Holiness Pentecostal doctrine would have it, then why does Paul need to tell the believers to *put off concerning the former manner of living, the old man* (Ephesian 4:22) even after they have been regenerated? It is because they still have the corrupting work of the old man in them. Paul tells them to put on the new man (Ephesians 4:24) *which is after God created in righteousness and true holiness.* Then Paul lists sins to be *put off* (Ephesians 4:25–32). Why is Paul telling them this if they have only the regenerated nature, and the old nature, that carnal man, is absent? It's clear from the Scriptures that as believers we have two natures, our new nature and our old nature, and that these natures are in constant battle for control in the life of a believer.

If we have only the new nature, the spiritual man, then why in Philippians does Paul tell them to *do all things without murmurings and disputings* (Philippians 2:14)? In Colossians, Paul warns them not to let any man cheat them *through philosophy and vain deceit after the tradition of, after the rudiments of the world, and not after Messiah.* Why warn them if believers have only the one nature given by God? It is because the old nature is still with us. Paul also tells these believers to *put thing[s] to death* [mortify] (Colossians 3:5). Why do so if you don't sin? If you don't sin because you only have God's nature after your rebirth, why does Paul also say to the Colossians *put off all these; anger, wrath, malice, blasphemy, filthy communication out of your mouth. Lie not one to another, seeing that you have put off the old man with his deeds* (Colossians 3:8). You are to put fleshly things off because you have put on the new man, but then he gives the list (Colossians 3:10–14) because the old nature is still with us.

Why does Paul tells believers not to *quench the Holy Spirit of God* (1 Thessalonians 5:19)? Is that something that our new nature would do? Hardly! Why did Paul tell them to *abstain from all appearances of evil*? If spiritual people do not retain their sin nature, as the Holiness Pentecostal doctrine would have it, why do they need to be warned and challenged not to live like the natural man? The fact is that the *old man*—the flesh, the sin nature—exists and often reigns in the lives of believers, or Paul would not have had to comment on or instruct them in these areas.

In the book of Hebrews, the author gives Jewish believers five warnings (Hebrews 2:1–4; 3:7–4:13; 5:11–6:12; 10:19–39; 12:14–29). Why would this be necessary if there is no sin nature in a believer?

In the book of James, chapters 1 and 2 both warn Jewish believers not to show favorites. If believers have not retained their sin nature (the old man, the fleshly nature), why would James say, in 4:7, 4:10, and 4:11, *submit yourselves therefore to God Resist the devil, ... humble yourselves in the sight of the Lord and speak no evil one of another.* In chapter 3, James warns and instructs believers about the destructiveness of the tongue even among believers; would this be necessary for those who have only a spiritual nature?

Why does Peter tell wives to submit to their husbands and not to dress like the woman of the world (1 Peter 3:1–4)? He admonishes them to *let none of you suffer as a murderer, or as a thief, or as an evil doer, or as a busybody in other men's matters* (1 Peter 4:15). These commands would not be needed for believers with only the new nature in the Spirit.

Look also at the epistle of John. If we don't still have a sinful nature, why would he say that we *walk in darkness* and admonish us not to *love this world*? John also says: *he that hates his brother is in darkness, and walks in darkness, and knows not whither he is going, because that darkness has blinded his eyes* (1 John 2:11). Another verse says *love not the world, neither the things that are in the world. If any man love the world, the love of the Father is not in him* (1 John 2:15). Only those who retained a sin nature would need such instruction.

Finally, look at Yeshua's words to the seven churches of Revelation. He put five of those churches on notice that He had corrections for them to heed and that believers in those churches should change their course, lest they be judged (Revelation 2–3).

This is only a small sampling of material in the epistles concerning the thinking, actions, and words of believers that would not have been needed or given unless believers do still have the old sin nature, the flesh which shows itself in carnal responses, actions, and thoughts. My Holiness Pentecostal friend is ignoring much Scripture that could correct (in fact, demolish) this erroneous doctrine!

As a final note, we must remember that the Law of Moses has no power to change or regenerate lives. It will even add to our fleshly actions, which have already been shown to produce *condemnation* and *death*.

Romans 8:2 — Law of the Spirit of Life in Christ Jesus

I have quoted numerous authors in presenting the fact that we will not receive any condemnation because of the ministry of the Holy Spirit in our lives as we today wrestle against our old nature and the law of sin and death. God did an amazing thing: He used flesh, the Flesh of the Lamb of God, to defeat the flesh. Douglas Moo expresses the concept of God.

> Paul indulges in a play on the word "flesh" that is obscured in the NIV. The law was weakened "by the flesh"; yet God also "condemned sin in the flesh." He won the victory over sin in the very realm where it seemed to rule unchallenged: in the "flesh." In claiming that Christ came "in the likeness of flesh" to offer himself as a sacrifice for our sins, Paul carefully balances Jesus' full humanity with his sinlessness. Christ did indeed become fully human by taking on "flesh." But calling that flesh "sinful" might suggest that Christ took on

fallen human nature. If so he would not have been qualified to be our sinless Redeemer. So Paul clarifies by adding the important word "likeness." In other words, Christ did not, like every other person since Adam, succumb to the tyranny of flesh. He did not himself sin, nor did he inherit the penalty of sin, namely, death. Paul uses the language of "interchange": Christ became what we are so that we could become what he is. By "condemning" sin in Christ as our sacrifice, he can now justly avoid "condemning" us who are in Christ.[193]

Moo's statement tries to capture for our human minds what God did in sending His Son. Because of that, there is a new reality in the life of every believer in Messiah. As Moo says, "Possessing the Spirit is the mark of being a new covenant believer."[194] Moo goes on to speak of the liberating power that is ours: "'The law of the Spirit,' then, denotes the authority or power exercised by the Holy Spirit. The Spirit exerts a liberating power through the work of Christ that takes us out of the realm of sin and the spiritual death to which sin inevitably leads."[195]

New Covenant believers are liberated by two works: the work of Messiah shedding His blood on the cross of Calvary and the work of the Holy Spirit in regenerating us and giving us all the blessing we have in Christ Jesus. But we have a second choice to make after salvation: Are we willing to be motivated and energized by the Holy Spirit that will give us victory and liberate us from the flesh? Sanford Mills points out that

> "[w]e must be motivated and energized by the Holy Spirit. Every step we take, every deed we do, every word we speak, must be an act of worship guided by the Holy Spirit in order that Christ may be glorified in us, His followers."[196]

The purpose of the ministry of the Holy Spirit is to give life. He does that in regeneration when we become born again of the Spirit, when we are reborn with a new spiritual nature. The New

Covenant believer is a miracle worked by God giving life to dead people, and it can be a miracle of victory over sin. It is a miracle that in this new life, that same New Covenant also presents to us the Law of Messiah. Mills describes what happens when the Holy Spirit enters into the life of a true believer in Messiah:

> The law of the "Spirit of life" operates in the life of the believer, and this law is life activated by the Spirit of God. ... The Holy Spirit is the life-giver. Whenever He enters a person it is for the purpose of giving life (Genesis 2:7); or for the purpose of creating eternal life (John 3:5–6); or for the purpose of calling one to receive the Word of God (Exodus 19:9); or for the ministry of the Gospel (Acts 13:2–4). In Romans 8:2 it is for the purpose of leading the believer to live a righteous life in Christ. ... When we accepted the Saviour we passed out of death into the glorious life-giving power of the Holy Spirit.[197]

We have passed from death to life by the ministry of the Holy Spirit. This transition is directly tied into the New Covenant of Jeremiah and Ezekiel which Yeshua inaugurated at Calvary.

Summary

In Galatians and 1 Corinthians we saw that the Law of Messiah has superseded the Law of Moses. The New (Covenant) came in because of the finished work of Messiah on the cross, and the old (covenant) went out because a greater-than-Moses was here. Messiah is the *Prophet like unto Moses* whom God told Israel would require of them His every word (Deuteronomy 18:18–19). It is because of Judaizers past and present, plus bad Christian theology, that the unbiblical notion of retention of the now-irrelevant Mosaic law of Moses has been inserted into the dispensation of grace. The Law of Messiah is now here.

What's more, believers are not taught the higher road, the higher plane of the Law of Messiah that dwarfs all other law systems. Believers are not taught the Law of the Spirit of Life, which holds the key to the victorious, empowering, overcoming life that He desires each of us to know. He desires not only to give regenerated life, but also to have us walk in the Law of Messiah in the everyday living of our new Christian lifestyle, with the power of the Holy Spirit in each of us to accomplish it. However, to do so we must learn to submit to Him and place ourselves as *living sacrifices* on God's altar and to *renew our minds* in His Holy Word.

Many in the Pentecostal and Charismatic movements have their hearts in the right place regarding the ministry of the Holy Spirit, but focus on the wrong issue. Spirituality is not endowed or proven by gifts of healings, working of miracles, or speaking in tongues. Paul is clear that it is the Holy Spirit Who decides who gets what gift (1 Corinthians 12). The gifts of the spirit are not for the individual alone: They are intended to edify, building up the whole of the body of Messiah and not dividing it between the gifted and the others. A spiritual nature is not an emotional experience that you must have. Rather, it is a new nature created by a personal spiritual relationship, a walk with Messiah, that we have been privileged to have because of the Holy Spirit's action; it has nothing to do with our begging, pleading, or choosing. Some Christians put experience and emotions first, but God has given us minds and He expects us to meditate on the Word so that it can transform our minds to do His will. Some have turned the will of God on its head by emphasizing experience or emotion as the authority.

Jesus said, in John 16:13–14, that the Holy Spirit *will not speak of Himself, for He shall glorify Me*. The Holy Spirit is a predominant participant in our spiritual walk, but it is a relationship rather than an experience. The Holy Spirit will exalt the Son always.

He is the lifegiver, He is to be submitted to. We are to walk in the Spirit, for He always yields to the Son and does the will of the Son, Who always yields to the will of the Father. The members of the Godhead that we call the Trinity—the Tri-unity of God—are equal in every way, yet in how they relate to mankind they yield to each other in complete submission.

There are no easy ways to really understand this. There are no shortcuts, so study Romans 6–8 and 1 John with much prayer and spiritual discernment. If knowledge is worth having, it will be worth the time you must take to discover it. Make it your priority. The books of Romans and 1 John are indispensable in learning what has been elusive to many believers: victory over the flesh and sin nature. But it should not be elusive or misunderstood. That is why it is so extremely important—foundational, even—to study and to understand: (1) to study the Scriptures from a Jewish perspective, (2) to interpret the Scriptures using a literal method, and (3) to study the Word with a clear picture of the covenants[198] and dispensations[199] that God has put in place. Four books in particular can help you see and grasp the spiritual realities that are ours, if we would only learn how to biblically walk in the Spirit so that we can prepare ourselves for the glorious eternal future that Messiah has prepared for us, His bride.

> *The Believer's Payday* by Paul N. Benware (Chattanooga, TN: AMG Publishers)
>
> *Salvation in Three Time Zones* by Dennis Rokser (Duluth, MN: Gospel Grace Press)
>
> *The Road to Reward* by Robert N. Wilkin (Denton, TX: Grace Evangelical Society)
>
> *Six Secrets of the Christian Life: The Miracle of Walking with God* by Zane Hodges (Denton, TX: Grace Evangelical Society)

You may be thinking, "Why don't you just tell us how?!" This walk with Christ is too personal, too individual, and too important for anyone to try to give you a condensed, simplistic, "10 Easy Steps" method for achieving it. You need to be in the Word, study the Word, and study the writing of people who are or were also in the Word.

Godly Paradigm	
Godly	**Carnal**
Mind	Emotions
Will	Will
Emotions	Mind

13

PARTICIPANTS IN THE LAW OF MESSIAH

The foundation of the Law of Messiah is the New Covenant. This is an unconditional covenant with two participants. The primary participant, revealed in Jeremiah 31:31, is the LORD, who makes this unconditional covenant with the second participant, Israel, also clearly identified in Jeremiah. You see the same two participants in Ezekiel 36, where more of the nature and purpose of the New Covenant is revealed. A third participant, unseen in the Hebrew Scriptures, is revealed in the New Testament. In the New Testament the spiritual benefits of this covenant are extended to the Gentiles, who are the third participant unseen and unidentified in the Hebrew Scriptures; Paul defines this as the mystery revealed in Ephesians (3:4–9) and Colossians (1:26). Back in Jeremiah, this unconditional covenant is clearly made between God and the *house of Judah* and *the house of Israel*, making the covenant exclusively Jewish, to the nation of Israel only.

A quick and simple Greek language lesson will be helpful here. In the Greek used in the New Testament, there are several tenses that give the reader information about the action taking place. There is a <u>present active indicative</u> tense, meaning the subject is acting. There is also a <u>present passive indicative</u>, which means that the subject is being acted upon[200] (for instance, the subject, God, is doing the action to/upon man). There is an <u>imperative</u> tense which indicates the giving of a command. For example, the imperative appears in cohortative or positive commands and in prohibitive or negative commands.[201]

Now let's put that into the context of our study. The New Covenant was God acting upon man (indicative) in giving us salvation (regeneration, justification, sanctification, reconciliation, imputation, redemption, and so on), as well as giving us the indwelling presence of the Holy Spirit Who regenerated us and removed our sin. God acted, not man. Man had no part in the salvation given except to believe by faith in the finished work of Messiah on the cross of Calvary. There are 33 positional truth[202] statements of the <u>action of God</u> in our salvation, which are borne out in Scripture in all that He did in saving us from our sins and placing us into His own family. These statements are then followed up by His commands, the imperatives, on how we are to walk this *new life in Christ*. This is the Law of Messiah, with well over 600 commands given to us by Yeshua and His apostles (indicative) that we, as the subject, are now to obey (imperatives) and live by daily. Please keep this in mind as you read on. Yeshua saved us (indicative) and then laid out commands (imperatives) on how we are to live and walk in Him. With this in mind, let's return to the participants in the Law of Messiah.[203]

Here we examine two of Paul's epistles, to the Romans and to the Ephesians. White states the following about Ephesians: "In Ephesians 1–3 Paul gives to the believers in the church the things that God has done for them [indicative], but then in chapters 4–6 Paul gives many commands [imperatives] on how the believer and the church is to live and walk before God and our fellow man."[204]

In the book of Romans, Paul also speaks about all that God has done for them (indicative) in chapters 1–8; then, in chapters 12–16, Paul again gives many commands (imperatives) on how the believer and the body of Messiah are to live and walk before God and our fellow man. White writes:

"Colossians 3:9 says that we have put on the new self [indicative] while Ephesians 4:22 commands us [imperative] to put on the new self [new man]. Galatians 3:27 says we who have been baptized into Christ have put on Christ [indicative], while Romans 13:14 commands us to put on the Lord Jesus Christ [imperative]."[205]

These things that God has done for us (indicative) are the 33 positional truths that He has bestowed upon us, and they are wonderful truths. But if we walk in such a manner as to tarnish or disregard those positional truths, we are walking in self, in darkness, in carnality, with a very ungrateful spirit toward our God Who has bestowed so much upon us. The commands (imperatives) that He has given us to obey we also are accountable for when we stand before Messiah at the reward seat (Bema Seat). Our unfaithful works, our disobedience to His commands (imperatives), will be destroyed by fire and we will have little or nothing in rewards to show for our earthly obedience or the lack thereof. That will affect our position in the eternal order as to our service to Him throughout that eternal order. Our position and standing were a mystery in the Hebrew Scriptures but now are revealed.

There is an aspect of this covenant that relates to the Gentiles. It is not expanded by the LORD in the Hebrew Scriptures, but is expanded by the Lord in the New Testament through the Apostle Paul. In Ephesians 3:9, Paul states *that it was a mystery, which from the beginning of the world has been hid in God, who created all things by Yeshua Messiah*. In Colossians 1:26–27, Paul unfolds the meaning of the mystery that was revealed:

> 26 *Even the mystery which has been hid from ages and generations, but now is made manifest to His saints:* 27 *To whom God would make known what is the riches of the glory of this mystery among the Gentiles; which is Messiah in you, the hope of glory.*

Remember, the New Covenant was given to the Jewish people in the Hebrew Scriptures: here Paul says that the Gentiles will

Chapter 13

be included in the New Covenant even though that fact was completely hidden by God from the Jewish people in the Hebrew Scriptures. Yet even in the Hebrew Scriptures God hints at the redemptive aspect of His will to the Gentiles, though He leaves it obscured and unexplained in the Hebrew Scriptures. Let me illustrate what I mean. Genesis 3:15 speaks of the promise again given by God concerning the redemption of the world, all the human race through the seed of the woman, but God does not explain how that redemption will be accomplished. It is not until Isaiah 7:14, with the revelation of the virgin birth, that Genesis 3:15 was explained — 3,000 years after the first announcement. In Genesis 12:3, God says to Abraham that in him *shall all families of the earth be blessed*, but once again waits until the days of Paul to explain how that would become a reality. Genesis 22:18 alludes to this when Yahweh says *in your seed all the nations of the earth shall be blessed*. Paul picks that up in Galatians 3:16 as referring to the Messiah. God repeats these same words to Isaac (Genesis 26:4) and to Jacob (Genesis 28:13–14), but again gives no further explanation. God sprinkles hints throughout the Hebrew Scriptures that the Gentiles will believe in Him, but He does not explain how that will happen, because (as Paul said) it is a mystery. Some passages from the Hebrew Scriptures are helpful illustrations:

> *His name shall endure forever: His name shall be continued as long as the sun: and men shall be blessed in Him: <u>all nations shall call Him blessed</u>.* (Psalms 72:17)

> <u>*All nations*</u> *whom you have made <u>shall come and worship before You, O Lord; and shall glorify Your name</u>.*
> (Psalms 86:9)

> *He shall not fail nor be discouraged, till He have set judgment in the earth: <u>and the isles shall wait for His law</u>.* (Isaiah 42:4)

> *I the LORD have called You in righteousness, and will hold Your hand, and will keep You, and give You for a covenant of the people, <u>for a light of the Gentiles</u>.* (Isaiah 42:6)

And He said, it is a light thing that You should be My servant to raise up the tribes of Jacob, and to restore the preserved of Israel: <u>I will also give You for a light to the Gentiles</u>, that You may be <u>My salvation unto the end of the earth</u>. (Isaiah 49:6)

Arise, shine: for Your light is come, and the glory of the LORD is risen upon You. For, behold, the darkness shall cover the earth, and gross darkness the people but the LORD shall arise upon You, and His glory shall be seen upon You. <u>And the Gentiles shall come to Your light</u>, and kings to the brightness of Your rising. (Isaiah 60:1–3)

And you shall swear, The LORD lives, in truth, in judgment, and in righteousness; and <u>the nations shall bless themselves in Him</u>, and <u>in Him shall they glory</u>. (Jeremiah 4:2)

O LORD, my strength, and my fortress, and my refuge in the day of affliction, the <u>Gentiles shall come unto You from the ends of the earth</u>, and shall say, Surely our fathers have inherited lies, vanity, and things wherein there is no profit. Shall a man make gods unto himself, and they are no gods? Therefore, behold I will this once cause them to know, I will cause <u>them to know Mine hand</u> and My might; and <u>they shall know that My name is the LORD</u>. (Jeremiah 16:19–21)

And <u>many nations shall be joined to the LORD in that day</u>, and <u>shall be My people</u>: and I will dwell in the midst of you, and you shall know that the LORD of hosts has sent me unto you. (Zechariah 2:11)

For from the rising of the sun even unto the going down of the same <u>My name shall be great among the Gentiles</u>: and in <u>every place</u> incense shall be offered unto My name, and a pure offering: for <u>My name shall be great among the heathen</u>, says the LORD of hosts. (Malachi 1:11)

These are some of the verses scattered throughout the Hebrew Scriptures that point to the fact that God was always interested in the salvation of the Gentiles. The Hebrew Scriptures are not just about Jewish people and their history: it is also the hope of the Gentiles that in some way God will include them, too. From Genesis 12 on, God wanted to use the covenant people of Israel to reveal Himself to the Gentiles. Israel generally failed at being the instrument of God to reveal Himself to the Gentiles, but the righteous remnant of Israel did not fail. Today you and I have the Word of God composed by God through more than 40 subauthors to reveal Himself to us Gentiles. The remnant also gave us the Messiah, the focus of all Scripture, to redeem Jewish people and Gentiles alike. To the surprise of Jewish believers, it was through Paul that the mystery of how God would accomplish that redemption was finally revealed. Under the New Covenant, the covenant of grace, God would save Gentiles without them becoming part of Israel or becoming Jewish, as is demonstrated by the salvation of the Samaritans (Acts 8) and then the Gentiles (Acts 10), and was finally confirmed at the Jerusalem Council (Acts 15). Paul opens up the mystery hidden in the heart of God. Paul, after stating in Romans 3 that God will save Jewish people and Gentiles alike, adds that He will justify them by His grace, redeem them, and satisfy His holy demands, all by His grace to us[206]: 29 *Is He the God of the Jews only? Is He not also of the Gentiles? Yes, of the Gentiles also.* 30 *Seeing it is one God, which shall justify the circumcision* [Jews] *by faith, and uncircumcision* [Gentiles] *through faith.* (Romans 3:29–30).

Coupling this with the two passages regarding the hidden mystery reveals that we as Gentiles were also included in the great plan of salvation to redeem us, justify us, reconcile us, and sanctify us through the blood of Messiah, the blood of the New Covenant. The salvation that initially appeared to have been promised only to the Jewish people is opened up to all of humanity, even as the first promise was given in Genesis 3:15 to all humanity.

Paul's doxology in Romans 11:33 shows that his own heart is overwhelmed: *O the depth of the riches both of the wisdom and knowledge of God! How unsearchable are His judgments, and His ways past finding out!*

14

What is the Law of Messiah?

My Prayer

I pray You, Lord God my Father, the awesome, magnificent Creator of the heavens and the earth; our only provider of salvation and future glorification of this mortal body when You will complete Your act of conforming me to the image of Your Son: Lead, guide, and instruct me, and enlighten the readers of this book, through Your Holy Spirit, as I move into uncharted waters in understanding the Law of Messiah.

As I study your Word, I am amazed at Your love for me and the world to provide so great a salvation. You have made me and all other believers a spiritual beneficiary of all Your spiritual blessings in heavenly places that we do not deserve. They are a total result of Your Son's finished work on the cross inaugurating the New Covenant, by His blood, the blood of the New Covenant. Lord, these last couple of years I have completely enjoyed sitting at Your feet learning truths that in years past I did not grasp the significance of, and am only now beginning to grasp the unfathomable riches of Your grace toward me. At the same time I know that I am not even approaching the depths of Your grace with my understanding.

Lord, my prayer asks that you help me to truly and convincingly communicate these marvelous truths to Your people. I am dust, I am merely one of Your servants, a man who is trying to communicate some of the riches of Your grace to my spiritual brothers and sisters in Christ, so I need Your Holy Spirit to take my inadequate words and thoughts and teach Your magnificent truths to Your people through Your Spirit using Your Holy Word that You have placed in our hands and hearts.

Lord, as I teach this subject, this Law of Christ, which is new to most believers, help them to focus on the laws You have placed in Your Word by Your apostles. May they not forget that our power to live this new life in Messiah comes from the teaching, leading, and instruction of the Holy Spirit, and our submission to Him; it is not within our human power. Help Your people to saturate their minds with Your Word so that we automatically respond to You by our heart's motivation and commitment rather than just outward actions.

Lord, we humans, even believers, all have a tendency to corrupt what You say. Preserve us so that we do not try to live the Law of Messiah by ourselves, by trying to live it in the flesh, in our carnality, and in the process take Your Law and walk in darkness and subvert Your Law, as Israel did with the Law of Moses. Lord, forbid that your people would use this as a measure or indication of spirituality. May they only judge themselves by Your standards. Lord, I fear perversion of this teaching that is new, but should not be new, for it has been with us since the days of the apostles and the Lord of glory Himself. It is not new, but it has never been clearly taught and explained.

Lord, may You take these words and glorify Yourself through the changed lives of believers, moved from living this life in the flesh and carnality to learning to walk in the Spirit.

Lord, You know my heart is to see the body of Messiah grow in the grace and knowledge of Jesus Christ. My prayer to You, O Lord, is that You would chasten anyone who would pervert this truth, as You promised to do to Your erring children.

I ask this in the matchless Name of our Lord and Savior, Yeshua ha Mashiach.

I move into this and the following chapters with trepidation. I do not want this material to be co-opted, ritualized and legalized by religionists and the traditions and biases of men. My concern is modern-day Judaizers who would legalize and ritualize the Word of God into a standard of external law observance, when in truth obedience must come from hearts motivated by love for our Savior Who has given us so much, and our submission to the teaching, leading, and guiding of the Holy Spirit Who regenerated us into the new life in Christ.

What is the Law of Messiah? We have learned what it is not. The first part of this book showed that the Law of Messiah is not a restatement of the Law of Moses or a renewal of the old law, for Messiah has fulfilled that law and rendered it inoperative by instituting His superior Law of Messiah. It is not the moral "part" of the Law of Moses; for those commandments are part of a unity; when you violate one law you violate all the law. We also saw that the Mosaic law is a ministration of *condemnation* and *death* because in our flesh we cannot keep it; thus it substantiates our sinfulness and complete inability to obey the law.

We have learned that the foundation of the Law of Messiah is love. Yeshua gave us an explicit command to love one another even as He and the Father loved us. We saw, too, that love is not the entirety of the Law of Messiah, nor is the Sermon on the Mount or other teachings of Yeshua. His teaching on love forms the foundation of His Law, but Yeshua, through the writings and teaching of the apostles, has given us hundreds of new laws which are different in nature and character from the old Mosaic law. Believers have been empowered to live out these new laws through the power of the Holy Spirit, Who resides in them because of the inauguration of the New Covenant by the blood of the Covenant through the Lamb of God, Yeshua.

Chapter 14

In 1 John 2:6 the apostle John sets a standard that applies to every true believer in Messiah: We are under a moral and legal obligation to be walking like Yeshua. John states:

> *He who is constantly saying that he as a habit of life is living in close fellowship with and dependence upon Him is <u>morally obligated just</u> as that One [Yeshua] conducted Himself, also himself in the manner spoken of to be conducting himself.* 1 John 2:6 (Expanded Wuest New Testament).[207]

Wuest focuses on the Greek tenses of these words to point out that we, as believers, are <u>morally obligated</u> to walk in this present life even as Yeshua Himself walked. That is not possible for humans except by the indwelling presence of the Holy Spirit, Who can empower us to live it and to walk it, not in our power but in His power. Notice how high John sets the bar. Such conduct can only be obtained or accomplished by the ministry of the Holy Spirit in the life of believers, because of the New Covenant for those who surrender to the Holy Spirit. We are under a legal obligation to Yeshua the Messiah, not to Moses; that obligation is not expressed by the externalities of the Mosaic law, but in the inward heart of every believer, which is again evidence of the outworking of the New Covenant in the hearts and lives of Jewish and Gentile believers in Messiah Yeshua. As Verbrugge put it,

> What is this "law of Christ"? Since *nomos* (law) has a wide variety of meanings and Paul is known to play with the meaning of this word, presumably he is referring to the life principle that manifested itself in Christ's own life and that shaped Paul's life, namely, the principle of self-sacrifice and of love as the summary of the law.[208]

Verbrugge is correct: *Nomos* refers to and is connected to the life principle seen in Christ's life, which was the same principle that shaped Paul's life, namely, self-sacrifice and love (to summarize the Law of Messiah). But his comments reveal an incomplete understanding of the Law of Christ, and he does not tell us what the Law of Messiah is. His statement concerning the foundation of the Law of Messiah is valid, but it does not explain what was built upon the foundation by the apostles of Messiah.

Love is the fulfilling of the Law of Messiah. This love is speaking of human relationships, but there is more to the Law of Messiah than love. What is lacking is the meat on the bones. Now we are getting closer, but love, the foundation, is still inadequate to express the entirety of the Law of Messiah.

This Law of Messiah includes our actions and our behavior, which come from our hearts that have been regenerated by the Holy Spirit through the New Covenant. In addition, this Law of Messiah includes instruction, correction, and warnings. The Law of Messiah has been divinely revealed by Messiah Himself through the teachings of His apostles. Certainly, the Law of Messiah encompasses love, but it consists of more than love: it includes the teachings that the apostles gave to individuals and to the churches. In the epistles of Paul, James, Peter, John, and the writer of Hebrews, there are well over 600 imperative commands, given by Yeshua Who is the Word of God (John 1:1–14; Revelation 19:13) through His apostles. These commands are just as authoritative as the laws given by God through Moses in the Old Testament. But Yeshua fulfilled the Mosaic law and rendered that law inoperative by His death, burial, and resurrection, and initiated the Law of Messiah instead.

The Law of Messiah is also a system of law given by Yeshua to His apostles as the standard that we as believers are to walk in. It governs our relationship to God and to humankind in general, as well as our relationship with our brothers and sisters in Messiah Yeshua. His new law comes in the form of imperative commands to teach, instruct, guide, correct, encourage, strengthen, and warn us about sin and false teachers. It also includes the ministry of

Chapter 14

the Holy Spirit that is to guide us into all truth. As we yield to Him and surrender to Him, He will give us the power to walk the Christian life in the Spirit, walking in the light and not in the flesh, in carnality and darkness.

In chapters 15 to 19, I unpack the Law of Messiah to help us grasp what I believe the Church and believers in general are oblivious to, although there are a few who have heard it before, at least to some degree. When I wrote my first book, *Discovering the Mystery of the Unity of God*, I discovered the centrality of the Messiah in the Hebrew Scriptures, and this opened my eyes to see and understand the nature and work of the second Person of the Godhead throughout the Hebrew Scriptures and the New Testament. Then I wrote a second book, on the New Covenant, *Israel's Only Hope: The New Covenant*. What I discovered in that study took my breath away: I sat in amazement at a Jewish covenant in which God has allowed me, a Gentile, to be a partaker with Jewish brothers and sisters in Messiah. I came to see and begin to understand and to grasp what the blood of the New Covenant, which Yeshua referenced at His last Passover with His disciples, actually did. For the first time in my life, I began to see how God has so richly blessed me in heavenly places with my salvation and all that goes along with salvation. Now I am standing at another threshold, just beginning to grasp the vast difference between the old, superseded Mosaic law and the Law of Messiah, which God has given to me to walk a Spirit-filled life so that I can give glory to my Sovereign God.

I invite you to join me on this spiritual journey to understand the breath and height of the love that God has bestowed upon us.

15

The Purpose of the Law of Messiah

Because the holiness of God has been revealed through the Law of Moses and fulfilled by Messiah, there is now a new standard of righteousness that God has given through the ministry of the Holy Spirit to empower the believer to walk in Messiah in holiness. That standard is the Law of Messiah. The believer can walk in Messiah by being submissive to the Holy Spirit, walking in the Spirit and in the light and not in carnality, the flesh, or darkness. Here I list some of the things that the Law of Messiah does in the heart and life of a true believer:

- The Law of Messiah can fully empower believers through the Holy Spirit: to instruct, correct, and guide us into all truth. It has no limitations.

- As a byproduct of the regeneration of the Holy Spirit through the New Covenant and the blood of Messiah, the Law of Messiah gives life which the Mosaic law could not provide (John 3:2–3; Titus 3:5; 1 Corinthians 3:7, 9).

- The Law of Messiah, through the ministry of the Holy Spirit, gives believers the power to have victory over sin (Romans 8:1–17). Mosaic law could not produce victory (2 Corinthians 3:7–9).

- The Law of Messiah gives new direction on being obedient to government authorities (Romans 13:1–7).

- The Law of Messiah gives the New Testament believer instruction—a new rule of conduct—on how to live and walk in the Spirit and in Messiah. Under this Law, both Jew and Gentile walk together as one new man in Messiah (Galatians 2:15; Ephesians 2:14–15, 4:4–6; 1 Corinthians 12:13).

- The Law of Messiah provides regeneration through the Holy Spirit because of the finished work of Messiah on the cross (John 3:3–5; Titus 3:5). The Holy Spirit uses the Word of God as the instrument for imparting life and regenerating us (1 Peter 1:23).

- The Law of Messiah provides instruction to fathers, wives, children, employees, and employers on how to live righteously in a godless world (Ephesians 5:21–6:9; Colossians 3:18–4:1).

- The Law of Messiah provides the fruit of the Spirit (Galatians 5:22–23).

- The Law of Messiah gives instruction to the leadership of the Church (1 Timothy 3; Titus 1:5–9).

- The Law of Messiah gives instruction to the local church (Ephesians 4:17–6:17).

- Under the Law of Messiah, we now confess our sins to restore fellowship with God (1 John 1:9), rather than offering sacrifices (Romans 6:10; Hebrews 10:10–12; 1 Peter 3:18).

- The Law of Messiah teaches cheerful giving to the Lord (2 Corinthians 9:7) and His work; there is no prescribed amount or tithe.

- The Law of Messiah tells us only to meet regularly for Bible study and worship; there are no prescribed days (Hebrews 10:25), in contrast to the three periods of corporate worship set out in the Law of Moses (Exodus 23:14–17).

- The Law of Messiah teaches believers to live distinct from the world (1 John 2:15), not by adopting specific modes of dress, outward appearance, or actions (as under the old law), but by living from the inner motivations of a Spirit-filled heart, separate from the evil world system (Romans 8:12–13; Colossians 3:5 9; 1 John 2:15–17).

- We obey the Law of Messiah <u>because</u> we have already been blessed (Ephesians 1:3 14).

- Under the Law of Messiah, we are given the indwelling (John 14:16 17; 1 Corinthians 3:16), the filling (Ephesians 5:18), the sealing (Ephesians 1:13–14), and the baptism of the Holy Spirit (1 Corinthians 12:13) to help us in our walk.

- The Law of Messiah gives spiritual empowerment and gifts to function in our lives for Him (Romans 12:3–16; 1 Corinthians 12:1–31; Ephesians 4:7 12).

- The Law of Messiah is the law of our King and High Priest (Hebrews 3:1).

- The Law of Messiah establishes better promises than the old Law of Moses (Hebrews 8:6).

- It establishes holiness in the lives of believers.

- The Law of Messiah places righteousness to the believer's account (Romans 4–5).

- Because of the New Covenant, the Law of Messiah gives us, as His bride, the power to live out a new lifestyle that was impossible before.

- The Law of Messiah gives believers a new motivation to live for Him.

In addition to these actions, effects, and purposes of the Law of Messiah, we also need to understand two key things about our relationship to the Law of Messiah, which are set out in the epistles to the churches. We must recognize these things as we study the Law of Messiah, our response to Him, and our submission to the Holy Spirit. <u>First</u> is the Law of Messiah itself, which includes more than 600 imperatives by the apostles as to how we are to live and walk before our God and fellow-believers. An "imperative" is a command to be obeyed: this is very simple. Second is the many admonitions also given by the apostles. An "admonition" is a gentle or friendly reproof, counsel or warning against a fault or oversight.[209] Put another way, the apostles gave primary commands (instructions) to the churches and secondarily issued admonitions based on those commands. We should obey both the imperative commands and the admonitions; we accomplish this by renewing our minds in and with the Word of God and submitting to the Holy Spirit to lead, guide, and direct us into all truth (which is part of His ministry to us).

Thus, as we submit to the Holy Spirit and His ministry in our lives, He give us victory over sin, the flesh, and the devil. When we submit to Him, He enables us to submit to the Law of Messiah (both imperative commands and admonitions) so that we can know what the abundant life really is on a daily basis.

Now that we see the purposes and actions of the Law of Messiah, we need to study the provisions of the New Covenant that can change spiritual defeat to spiritual life and victory.

16

PROVISIONS OF THE LAW OF MESSIAH

The provisions of the Law of Messiah are directly connected to the New Covenant. Without the New Covenant, there would be no Law of Messiah. The key New Covenant passages spoken of are Jeremiah 31 and Ezekiel 36, which is the covenant that allows all the other covenants to be fulfilled, because it provides what no other covenant (including the Mosaic Covenant) could provide. Let's review each covenant's purpose and distinct area:

Abrahamic Covenant—Guarantees Israel's national existence (but not salvation); they are indestructible as a people and as a nation.

Land Covenant—Guarantees the land given to Abraham, Isaac, Jacob and their descendants; is not transferable to any other people or group.

Mosaic Covenant—Gives the Israelites a standard to be lived by until the ultimate perfect sacrifice is given by Messiah; it does not provide salvation.

Davidic Covenant—Guarantees to David that one of his sons (1 Chronicles 17:11) will reign on his throne forever in physical Jerusalem.

New Covenant—The last covenant, given specifically to Israel, is the New Covenant, which was inaugurated by the blood of the Lamb of God on the cross of Calvary in His death, burial, and then resurrection victorious over death. So, what does the New Covenant provide to Jewish and Gentile believers in Messiah? What does the New Covenant bring to our progressive understanding of God's Word? Remember, the Law of Messiah would have no purpose, or even have come into existence, without the New Covenant. Thus, the New Covenant and the Law of Messiah are inseparably linked.

None of the other covenants says anything about the regeneration of the human heart. How does God give man a new heart, a circumcised heart without sin (Deuteronomy 30:6; Colossians 2:11–13)? In Genesis, God clearly points out that the human heart is depraved (Genesis 6:5, 8:21; Jeremiah 17:9) and can merit nothing before a holy God. These issues are answered in the New Covenant and what it provides put in motion a new law, the Law of Messiah. Let's first examine Jeremiah and Ezekiel:

> 31 *Behold, the days come, says the LORD, that I will make a New Covenant with the house of Israel, and with the house of Judah:* 32 *Not according to the covenant that I made with their fathers in the day that I took them by the hand to bring them out of the land of Egypt; which My covenant they broke, although I was an husband unto them says the LORD.* 33 *But this shall be the covenant that I will make with the house of Israel; after those days, says the LORD,* <u>*I will put My law in their inward parts, and write it in their hearts;*</u> *and will be their God, and they shall be My people.* 34 *And they shall teach no more every man his neighbour, and every man his brother, saying know the LORD: for they shall all know Me, for the least of them unto the greatest of them, says the LORD:* <u>*for I will forgive their iniquity, and I will remember their sin no more.*</u> (Jeremiah 31:31–34)

> 26 <u>*A new heart also will I give you,*</u> *and* <u>*a new Spirit will I put within you*</u> *and I will take away the stony heart out of your flesh, and I will give you an heart of flesh.* 27 <u>*And I will put My Spirit within you,*</u> *and cause you to walk in My statutes, and you shall keep My judgments, and do them.* (Ezekiel 36:26–27)

Before we investigate the provisions of the New Covenant (underlined in the quotations), we should review the background.

In verse 31, the words the *days come* are a prophetic future statement about something that was not happening or going to happen in Jeremiah's day. God speaks of a *new covenant*, not an old or renewed one as many try to read it. Lastly, this verse says the covenant will be given to the *house of Israel* and the *house of Judah*; thus, it is a Jewish covenant, not given to the Church.

Verse 32 contrasts the New Covenant with the old system given at Sinai, which had been repeatedly violated and *broken* even though God as their *husband* had nourished them, guided them, and provided for them in every possible way.

In verse 33, the LORD again repeats who the New Covenant is for and with: the *house of Israel*. God says that He will write His law on their *inward parts* and *their hearts*, hearts of flesh in contrast to the old writing on stone (Exodus 31:18; 2 Corinthians 3:7). The net result will be that finally Israel will live and walk after their God; for He will be *their God* and they will finally live out, in a practical manner, the fact that He is their God.

Verse 34 tells us that this covenant will affect every Jewish person living when the New Covenant is implemented when the *days come*, for they will all know Him. God will *forgive their iniquity and will remember their sin no more*. Israel will be a saved nation. All of Israel's sin and iniquity will no longer be remembered by God, illustrated in Zechariah 3.

Then, in Ezekiel, God gives some additional information about what He will do to and with Israel. Ezekiel 36:26–27 is related to Jeremiah as an expansion and reiteration of the New Covenant promises. In these verses God states that He will do something supernatural in the hearts and lives of every Jewish person living at that time. Paul says in Romans 11:26 that *all Israel shall be saved*, and the prophet Zechariah says in 3:9 that all this will happen in *one day*.

In verse 26 God repeats the promise given in Jeremiah that He will give Israel a new heart. On top of that, He will put a *new Spirit* within them (John 14:17). This is completely new: in the old economy the Holy Spirit would only come upon them [selectively and] temporarily and not indwell them. God repeats that He will do a heart transplant in every Jewish person living at that time. In verse 27, God again says that He *will put My Spirit within you* who will cause Israel to *walk in* His *statutes* and *keep* His *judgments and do them.*

Three Key Concepts of the New Covenant

Now let's explore those three key things that God will do for Israel in the future, under the New Covenant which Messiah inaugurated on the cross with His blood.

First, God will *circumcise* the depraved heart of the Jewish people (Deuteronomy 30:6). In other words, He will regenerate the uncircumcised Jewish heart to walk after Him in complete obedience. The heart is totally corrupt and wicked from its youth (Genesis 8:21), but God will change the heart by the power of the Holy Spirit, as Yeshua taught Nicodemus in John 3. So, the first key concept is regeneration.

Second, sin will be removed, never to be remembered again and never to be charged against them, again because of the blood of the perfect Lamb of God. In the New Testament this is expanded to cover the sin of Gentiles. That also is completely different from what the Law of Moses taught in the sacrificial system, under which sacrifices had to be offered multiple times because of the ever presence of sin. Even sacrifices offered on the Day of Atonement only covered sin for a year; the following year they had to be done again. The root word translated as atonement means "to cover." In the Hebrew Scriptures, sins were not removed but covered until the ultimate sacrifice of Messiah, the Lamb of God Who came and died on the cross. At death, Old Testament saints did not go to heaven but to Hades, the place of the dead which was also called Paradise or the bosom of Abraham, which is what Yeshua referenced in Luke 16:19 31 with regard to Lazarus and the rich man. Thus, the second key concept is the <u>removal of sin</u>.

Third, in the Hebrew Scriptures the Holy Spirit came upon a person in order to fulfill a task, and once that task was completed the Holy Spirit left. The Holy Spirit's ministry to Israel was temporary and had absolutely nothing to do with salvation. However, in the economy of grace the Holy Spirit will indwell believers permanently. This was a new work that the Holy Spirit would do, as Yeshua said in John 14:17. Here we see a complete contrast in both the purpose and the style of the ministry of the Holy Spirit. So, the third key concept is the <u>indwelling of the Holy Spirit</u>.

The New Covenant teaches three things: [1] the human heart will be **regenerated** by the Holy Spirit (as Paul discussed in depth in Romans 7–8); [2] the removal of sin by the blood of Messiah (that is, the blood of the New Covenant will **remove sin** rather than just covering it); [3] and the **indwelling of the Holy Spirit** in each and every believer in Yeshua. These three provisions are inherent in every page of the epistles written by the apostles.

The New Covenant is conveyed in a new Law of Messiah which is active in the life of every believer in Messiah. This new Law has a focus completely different from that of the old, superseding the Mosaic law. Perhaps most importantly, it is unlimited in scope: what the Law of Moses did not provide and could not do, the Law of Messiah does.

- In the Law of Messiah, there are no lists of do's and don'ts. Now, out of a heart of love and gratitude, we serve our God with thankfulness for all the spiritual blessings we have in Messiah (Ephesians 1:3).

- The Law of Messiah is based on the unconditional, unilateral New Covenant.

- In the Law of Messiah, His sacrifice is completely adequate to remove our sin; no further sacrifice or work is needed.

- The Law of Messiah imposes no dietary regulations.

- The Law of Messiah has no clothing regulations. All believers are simply to dress modestly, with attention drawn to the heart and not to the body.

- The sign of the New Covenant is regeneration.

- The token of the New Covenant is the indwelling ministry of the Holy Spirit in all believers.

- Under the Law of Messiah, we can (and should) be sinning less, whereas under the Law of Moses we sinned more.

The purposes of the Law of Messiah are made clear by the indwelling ministry of the Holy Spirit. However, in the past century the subject of the Holy Spirit has become very divisive among true believers in Messiah, because of misplaced emphasis on the Holy Spirit's ministry in the lives of believers—and division is not the work of the Holy Spirit. It is important that we understand the ministry of the Holy Spirit, Who enables us to live obediently to Messiah, but I cannot provide a detailed study of the Holy Spirit here. There are numerous biblical books on the Holy Spirit that would be very beneficial to read.[210] However, a thorough study of Scripture would reveal even more. The following is just a sampling of the ministry of the Holy Spirit in our lives:

- The Holy Spirit regenerates us, makes us alive (Ephesians 2:5; Titus 3:5).

- The Holy Spirit is our teacher, guiding us into all truth (John 16:13; 1 Corinthians 2:10–11).

- The Holy Spirit does not operate in the sphere of the flesh, carnality, and darkness (Romans 8:2–8).

- The Holy Spirit intercedes on our behalf (Romans 8:26–27).

- The Holy Spirit gives us joy and peace (Galatians 5:22–23).

- The Holy Spirit gives us gifts for ministry (1 Corinthians 12:4–7).

- The Holy Spirit gives us boldness to witness (Acts 4:31).

- The Holy Spirit gives us power to live the Law of Messiah (Ephesians 3:16).

- The Holy Spirit gives us power to live godly lives (Romans 8:1–2).

- The Holy Spirit helps us to pray when we do not know how or what to pray (Ephesians 6:18).

- The Holy Spirit gives us *the spirit of wisdom and revelation in the knowledge of Him* (Ephesians 1:17–18) to illuminate our hearts and minds.

The Holy Spirit's ministry to us is very significant—in fact, indispensable—and should not be neglected. However, we often shy away from studying the work of the Holy Spirit, sometimes because of the abuses of that doctrine and sometimes because we are just biblically illiterate concerning the doctrine of the Holy Spirit. Neither should be the case, which is why, by studying the Scriptures through the lens of its Jewish perspective and by taking the Scriptures literally and dispensationally, we can be guided through the minefields of incorrect doctrine and unbiblical practices that have often destroyed believers' walk with Messiah.

17

THE UNDERLYING PRINCIPLE OF FREEDOM FOR BELIEVERS UNDER THE LAW OF MESSIAH

The believer in Yeshua ha Mashiach is free from the necessity of keeping any commandment of the Law of Moses. However, it is crucial to note that he is also free to keep parts of the Mosaic law if he so desires, even though it does not earn him extra merit points.

The biblical basis for this freedom to keep the law is evident in the actions of Paul, the greatest exponent of freedom from the Mosaic law. His vow in Acts 18:18 is based on the Law of Moses as set out in Numbers 6:2, 5, 9, and 18. His desire to be in Jerusalem for Pentecost in Acts 20:16 is based on Deuteronomy 16:16. The strongest example is Acts 21:17–26, where we see Paul himself keeping that law.

For example, if a Jewish believer feels the need to refrain from eating pork, he is free to so refrain. The same is true for all the other commandments. However, there are two dangers that must be avoided by both Messianic Jewish believers (or Gentiles) and those who choose to keep portions of the Law of Moses. First is the belief that a person who keeps that law is thereby contributing to his own justification and sanctification. This notion is false and must be avoided. The second danger is that one may demand or expect others to keep the law as well.[211] This is equally wrong; in fact, it is outright legalism. Ones who exercise their freedom to keep the law must recognize and respect others' freedom not to do the same. This is the principle of Christian liberty that Paul taught in Romans 14:1–23 and 1 Corinthians 10:23–33.

Chapter 17

The solution to these problems lies in discovering what the Bible says about the Messianic believer's relationship to the law, especially the Ten Commandments, and to the new set of laws, the Law of Messiah, which both Jewish and Gentile believers are bound to keep because of the New Covenant.

The most immediate problem that seems to face the new Jewish believer in Messiah is his relationship to the Law of Moses. To what extent is the Messianic Jew to keep the Law of Moses? We have clearly shown throughout this book that the Law of Moses is not binding on believers, whether Jewish or Gentile, and thus believers have no need to practice, observe, or obey that old law.

There are, of course, other cultural and relational factors bearing on Messianic believers who feel the need to place themselves back under the Law of Moses. Because Jewish believers are rejected by the larger unbelieving Jewish community, and are viewed as traitors to their fathers who have over the centuries suffered so much at the hands of Christian anti-Semitism, they have what might be called Jewish separation anxiety. They have a great desire to be connected with their physical Jewish brothers and sisters. So they observe the law, and wear the Jewish religious attire, in the irrational hope that by being "more Jewish" they will be accepted by the larger Jewish community. That will never happen unless they recant their faith in Messiah Yeshua. They cannot be more Jewish if they are already Jewish. In fact, they are more Jewish than the larger unbelieving Jewish community, because they have accepted the *Prophet like Moses*, Yeshua, as their Messiah and Savior; you cannot get any more Jewish than that! Jewish believers are still accountable to a law, but it is the Law of Messiah and Redeemer, your Savior who made the covenant with Abraham, Isaac, and Jacob, Who is the same one Who will restore Israel and Who Himself will physically sit on the throne of His father David.

The Underlying Principle of Freedom for Believers Under the Law of Messiah

Today we see Gentile Christians placing themselves under a law that was given to Jewish people, who through faulty teaching are trying to keep aspects of that law, but by doing so stand guilty of breaking the whole Mosaic law. We have Gentile Christians who think that because they are in Abraham, they are Jewish. It needs to be remembered that Arabs can also claim to be of Abraham as well. We also have Jewish believers who cling to the law that was fulfilled in the death of Messiah on the Cross, despite the biblical fact that His inauguration of the New Covenant totally and completely replaced the Mosaic law with the Law of Messiah. The Mosaic law could not bring about God's circumcision of the heart (Colossians 2:11); the New Covenant is the only covenant made with Israel that can regenerate the heart.

Today many Messianic Jews and Gentiles adhere to and teach what is sometimes called Torah observance, which is a partial keeping of the Law of Moses. They are very inconsistent in what laws they choose to obey, although they demand that others are to be like them in Torah observance. Like their unbelieving Jewish brethren, these believers are clinging to a law that is no longer relevant before God, instead of placing their faith solely in Messiah and accepting the truth that the New Covenant has replaced the old. Righteousness and godly living do not come from the law that has been rendered inoperative, but from the Law of Messiah, established by the blood of the New Covenant which Messiah shed on the cross of Calvary.

Certainly, you have the freedom and right to keep kosher, to keep the feasts, and so on; Messiah gives you the liberty to do so. However, you do <u>not</u> have the right to cause other believers to lose their focus on Messiah and the ministry of the Holy Spirit that would empower them to live the victorious life that the Law of Moses could not give. The Law of Messiah includes all the individual commandments from Messiah and the apostles that are applicable to a believer in Messiah.

Chapter 17

A couple of other observations might assist those who wonder if they should try to keep the Mosaic law. First, within Judaism, the rabbis have focused only and completely on the rabbinic law, which is not Mosaic law, but rather a reinterpretation of the Mosaic law that has been formed into man-made law by rabbis over the centuries. Second, the Mosaic law has, in various ways, inappropriately dominated the teaching and lifestyle of many within the church since the establishment of the Church in Acts 2. Those believers have also been lax in understanding the Law of Messiah that they are responsible to God to keep.

18

THE UNIQUENESS OF THE LAW OF MESSIAH

The Law of Messiah is intrinsically different from the Law of Moses. Remember that on a very basic level the Law of Moses was holy (Romans 7:12), and one of its purposes was to lead Israel to Messiah as a tutor/guardian who would guide the student in grasping his studies (Galatians 3:24 25). Because Israel could not keep the Law of Moses, that law also became the ministration of *condemnation* and *death* (2 Corinthians 3:7, 9). In contrast, the New Covenant gave regenerated life (2 Corinthians 3:6), a circumcised heart (Colossians 2:11), and the enabling power of the Holy Spirit so that believers could walk and live according to the New Covenant standards, which are expressed in the Law of Messiah.

The Law of Messiah is comprised of many imperative commands given in the epistles, which observant believers can live and walk by in the enabling power of the Holy Spirit (You will find a complete listing of all these imperatives in the appendix) In this chapter, I set out some of the categories and samples of the imperative commands that each believer is to obey.

The Law of Messiah is unique, and its difference is in sharp contrast to the Mosaic law, which is old, decayed, and vanished away (Hebrews 8:13). We New Covenant believers, under the Law of Messiah, live in Messiah and can have victory over the habitual sin in our lives on a daily basis because of the indwelling Holy Spirit of God, Who regenerated us unto life (Titus 3:5); Who enables us to walk in the light, not in carnality, the flesh which is darkness (1 John 1:5–7); and Who ensures that death no longer has a place in our lives (Romans 6:11–13).

In this section I include not only limited aspects of the Law of Messiah, but also the admonitions of the apostles as they taught the Church in their epistles, so that you can observe the contrasts between the old law and the New Law. You will quickly see that although many of the themes in the two covenants are similar, their instructions differ markedly. The points I discuss are only examples of the areas of change and difference between these two laws; you can greatly expand this list through study of the Scriptures.

Moses = Condemnation and Death; Messiah = Life

As I have said many times before, the two laws are as different as day and night, cold and hot. *Condemnation* and *death* is the net result of the Law of Moses (2 Corinthians 3:6 14; 15:56). Though the law was holy, man was unholy and unable to keep God's holy law (Romans 2:25), so *condemnation* and *death* were the outcome (Romans 6:23).

Compare that with the regenerating work of the Holy Spirit which gave life (2 Corinthians 3:6c): through the New Covenant Law of Messiah, we were born again from above (John 3:3–6) and made alive (Romans 6:3–4; Ephesians 2:5). The writer of Hebrews is clear that Messiah came to take away the first law, the Mosaic law, and establish the second, the New Covenant and Law of Messiah (Hebrews 10:9; 9:14–15).

Moses = Priests and Sacrifices; Messiah = Churches, Elders, and Deacons

In the Old Testament economy of law, priests officiated in the Tabernacle and the Temple, doing the sacrifices prescribed in the books of Leviticus and Hebrews. The ministering of the priests was an unending job (Hebrews 10:11), for the offerings did not remove sin but merely covered sin (Hebrews 10:11), so the offerings had to be repeated time and again. The root meaning of "atonement" (as in Yom Kippur, the Day of Atonement) is simply "to cover." A death was required to cover sin, so priests most frequently offered the lamb as a substitute. Death is the epitaph of sin (Romans 4:15; 5:20).

Under the Law of Messiah, the demand of death for sin has been satisfied once and for all by the death of Messiah. Now, instead of priests, we have the Church (the universal church, people from every nation and ethnicity making up the body of Messiah); locally, we have elders and pastors along with deacons who teach the Scriptures and work to meet the needs of the local church (2 Timothy 3:1–13; Acts 6:1–7). These elders and deacons make no sacrifices; instead, they teach, instruct, encourage, correct, admonish, and care for the spiritual and physical needs of the local church as it walks in Messiah.

Moses = General Israeli Society; Messiah = Family Unit, Marriage, Employment

In the Old Testament economy, the law was given to national, ethnic, physical Israel and not to Gentiles (Exodus 24:1–8; Ephesians 2:11–13) [or the nations]. It formed a system of law to be obeyed by and to govern the actions of the people of Israel. It governed and controlled Israel's entire religious life, social (family) life, and civil life.

In contrast, under the economy of grace—that is, under the Law of Messiah—the Law will govern every sphere of life for the believer in Messiah; it is not for an earthly nation of people. The Law includes family life (the union of a man and woman with their offspring) among all the ethnicities of the earth. It governs how a husband and wife relate to each other (Ephesians 5:18–33; Colossians 3:18–21; 1 Peter 3:1–7), how to raise children (Ephesians 6:1–4; Colossians 3:20), how to work for your employer (Ephesians 6:5–8; Colossians 3:22–25), and how the employer is to treat employees (Ephesians 6:9; Colossians 4:1). The Law of Messiah is carefully laid down to create the most harmonious life possible among human beings, no matter what their station is life is, and among all cultures, nations, and peoples. Thus, the whole focus of law is different. In the old, you had law to be obeyed; in the new, though you still have law, the nature of that law is entirely different.

Moses = Tribal Heads; Messiah = Governments

Under the Law of Moses, you were responsible to the leadership in each city and tribe, and to the king. In the Law of Messiah, we are equally responsible to the leadership on a local, state, and federal level. The Law of Moses was all focused on the leadership of Israel. However, we under grace are from many nations and peoples; the laws of each nation are different, and we are responsible to obey the law of the nation we live in. I am not responsible for abiding by the law of the United Kingdom, China, Russian, South Africa, Iran, or Brazil, but I am responsible for obeying the laws of the United States of America where my earthly citizenship is. The principles laid down by Paul are clear, and they apply to and work in every nation under the sun where believers live (Romans 13:1–7). Peter states that we as believers are to *honor the king* (1 Peter 2:17) and *submit to the ordinance* of men (1 Peter 2:13) unless that nation tells us to violate the Scriptures.

Moses = Idolatry and False Prophets; Messiah = False Teachers, Discerning

Idolatry and false prophets were noted often in the Law of Moses. Warnings against the practice of idolatry are repeated often, and the standard against false prophets is both noted clearly (Deuteronomy 18:20–22; 13:1–5) and illustrated by examples (Jeremiah 23:13–21; 28:1–17).

Under the Law of Messiah, local churches, elders, and pastors are warned about false teachers who present error. Paul calls them *dogs* and *evil workers* in Philippians 3:2, and in Colossians 2:8 he calls out those who use *worldly philosophy* and deceit to obtain wealth and a following that makes them look authentic. Paul called the Judaizers *anathema* (cursed) for combining truth with error. John states that anyone who does not hold to the doctrine of Christ is not to be received, and says we should not even bid them well (2 John 9–11); Jude warns believers in the same way (Jude 3–4). Unfortunately, in the today's Church, many pastors, elders, and deacons are completely ignoring these warnings and thus are responsible for openly allowing falsehood and error into the church; they are violating the Law of Messiah.

Moses = Distinction/Separation; Messiah = Separation

Under Moses, Israel was to keep itself as a distinct people separate from the nations that surrounded them and the peoples of the earth. They were to keep their faith pure and not introduce the pagan beliefs and practices of neighboring nations into their national life. They were to be separated unto the LORD in all aspects of their national life. That included not only their worship of the LORD, but also how they ate, dressed, circumcised their sons, met for worship on the Pilgrim Feasts, and many more things. What we see in the book of Judges concerning the days of Israel's judges is what they did by disobeying and compromising their law, thus bringing judgment upon themselves.

Under the Law of Messiah, believers can eat anything they wish (Acts 10:9–15), and dress modestly (1 Timothy 2:9; 1 Peter 3:3–4). We are to be distinct from the world system (Romans 12:2; 1 John 2:15–17), which is under the control of Satan (Matthew 4:8–11; John 12:31; 2 Corinthians 4:4; 1 John 5:19). We are to be constantly on guard against error (2 Corinthians 6:14–18). Our distinction and separation from the world is largely spiritual, manifesting as an inner quality of life. As an example, under the Law of Messiah, in China believers can dress like the Chinese, and believers in India can dress according to their national culture and it is okay. This is true of any culture or nation as long as the cultural mores and demands do not violate the clear commands of the Scriptures.

Moses = Widows, Poor, and Needy; Messiah = Widows, Poor, and Needy

In the Mosaic law, God gives explicit instructions to care for widows and orphans, the poor and needy. As the kingdoms of Israel and Judah corrupted themselves, the prophets referred to these laws in urging Israel to repent and return to obedience to the law (Exodus 22:20–24; Deuteronomy 27:19; Proverbs 28:27, 29:7; Isaiah 1:17; Zechariah 7:9–10).

In the Law of Messiah, believers are taught that both they and their Church should care for widows, the poor, and the needy, and also are taught to care for the members of their congregation as well as others (1 Timothy 5:3–16; James 1:27).

Moses = Passover; Messiah = Lord's Table

In Exodus 12 the Passover was inaugurated for Israel to practice until the ultimate sacrifice was given by God in 30 AD, in the Person of Yeshua when He died on the cross. Under the Law of Moses, the Passover was both forward- and backward-looking; backward in that they were to celebrate their redemption from Egypt, and forward in that they celebrated a future Passover Lamb that God would provide.

On Passover 30 AD, Yeshua became the voluntary sacrificial offering for the sins of Israel as well as Gentiles. Gentiles are not obligated to practice the Feast of Passover because the ultimate Lamb of God has already been sacrificed. For Jewish people today, the feast is optional: it can be practiced or not as desired.

The blood of the Messiah inaugurated the New Covenant on the day of Passover. It was on that day that Yeshua celebrated Passover with his disciples and established a new ordinance called the Lord's Table or the Communion Service. Today we do it in observance of what Yeshua asked us to do to remember what He did on that unique Passover Day. We now remember the matzo (bread) that represents the body of Messiah and the cup which represents the blood of Messiah, the Blood of the New Covenant, and all the ramifications of what these two items mean to us (Matthew 26:20 30; Luke 22:14 20; 1 Corinthians 11:23 27; 5:7). Look at these two elements:

The Lord's Table

Unleavened Bread (Matzo)	Wine (The Cup)
His body — sinless life	The wine represents the blood of the Exodus
His Scourging with a Roman whip in our place	Passover Lamb
He was pierced like the appearance of the Passover matzo bread	His blood
	The Blood of the New Covenant regenerated us, removed our sin, and gave us the indwelling of the Holy Spirit
Afikomen released us from the power and penalty of sin	

Moses = Physical Blessings; Messiah = Spiritual Blessings

Blessings are promised throughout the Scriptures. Israel is promised physical blessing that is all related to their walk with the LORD. If they are obedient to His law, Israel will be blessed, as Deuteronomy 28:1–14 tells us. Throughout the Scriptures the Jewish people are promised by God that the Land will be restored to them and that the Messiah will reign on David's throne. These and much more all relate to the physical blessings promised to Israel.

Chapter 18

However, for the Church, which is the body of Messiah, no physical blessings are promised—but there are promises of spiritual blessings (Ephesians 1:3). Those spiritual blessings come directly from the Blood of the New Covenant. The obedience to the Law of Messiah will give us spiritual rewards (1 Corinthians 9:24–27) which will determine our lives and positions in the eternal order by our service to God.

Moses = Physical Cleanness (Women); Messiah = Spiritual Cleanliness (Women)

The Law of Moses established ritual immersions and sacrifices for a woman 40 days (son) or 80 days (daughter) after the birth of a child (Leviticus 12:6–8; Luke 2:22–24). Women were considered ritually unclean during the monthly menstrual cycle (Leviticus 15:19). Physical cleanliness under the law was strictly adhered to.

However, under the Law of Messiah, there is no such requirement to fulfill at childbirth or during a monthly menstrual cycle. Why? Since the commands in the Law of Messiah now pertain to Gentiles worldwide; because now the Gospel is to be taken throughout the world to many other cultures, these ritual acts under the Law of Moses were not passed on. Now the focus of God is not on a chosen people but on all peoples of the earth, and on the spiritual inward character of all believers from every nation, not their physical characteristics and customs.

Moses = Holy Spirit Temporary; Messiah = Holy Spirit Permanent

In the Old Testament economy, the Holy Spirit's relationship to humans was temporary. The Holy Spirit came upon Moses, the 70 elders of Israel, Samson, and King Saul—and departed them when His task was completed. That was His ministry in the Old Testament economy of the Law of Moses. Yeshua said in John 14:17 that the Holy Spirit was *with* them but shall be (future) *in* them. Likewise, Ezekiel 36:26–27, in a New Covenant passage, clearly states that the Holy Spirit will indwell all believers. In the New Testament economy, the new ministry of the Holy Spirit in the New Covenant not only involves indwelling (1 Corinthians 3:16), but also filling (Ephesians 5:18), sealing (Ephesians 1:13–14), and baptism (1 Corinthians 12:13), which were unknown in the old economy.

Moses = Land Stipulations; Messiah = Integrity of Heart

In Israel, the tribal designations of the landholding were then further subdivided into families. This was very important to with the family's inheritance, so the markers that designated the boundaries of each family's land was a very big deal. To move a boundary marker was a very serious offense. Moving a boundary not only broke the Law of Moses, but also suffered a curse attached to it (Deuteronomy 19:14, 27:17; Hosea 5:10).

In the new economy of grace, the Law of Messiah governs the integrity of the heart of believers walking in the Spirit and walking in the light. Even though there are no specific statements about property borders, we are told to walk as Messiah Himself walked (1 John 2:6).

Moses = Love God and Neighbors; Messiah = Love Greatly Intensified

Under the Law of Moses, Israel was to love God and love their neighbors. Moses expressed in several places that they were to love the LORD their God (Deuteronomy 6:5; 10:12; 11:13, 22; 30:16) and to love their neighbors (Leviticus 19:18, 34; Matthew 22:36–40). These commands of the law governed many interpersonal connections.

The Law of Messiah teaches love, but in this respect the action of love is more intense than what the law in the old economy taught.

Chapter 18

Under the New Covenant, we are to love the Lord and serve Him and to love people. This moves the focus of love from a human standard to a standard directed toward God. Yeshua said we are to love each other so that the world will know we are Yeshua's disciples (John 13:35; 15:9–10, 13). The word for "love" in the Greek is *agape*, meaning self-sacrificial love. God's love and the love of believers are expressed in the following terms:

- <u>God loved us</u> *while we were yet sinners, Messiah died for us* (Romans 5:8)

- *Who shall separate us from the <u>love</u> of Messiah? For I am persuaded, that neither death, nor life, nor angels, nor principalities, nor powers, nor things present, nor things to come, nor height, nor depth, nor any other creature, shall be able to separate us from the <u>love</u> of God, which is in Messiah Yeshua our Lord.* (Romans 8:35, 38–39)

- <u>Love</u> *should be without hypocrisy, <u>without a two-faced character, no play acting</u>.* (Romans 12:9)

- <u>Love</u> *does no ill to his neighbor* [or <u>love does no evil</u>]. (Romans 13:10)

- <u>By love</u> *serve one another.* (Galatians 5:13)

- *The fruit of the Spirit is <u>love</u>* [this is listed first by Paul for emphasis]. (Galatians 5:22)

- *Rooted and grounded in <u>love</u> ... to know the <u>love</u> of Messiah.* (Ephesians 3:17 19)

- *With all lowliness and meekness, with longsuffering* [patience,] *forbearing one another in <u>love</u>* [Love is the key, the foundation of all our life responses]. (Ephesians 4:2)

- *Speaking the truth in <u>love</u> ... makes increase of the body unto the edifying of itself in <u>love</u>* [speak truth in love, not with conflicting shades of meaning, for we are to build up the body of Messiah]. (Ephesians 4:15 16)

- *Walk in <u>love</u>, as Messiah also has <u>loved</u> us* [our walk carries with it love in every sphere of life]. (Ephesians 5:2)

- *I pray that your <u>love</u> may abound yet more and more in knowledge and in all judgment* [Paul commends love to be used with knowledge and in all our judgments and decisions]. (Philippians 1:9)

- *Fulfill you my joy, that you be likeminded, having the same <u>love</u>, being of one accord, of one mind* [here Paul unites love with being in complete unity and of the same mind]. (Philippians 2:2)

- [That the Colossians'] *hearts might be comforted, being knit together in <u>love</u>* [Believers are to be knit together as one would knit a garment]. (Colossians 2:2)

- *Husbands, <u>love</u> your wives* [the act that a wife needs from her husband]. (Colossians 3:19)

- *Remember without ceasing your work of faith, and labour of <u>love</u>, and patience of hope in our Lord Yeshua Messiah* [Our work and labor for Yeshua is to be characterized by love. It is an act of love, not done because of dread or just to be compliant]. (1 Thessalonians 1:3)

- *And the Lord make you to increase and abound in <u>love</u> one toward another, and toward all men* [Believers are to increase and abound in self-sacrificial love toward other believers]. (1 Thessalonians 3:12)

- *But as touching brotherly <u>love</u> you need not that I write unto you: for you yourselves are taught of God to <u>love</u> one another* [We are to love our brethren]. (1 Thessalonians 4:9)

- *And to esteem them* [elders] *very highly in <u>love</u> for their work's sake. And be at peace among yourselves* [Elder leaders are to be loved for the work they do for the local body of believers so that there is always peace between you and them]. (1 Thessalonians 5:13)

- *For whom the Lord <u>loves</u> He chastens and scourges every son whom He receives* [God the Father in love will discipline believers whom He loves]. (Hebrews 12:6)

The First Epistle of John also has a plethora of references to love in the context of believers.

Paul gives the best description of this intensified love in any of the Scriptures where love is expounded upon. Love is the key; it is the foundation underlying all the Law of Messiah given to the Church by Yeshua and His apostles. Notice the quality of the heart if love is exercised by God in the believer's life, and notice as well the inward motivation from the heart that Paul brings to light in 1 Corinthians:

1 If I speak in the tongues [languages] *of men and of angels, but have not love, I am a noisy gong or a clanging cymbal. 2 And if I have prophetic powers, and understand all mysteries and all knowledge, and if I have all faith, so as to remove mountains, but have not love, I am nothing. 3 If I give away all I have, and if I deliver up my body to be burned, but have not love, I gain nothing.* 4 Love is patient and kind; love does not envy or boast; it is not arrogant or rude. 5 *It does not insist on its own way; it is not irritable or resentful; 6 it does not rejoice at wrongdoing, but rejoices with the truth. 7 Love bears all things, believes all things, hopes all things, endures all things.*

8 Love never ends. As for prophecies, they will pass away; as for tongues [languages], *they will cease; as for knowledge, it will pass away. 9 For we know in part and we prophesy in part, 10 but when the perfect comes, the partial will pass away. 11 When I was a child, I spoke like a child; I thought like a child, I reasoned like a child. When I became a man, I gave up childish ways. 12 For now we see in a mirror dimly, but then face to face. Now I know in part; then I shall know fully, even as I have been fully known.*

13 *So now faith, hope, and love abide, these three, but the greatest of these is love.* (1 Corinthians 13:1–13, ESV)

The intensification of love in the New Covenant shows again the foundation that Yeshua laid down. Paul highlighted love to show the significance of the Law of Messiah and how it is to be lived in believers' lives.

Moses = No Demonic Adversaries; Messiah = Demonic Adversaries, Spiritual Warfare

There are almost no references to demonic activity in the Hebrew Scriptures. The strongest possibility is the sons of God in Genesis 6:2, but that is before the Law of Moses. Demonic powers are referenced in Daniel 10:12–13, when the message to Daniel was delayed by the prince of the kingdom of Persia, but Michael came and helped the angel so that he could give God's message to Daniel. Although very little is said about demonic forces in the Hebrew Scriptures, they were nonetheless active during this time.

In contrast, the New Testament says a great deal about demons. The Gospels are still in the period of the Mosaic law and not in the new economy of Grace. At the end period of the Mosaic law system, during the ministry of Yeshua, demons were very active because of His personal presence on earth. From the coming of the Holy Spirit at Pentecost to the Rapture of the Church, demonic powers are mentioned often in the dispensation of grace. Before and during the economy of grace, the New Testament records demonic possession, and fighting against principalities and powers. This again highlights a sharp difference between the Law of Moses and the Law of Messiah.

- *People who worship idols are worshipping demons.* (1 Corinthians 10:19–21; Revelation 9:20)

- *And no wonder! For Satan himself transforms himself into an angel of light. Therefore, it is no great thing if his ministers also transform themselves into ministers of righteousness, whose end will be according to their works.* (2 Corinthians 11:13–14)

- *Put on the whole armor of God, that you may be able to stand against the wiles of the devil. For we do not wrestle against flesh and blood, but against principalities, against powers, against the rulers of the darkness of this age, against spiritual hosts of wickedness in the heavenly places.* (Ephesians 6:11–12)

- *In the latter days, people will give in to deceiving spirits and doctrines of demons* (1 Timothy 4:1–3)

- *Evil earthly wisdom comes from demons* (James 3:13–16)

Moses = Nothing in Relationship to the Flesh; Messiah = Make No Provisions for Flesh

There was nothing in the Mosaic law that could deal with the fleshly, inward evil impulses and desires of the heart except meditation on His Word (Joshua 1:8; Psalm 1:2). There were men who had great spiritual integrity, but the average citizen of Israel had nothing to help him overcome the evil imaginations of the heart (Genesis 6:5, 8:21) or the deceitfulness of the heart (Jeremiah 17:9). There were only three periods of corporate worship (Exodus 23:14 17; 34:23), and no indwelling of the Old Testament believer by the Holy Spirit, just a system of law that they were to obey. Within themselves there was no power to overcome their own sinful hearts (Job 5:7). They were told to meditate on the Word of God, but where were they to get it? Individuals did not have personal copies of scrolls of Scripture unless they were very wealthy. The priests were to teach the people the law, the commandments and statutes, but they themselves did not have the power to overcome their own evil hearts; as the northern and southern kingdoms of Israel and Judah became corrupt, so did the priesthood. Israel was given a holy law by God, with only their consciences from the days of Adam and the dispensation of conscience and their own self-will to focus on obeying that law. The Old Testament believer was thus at a great disadvantage compared to believers in the economy of grace and the New Covenant Law of Messiah.

Under the New Covenant in the economy of grace, Paul tells believers to *Put you on the Lord Yeshua Messiah, and make no provision for the flesh, to fulfill the lusts thereof* (Romans 13:14). We do so by yielding in submission to the indwelling Holy Spirit, Who will give us the enabling power to overcome the sinful heart that we still possess. Go back and look again at Paul's teaching in the book of Romans, specifically chapters 6–8, and in this book's discussion of the three kinds of people in chapter 8. We have the same conscience to help us as the Old Testament believer had, but we all have a copy of the Living Word of God to study and meditate on, in addition to the indwelling presence of the Holy Spirit Who teaches us, guides us, and leads us into all truth. God has given us every possible advantage and encouragement to live holy lives, yet today most believers live spiritually no better than their Old Testament counterparts did. What a point of condemnation on the head of New Testament believers; sin still reigns!

Chapter 18

Moses = Discipline; Messiah = Discipline

Under the Law of Moses, God disciplined His people even as He does New Testament believers. However, the nature of the discipline was more severe than what a believer in the New Testament experiences. Under Mosaic law, if people violated the law and turned away from living for God, they received God's curse, as recorded in Deuteronomy 28:15–68. Under that law, the death sentence was prescribed for idolatry (Deuteronomy 13:1–10; 17:2–5); blasphemy (Leviticus 24:11–16); Sabbath breaking (Exodus 31:14–15; 35:2); dishonoring parents (Deuteronomy 21:18–21; Exodus 21:17); premeditated murder (Exodus 21:12–14); adultery, homosexuality, and various forms of incest (Leviticus 20); theft in the form of kidnapping (Exodus 21:16); false witness, and perjury in capital cases (Deuteronomy 19:15–21). The punishment for these sins was death in the form of stoning. This death penalty applied to other cases as well:

- If a man knew his ox was prone to hurt people and his ox killed someone, the owner of the ox would be put to death. (Exodus 21:29)

- A witch would be put to death. (Exodus 22:18)

- Those who participated in sexual bestiality would be put to death. (Exodus 22:19)

- Those who gave their children to a false god would be put to death. (Leviticus 20:2)

- Incestuous polygamy would be punished by death. (Leviticus 20:14)

- False prophets would be put to death. (Deuteronomy 13:5–10)

- A man who would not listen to the priest or judge would be put to death. (Deuteronomy 17:12)

- A man who raped a woman, and the woman who is raped, if she does not cry out when help is nearby, would be put to death. (Deuteronomy 22:23 24)

The discipline of God was intended to get Israel to repent, as Amos proclaims to disobedient Israel in Amos 4:6–12. In verses 6, 8, 9, 10, and 11, note the words *yet have you not returned unto me*. Look as well at Jeremiah 15:7, which says they returned not from their ways. Jeremiah uses the key word *shoove*, meaning "to return," repeatedly throughout his book.

Under the Law of Messiah and the New Covenant, there is no death penalty for the Church! However, in specific instances God may execute a person, as for the sin of Ananias and Sapphira in lying to the Holy Spirit (Acts 5:1–11). Some also received death by the hand of the Lord because of their abuse of the Lord's Table (1 Corinthians 11:30). Beyond this, there is a reference to the Church turning an unrepentant sinner over to Satan for the destruction of his flesh (1 Corinthians 5:5). Nevertheless, the difference between law and grace in this respect is tremendous.

Moses = Cities of Refuge; Messiah = Controlled by the Spirit

Under the Law of Moses, "cities of refuge" were created to protect individuals who had accidently killed someone. These cities provided a place of safety against a family member of the person slain, called the "avenger of blood," until judgment could be made (Leviticus 35:9–15; Deuteronomy 4:41–45; Joshua 20).

Now, because we do not operate under the old economy but under the laws of many nations, there are no cities of refuge. What becomes abundantly clear in the Law of Messiah and the New Covenant is that Messiah is our refuge (John 6:37; Romans 5:11; Hebrews 6:18). Under a nation's legal system, there may be consequences for one who causes the careless or accidental death of another person. We would stand before the legal court system, but do not have to worry about fleeing from an avenger of blood. Once again, the Law of Moses and the Law of Messiah are quite different in this respect.

Moses = Tithing; Messiah = No Tithing

The Law of Moses prescribed tithes to be given, although a "tithe" was not necessarily 10% of one's income; that was done only once by Abram (Genesis 14:20; Hebrews 7:4 [no percentage mentioned]) before the Law of Moses was given. The Mosaic law required three tithes, two of which were annual tithes of a tenth to provide for the Levites as they ministered before the LORD and on behalf of the people. The law also specified a third offering on the third year which amounted to another 10%. Thus, the actual average of tithes for a three-year period was closer to 23%. The tithe on the third year was aimed at the agricultural community of Israel, with their offerings to be placed in tribal or communal storehouses for the stranger (foreigner), the poor, widows, and orphans. This was God's "welfare" system to help the unfortunate (Genesis 14:19–20, 28:20–22; Leviticus 27:30–34; Numbers 18:21, 26; Deuteronomy 12:5–6, 14:27–29; 2 Chronicles 31:4–5; Nehemiah 10:35–37; Malachi 3:8–12). This system of tithing was rendered inoperative with the rest of the Mosaic law and does not apply to the Church.

We are no longer a national community as Israel was. Believers are in nations all around the world, so a communal tithing system simply would not work. Nowhere in the New Covenant of the Law of Messiah do we find God commanding a 10% tithe of your income! However, God does lay down principles to guide us in giving to His work and toward helping the poor and needy in our churches and communities. The principle comes from Paul in 2 Corinthians 9:6–7, where he taught giving based on how God has prospered us. Paul intensifies a believer's heart attitude in giving. The word *giver* in English is from Greek root word *didomi*. We are to be giving not just "cheerfully," as the

English text states, for that word in the Greek is an intensification of how to give: "hilariously."[212] Believers are admonished to give to help others and to help those in need when one has the means to do so, but each time the heart attitude of the believing giver is emphasized (Romans 12:6–8; 2 Corinthians 9:6–7; 1 Timothy 6:17–19; Hebrews 13:15; James 2:15–16; 1 John 3:17).

Moses = Nothing about Spiritual Character; Messiah = Spiritual Character Stressed

It seems odd that spiritual character is not emphasized in the old law, although godly behavior appears to be defined and created by obedience to the Law of Moses. In the old economy of law, it seems that Israel could obey the law without faith and still be blessed by God. The goal was for Israel to repent, change their minds and actions, and express their faith by obedience to the holy Law of Moses. The Prophet Jeremiah constantly uses the word for "repent" [*shoove*] in addressing Judah regarding its backsliding so that the Judeans would turn back to God in faith. It was Habakkuk who said *the just shall live by faith*. Josiah was a godly king who set forth reforms that the people obeyed, but they only obeyed on the surface level. There was a repentance movement, but it was not in most people's hearts to repent and live by faith (2 Chronicles 34–35). Spiritual character exhibited by faith does not stand out as a key element of the desired repentance. Of course, there were many who did exercise faith, as Hebrews 11 attests. Israel was to live by the holy standard of God (Leviticus 19:2), but because of its heart, it could not (Ecclesiastes 7:20; Jeremiah 17:9).[213]

In the new economy of grace, emphasis is constantly laid on the spiritual character of the believer, because of the indwelling presence of the Holy Spirit Who gives us life and enables victory over sin. The new economy, with its focus on grace and the Law of Messiah, urges us in every possible way to yield to the Holy Spirit and let Him build spiritual character in us so that the Father can conform us to the image of His son.

Moses = For a Nation; Messiah = For All the Peoples of the Earth

As I have said before, the Law of Moses was for Israel and Israel alone. Believers now are not physical Israel; we are the Church baptized into the body of Messiah from every nation and ethnicity on the earth. The two law systems do not mix and are not meant to agree. They are different because now we are dealing with a different administration of God, called grace, which came from the New Covenant.

Moses = All to Obey, No Exceptions; Messiah = Christian Liberty

The Law of Moses was a blanket deal: all of Israel was obligated to obey the Law. There were no exceptions. The poor and destitute had to obey all of it, the rich and the king had to obey all of it, even the priests were obligated to obey all of it.

The Law of Messiah is also a blanket deal, yet in the Law of Messiah, there are grey areas at the individual-human level. These areas are not identified as sin, but may be considered sin by some of the body of Messiah because of their former background or cultural upbringing. This Law requires believers to use their Christian liberty so that other believers who are weak in a given area do not stumble. Under the old economy, there was no such thing as using one's liberty not to offend another believer.

Moses = Servants or Slaves; Messiah = We Are All Servants/ Bond Slaves

Under the Mosaic law, the term *servants and slaves* simply meant just that: servants and slaves. The law regulated how servants and slaves should be treated. Old Testament saints were called servants of God, but never slaves. God refers to Abraham as His servant (Genesis 26:24), and Moses was referred to by others as God's servant (Exodus 14:31; Numbers 12:7–8; Deuteronomy 34:5; Joshua 1:2; Malachi 4:4); David was called *My servant* (2 Samuel 7:5, 8), as was Isaiah (Isaiah 20:3), and God also referred to the prophets as His servants (2 Kings 17:13; Jeremiah 7:25; 26:5). In Isaiah God refers to two servants of the LORD: the first is the Messiah as the Servant of the LORD (Isaiah 42:1–7; 49:1–6; 50:4–11; 52:13–53:12) and the second is Israel (Isaiah 41:8; 43:10; 44:1). In Zechariah 3:8 Messiah is called *My servant the Branch*. In these instances God called His people, the prophets, and the Messiah *servants*.

Under the Law of Messiah, believers in the New Covenant are referred to both as *servants* and as *slaves* or *bond slaves* (Romans 6:16–18; 2 Corinthians 4:5; Colossians 4:12; 2 Timothy 2:24; Revelation 1:1). The term "slave" in the Greek is *doulos*, meaning one who is purchased or owned by a master: a bond slave or *bondservant*. Throughout the New Testament, the writers of Scripture refer to themselves as a *bondservant*, slave, or servant, terms which they applied metaphorically to someone who was absolutely devoted to Jesus, such as Paul, Timothy, James, Peter, and Jude (Romans 1:1; Galatians 1:10; Philippians 1:1; Titus 1:1; James 1:1; 2 Peter 1:1; Jude 1:1). In the New Covenant Christians refer to themselves and other believers as servants or bondservants of Messiah.

Moses = Jewish Culture Only; Messiah = Cultures Conforming to Godly Lifestyle

In Israel, under the Law of Moses everything pertained to Jewish people, directing them to keep themselves distinct from the world and to be His *witnesses* to all the other peoples of the earth. That law applied specifically and only to Israel: Jewish people with all their covenants and promises. Everything in the law was linked to their biblical culture.

Chapter 18

The Law of Messiah applies to believers who are Jewish, but it also includes all other peoples and cultures who have embraced Yeshua as their personal Savior from sin. The emphasis in this dispensation of grace has shifted to the believing peoples of the nations plus Jewish people who make up the body of Messiah. Now we who are from the non-Israeli nations have a biblical culture in the Law of Messiah which is separate and distinct from the world system, the nations, and the sinful aspects of any given culture. We now are to live unto Christ through the Holy Spirit within our diversities of ethnicities in Messiah Who binds us together in Himself by obedience to the Law of Messiah.

Moses = Law; Messiah = Grace

Israel alone committed themselves to the keeping of the Law of Moses (Exodus 24). That law was given to Israel and not to the Gentiles. In the old economy of the Mosaic law, Gentiles could become part of Israel by becoming circumcised and being obedient to the law.

Under grace, the Law of Messiah was given for all believers, whether Jewish or Gentile. This Law of the new economy was given to all the peoples of the earth, including Israel. The Holy Spirit regenerated them because of their belief in the death, burial, and resurrection of Messiah from the grave. The Holy Spirit enables us to live a godly life and indwells, fills, seals, and baptizes us into the body of Messiah, making us *one new man* in Messiah.

Thus, these two systems of law have completely different purposes. Both are given to believers, but the focus and emphasis of the Law of Messiah gives all cultures and ethnicities the power to live for Him without becoming Jewish or adhering to Jewish law.

Messiah = Model Christian Character Inward

The Law of Messiah of the New Covenant, as acted upon by the believer, can present to the world the most beautiful picture or model of how Christ is to radiate through our lives. We can present godly character as at no other time in the history of man. The old economy could not produce this kind of Holy Spirit-guided, inward response. If you carefully read all the imperative commands making up the Law of Messiah, you will find that the Lord is thereby dealing with our inward character and response to all of life. The law of the old economy dealt strictly with external obedience, but in the Law of the new economy God deals with us regarding our inward response, from the heart that was circumcised by Messiah (Colossians 2:11–13) through the ministry of the Holy Spirit.

Messiah = Gifts of the Spirit

As part of the body of Messiah, we have something given to us when we were regenerated and placed into the body of Messiah: gifts of the Holy Spirit, which were unknown and unheard of in the old economy. 1 Corinthians 12:4–11 explains that it is the Holy Spirit Who gives the gifts; none of our begging or praying for a gift has any effect. God knows where we are to fit in the body and He gives gifts accordingly. We are to submit to Him, learn the gift or gifts that we have, and use those gifts to bring glory and honor to His Name. Here is a listing of gifts that God sovereignly gives (Romans 12:6–8; Ephesians 4:11; 1 Corinthians 12:7–11): (1) prophecy; (2) service; (3) teaching; (4) exhortation; (5) giving; (6) administration or leadership; (7) mercy, (8) apostleship; (9) evangelism; (10) pastor-teacher; (11) singleness; (12) wisdom; (13) knowledge; (14) faith; (15) healings; (16) miracles; (17) discernment of spirits; (18) tongues (languages); and (19) interpretation of tongues (languages).[214]

Chapter 18

In the old economy God did give gifts, but they were temporary. When the project was done, the gifting of the Holy Spirit would leave, as in the cases of Bezaleel and Othniel (Exodus 31:2–3, 28:3; Judges 3:9–10).[215] So, as you view the gifting of the Holy Spirit in both testaments, you will see the temporary nature of the gifting in the old economy, and the permanent nature of His gifting in the new economy: again, a sharp contrast between the two system.

Messiah = Christian Admonitions

Throughout the epistles, the apostles gave us commands from the Lord, and embedded in those commands and their immediate context are admonitions as to how to live this new lifestyle in Messiah to the glory and praise to God. To illustrate, in 2 Corinthians Paul gives his first and second imperative commands in 5:17 and 5:20 (in the following the imperative commands are underlined), but then look at the admonition that Paul puts in between the commands:

> 17 *Therefore, if anyone is in Messiah, he is a new creation; old things have passed away;* <u>behold</u>, *all things have become new.* 18 *And all things are of God, who has reconciled us to Himself by Yeshua Messiah, and has given to us the ministry of reconciliation;* 19 *To wit, that God was in Messiah, reconciling the world unto Himself, not imputing their trespass unto them; and has committed unto us the word of reconciliation.* 20 *Now then we are ambassadors for Messiah, as though God did beseech you by us: we pray you in Messiah's stead, be you* <u>reconciled</u> *to God.*

In verse 18, the admonition is He *has given to us the ministry of reconciliation*; in verse 19, it is He *has committed unto us the word of reconciliation*, thereby making us *ambassadors for Messiah*. Before the imperative *behold* in verse 17 is an admonition to us, reminding us that we are *a new creature* in Messiah. This is the work of the New Covenant in our regeneration; we have been reborn and reconciled to God by that ministry of the Holy Spirit. This new creation is also a reflection of the creation of man in Genesis 1:26. We are a new creation in Messiah, with a new nature, reborn as He makes us alive.

We still have two natures, one that draws us to sin and a second one that cannot sin. It is a conscious choice on our part. It all depends on what we submit to: the flesh (the sin nature in us), or the work of the Holy Spirit in our lives, by yielding to Him. In verse 20 Paul adds *be you reconciled to God* not just on a theological basis, but also on a practical, daily-living basis. The commands are there and the admonitions are also there. This is the Law of Messiah based on the foundation of love. Ephesians 4:17–20 leads up to eleven imperative commands in verses 25–31. Notice the underlined words:

> 17 *This I say therefore, and testify in the Lord, that you henceforth <u>walk not</u> as other Gentiles walk in the vanity of their mind,* 18 *Having the*[ir] *understanding darkened, being alienated from the life of God through the ignorance that is in them, because of the blindness of their heart:* 19 *Who being past feeling have given themselves over unto lasciviousness, to work all uncleanness with greediness.* 20 *But <u>you have not so learned</u> Messiah.*

Paul admonishes the Ephesians (and us) to live for Messiah and states four ways that we are not to walk as the Gentiles:

(1) first *in the vanity of the* unregenerated *mind*; (2) their *understanding darkened* because there is no light in them; (3) *alienated from the life of God through the*[ir] *ignorance*; and (4) *because of the blindness of their heart*[s]. These are the characteristics of the walking dead. We as believers are not to express these characteristics, for we have not learned to do so through Messiah. What He gives us is victory and a joyful life if we choose to submit to Him in every area of our lives.

Paul then issues eleven imperative commands related to our walk. He tells us of things to *put off* and things to *put on*, and reminds us that we are not to *grieve the Holy Spirit* Who regenerated us (New Covenant), ministers within us, and also enables us with power to overcome the sinful nature within us. The Christian has absolutely no excuse when he stands before Messiah at the Bema Seat, for it is clearly stated in Scriptures how our lives are to be lived out. Nevertheless, many believers walk just like the natural man walks, the exact opposite of what Paul commanded.

Summary

Each of the contrasts discussed in this chapter could be greatly expanded upon, and there are others that we did not touch upon. This material just give you a basic idea of the tremendous differences between the Law of Moses and the Law of Messiah. Today many in the Church, both Jewish and Gentile believers, are preoccupied with the necessity and possibility of Mosaic law observance, to varying degrees. For 20 centuries, we in the Church have not recognized the Law of Messiah that comes from the New Covenant, because the vast majority of believers have absolutely no idea of the ramifications of the New Covenant for the believer in Messiah and how that covenant relates to them.

19

THE LAW OF MESSIAH

The Law of Messiah constitutes a whole new Law, instituted not to burden believers but to release them from a system that was holy, yet unachievable. The Law of Messiah elevates us to a higher standard than can be reached and obeyed through the Law of Moses. The fact is that we will not keep the newer Law perfectly, but when we do sin we have *an advocate with the Father* in the person of Messiah (1 John 2:1), so that when *we confess our sins He is faithful and just to forgive us our sins* (1 John 1:9). The new law gives us direction and encouragement throughout our lives if we yield and surrender to the ministry of the Holy Spirit.

In this chapter I try to show some of what the Law of Messiah requires and how it functions. This is only an initial attempt to categorize the commands that we as believers are to submit to, using a sampling of verses in which Paul, Peter, James, John, and the author of Hebrews gave us information to help us see the significance of this Law to every believer and learn how to obey it. The categories that I have used will and should be revised and refined by future believers.

My purpose in focusing on the Law of Messiah is for believers from all the nations to become more aware of the commands of our Lord and His apostles. I hope to emphasize the inner character that believers are to model by the enabling power of the Holy Spirit. Messiah has given these new laws so that we can walk in Him and emulate His Law, His character, and His person in each of our lives by the power of the Holy Spirit that now resides in each and every believer. 2 Timothy 3:16 gives the following four-part classification of Scripture to accomplish His net result (verse 17):

16 *All Scripture is given by inspiration of God, and is profitable for doctrine, for reproof, for correction, for instruction in righteousness:* 17 *That the man of God may be perfect, thoroughly furnished unto all good works.*

These four areas — doctrine, reproof, correction, and instruction in righteousness — are the focal points of the epistles that set out doctrine (as Paul does in Romans when teaching the depravity of man, our justification, our sanctification, and our glorification); reprove Christians (as Paul does the Corinthians); correct (as Paul does in Galatians and the author of Hebrews does to the Jewish believers in Judea); and lastly instruct believers on how to live the Christian life (as in all the apostles' epistles). In addition, the epistles interact and interchange these subjects throughout, so each epistle serves not just purpose but several.

It is best to read this chapter with your Bible close at hand. The verses here are quoted from the New King James Version. Some are self-explanatory, but for others you will need to look at the immediate context of the verses that surround the imperative commands to grasp their full meaning. There are more than 600 imperatives in these selected passages in the Gospels that relate to the future Church, the Acts of the Apostles and the Epistles of the New Testament, which are expressed as commands. In each verse, the word corresponding to the Greek imperative command is bolded. (See the appendix for more examples of imperatives)

Christian Character

The Law of Messiah covers all areas of life, and the tone of this Law is completely different from the Law of Moses as it relates to the character of the believer. The Holy Spirit that was promised to believers is now indwelling us, filling us, sealing us, and baptizing us into the body of Messiah. Our salvation is secure because of

Messiah's finished work on the cross, which initiated the New Covenant by His blood and enable God to justify, sanctify, and reconcile us to Himself. This is the work of the Holy Spirit, Who now resides in us to guide us into all truth and teach us the Word of God, and Who will give us victory over the *old man* (our flesh) when we submit to Him.

*We **are to display** the character of Messiah by putting on Christ.* (Romans 13:14)

***Live** your life by being reconciled.* (2 Corinthians 5:20)

Do not be unequally yoked together with unbelievers. (2 Corinthians 6:14)

*Wherefore **come** out from among them and **be** ye separate.* (2 Corinthians 6:17)

***Be** complete [perfect], **be** of good comfort, **be** of one mind, **live** in peace.* (2 Corinthians 13:11)

*Therefore, putting away lying, **let** each one of you **speak** truth with his neighbor: for we are members one of another.* (Ephesians 4:25)

***Let** him that stole steal no more, but rather **let** him labor, working with his own hands.* (Ephesians 4:28)

***Let** no corrupt communication proceed from the mouth but that which is good to the use of edifying.* (Ephesians 4:29)

***Let** all bitterness, and wrath, and anger, and clamor and evil speaking be put away from you, with all malice.* (Ephesians 4:31)

***Be** you kind one to another, tenderhearted, forgiving one another, even as God for Christ's sake has forgiven you.* (Ephesians 4:32)

Do *all things without complaining and disputing.* (Philippians 2:14)

Mortify *[put to death] therefore your members: fornication, uncleanness, passion, evil desire, and covetousness, which is idolatry.* (Colossians 3:5)

Put *off all these: anger, wrath, malice, blasphemy, filthy language out of your mouth.* (Colossians 3:8)

Do not ***lie*** *to one another, seeing that you have put off the old man with his deeds.* (Colossians 3:9)

Put *on therefore, as the elect of God, holy and beloved, tender mercies, kindness, humbleness of mind, meekness, longsuffering.* (Colossians 3:12)

Abstain *from all appearance of evil.* (1 Thessalonians 5:22)

But ***refuse*** *profane and fables, and* ***exercise*** *yourself rather unto godliness.* (1 Timothy 4:7)

Let *everyone that names the Name of Messiah depart from iniquity.* (2 Timothy 2:19)

Flee *youthful desires [lust] but pursue righteousness.* (2 Timothy 2:22)

Learn *to maintain good works ... that they not be unfruitful.* (Titus 3:14)

Pursue *peace with all men.* (Hebrews 12:14)

Don't ***forget*** *to do good.* (Hebrews 13:16)

Therefore, ***get rid*** *of all moral filth and the evil that is so prevalent and humbly receive with meekness the implanted word.* (James 1:21 [NIV])

Be *doers of the word and not hearers only.* (James 1:22)

Let *him turn away from evil, and* ***do*** *good;* ***let*** *him* ***seek*** *peace and* ***pursue*** *it.* (1 Peter 3:11)

Do *not* ***be afraid*** *of their threats.* (James 3:14)

Let *him* ***show*** *by good conduct that his works are done in meekness.* (James 3:13)

If you have bitter envying and strife in your hearts, ***glory*** *not, and* ***do not lie*** *against the truth.* (James 3:14)

Purify *your hearts, you double minded.* (James 4:8)

Do not speak *evil of one another.* (James 4:11)

Do not grumble *against one another.* (James 5:9)

Keep *your oath that you swore,* ***let*** *your yes be yes, and your no be no; lest you fall into condemnation.* (James 5:12)

And if you address as Father the One who impartially judges according to each man's work, ***conduct*** *yourselves in fear during the time of your stay upon earth.* (1 Peter 1:17)

Sanctify *the Lord God in your hearts: and* ***be ready*** *always to give an answer to every man that asks you a reason of the hope that is in you with meekness and fear.* (1 Peter 3:15)

But the end of all things is at hand: ***be*** *serious* [sober] *and watchful in your prayers.* (1 Peter 4:7)

Now that you have read these directives, think: How well have you done in fulfilling the Law of Messiah in your daily life? Notice the inward nature of this Law of Messiah that we are obligated to do (1 John 2:6). Remember, we do not do these things to receive God's favor; rather, we do them because we have been blessed with every spiritual blessing in Messiah

(Ephesians 1:3). All of that relates back to the New Covenant and everything that Yeshua did for us on the cross of Calvary by the shedding of His blood. The writer of Hebrews says we do not want to be accused of treading underfoot the precious blood of Messiah as a worthless thing (Hebrews 10:29). Do we care? It should be very important to us.

Christian Liberty

With Christian liberty, you are expressing love to your neighbor; this is the foundational commandment of our Lord. Such love is expressed to a fellow believer who is not as far along spiritually as you are. For example, there are things in his life experience before he was saved that are now stumbling blocks for him, sin for him to commit, whereas for us those things are not sin and it does not bother us to do them. In such a situation, we exercise love for our brother by personally withdrawing from an event or not participating in something in deference to our brother; this is called Christian liberty. Notice that the passages in Romans and 1 Corinthians relate to your Christian liberty being exercised in the Law of Messiah. Remember that foundational love statement of Messiah in John 13:34–35:

> 34 *A new commandment I give unto you, that you love one another; as I have loved you, that you also love one another.*
> 35 *By this shall all men know that you are my disciples, if you have love one to another.*

If you violate this new commandment of Messiah's Law, you are sinning in two ways. First, you have violated a direct command from your Savior. Second, you are potentially destroying another brother for whom Messiah equally died by causing that brother to stumble.

The context here has to do with meat offered to idols and then sold in the marketplace. The underlying principle has many applications in today's culture.

Let *not him who eats **despise** him who does not eat, and **let** not him who does not eat **judge** him who eats.* (Romans 14:3)

*Therefore **let** us not judge one another anymore, but rather **resolve** this, not to **put** a stumbling block or a cause to fall in our brother's way.* (Romans 14:13)

Do not destroy *with your food the one for whom Messiah died.* (Romans 14:15)

*Therefore **do not let** your good be spoken of as evil.* (Romans 14:16)

Do not destroy *the work of God for the sake of food.* (Romans 14:20)

*But **beware** lest somehow this liberty of yours become a stumbling block to those who are weak.* (1 Corinthians 8:9)

Let *no one seek his own, but each one the other's well-being.* (1 Corinthians 10:24)

Eat *whatever is sold in the meat markets.* (1 Corinthians 10:25)

Eat *whatever is set before you, asking no question for conscience' sake.* (1 Corinthians 10:27)

*But if anyone says to you, this was offered to idols, **do not eat** it for the conscience' sake of the one who told you.* (1 Corinthians 10:28)

Whether you eat or drink, do all to the glory of God. (1 Corinthians 10:31)

Stand fast *therefore in the liberty wherewith Messiah has made us freed, and **do not be entangled** again with a yoke of bondage.* (Galatians 5:1)

Chapter 19

How much spiritual sensitivity have you shown in relation to another brother fulfilling the Law of Messiah?

Christian Home and Marriage

Today the home is a strategic area in a sin-filled world, where divorce is accepted, adultery is accepted, pornography in print and on the Internet is accepted, and homosexuality and lesbianism are now protected under the law of the land. We live in a sexually perverted society. Now more than ever, Christians should highlight godly, happy marriages in which both partners exercise their calling in marriage: to be an example to a world that has lost sight of the fulfillment for both sexes in marriage, by fulfilling the Law of Messiah and displaying the interdependence of husband and wife. The home today is often a disgrace to God as Christians operate in a self-centered worldly mold. Remember, we are bondservants of the Lord: we have no rights. All is in relation to our Lord, not to self-will or desires! In this section we look at the Law of Messiah regarding men (husbands), women (wives), and the parenting of children.

Men (husbands), you are the responsible head of your home, your wife, and your children; you are responsible for meeting not just the physical needs of your family, but also the spiritual needs of your family. Many Christian men today have abdicated their spiritual responsibility in the home for the temporary pleasures of this world. They often allow their children to control the home according to what they want to do, rather than the father exercising his God-given responsibility. Paul addressed many words to men in 1 Corinthians, Ephesians, and Colossians. Again, these are commands and a part of the Law of Messiah, specifically as it relates to men and their relationship before God and their family.

Nevertheless, to avoid fornication, ***let*** *each man have his own wife.* (1 Corinthians 7:2)

Let *the husband render to his wife the affection due her.* (1 Corinthians 7:3)

***Do not deprive** one another except with consent for a time.* (1 Corinthians 7:5)

*But if they cannot exercise self-control, **let** them marry.* (1 Corinthians 7:9)

*Are you bound to a wife? **Do not seek** to be loosed. Are you loosed from a wife? **Do not seek** a wife.* (1 Corinthians 7:27)

*But if any man is behaving improperly toward his virgin, if she is past the flower of youth, and thus it must be, **let** him do what he wishes; he does not sin; let them marry.* (1 Corinthians 7:36)

*Husbands, **love** your wives even as Messiah also loved the church, and gave Himself for it.* (Ephesians 5:25)

*Nevertheless **let** each one of you in particular so **love** his own wife as himself.* (Ephesians 5:33)

*Husbands, **love** your wives and **do not be bitter** toward them.* (Colossians 3:19)

Other than the Lord, is your love focused on your wife alone? We men tend to be insensitive to the heart needs of the wife; we need to exercise the same agape love that He did for us. Again, the Law of Messiah deals with a man's heart attitude toward his wife. Is that your focus as you walk with the Lord in His guidance and direction through the indwelling presence of the Holy Spirit in your marriage relationship?

Women (wives), you are to submit to your husband, for he is your head. Your responsibility is to honor and respect your husband (1 Peter 3:1–6). Women may recoil at this statement. This is not an issue for men, as they have to be in submission daily at work, so they submit, but in the home it is the wife who is to submit. Men must not abuse their position in the family, but as Peter said, give honor lest your prayers be hindered (1 Peter 3:7). Women as mothers are to stay home if possible and instill in the lives of their children a biblical worldview. Here are a few things that a believing women should remember.

Let *each woman have her own husband.* (1 Corinthians 7:2)

Let *the husband render to his wife the affection due her and likewise also the wife to her husband.* (1 Corinthians 7:3)

But even if she does depart, ***let*** *her remain unmarried or* ***be*** *reconciled to her husband.* (1 Corinthians 7:11)

And a woman who has a husband who does not believe, if he is willing to live with her, ***let her not divorce*** *him.* (1 Corinthians 7:13)

But if the unbeliever departs, ***let*** *him depart; a brother or a sister is not under bondage in such cases.* (1 Corinthians 7:15)

Wives, ***submit*** *to your own husbands, as to the Lord.* (Ephesians 5:22)

Wives, ***submit*** *to your own husbands, as is fitting in the Lord.* (Colossians 3:18)

There are many more admonitions in the Scriptures that apply to the husband-and-wife relationship. Men, how well do you love (*agape*, self sacrificial love) your wife before the Lord? Women, how well do you respond to your husband in honor?

Christian Woman in the Church

A woman's place in the church is often a very challenging and confrontational issue for Christian women and men. Women are never referred to as pastors and leaders in the Church. Leadership is given to men both in the home and in the church. Women have leadership positions over the women and children in the Church under the oversight of spiritual men in the Church. This is a hot-button issue today for two reasons.

First, the ideas of the secular women's liberation movement, stating that women are equal to men, have permeated the Church, leading some to argue that women can function in the Church just like men. Women are equal to men spiritually before God. But, in the local church and the home, God has set up male leadership. In Luke 2:52 you will find that Jesus, as a youth, submitted Himself to Mary and Joseph, who were actually his inferiors. This illustrates that submission has absolutely nothing to do with superiority and inferiority, but everything to do with being obedient in your position.

The second problem, which has exasercbated the first issue, is the attitude and actions of men who use their authority to abuse women. You can be sure that at the Bema Seat of Messiah, many of the works of male oppression and inequality in action and word will not garner any reward; they will be wood, hay, and stubble to be burned up. Men, examine your position before God and be responsible for obeying the biblical commands and admonitions that the Scriptures have given you to obey.

***Let** the woman keep silent in the churches.*
(1 Corinthians 14:34)

*If they [women] want to learn... **let** them ask their own husbands at home.* (1 Corinthians 14:35)

*For if a woman is not covered, **let** her also **be shorn**. But if it is shameful for a woman to be shorn or shaved, **let** her **be covered**.* (1 Corinthians 11:6)

***Judge** among yourselves. Is it proper for a woman to pray to God with her head uncovered?* (1 Corinthians 11:13)

Chapter 19

Christian Parenting

Fathers, here is another responsibility for you: being reasonable and patient with your children. It is also your responsibility to train your children in the Scriptures in the home. It is not the church's responsibility, it is yours. The desired result is that your children who have seen your example demonstrated before them in their childhood will love the Lord their God when they become adults with their own families.

*Fathers, **do not provoke** your children to wrath: **Bring** them up in the training and admonition of the Lord.* (Ephesians 6:4)

*Fathers, **do not provoke** your children, lest they become discouraged.* (Colossians 3:21)

Many children have had their lives destroyed by fathers who scarred them physically, emotionally, and spiritually. So men, be biblical and godly and stand tall before the Lord in the future: you are to instill in your children wisdom and the ability to use that wisdom when they become adults with their own families.

Children are to obey their parents; the hope is that in the future they will walk in Christ and have had a model for their own families. Parents, if you do not teach your children human authority and responsibility, it will be very hard for them to learn to listen to and obey our heavenly Father.

*Children, **obey** your parents in the Lord, for this is right.* (Ephesians 6:1)

***Honor** your father and mother, which is the first commandment with promise.* (Ephesians 6:2)

*Children, **obey** your parents in all things, for this is well pleasing to the Lord.* (Colossians 3:20)

Many children today show great dishonor and disrespect for their parents. Even as adults, many children dishonor their parents in how they speak to them and how they treat them. Parents, remember that you are an example to your children, so if you want honor from your children, show them how to honor you by honoring your own parents. You might say that your parents don't deserve honor. The Law of Messiah states we <u>are</u> to honor our parents, whether you think they deserve it or not.

Christian Employee or Employer

The Law of Messiah lays out guidelines for both employers and employees. Employers are to be fair and treat their workers honorably, paying fair wages and treating their workers with respect. They are to be obedient and serve their employees well; and the same is true for employees as they work for their employer. Notice, in the book of Philemon, how Paul encourages and gives honor to both the slave (employee) and the master (employer).

Employers (Masters):

*And you masters, **do** the same things to them, giving up threatening.* (Ephesians 6:9)

*Master, **give** your bondservants what is just and fair.* (Colossians 4:1)

*You therefore **receive** him, that is, my own heart.* (Philemon 12)

***Receive** him as you would me.* (Philemon 17)

*If he has wronged you or owes anything, **put** that on my account.* (Philemon 18)

*Yes, brother, **let** me have joy from you; refresh my heart.* (Philemon 20)

Indeed, the wages of the laborers who reaped your fields, which of you kept back [wages] *by fraud, their cries reach the ears of God.* (James 5:4)

Employees (Slaves):

Servants, **be** *obedient to those who are your masters.* (Ephesians 6:5)

Servants, **obey** *in all things your masters according to the flesh.* (Colossians 3:22)

Let *as many bondservants as are under the yoke* **count** *their own masters worthy of all honor.* (1 Timothy 6:1)

And those who have believing masters, **let** *them not despise them, because they are brethren, but rather* **serve** *them because those who are benefited are believers and beloved.* (1 Timothy 6:2)

Christian Walk

Many books could be written on the subject of the Christian walk. Here I only give a few examples for believers who put their focus on walking in Christ and not the world system. The instructions given in these verses have no counterpart in the Law of Moses; they are unique to the New Commandment and the Law of Messiah. Basically, our walk consists of being an example to other believers, being dead to sin, and not letting sin reign in our bodies. The imperative commands in these verses (among others) show how we are to walk.

Reckon *yourselves to be dead indeed to sin.* (Romans 6:11)

Therefore **do not let** *sin reign in your mortal body.* (Romans 6:12)

Do not present *your members as instruments of unrighteousness to sin.* (Romans 6:13)

*But **present** yourselves to God as being alive from the dead.* (Romans 6:13)

***Present** your members as slaves of Righteousness.* (Romans 6:19)

***Do not boast** against the branches.* (Romans 11:18)

*Therefore **let** no one boast in men.* (1 Corinthians 3:21)

*Therefore I urge you, **imitate** me* [Paul]. (1 Corinthians 4:16)

***Become** like me* [Paul]. (Galatians 4:12)

Integrity: Concerning things which I write to you, indeed, before God, I do not lie. (Galatians 1:20)

***Walk** in the Spirit.* (Galatians 5:16)

*Therefore **be** imitators of God as dear children.* (Ephesians 5:1)

***Walk** in Love.* (Ephesians 5:2)

***Walk** as children of light.* (Ephesians 5:8)

***See** that you **walk** circumspectly, not as fools, but as wise.* (Ephesians 5:15)

*The things which you learned, received, heard and saw in me, these **do**.* (Philippians 4:9)

*As you have therefore received Messiah Yeshua the Lord, so **walk** in Him.* (Colossians 2:6)

***Walk** in wisdom toward them that are without, redeeming the time.* (Colossians 4:5)

***Arm** yourselves also with the same mind as Messiah.* (1 Peter 4:1)

Chapter 19

> **Behold** *what manner of love the Father has bestowed on us, that we should be called the sons of God.* (1 John 3:1)

In the old economy there is nothing like these commands, because here we are dealing with the inner motivation of the heart, which has a direct connection to the New Covenant. These commands are more of the Law of Messiah that all believers are to live by daily.

Christian Position in Life

Are you happy with your position in life? Are you happy with yourself and your talents (or lack of them)? Are you content with your job? It took me 50 years to figure this out, but now I am completely content with who I am. The Scriptures state that we are to be content in whatever state we are in, as these verses show.

> *As the Lord has called each one, so **let** him walk.* (1 Corinthians 7:17)

> ***Let** each one remain in the same calling in which he was called.* (1 Corinthians 7:20)

> ***Let** each one remain with God in the state in which he was called.* (1 Corinthians 7:24)

You must be content with yourself, with all your shortcomings. You are responsible to be faithful stewards of what He has given you and your position in life. I completely concur with the admonition of Paul:

> *Therefore, the prisoner of the Lord, beseech you that you walk worthy of the vocation wherewith you are called.* (Ephesians 4:1).

On a personal note, at 73 years of age, this whole section has become very important to me in being content. On my dresser I have a plaque that encourages me to press on and not retire, living

for Him with the abilities He has given to me: "You are never too old to set another goal or to dream a new dream."
—C. S. Lewis

Christian Practice

How do you practice your faith? That is, how do you live out your faith? Is it according to the Law of Messiah? Do you understand the working of the Holy Spirit in your life, Who regenerated you to walk in the newness of life on a daily basis in Messiah? How wonderful it would be if we as believers would only grasp the *unfathomable riches of His grace* to us, and then walk in it and let it be our character—actually, His character in and through us. Here are some imperative commands for us to abide by:

That no flesh should glory in His presence. But of him are you in Messiah Yeshua, who of God is made unto wisdom, and righteousness, and sanctification, and redemption: That, according as it is written, He that glories, **let him glory** *in the Lord.* (1 Corinthians 1:29 31; 2 Corinthians 10:17)

Therefore **judge** *nothing before the time, until the Lord comes, Who both will bring to light the hidden things of darkness, and will make manifest the counsels of the hearts: and then shall every man have praise of God.* (1 Corinthians 4:5)

For you are bought with a price: therefore **glorify** *God in your body, and in your spirit, which are God's.* (1 Corinthians 6:20)

You are bought with a price; **do not become** *slaves to human beings.* (1 Corinthians 7:23)

Don't complain [or **murmur**], *as some of them also murmured and were destroyed of the destroyer.* (1 Corinthians 10:10)

Therefore **let** *him who thinks he stands take heed lest he fall.* (1 Corinthians 10:12)

Chapter 19

Give *no offense, neither to the Jews, nor to the Gentiles, nor to the church of God.* (1 Corinthians 10:32)

If any man love not the Lord Yeshua Messiah, ***let*** *him* ***be*** *Anathema Maranatha* [curse]. (1 Corinthians 16:22)

Examine *yourselves whether you* ***be*** *in the faith.* (2 Corinthians 13:5)

Bear *you one another's burdens, and* ***do*** *fulfill the Law of Messiah.* (Galatians 6:2)

For if a man think himself to be something, when he is nothing, he deceives himself. But ***let*** *every man examine* [prove] *your own work.* (Galatians 6:4)

Let *no one trouble me: for I bear in my body the marks of the Lord Yeshua.* (Galatians 6:17)

Let *this Mind be in you, which was also in Messiah Yeshua.* (Philippians 2:5)

Be *careful for nothing: but in everything by prayer and supplication with thanksgiving let your requests be made known unto God.* (Philippians 4:6)

Finally, brethren, whatsoever things are true, honest, just, pure, lovely, good ***report***; *if there be any virtue, and if there be any praise,* ***Meditate*** *on these things.* (Philippians 4:8)

If you then be risen with Messiah, ***seek*** *those things which are above.* (Colossians 3:1)

Set *your affection [mind] on things above, not on things on the earth.* (Colossians 3:2)

Peace of God ***rule*** *in your hearts, to the which also you are called into one body,* ***be*** *thankful.* (Colossians 3:15)

Let *the word of Messiah dwell in you richly in all wisdom; teaching and admonishing one another in psalms and hymns and spiritual songs, singing with grace in your hearts to the Lord.* (Colossians 3:16)

And whatsoever you do, ***do*** *heartily to the Lord, and not unto man.* (Colossians 3:23)

Be *at peace among yourselves.* (1 Thessalonians 5:13)

Warn *them that are unruly,* ***uphold*** *the weak,* ***be*** *patient with all men.* (1 Thessalonians 5:14)

Pursue *what is good.* (1 Thessalonians 5:15)

In everything ***give*** *thanks.* (1 Thessalonians 5:18)

Test *all things; hold fast that which is good.* (1 Thessalonians 5:21)

Humble *yourselves in the sight of the Lord, and He shall lift you up.* (James 4:10)

Humble *yourselves under the mighty hand of God.* (1 Peter 5:6)

Add *to your faith virtue; and to virtue knowledge; and to knowledge temperance; and to temperance patience; and to patience godliness; and to godliness brotherly kindness; and to brotherly kindness love.* (2 Peter 1:5)

But ***grow*** *in the grace and knowledge of our Lord and Saviour Yeshua Messiah.* (2 Peter 3:18)

Remember *the words which were spoken before of the Apostles.* (Jude 17)

These are commands of the Law of Messiah that we are to follow in our daily lives as true believers in Messiah who are walking in the Spirit. How is your walk? How many of these commands have you disobeyed? Do you take obedience seriously, or ignore it, or simply lay it aside?

Christian Giving

Our manner of giving is from the heart as God has prospered us. The Law of Messiah demands no tithe; instead, we are instructed simply to lay aside and give to the work of the Lord. No percentages or amounts are set. You are just to give as God has prospered you. The first verse is a command and the second verse is an admonition:

> *Collection for the saints, **do** also ... first day **lay** something aside.* (1 Corinthians 16:1, 2)

> *Every man according as he purposed in his heart, so **let him give**; not grudgingly, or of necessity: for God loves a cheerful giver.* (2 Corinthians 9:7)

Among other things, this means you should not give funds to prosperity preachers, who call it "seed money." They are milking you while they become wealthy at your expense. What they are doing is immoral and God will judge them. Be good stewards of your giving and, as much as is humanly possible, see that the organizations and missionaries you support are faithful themselves.

Christians and Government

Because the Church is not Israel, we are individual members of the body of Messiah. We are also individual citizens of the countries on the earth. The earthly laws vary from country to country, so in the Law of Messiah, the Lord has given us instruction as to how we should treat our government; that is, how we can honor and conduct ourselves in each individual country. We are to obey the law of the land unless it tells us to violate our biblical beliefs. Verses from Paul and Peter, who were killed for their belief in

Messiah by a corrupt pagan government, illustrate these points.

__Let__ every soul be subject to the governing authorities. (Romans 13:1)

__Do__ what is good, and you will have praise from the same. (Romans 13:3)

But if you do evil, __be__ afraid; for he [government official] *does not bear the sword in vain.* (Romans 13:4)

__Render__ therefore to all their dues; tribute to whom tribute is due; custom to whom custom; fear to whom fear; honor to whom honor. (Romans 13:7)

__Honor__ the King [or President]. (1 Peter 2:17)

__Submit__ yourselves to every ordinance of man for the Lord's sake; whether it be to the king, a supreme; or unto governors, as unto them that are sent by him for the punishment of evildoers, and for the praise of them that do well. (1 Peter 2:13–14)

If you live under a wicked government, such as North Korea or Iran, for example, you can be severely persecuted or killed merely for being a Christian. As America drifts from its Christian foundations, it is more likely that we can be imprisoned for speaking out against certain groups and sins. The Law of Messiah does not protect us from wicked countries, wicked earthly laws, wicked officials, or wicked judges, so we must be willing to stand fast in Him.

Christian Prayer

Prayer is a very important component of a Christian life. The Lord speaks to us through the teaching ministry of the Holy Spirit using the written Word of God. The Bible is God speaking to man and our response is communicating with God through prayer. In the Law of Messiah, Paul, Peter, and James give us commands in relationship to our prayer life.

> *Be careful for nothing, but in everything by prayer and supplication, with thanksgiving, **let** your requests be made known to God.* (Philippians 4:6)
>
> ***Continue** earnestly in prayer, being vigilant in it with thanksgiving.* (Colossians 4:2)
>
> ***Pray** without ceasing.* (1 Thessalonians 5:17)
>
> *Brethren, **pray for us** [Christian leadership].* (1 Thessalonians 5:25)
>
> *Finally, brethren, **pray** for us, that the word of the Lord may have free course, and be glorified.* (2 Thessalonians 3:1)
>
> ***Pray** for us; for we are confident that we have a good conscience.* (Hebrews 13:18)
>
> *Is anyone among you suffering? **Let** him pray.* (James 5:13)
>
> Pray for one another. (James 5:16)
>
> *Therefore be serious and watchful in your prayers.* (1 Peter 4:7)

Today in America, local churches are abandoning prayer for reasons of self-interest, or pleasure, or convenience. We need to focus solely on God, for He is our power and strength, not the government or a political party. Given the massive problems this country is facing, only with repentance and spiritual intercession to God will we get lasting results. Only through prayer and Christians living out their daily walk in obedience to the Law of Messiah is there hope for our country, our society, and our families.

Christian Leadership in the Church

In the Church there are no kings, no priests or popes. Our head is Christ, the Messiah; He alone is our Mediator and High Priest. We are not under bishops, cardinals, or apostles today. We are under Messiah. Biblically, each church is under Messiah and is responsible to Him. Each church is to be self-governing and not controlled by synods, presbyters, or conventions. Each individual church depends on the leadership of the elders for spiritual oversight. The pastor or teaching elder takes on the responsibility of teaching the Word of God to that local church. You will find that Paul gives a clear standard for elders, for they are not just filling an opening. The position is to be filled with a spiritual qualified man. Consider the guidelines that Paul gave to young Timothy and Titus as they pastored a local church:

*Therefore **take heed** to yourselves and to all the flock, among which the Holy Spirit has made you overseers.* (Acts 20:28)

*These things **command** and teach.* (1 Timothy 4:11)

***Let** no one despise your youth; but **be** an example of the believers, in word, in manner of living, in love, in spirit, in faith, in purity.* (1 Timothy 4:12)

*Till I come, **give** attention to reading, to exhortation, to doctrine.* (1 Timothy 4:13)

***Do not neglect** the gift that is in you.* (1 Timothy 4:14)

***Meditate** on these things and give yourself entirely to them.* (1 Timothy 4:15)

***Take heed** to yourself and to the doctrine, continue in them.* (1 Timothy 4:16)

***Do not rebuke** an older man, but **exhort** him as a father.* (1 Timothy 5:1)

*And these things **command**, that they may be blameless.* (1 Timothy 5:7)

***Let** the elders who rule well **be** counted worthy of double honor.* (1 Timothy 5:17)

***Do not receive** an accusation against an elder except from two or three witnesses.* (1 Timothy 5:19)

*Those who are sinning **rebuke** in the presence of all, that others also may fear.* (1 Timothy 5:20)

***Do not lay hands** on anyone hastily, nor share in other people's sins: keep yourself pure.* (1 Timothy 5:22)

***Let** as many servants as are under the yoke **count** their own masters worthy of all honour, that the Name of God and His doctrine be not blasphemed. And they that have believing masters, **let** them not **despise** them, because they are brethren; but rather **do** them service, because they are faithful and beloved, partakers of the benefit. These **teach** and **exhort** these things.* (1 Timothy 6:1–2)

*Perverse disputings of men of corrupt minds, and destitute of the truth, supposing that gain is godliness: from such **withdraw** yourself.* (1 Timothy 6:5)

***Flee** these things and **pursue** righteousness, godliness, faith, love, patience, gentleness.* (1 Timothy 6:11)

***Fight** the good fight of faith, **lay** hold on eternal life.* (1 Timothy 6:12)

***Command** those who are rich in this present age not to **be** high-minded, nor **trust** in uncertain riches, but in the living God.* (1 Timothy 6:17)

***Guard** what was committed to your trust.* (1 Timothy 6:20)

Hold fast *the pattern of sound words which you have heard from me.* (2 Timothy 1:13)

Keep *by the Holy Spirit who dwells in us.* (2 Timothy 1:14)

Be strong *in the grace that is in Messiah Yeshua.* (2 Timothy 2:1)

Commit *these to faithful men who will be able to teach others also.* (2 Timothy 2:2)

Consider *what I say; and the Lord give you understanding in all things.* (2 Timothy 2:7)

Remind *them of these things.* (2 Timothy 2:14)

Be diligent [study] *to present yourself approved to God.* (2 Timothy 2:15)

But **shun** *profane and idle babblings.* (2 Timothy 2:16)

Flee *also youthful lust: but* **follow** *righteousness, faith, love, peace, with them that call on the Lord out of a pure heart.* (2 Timothy 2:22)

But **continue** *in the things which you have learned.* (2 Timothy 3:14)

Preach *the word,* **be ready** *in season and out of season,* **convince, rebuke, exhort,** *with all longsuffering and teaching.* (2 Timothy 4:2)

But **be watchful** *in all things,* **endure** *afflictions,* **do** *the work of an evangelist,* **fulfill** *your ministry.* (2 Timothy 4:5)

You also must **beware** *of him, for he has greatly resisted our words.* (2 Timothy 4:15)

Chapter 19

Speak *the things which are proper for sound doctrine.* (Titus 2:1)

Exhort *the young men to be sober minded.* (Titus 2:6)

Speak *these things,* **exhort***, and* **rebuke** *with all authority,* **let** *no one despise you.* (Titus 2:15)

But **avoid** *foolish disputes, genealogies, contentions, and striving against the law; for they are unprofitable and vain.* (Titus 3:9)

Reject *a divisive man after the first and second admonition.* (Titus 3:10)

Remember *those in the church who rule over you,* **follow** *them faithfully.* (Hebrews 13:7)

Is any sick, **call** *for the elders.* (James 5:14)

Shepherd *the flock of God which is among you, serving as overseers.* (1 Peter 5:2)

Here are some admonitions of Paul concerning elders:
If any be blameless, the husband of one wife, having faithful children not accused of riot or unruliness, For a bishop **must be blameless***, as the steward of God; not self-willed, not soon angry, not given to wine, no striker, not given to filthy lucre; but a lover of hospitality, a lover of good men, sober, just, holy, temperate; Holding fast the faithful word as he has been taught, that he may be able by sound doctrine both to exhort and to convince the gainsayers.* (Titus 1:6–9)

A bishop then **must be blameless***, the husband of one wife, vigilant, sober, of good behavior, given to hospitality, apt to teach; not given to wine, no striker, not greedy of filthy lucre, but patient, not a brawler, not covetous; One that rules well his own house, having his children in subjection with all gravity; not a novice, lest being lifted up with pride he fall* *into the condemnation of the devil. Moreover he must have a good report of them which are without.* (1 Timothy 3:2–7)

There are also a few statements on deacons, and then an admonition from Paul to Timothy.

Brethren, **seek** *out from among you seven men of good reputation.* (Acts 6:3)

But **let** *these also first* **be tested***, then* **let** *them* **serve** *as deacons.* (1 Timothy 3:10)

Let *deacons* **be** *the husbands of one wife.* (1 Timothy 3:12)

Likewise **must the deacons be grave***, not double tongued, not given to much wine, not greedy of filthy lucre; holding the mystery of the faith in a pure conscience. And* **let** *these also first* **be** *proved; then* **let** *them use the office of a deacon, being found blameless. Even so* **must their wives be** *grave, not slanderers, sober, faithful in all things.* **Let** *the deacons* **be** *the husbands of one wife, ruling their children and their own houses well.* (1 Timothy 3:8–12)

Church Discipline

In Matthew 18:15–19, Yeshua lays down the procedure for church discipline—yet most churches do not follow the commands of Yeshua. Here are the commands, step by step.

Moreover if your brother sins against you, **go** *and tell him his fault.* (Matthew 18:15)

But if he will not hear, **take** *with you one or two more, that in the mouth of two or three witnesses every word may* **be** *established.* (Matthew 18:16)

And if he refuses to hear them, tell it to the church: but if he neglects to hear the church, **let** *him* **be** *to you like a heathen and a tax collector.* (Matthew 18:17)

*Those who are sinning **rebuke** in the presence of all.*
(1 Timothy 5:20)

*If any man obey not our word by this epistle, **note** that man, and **do not keep** company with him.* (2 Thessalonians 3:14)

*Yet **count** him not as an enemy, but **admonish** him as a brother.* (2 Thessalonians 3:15)

***Do not despise** the discipline of the Lord.* (Hebrew 12:5)

God will exercise discipline on rebellious believers as He did with Ananias and Sapphira in Acts 5. Hebrews 12 tells believers not to despise the chastening of the Lord. God, in His own way, will chastise or discipline believers if they walk contrary to the Law of Messiah.

Lord's Table

The Lord's Table, also called the Communion Service, is one of the ordinances of the Church, and the Apostle Paul gives instructions on doing it. He also references the Last Passover that Yeshua participated in regarding the use of the bread and the cup. Here are some of Paul's instructions.

***Take** and eat, this is My body which is broken for you: this **do** in remembrance of Me.* (1 Corinthians 11:24)

***Do** this in remembrance of Me.* (1 Corinthians 11:25)

***Let** a man examine himself as he eats of the bread, **let** a man examine himself as he drinks of the cup.* (1 Corinthians 11:28)

***Wait** on each other.* (1 Corinthians 11:33)

*If hungry **eat** at home.* (1 Corinthians 11:34)

In repeating the words of Yeshua, in remembrance of Me, what are we, as believers, to remember? First, the unleavened bread (Jewish matzo) represents His body which was striped or scourged, and pierced in our place. The matzo that is taken also is the Jewish *afikoman*, signifying that we have been released from the power and penalty of sin. The cup represents His blood, the blood of the New Covenant. The New Covenant is the instrument that Yeshua used to have us regenerated by the indwelling ministry of the Holy Spirit when we believed. This expression of the bread and cup are briefly presented in our Communion Services and show an elementary understanding of exactly what Yeshua accomplished on the cross.

Christian Service and Rewards

As believers, we are to bring glory to God's Name in our service for Him. Our service must be in harmony with the Law of Messiah in all respects. Rewards are given to those in Christ who have served Him while *walking in the Spirit* and *walking in Christ.* You can be doing good deeds for Christ, but if you do them in the flesh, they are wood, hay and stubble. Several verses deal with service and rewards.

> ***Know*** *you not that they which* ***run*** *in a race run all, but one receives the prize? So run, that you may obtain. And every man that strives for the mastery is temperate in all things. Now they do it to obtain a corruptible crown: but we an incorruptible.* (1 Corinthians 9:24–25)

> ***Let*** *no one cheat or beguile you of your rewards.* (Colossians 2:18)

> ***Knowing*** *that of the Lord you shall receive the reward of the inheritance: for you serve the Lord Messiah.* (Colossians 3:24)

> *Take heed and* ***fulfill*** *your field of service.* (Colossians 4:17)

> *God will not forget our work and labor of love shown toward His name.* (Hebrews 6:10)

Look *to yourselves, that you may receive a reward.* (2 John 8)

Christian Obedience in Ministry

Are we obedient to the promptings of God? In 2 Corinthians 3:6, Paul states that all believers are *ministers of the New Covenant,* and in 2 Corinthians 5:17–20 he continues to teach that we have the *word of reconciliation* and the *ministry of reconciliation* to a lost world. We are all in the ministry for our Lord. Do we obey as Peter, John, Philip, and Ananias did? These commands are in the book of Acts, as Luke gives them to us.

Go, stand *in the temple and* **speak** *to the people all the words of this life.* (Acts 5:20)

Go *near and* **overtake** *this chariot.* (Acts 8:29)

Arise *and go into the city, and you will be told what you must do.* (Acts 9:6)

Arise *and* **go** *to the street called Straight, and* **inquire** *at the house of Judas for one called Saul of Tarsus,* **behold***, he is praying.* (Acts 9:11)

Go*, for he is a chosen vessel of Mine to bear My name before Gentiles.* (Acts 9:15)

Arise *and* **make** *your bed.* (Acts 9:34)

Gird *yourself and* **tie** *on your sandals.* (Acts 12:8)

Put *on your garment and* **follow** *me.* (Acts 12:8)

Separate *to Me Barnabas and Saul the work to which I have called them.* (Acts 13:2)

Do not be afraid, *but* **speak***, and* **do not keep silent***.* (Acts 18:9)

Your calling may not be as direct as those depicted in the book of Acts, but many believers know they have been called to serve and yet withdraw themselves in disobedience. We are to go and evangelize and teach sound doctrine to unbelievers.

Christian Separation

In the old economy under the Law of Moses, Israel was to be separate and distinct from the pagan nations around them. In the new economy of grace, we are also to be a separate and distinct people, but we who have believed in Yeshua are from many nations. Now we are to be separate from the world system that we live in by being obedient to the Law of Messiah, which transcends the limited provisions made for Israel under the old law. However, what we see today in the Church are multitudes of Christians who are currently not separating themselves from the pagan world system around them. Many are living in church ritualism and tradition instead of living by the commands given to us in the New Testament and the Law of Messiah which comes out of His New Covenant. Commands regarding our separation come from the Apostles Paul, Peter, and John.

Do not be partakers with the world. (Ephesians 5:7)

Have *no fellowship with darkness.* (Ephesians 5:11)

Be holy *in all your conduct.* (1 Peter 1:15)

Be holy, *for I am holy.* (1 Peter 1:16)

Do not love *the world, neither the things that are in the world. If any man love the world, the love of the Father is not in him.* (1 John 2:15)

If there come any unto you, and bring this doctrine (see verse 9), **do not receive** *him into your house, neither* **bid** *him God's speed or greet him.* (2 John 10)

How do we measure up to the Law of Messiah? Separation of believers from the world is a very real problem in the church today, as more and more worldly matters are incorporated into the Church and into the lives of individual believers. Instead of separating from the world, the Church has become rich and in need of nothing (Revelation 3:17), but its power to affect the lives of unbelievers has been greatly tarnished and reduced.

Christian Spiritual Warfare

In the old economy, there is no correlate to the commands regarding spiritual warfare. As Christians, we often live in a world against which we have no defenses, and all too often the only offensive weapon has been to throw our sword, our bible aside. By not obeying the Law of Messiah, we have made ourselves very vulnerable to the world and the devil. How prepared are we to defend ourselves from our enemy who seeks to destroy us and ruin our testimony with his world system? Look at Paul's command in the book of Ephesians.

Be strong *in the Lord and in the power of His might.* (Ephesians 6:10)

Put *on the whole armor of God.* (Ephesians 6:11)

Therefore **take** *up the whole armor of God.* (Ephesians 6:13)

Stand *therefore, having girded your waist with truth, having put on the breastplate of righteousness.* (Ephesians 6:14)

And **take** *the helmet of salvation, and the sword of the Spirit.* (Ephesians 6:17)

Are we, as soldiers of the cross, putting on our defense armor and our offensive weapon, the sword known as the word of God? Most Christians are dressed not for spiritual warfare, but in the clothing of accommodation to the world system. Thus we are defeated because we do not put on and obey the Law of Messiah.

Christian Warnings

In the Law of Messiah, the Lord has given us many warnings to obey, intending to open our eyes and thus help us to have victory over our own sinful nature and the pressures of Satan's sinful world. Sadly, many believers have not taken God seriously, and have ignored the warnings about their own spiritual defeats. Look at the commands Paul has given us in the Law of Messiah with the prayer that believers will take them seriously.

Because of unbelief they were broken off, and you stand by faith. ***Do not be haughty****, but fear.* (Romans 11:20)

Consider *the goodness and severity of God: on those who fell* [context of discipline]. (Romans 11:22)

And ***be not conformed*** *to this world, but* ***be you transformed*** *by the renewing of your mind.* (Romans 12:2)

Bless *them which persecute you:* ***bless****, and* ***curse*** *not.* (Romans 12:14)

Do not be overcome *with evil, but* ***overcome*** *evil with good.* (Romans 12:21)

Make *no provisions for the flesh.* (Romans 13:14)

But ***let*** *each one take heed how he builds upon the foundation laid by Messiah.* (1 Corinthians 3:10)

Do not be entangled *with the yoke of the law.* (Galatians 5:1)

Behold, I Paul say unto you, that if ***indeed*** *you be circumcised, Messiah shall profit you nothing.* (Galatians 5:2)

Beware *of dogs,* ***beware*** *of evil workers and* ***beware*** *of false circumcision.* (Philippians 3:2)

Beware *lest anyone cheat you through philosophy and empty deceit.* (Colossians 2:8)

> **Warn** those who are unruly. (1 Thessalonians 5:14)
>
> But **know** this, that in the last days perilous times will come. (2 Timothy 3:1)
>
> A form of godliness denying its power, from such people **turn away**. (2 Timothy 3:5)
>
> You also **must beware** of him, for he has greatly resisted our words. (2 Timothy 4:15)
>
> **Beware** of the evil heart of unbelief. (Hebrews 3:12)
>
> See that you **do not refuse** Him who speaks. For if they did not escape who refused Him who spoke on earth, much more shall we not escape if we turn away from Him who speaks from heaven. (Hebrews 12:25)
>
> **Do not be carried away** by various and strange doctrines. (Hebrews 13:9)
>
> **Beware** lest you fall from your steadfastness. (2 Peter 3:17)

Throughout the epistles the apostles gave us warnings, but do we heed them or ignore them, basically saying that our wisdom is better than God's? Remember that these words of warning are commands given by our Lord through the apostles.

Deception

Unless we are anchored in the word of God, we are susceptible to being deceived by false teachers, philosophy, cults, and religionists. Deception comes in the form of truth mixed with error, with the enemy's intended purpose being to lead those astray who follow it by deception. This is very prevalent in false "Christianity" which uses enough truth to draw the unwary into their deception. The commands in these verses are also another form of warning that the Law of Messiah gives to us.

> *If any man defile the temple of God, him shall God destroy; for the temple of God is holy, which Temple you are.* ***Let no one deceive*** *himself. If any man among you seems to be wise in this world,* ***let him become*** *a fool, that he may be wise.* (1 Corinthians 3:17–18)

> *Do you not know that the unrighteous will not inherit the kingdom of God?* ***Do not be deceived.*** *Neither fornicators, nor idolaters, nor adulterers, nor homosexuals nor sodomites, nor abusers of themselves with mankind, nor thieves, nor covetous, nor drunkards, nor revilers, nor extortioners, shall inherit the kingdom of God.* (1 Corinthians 6:9–10)

> ***Be not deceived***: *evil communications corrupt good manners.* (1 Corinthians 15:33)

> ***Do not be deceived***, *God is not mocked; for whatever a man sows, that he will also reap.* (Galatians 6:7)

> ***Let*** *no one deceive you with empty words.* (Ephesians 5:6)

> ***Do not be deceived***, *my beloved brethren...* (James 1:16)

> ***Let*** *no one deceive you.* (1 John 3:7)

If we are not anchored in the Word—in the doctrine of our Lord given through the apostles—we can be and are deceived by Satan and our sinful flesh. We need to face reality; we can be easily deceived by our enemies if we are not anchored to the Solid Rock, Messiah, and His Law, the Law of Messiah.

Spiritual Discernment

These commands could also go in the section about warning. Today spiritual discernment is at an all-time low, even among believers. We desperately need spiritual discernment, because of all the false and apostate Christian teachers, pastors, and educators who have chosen to walk a carnal, humanistic, secular pathway and have laid down or thrown the Bible away. In general, our churches show very little interest in studying the Bible to know our God, for they have been so thoroughly immersed in the humanistic culture of the day. Do you exercise biblical discernment as to what you hear on television, radio, or the Internet, even from so-called pulpits?

> *Therefore **do not be unwise**, but understand what the will of the Lord is* (Ephesians 5:17)

> *Brethren, **be** followers together of me, and **mark** those who walk [so], as you have us for a pattern. For many walk, of whom I have told you often, and now tell you even weeping, that they are the enemies of the cross of Messiah.*
> (Philippians 3:17–19)

Christian Trials and Persecution

These commands in the Law of Messiah are difficult to obey, for no one enjoys trials and persecution. In our day there is much false teaching on the "prosperity gospel," which claims that all the promises in the Hebrew Scriptures were given to us. They were not given to us: they were given to national, physical, ethnic Israel. In the New Covenant, we are not promised physical blessing, although many of the prosperity preachers use that as a measure or indicator of "spirituality." To counter this, I recommend a DVD by Justin Peters, who with grace and truth confronts these people and teaches believers what they are really all about.[216] We as believers will suffer, we will be persecuted. We have been sheltered in the United States, but anti-Christian forces are making huge strides in claiming this country for a humanistic, secularistic worldview; they will tolerate anything but Christians. So prepare yourself; trials and persecution like the rest of the world receives are coming!

> *And they stoned Stephen as he was calling on God and saying, "Lord Yeshua, **receive** my spirit.* (Acts 7:59)

If your enemy hunger, ***feed*** *him; if he thirst,* ***give*** *him drink: for in so doing you shall heap coals of fire on his head.* (Romans 12:20)

Remember *my bonds* [Paul]. (Colossians 4:18)

Be not *therefore* ***ashamed*** *of the testimony of our Lord, nor of me His prisoner: but be a partaker of the afflictions of the gospel according to the power of God.* (2 Timothy 1:8)

But ***call*** *to remembrance the former days, in which, after you were illuminated, you endured a great fight of afflictions.* (Hebrews 10:32)

Remember *them that are in bonds, as bound with them; and them which suffer adversity, as being yourselves also in the body.* (Hebrews 13:3)

Count *it all joy when you fall into many different trials.* (James 1:2)

No man can say [when] *he was tempted, I am tempted of God: for God cannot be tempted with evil, neither tempts He any man: but every man is tempted, when he is drawn away of his own lust, and enticed.* (James 1:13)

Take*, my brethren, the prophets, who have spoken in the Name of the Lord, for an example of suffering, affliction, and patience.* (James 5:10)

Indeed those who endure are blessed. (James 5:11)

[Are] *any among you afflicted?* ***Let him pray****. Is any merry?* ***Let him sing*** *psalms.* (James 5:13)

But if you suffer for righteousness' sake happy are you: and ***be not afraid*** *of their threats, neither be troubled.* (1 Peter 3:14)

Think *it not strange concerning the fiery trial which is to try you, as though some strange thing happened unto you.* (1 Peter 4:12)

Rejoice *insomuch as you are partakers of Messiah's suffering.* (1 Peter 4:13)

Let none of you suffer as a murderer, thief, evil doer, or a busybody. (1 Peter 4:15)

If any man suffer as a Christian, **let** *him not* **be ashamed***.* (1 Peter 4:16)

But **let** him glorify God on his behalf. (1 Peter 4:16)

If you suffer, ***commit*** *their souls to Him.* (1 Peter 4:19)

Summary

The expanse of the Law of Messiah is all encompassing, and in this chapter I have only categorized examples of its commands underinto 23 topics.Many more categories and topics could be extracted, and I have reproduced only about half of all the imperative commands in the epistles.

There are commands that relate to spiritual gifts to the Church, to Christian anger and encouragement, and to Christian hypocrisy. There are commands (in the book of Philippians) that we are to have joy and rejoicing in Messiah because of what He has done for us, regardless of our worldly situation. There are commands as to how the Church is to treat widows, the rich and powerful, and the poor. There are commands on how we are to deal with the devil and disobedient brothers and sisters in the Lord. Other commands tell us to be consistent in our walk with the Lord. We are not to marvel that the world hates us, for it hated Messiah and we are not above our Lord. We are warned about idolatry. There are commands relating to the ministry of the Holy Spirit in our lives and commands on loving each other. There are commands on how to respond when tempted sexually, on turning away from evil, and on the proper use of the tongue. I am giving these further examples because they, and all the others that I have not pointed out, are God's commands equal to the ones I did list under the subheadings in this chapter. All His commands constitute the Law of Messiah, and must be obeyed.

You are under grace, praise God, but that grace was never given to you as a license to sin and live as you wish. Many Christians will have a rude awaking when they get to heaven and will experience great shame before Messiah at the Bema Seat. License is a total lack of understanding of the New Covenant and what God did for us out of His love for us. Being a Christian is not merely a way to escape hell; rather, it is a personal relationship with our Creator and Savior. Far too many believers today have ignored or belittled the precious blood of the Messiah and all the spiritual benefits we have which will someday blossom into rewards for the faithful, who will take up positions of authority and service to our Messiah in the eternal future order. Please take your salvation seriously, for your eternal rewards and service depend on it.

20

THE LAW OF MESSIAH AND OUR SANCTIFICATION: WHAT DOES IT MATTER?

As I worked on this manuscript, I discovered something that I had not seen before in my study of the Law of Messiah. I found that the Law of Messiah falls under the general doctrine of our sanctification, our salvation. In its simplest form, "sanctification" means being set apart by God for holy use. Sometime ago I read a very good book that deals with our sanctification in Christ. The author, Dennis Rokser, pastor of Duluth Bible Church, asks three probing questions designed for believers:

- Have you ever been saved?
- Are you being saved?
- Do you know with certainty that you will be saved?

Believers say yes, I believed and trusted in Jesus Christ as my personal Savior. For me, that was on July 23, 1960. On that day the Holy Spirit regenerated me, justified me, and sanctified me, and He will glorify me in the future. In the first stage of His sanctification He saved me from the penalty of sin. That is my justification: an act of God that occurred 59 years ago, in the past. That is stage one of God's sanctification.

I know from the promises in Scripture that my salvation 59 years ago will someday lead me to stage three of my sanctification, which will be my glorification when I will be saved from the very presence of sin here on earth. At death or at the rapture of the Church, I will leave my sinful flesh and nature behind me, and I will be made whole and complete; that will be my sanctification future, my glorification. He will conform me to the image of His

Chapter 20

Son when I go through the portals of death and stand in the very presence of my Savior and see Him face to face. My salvation then will be completed.

I have been saved (past tense), and I will be saved (future tense) as I leave this world behind and enter the presence of my God and Savior. By those two acts of God — one past, my justification; and one yet to come in the <u>future</u>, my glorification — I will have completed the first and last stages of my sanctification.

I skipped over the second stage because I want to spend a little more time on that stage. That second part of my salvation is the only part of my earthly experience in which I have some control over my final position in the eternal order.

That leads to a question: What about now, today? I live in a sinful world and I have to be on guard against my sinful nature — my flesh and my carnality — on a moment-by-moment and daily basis, a fact that the Law of Moses exposes. Not only that, I must put on the whole armor of God to be able to stand against the outside forces of the devil (Ephesians 6:10–17). We have to deal with a two-pronged attack against us: firstly our sin nature within, and secondly the forces of evil from without. These things plague all believers, and it takes a moment-by-moment, focused walk with Christ to walk in the Spirit... to walk in Christ in this present evil world. But I have a new nature given to me when I was born again, when I was regenerated and reconciled to God. He made me a new creation in Messiah (1 Corinthians 5:17). This justification, sanctification, regeneration, and reconciliation are all possible <u>only</u> because of the finished work of Messiah on the cross when He shed His blood at Calvary, thereby inaugurating the New Covenant.

What do I do with my salvation and my sanctification presently, right now, here on earth? God did not justify me in the past, nor will He glorify me in the future just to let me run uncontrolled in fleshly selfishness with complete license to live as I want in this present sinful world (Judges 21:25). This aspect of our sanctification is repeatedly ignored and violated by most Christians with no pain in our spirit. Why? In my salvation present, how do I live for Him and not for self? Today the lives of Christians suffer horribly with lack of spiritual discernment and uncontrolled living. The lives of Christians in America today are largely uncommitted to God, without accountability or responsibility before Him, the *Lord of hosts* who is *Holy, Holy Holy* (Isaiah 6:3). Many believers today go to church, participate in entertaining "worship," and listen to seeker-sensitive, nonconvicting messages with no meat to build them up spiritually, let alone build the body of Messiah. They are not discerning in doctrine, for many have fallen into doctrinal error and do not even have a clue as to their real spiritual nature before a holy God. The Church today neglects to teach believers their responsibility and accountability to walk in all spheres of life in a Christlike manner and to count the extravagant love of God and Christ for us as greatest value. Look at the words of Paul to Timothy, where he gives a brief evaluation of Christians in the last days:

> 1 *But understand this, that in the last days there will come times of difficulty. 2 For people will be lovers of self, lovers of money, proud, arrogant, abusive, disobedient to their parents, ungrateful, unholy, 3 heartless, unappeasable, slanderous, without self-control, brutal, not loving good, 4 treacherous, reckless, swollen with conceit, lovers of pleasure rather than lovers of God, 5 having the appearance of godliness, but denying its power. Avoid such people. 6 For among them are those who creep into households and capture weak women, burdened with sins and led astray by various passions, 7 always learning and never able to arrive at a knowledge of the truth, 8 Just as Jannes and Jambres opposed Moses, so these men also oppose the truth, men corrupted in mind and disqualified regarding the faith. 9 But they will not get very*

far, for their folly will be plain to all, as was that of those two men. (2 Timothy 3:1–9, ESV)

1 *I charge you therefore before God, and the Lord Jesus Christ, who shall judge the quick* [the living] *and the dead at His appearing and His kingdom;* 2 *Preach the word; be instant [ready] in season, out of season; reprove, rebuke, exhort with all longsuffering and doctrine.* 3 *For the time will come when they will not endure sound doctrine; but after their own lusts* [desires] *shall they heap to themselves teachers, having itching ears*; 4 *And they shall turn away their ears from the truth, and shall be turned unto fables.* (2 Timothy 4:1–4)

26 *For this reason God gave them up to dishonorable passions. For their women exchanged natural relation for those that are contrary to nature;* 27 *and the men likewise gave up natural relations with woman and were consumed with passion for one another, men committing shameless acts with men and receiving in themselves the due penalty for their error.* 28 *And since they did not see fit to acknowledge God, God gave them up to a debased mind to do what ought not to be done.* 29 *They are full of envy, murder, strife, deceit, maliciousness. They are gossips,* 30 *slanderers, haters of God, insolent, haughty, boastful, inventors of evil, disobedient to parents,* 31 *foolish, faithless, heartless, ruthless.* 32 *Though they know God's righteous decree that those who practice such things deserve to die, they not only do them but give approval to those who practice them.* (Romans 1:26–32, ESV)

Sadly, that is the attitude of many believers and the situation today in the Church. Let me add one more attitude that is a hallmark of the 21st-century church. Apathy reigns supreme in the hearts of even good moral believers, and the net result is that they are powerless to affect the world for Messiah. The believing Church in America is not walking in Christ, nor are they walking in the Spirit. However, God has an answer! He has also provided sanctification present, to save us from the power of sin NOW, today.

Too many believers in Messiah today have a false sense of security, thinking that because they have accepted Jesus as their Savior and have [as a possession] eternal life, that is all they need. That is true of salvation, but there is more to our eternal destiny in the new eternal order after the present heavens and earth are destroyed. Peter references the fact that many Christians deny that God once destroyed the world by water and will again destroy the world, this time by fire. Look at Peter's statements:

6 Whereby <u>the world that then was</u>, being <u>overflowed with water</u>, perished: 7 But the heavens and the earth, which are now, by the same word are kept in store, <u>reserved unto fire</u> against the day of judgement and perdition of ungodly men.

9 The Lord is not slack concerning His promise, as some men count slackness; but is longsuffering to us ward, not willing that any should perish, but that all should come to repentance. 10 But the day of the LORD will come as a thief in the night; in which <u>the heavens shall pass away with a great noise, and the elements shall melt with fervent heat,</u> the earth also and the works that are there shall be burned up. 11 <u>Seeing then</u> that all these things shall be dissolved, <u>what manner of persons ought you to be in all holy living</u> [your lifestyle] <u>and godliness</u>. 12 Looking for and hasting unto the coming of the day of God, <u>wherein the heavens being on fire shall be dissolved, and the elements shall melt with fervent heat?</u> 13 Nevertheless we, according to His promise, look for <u>new heavens</u> and a <u>new earth</u>, wherein dwells righteousness. 14 Wherefore, beloved, seeing that you look for such things, <u>be diligent that you may be found of Him in peace, without spot, and blameless.</u> (2 Peter 3:6–7, 9–14)

Chapter 20

God was longsuffering in Noah's lifetime, for God gave man 120 years to repent, but they did not, and they were destroyed by something they had never seen before: 40 days of rain! Now the 21st-century human thinks that God will not keep His promise; Peter said that in the *last days scoffers, walking after their own desire will deny* His coming (2 Peter 3:3). Think about what is in your hands, your wealth, your fame, your power, your integrity, your word, your prestige. Where do you spend your time: in sports, at the job, in your hobbies? Are you infatuated with yourself? Just remember the words of Solomon from Ecclesiastes when you devote your time to things and worship the work of your hands, or the power of your mind:

> 1 *The words of the Preacher the son of David, king in Jerusalem.* 2 *Vanity of vanities, says the Preacher, vanity of vanities; all is vanity.* 3 *What profit has a man of all his labour which he takes under the sun?* (Ecclesiastes 1:1–3).

Life moves fast, and before you know it life is over. Did all that you spent your life on prepare you for death, and did it prepare you to meet your God? Will the Father say of you *"Well done, good and faithful servant,"* or will you stand in shame before Him (I John 2:28)? My brothers and sisters in Christ, what are you spending your lives on? Are you putting spiritual treasures first, or earthly treasures that you cannot take with you and will not give you any rewards for eternity? Your sanctification in this life is in your hands: this is stage two, the Holy Spirit's ability to give you power over sin. Is that your focus?

He will create a new heaven and a new earth for His redeemed sons and daughters to dwell in forever (Revelation 21:1–2). Here is a summary of the three stages; I want you to be particularly aware of stage two.

>Stage One: Justification—Saved from the penalty of sin (past tense)

(Titus 3:5; Ephesians 2:8–9; Luke 7:50)

Stage Two: Sanctification—Being saved from the <u>power of sin</u> (present tense)
(1 Timothy 4:16; James 1:21; Philippians 2:12–13)

Stage Three: Glorification—Will be saved from the <u>presence of sin</u> (future tense)
(Romans 5:9–10; Romans 13:11; 1 Corinthians 3:15)[217]

Now, because we have been saved in the past, being justified by the work of Messiah at Calvary, there is another facet to our walk with Messiah other than knowing that our salvation keeps us from hell. God wants us to live for Him so that we can be rewarded by Him at the Bema Seat (Judgment or Reward Seat). Perhaps you have not considered future rewards. Do you think that all believers will share in the eternal order equally, on the same level? Will disobedient saints have an equal share with the apostles, with men and woman who counted their faith so precious to them that they were willing to suffer for the Name of Christ as well as be martyred for Christ? Will disobedient saints serve equally with faithful saints[& Elizabeth] [I do want these names included] who lived their lives faithfully before Christ? This is a subject that I have not heard preached on for more than 30 years: the rewards of Christ to believers who labored faithful to Him in the power of the Holy Spirit who regenerated them. We will look at two examples, one a human illustration of rewards for being faithful and then Scriptures that point to a time of rewards for faithful service.

A human illustration of the Judgment (Bema) Seat of Christ

Mr. Smith had three sons who worked with him in his business. His oldest son, Al, was a diligent worker who was never late for work and often stayed late if needed. He did whatever he was asked to do and was willing to do some of those dirty jobs that everyone else avoided. He often ate lunch with his dad and asked many questions in order to understand the business better. These frequent lunch conferences helped Al understand his father's business.

Mr. Smith's second son was Ben. Ben worked hard and was fairly dependable, but had many interests outside of work. Ben's mind was frequently on these other interests and because of them he was often unwilling to give extra time to the job. However, he got along fine with his dad, and his work was usually good.

Carl, the third son, was more of a "free spirit." Carl's definition of being on time to work was arriving within 25 minutes of starting time. His work was generally acceptable, but he made many mistakes, largely because his mind was elsewhere and also because he really didn't understand the procedures and policies of the business. The policies and procedures that he did understand seemed pretty silly to him, so he did not take them seriously. Although Carl was not "on the same page" as his father, he had no significant conflicts with him.

Mr. Smith loved his three sons dearly. Each was precious to him and he loved them equally. But when Mr. Smith got ready to retire, which son did he put in charge of his business, along with a significant pay increase and some nice perquisites? One does not need a PhD in human behavior or a master's degree in business administration to answer that question. Carl was a reluctant worker, and Ben had divided loyalties. Al knew his father and his father's business and had been faithful and diligent. Is there any doubt that the position and the perks go to Al?

Our heavenly Father loves His children dearly and equally, and the Bible is quite clear that He is not a respecter of persons (Ephesians 6:9). But when it comes to rewarding His children, He will deal with each of them fairly. Those who know Him well and who have obediently and faithfully carried on His business in this world will be rewarded in a greater way than other children who have been careless, self-focused, and unfaithful.[218]

Biblical References to Rewards at the Judgment (Bema) Seat of Christ

Look at just a few verses that teach rewards for obedience and faithfulness, as there are too many to quote them all.

> 24 *Know you not that they which run in a race run all, but one receives the prize? So run, that you may obtain. 25 And every man that strives* [competes] *for the mastery* [games exercises] *is temperate* [self-controlled] *in all things. Now they do it to obtain a corruptible crown* [wreath]; *but we an incorruptible. 26 I therefore so run, not as uncertain* [without aim]; *so fight I, not as one that beats the air: 27 But I discipline* [buffet] *my body and bring it into subjection, less when I have preached to others, I myself should become disqualified* [disapproved]. (1 Corinthians 9:24–27)

> *And now, little children abide in Him; that, when He shall appear, we may have confidence, and not [shrink away or] be ashamed before Him at His coming.* (1 John 2:28)

> 23 *Whatsoever you do, do it heartily, as to the Lord, and not unto men; 24 Knowing that of the Lord you shall receive the reward of the inheritance; for you serve the Lord Christ. 25 But he that does wrong shall receive for the wrong which he has done: and there is no respect of person.* (Colossians 3:23–25)

> 12 *Now if any man build upon this foundation gold, silver, precious stones, wood, hay, stubble: 13 Every man's work shall be made manifest* [evident]: *for the day shall declare it, because it shall be revealed by fire; and the fire shall try* [test the quality of] *every man's work of what sort* [quality] *it is. 14 If any man's work abide which he has built thereupon, he*

shall receive a reward. 15 *If any man's work shall be burned* [up], *he shall suffer loss: but he himself shall be saved: yet so as by fire.* (1 Corinthians 3:12–15)

9 *Know you not that the unrighteous shall not inherit the kingdom of God? Be not deceived: neither fornicators, nor idolaters, nor adulterers, nor effeminate* [effeminate by perversion], *nor abusers of themselves with mankind* [homosexuals], 10 *Nor thieves, nor covetous, nor drunkards, nor revilers, nor extortioners* [swindlers], *shall inherit the kingdom of God.* 11 *And such were some of you: but you are washed, but you are sanctified, but you are justified in the Name of the Lord Jesus, and by the Spirit of our God.* (1 Corinthians 6:9–11)

19 *Now the works of the flesh are manifest* [evident], *which are adultery, fornication, uncleanness* [impurity], *lasciviousness* [sensuality], 20 *idolatry, witchcraft [sorcery], hatred, variance, emulations, wrath* [outbursts of anger], *strife* [disputes], *seditions, heresies,* 21 *envying, murders, drunkenness, revellings* [carousing], *and such like: of the which I tell you before, as I have also told you in time past, that they which do such things shall not inherit the kingdom of God.* (Galatians 5:19–21)

5 *For this you know, that no whoremonger [immoral], nor unclean* [impure] *person, nor covetous man, who is an idolater, has any inheritance in the kingdom of Christ and of God.* 6 *Let no man deceive you with vain* [empty] *words: for because of these things comes the wrath of God upon the children of disobedience.* 7 *Be not ye therefore partakers with them.* 8 *For you were sometimes* [formerly] *darkness, but now are you light in the Lord: walk as children of light.* (Ephesians 5:5–8)

> *To an inheritance incorruptible, and undefiled, and that fades not away, reserved in heaven for you.* (1 Peter 1:4)

> *Wherefore, my beloved, as you have always obeyed, not as in my presence only, but now much more in my absence, work out your own salvation with fear and trembling.* (Philippians 2:12)

> *But why do you judge your brother? Or why do you set at naught your brother [regard your brother with contempt]? For we shall all stand before the judgment seat* [Bema Seat] *of Christ.* (Romans 14:10)

> *For we must all appear before the judgment seat [Bema Seat] of Christ, that every one may receive the things done in his body, according to that he has done, whether it be good or bad.* (2 Corinthians 5:10)

These verses are really self-explanatory. Each verse speak of rewards for faithful service and lists sins that will not enter the kingdom of Christ in the eternal order with the new heavens and new earth. Those sins listed will be wood, hay, and stubble and will be burned with fire, so the believer who committed these sins will have them purged by fire. Only those things done in accordance to and with the Law of Messiah because of the New Covenant will enter His kingdom.

Read Luke 19:11–27, where Yeshua gives the parable of a nobleman who gave three different amounts of money to three servants to invest. Two did well and one sat on it and did nothing. The first two were rewarded and the last servant was reprimanded. The first two were commended by the Lord—*well done, you good and faithful servant* (Luke 19:17)—and they were each rewarded. Is Jesus going to say that to all believers? No! The unfaithful servant lost the money he was given (though not his salvation), and he was reprimanded for his unfaithfulness as a servant.

Chapter 20

What Is the Bema Seat of Christ?

Over the years, three views have emerged as to what will happen at the Judgment (Bema) Seat of Christ. The first two are erroneous.

The first—erroneous—view holds that the Bema Seat does not deliver an individual personal judgment for sin, and you will not personally be punished for that sin and have to do penitence. Your salvation is secure; however, the works that you do (rather than you personally) will be judged by fire. So you may enter the kingdom with no or little to show for your lack of service in your present sanctification.

The second view—also erroneous—is that this is not a time of rejoicing, but rather a time of shame and regret that we did not serve Him better in our earthly life in our present sanctification, because of our selfishness and apathy about serving Him in righteousness by the power of the Holy Spirit.

The third (correct) view of the Judgment (Bema) Seat of Christ emphasizes the fact that each Christian must give an account of his and her life before the omniscient and holy Messiah. All the works that have been done in the energy and power of the flesh (carnality) will be regarded as worthless and no reward will be given for them. However, all the works done through the power of the Holy Spirit will be graciously rewarded because of how we served Him in our present sanctification.

This means that all believers will stand glorified before the Messiah without their sin nature. Their worthless works will be burned by fire and only their works of gold, silver, and precious stones (works done through the Holy Spirit) will remain. So each believer will be rewarded based on the justification and sanctification of his or her life through the power of the Holy Spirit and Messiah's blood sacrifice on the cross for all sin. At that Bema Seat we will stand before Him only with our new nature given to us at salvation <u>past</u>, and having been saved in our <u>present</u> life, in the quality of our service we will in the <u>future</u> be glorified. The rewards and positions will be given out based on the good works that we did on earth while we were dealing with our present sanctification.

To briefly summarize, Chafer writes concerning the Bema seat, "It cannot be too strongly emphasized that the judgment is unrelated to the problem of sin, that it is more for the bestowing of rewards than rejection or failure."[219] The emphasis is on God's motivation for rewarding His faithful servants. However, the fact is that believers have turned a deaf ear to the words of Messiah through the Apostle Paul. Today believers are more interested in having a good feeling in the church, with complacency and apathy about their faith. Here are four reasons for the lack of teaching about future rewards to believers.

1. Reason one is that in the Church it is viewed that all believers are the same and will always be the same.

2. Reason two is the diminishing of emphasis in this biblical truth; thus, the Church has shifted its focus away from rewards.

3. Reason three is the diminished teaching of the doctrine of Christ's judgment seat because it has been replaced by an emphasis on positional truth. Emphasis is only on what God has done for us, to the neglect of our living a life of love for Him because of those positional truths.

4. Reason four is because of inadequate teaching of theology concerning "good works," because good works have been associated by many as part of staying saved. However believers are instructed, because of their salvation and justification to do good works <u>because</u> they are saved, not to keep their salvation.[220]

This teaching is important because it will determine your position of service (authority in the eternal order) in the new heavens and the new earth forever, for eternity. Many believers will have mediocre jobs of service, while others will have positions of authority in their service before Messiah. There is nothing more important in relation to our time spent on earth than our faith and trust in the finished work of Messiah on the cross. The whole area of teaching faithfulness and living faithfully should trump every other endeavor on earth today.

Why Spend Time on This?

Let me refocus on the subject of this book. The Law of Moses has been rendered inoperative as a system of law to be kept: it has been laid aside and trumped by another Law. Believers in Messiah have, through the New Covenant, made themselves subject to a new law system called the Law of Messiah. Within this new law, believers are instructed on how to relate to God during our service to Him. Also, this new Law presents to believers how they are to live before fellow believers and people in general. This Law gives us exhortations, things to be aware of, things to flee from, instruction in a multitude of areas, comfort, and correction. All of these and more are designed to help us walk in Christ, and to walk in the power of the Holy Spirit, Who regenerated us to live lives that bring glory and honor to His Name. The Law of Messiah is now our focus, our motivation, a new lifestyle that believers in Messiah are to walk in during their pilgrimage through life in preparation for the eternal state. The Holy Spirit and our yielding or submitting to Him are key and are central for a victorious life in Christ on earth. This is the time, through the Law of Messiah, that He has given to us all the information that we need to walk by the power of the Holy Spirit in faithfulness and righteously before Him in love.

There are no easy step plans and no three- and five-point systems for being successful in the Christian walk. Success requires a daily, moment-by-moment surrendering and yielding of ourselves to the Holy Spirit. It is a daily conscious desire to walk in the light after the leading and guiding of the Holy Spirit in our lives. In the imperative commands of the Law of Messiah you will find your map to navigate through all the temptations and the fiery arrows that come our way, whether sent by the devil or by our own sinful nature. What we as believers are up against in our walk with Christ are our own self-centered heart desires, as James so clearly expresses:

> 13 *Let no man say when he is tempted, I am tempted of God: for God cannot be tempted with evil, neither tempts He any man:* 14 *But every man is tempted, when he is drawn away of his own lust* [desires] *and enticed.* 15 *Then when lust has conceived, it brings forth sin: and sin, when it is finished, brings forth death.* 16 *Do not err* [be deceived], *my beloved brethren.* (James 1:13–16)

Because of the temptation recognized in James, God through the Law of Messiah has given us the guidelines and the power to walk by so that we can bring glory and honor to Him in our daily lives. God has not just given us the Law of Messiah as an effective law system, He has also given us the Holy Spirit's power that we desperately need in our daily walk because we battle not only with our old nature of sin, but also with demonic spiritual forces. The entire Law of Messiah is designed by God to aid us in walking through the <u>present</u> stage of our sanctification.

Appendix

Imperative Commands

This appendix lists all the imperative commands in the Greek text that apply to the dispensation of grace. There are some commands that are personal in nature, such as when Paul asks Timothy to bring the parchments (Scriptures) and his cloak (his outer coat). Some of them are from the Hebrew Scriptures, especially from book of Acts in quotations from the Greek Septuagint (e.g., Acts 2:22 and 24). There are other incidents, particularly in the book of Acts, where the command(s) only applied to the individual addressed or to unbeliever in the narrative of the text. I did not include the Gospels except where Yeshua made reference to the future Church. In all, 497 verses are referenced, which contain 627 total imperative commands. For believers today, they carry the same weight that the law of the old economy carried.

Gospels

Matt 16:24   Then Yeshua said to His disciples, "If anyone desires to come after Me, let him **deny** himself, and take up his cross, and **follow** Me.

Matt 18:15   Moreover, if your brother sins against you, **go** and **tell** him his fault between you and him alone. If he hears you, you have gained your brother.

Matt 18:16   But if he will not hear, **take** with you one or two more, that by the mouth of two or three witnesses every word may be established.

Matt 18:17   And if he refuses to hear them **tell** it to the church. But if he refuses even to hear the church, let him be to you like a heathen and a tax collector.

Appendix

Matt 19:6 So then, they are no longer two but one flesh. Therefore what God has joined together, let not man **separate**.

Matt 28:19 Go therefore and make **disciples** of all the nations, baptizing them in the name of the Father and of the Son and of the Holy Spirit.

Mark 16:15 And He said to them, "Go into all the world and **preach** the gospel to every creature.

John 14:1 Let not your heart be troubled; you believe in God, **believe** also in Me.

John 15:4 **Abide** in Me, and I in you.

John 15:7 If you abide in Me, and My words abide in you, you will **ask** what you desire, and it shall be done for you.

John 15:9 As the Father loved Me, I also have loved you; **abide** in My love.

John 15:18 If the world hates you, you **know** that it hated Me before it hated you.

John 15:20 **Remember** the word that I said to you, A servant is not greater than his master.

John 17:11 Holy Father, **keep** through Your name those whom You have given Me, that they may be one as We are.

John 17:17 **Sanctify** them by Your truth.

Acts

Acts 6:3 Therefore, brethren, **seek** out from among you seven men of good reputation, full of the Holy Spirit and wisdom, whom we may appoint over this business;

Acts 8:22 **Repent** therefore of this your wickedness, and **pray** God if perhaps the thought of your heart may be forgiven you.

Acts 15:29 That you **abstain** from things offered to idols, from blood, from things strangled, and from sexual immorality.

Acts 16:31 So they said, "**believe** on the Lord Yeshua Messiah, and you will be saved, you and your household."

Acts 20:28 Therefore **take** heed to yourselves and to all the flock, among which the Holy Spirit has made you overseers....

Acts 20:31 Therefore **watch**, and remember that for three years I did not cease to warn everyone night and day with tears.

Romans

Rom 2:17 **Indeed** you are called a Jew, and rest on the law, and make your boast in God.

Rom 3:4 Indeed, **let** God be true but every man a liar. As it is written: "That you may be justified in your words, and may overcome when you are judged."

Rom 6:11 Likewise you also, **reckon** yourselves to be dead indeed to sin, but alive to God in Christ Jesus our Lord.

Rom 6:12 Therefore do not let sin **reign** in your mortal body, that you should obey it in its lusts.

Rom 6:13 And do not **present** your members as instruments of unrighteousness to sin, but **present** yourselves to God as being alive from the dead, and your members as instruments of righteousness to God.

Rom 6:19   For just as you presented your members as slaves of uncleanness, and of lawlessness leading to more lawlessness, so now **present** your members as slaves of righteousness for holiness.

Rom 9:33   As it is written: "**Behold** I lay in Zion a stumbling stone and rock of offense, and whoever believes on Him will not be put to shame."

Rom 11:9   And David says, "Let their table **become** a snare and a trap, a stumbling block and a recompense to them."

Rom 11:10   Let their eyes be **darkened**, so that they do not see, and bow down their back always.

Rom 11:18   Do not **boast** against the branches. But if you do boast, remember that you do not support the root, but the root supports you.

Rom 11:20   Do not be **haughty**, but **fear**.

Rom 11:22   Therefore **consider** the goodness and severity [sternness] of God: on those who fell, severity [sternness]; but toward you, goodness, if you continue in His goodness.

Rom 12:2   And do not be **conformed** to this world, but be **transformed** by the renewing of your mind, that you may prove what is that good and acceptable and perfect will of God.

Rom 12:14   **Bless** those who persecute you; **bless** and do not curse.

Rom 12:16   Be of the same mind toward one another. Do not set your mind on high things, but associate with the humble. Do not **be** wise in your own opinion.

Rom 12:19   Beloved, do not avenge yourselves, but rather **give** place to wrath; for it is written, "Vengeance is Mine, I will repay," says the Lord.

Rom 12:20 Therefore "If your enemy is hungry, **feed** him; if he is thirsty, give him to **drink**; For in so doing you will heap coals of fire on his head."

Rom 12:21   Do not **be overcome** by evil, but **overcome** evil with good.

Rom 13:1   Let every soul be **subject** to the governing authorities. For there is no authority except from God, and the authorities that exist are appointed by God.

Rom 13:3   Do you want to be unafraid of the authority? **Do** what is good, and you will have praise from the same.

Rom 13:4   But if you do evil, be **afraid**; for he does not bear the sword in vain; for he is God's minister ... .

Rom 13:7   **Render** therefore to all their due; taxes to whom taxes are due, customs to whom customs, fear to whom fear, honor to whom honor.

Rom 13:8   **Owe** no one anything except to love one another, for he who loves another has fulfilled the [Mosaic] law.

Rom 13:14   But put **on** the Lord Yeshua Messiah, and **make** no provision for the flesh, to fulfill its lusts.

Rom 14:1   **Receive** one who is weak in the faith, but not to dispute doubtful things.

Rom 14:3   Let not him who eats **despise** him who does not eat, and let not him who does not eat **judge** him who eats, for God has received him.

Rom 14:5   One person esteems one day above another; another esteems every day alike. Let each be **fully** convinced in his own mind.

Rom 14:13   Therefore let us not judge one another anymore, but rather **resolve** this, not to put a stumbling block or a cause to fall in our brother's way.

Rom 14:15   Do not **destroy** with your food the one for whom Messiah died.

Rom 14:16   Therefore do not let your good **be** spoken of as evil.

Rom 14:20   Do not **destroy** the work of God for the sake of food. All things indeed are pure, but it is evil for the man who eats with offense.

Rom 14:22   Do you have faith? **Have** it to yourself before God.

Rom 15:2   Let each of us **please** his neighbor for it is good, leading to edification.

Rom 15:7   Therefore **receive** one another, just as Messiah also received us, to the glory of God.

Rom 15:10   And again he says: "**Rejoice**, O Gentiles, with His people!"

Rom 15:11   And again: "**Praise** the Lord, all you Gentiles! **Laud** Him, all you peoples!"

Rom 16:16   **Greet** one another with a holy kiss. The churches of Messiah greet you.

Rom 16:17   Now I urge you, brethren, note those who cause divisions and offenses, contrary to the doctrine which you learned, and **avoid** them.

1 Corinthians

1 Cor 1:31 … that, as it is written, "He who glories, let him **glory** in the Lord."

1 Cor 3:10 According to the grace of God which was given to me, as a wise master builder I have laid the foundation, and another builds on it. But let each one **take** heed how he builds on it.

1 Cor 3:18 Let no one **deceive** himself. If anyone among you seems to be wise in this age, let him become a fool that he may become wise.

1 Cor 3:21 Therefore let no one **boast** in men. For all things are yours:

1 Cor 4:1 Let a man so **consider** us, as servants of Messiah and stewards of the mysteries of God.

1 Cor 4:5 Therefore **judge** nothing before the time, until the Lord comes, who will both bring to light the hidden things of darkness and reveal the counsels of the hearts.

1 Cor 4:16 Therefore I urge you, **imitate** me [Paul].

1 Cor 5:7 Therefore **purge** out the old leaven, that you may be a new lump, since you truly are unleavened.

1 Cor 6:9 Do not be **deceived**.

1 Cor 6:18 **Flee** sexual immorality.

1 Cor 6:20 For you were bought at a price; therefore **glorify** God in your body and in your spirit, which are God's.

1 Cor 7:2 Nevertheless, because of sexual immorality, let each man **have** his own wife, and let each woman **have** her own husband.

Appendix

1 Cor 7:3   Let the husband render to his wife the affection **due** her, and likewise also the wife to her husband.

1 Cor 7:5   Do not **deprive** one another except with consent for a time, that you may give yourselves to fasting and prayer...

1 Cor 7:9   But if they cannot exercise self-control, let them **marry**.

1 Cor 7:11 But even if she does depart, let her **remain** unmarried or be **reconciled** to her husband.

1 Cor 7:12 But to the rest I, not the Lord, say: If any brother has a wife who does not believe, and she is willing to live with him, let him not **divorce** her.

1 Cor 7:13 And a woman who has a husband who does not believe, if he is willing to live with her, let her not **divorce** him.

1 Cor 7:15 But if the unbeliever departs, let him **depart**; a brother or a sister is not under bondage in such cases.

1 Cor 7:17 But as God has distributed to each one, as the Lord has called each one, so let him **walk**.

1 Cor 7:18 Was anyone called while circumcised? Let him not **become** uncircumcised. Was anyone called while uncircumcised? Let him not be **circumcised**.

1 Cor 7:20 Let each one **remain** in the same calling in which he was called.

1 Cor 7:21 Were you called while a slave? Do not be **concerned** about it, but if you can be made free, rather **use** it.

1 Cor 7:23 You were bought at a price; do not **become** slaves of men.

1 Cor 7:24   Brethren, let each one **remain** with God in the state in which he was called.

1 Cor 7:27   Are you bound to a wife? Do not **seek** to be loosed. Are you loosed from a wife? Do not **seek** a wife.

1 Cor 7:36   But if any man thinks he is behaving improperly toward his virgin, if she is past the flower of youth, and thus it must be, let him **do** what he wishes. He does not sin; let them **marry**.

1 Cor 8:9   But **beware** lest somehow this liberty of yours become a stumbling block to those who are weak.

1 Cor 9:24   Do you not know that those who run in a race all run, but one receives the prize? **Run** in such a way that you may obtain it.

1 Cor 10:7   And do not **become** idolaters as were some of them.

1 Cor 10:10   Nor **complain**, as some of them also complained, and were destroyed by the destroyer.

1 Cor 10:12   Therefore let him who thinks he stands take **heed** lest he fall.

1 Cor 10:14   Therefore, my beloved, **flee** from idolatry.

1 Cor 10:15   I speak as to wise men; **judge** for yourselves what I say.

1 Cor 10:18   **Observe** Israel after the flesh: Are not those who eat of the sacrifices partakers of the altar?

1 Cor 10:24   Let no one **seek** his own, but each one the other's well-being.

Appendix

1 Cor 10:25   **Eat** whatever is sold in the meat markets, asking no questions for conscience sake.

1 Cor 10:27   If any of those who do not believe invites you to dinner, and you desire to go, **eat** whatever is set before you, asking no question for conscience sake.

1 Cor 10:28   But if anyone says to you, "This was offered to idols," do not **eat** it for the sake of the one who told you, and for conscience sake …

1 Cor 10:31   Therefore, whether you eat or drink, or whatever you do, **do** all to the glory of God.

1 Cor 10:32   **Give** no offense, either to the Jews or to the Greeks or to the church of God.

1 Cor 11:1   **Imitate** me, just as I also imitate Messiah.

1 Cor 11:6   For if a woman is not covered, let her also be **shorn**. But if it is shameful for a woman to be shorn or shaved, let her be covered.

1 Cor 11:13   **Judge** among yourselves.

1 Cor 11:24   And when He had given thanks, He broke it and said, "**Take, eat**; this is My body which is broken for you; **do** this in remembrance of Me."

1 Cor 11:25   In the same manner He also took the cup after supper, saying, "This cup is the New Covenant in My blood. This **do**, as often as you drink it, in remembrance of Me."

1 Cor 11:28   But let a man **examine** himself, and so let him **eat** of the bread and **drink** of the cup.

1 Cor 11:33   Therefore, my brethren, when you come together to eat, **wait** for one another.

Appendix

1 Cor 11:34 But if anyone is hungry, let him **eat** at home, lest you come together for judgment, and the rest I will set in order when I come.

1 Cor 12:31 But earnestly **desire** the best gifts.

1 Cor 14:1 **Pursue** love, and **desire** spiritual gifts, but especially that you may prophesy.

1 Cor 14:12 Even so you, since you are zealous for spiritual gifts, let it be for the edification of the church that you **seek** to excel.

1 Cor 14:13 Therefore let him who speaks in a tongue **pray** that he may interpret.

1 Cor 14:20 Brethren, do not **be** children in understanding; however, in malice be **babes**, but in understanding **be** mature.

1 Cor 14:26 Let all things be **done** for edification.

1 Cor 14:27 If anyone speaks in a tongue, let there be two or at the most three, each in turn, and let one **interpret**.

1 Cor 14:28 But if there is no interpreter, let him **keep** silent in church, and let him **speak** to himself and to God.

1 Cor 14:29 Let two or three prophets **speak**, and let the others **judge**.

1 Cor 14:30 But if anything is revealed to another who sits by, let the first **keep** silent.

1 Cor 14:34 Let your women **keep** silent in the churches, for they are not permitted to speak...

1 Cor 14:35 And if they want to learn something let them **ask** their own husbands at home...

1 Cor 14:37 If anyone thinks himself to be a prophet or spiritual, let him **acknowledge** that the things which I write to you are the commandments of the Lord.

1 Cor 14:38 But if anyone is ignorant, let him be **ignorant**.

1 Cor 14:39 Therefore, brethren, **desire** earnestly to prophesy, and do not **forbid** to speak with tongues.

1 Cor 14:40 Let all things be **done** decently and in order.

1 Cor 15:33 Do not be **deceived**: "Evil company corrupts good habits."

1 Cor 15:34 **Awake** to righteousness, and do not sin; for some do not have the knowledge of God, I speak this to your shame.

1 Cor 15:51 **Behold**, I tell you a mystery: We shall not all sleep, but we shall all be changed.

1 Cor 15:58 Therefore, my beloved brethren, **be** steadfast, immovable, always abounding in the work of the Lord, knowing that your labor is not in vain in the Lord.

1 Cor 16:1 Now concerning the collection for the saints, as I have given orders to the churches of Galatia, so you must **do** also:

1 Cor 16:2 On the first day of the week let each one of you **lay** something aside, storing up as he may prosper, that there be no collections when I come.

1 Cor 16:10 And if Timothy comes, **see** that he may be with you without fear; for he does the work of the Lord, as I also do.

1 Cor 16:11 Therefore let no one despise him. But **send** him on his journey in peace …

1 Cor 16:13   **Watch**, **stand** fast in the faith, be brave, be strong.

1 Cor 16:14   Let all that you do be **done** with love.

1 Cor 16:18   For they refreshed my spirit and yours. Therefore **acknowledge** such men.

1 Cor 16:20   All the brethren greet you. **Greet** one another with a holy kiss.

1 Cor 16:22   If anyone does not love the Lord Yeshua Messiah, let him **be** accursed. O Lord, **come**!

2 Corinthians

2 Cor 5:17   Therefore, if anyone is in Christ, he is a new creation; old things have passed away; **behold**, all things have become new.

2 Cor 5:20   … we implore you on Christ's behalf, be **reconciled** to God.

2 Cor 6:2   **Behold**, now is the accepted time; **behold**, now is the day of salvation.

2 Cor 6:9   … as dying, and **behold** we live; as chastened, and yet not killed

2 Cor 6:13   Now in return for the same (I speak as to children), you also be **open**.

2 Cor 6:14   Do not **be** unequally yoked together with unbelievers.

2 Cor 6:17   Therefore "Come out from among them and **be separate**," says the Lord. "Do not **touch** what is unclean, and I will receive you."

2 Cor 7:2   **Open** your hearts to us.

Appendix

2 Cor 7:11   For **observe** this very thing, that you sorrowed in a godly manner:

2 Cor 8:11   But now you also must **complete** the doing of it; that as there was a readiness to desire it, so there also may be a completion out of what you have.

2 Cor 8:24   Therefore **show** to them, and before the churches the proof of your love and of our boasting on your behalf.

2 Cor.10:7   If anyone is convinced in himself that he is Christ's let him again **consider** this in himself, that just as he is Christ's, even so we are Christ's.

2 Cor 10:11 Let such a person **consider** this, that what we are in word by letters when we are absent, such we will also be in deed when we are present.

2 Cor 10:17 But "he who glories, let him **glory** in the Lord."

2 Cor 11:16 I say again, let no one think me a fool. If otherwise, at least **receive** me as a fool, that I also may boast a little.

2 Cor 12:13 **Forgive** me this wrong!

2 Cor 12:16 But **be** that as it may, I did not burden you.

2 Cor 13:5   **Examine** yourselves as to whether you are in the faith. **Test** yourselves.

2 Cor 13:11 Finally, brethren, **farewell**. Become **complete**. Be of **good** comfort, **be of one mind**, **live** in peace; and the God of love and peace will be with you.

2 Cor 13:12 **Greet** one another with a holy kiss.

Galatians

Gal 1:8　　　But even if we, or an angel from heaven, preach any other gospel to you than what we have preached to you, let him **be** accursed.

Gal 1:9　　　As we have said before, so now I say again, if anyone preaches any other gospel to you than what you have received, **let** him **be** accursed.

Gal 1:20　　　Now concerning the things which I write to you, **indeed**, before God I do not lie

Gal 3:7　　　Therefore **know** that only those who are of faith are sons of Abraham.

Gal 4:12　　　Brethren, I urge you to **become** like me, for I become like you.

Gal 4:21　　　**Tell** me, you who desire to be under the law, do you not hear the law?

Gal 4:27　　　For it is written: "**Rejoice**, O barren, you who do not bear! Break **forth** and **shout**, you who are not in labor! ...

Gal 4:30　　　"**Cast** out the bondwoman and her son, for the son of the bondwoman shall not be heir with the son of the freewoman."

Gal 5:1　　　**Stand** fast therefore in the liberty by which Messiah has made us free, and do not be **entangled** again with a yoke of bondage.

Gal 5:13　　　For you, brethren, have been called to liberty; only do not use liberty as an opportunity for the flesh, but through love **serve** one another.

Gal 5:15　　　But if you bite and devour one another, **beware** lest you be consumed by one another!

Appendix

Gal 5:16　　I say then: **Walk** in the Spirit, and you shall not fulfill the lust of the flesh.

Gal 6:1　　Brethren, if a man is overtaken in any trespass, you who are spiritual **restore** such a one in a spirit of gentleness, considering yourself lest you also be tempted.

Gal 6:2　　**Bear** one another's burdens, and so **fulfill** the Law of Messiah.

Gal 6:4　　But let each one **examine** his own work, and then he will have rejoicing in himself alone, and not in another.

Gal 6:6　　Let him who is taught the word **share** in all good things with him who teaches.

Gal 6:7　　Do not be **deceived**, God is not mocked; for whatever a man sows, that he will also reap.

Gal 6:11　　**See** with what large letters I have written to you with my own hand!

Gal 6:17　　From now on let no one **trouble** me, for I bear in my body the marks of the Lord Yeshua.

Ephesians

Eph 2:11　　Therefore **remember** that you, once Gentiles in the flesh, who are called uncircumcision by what is called circumcision made in the flesh by hands.

Eph 4:25　　Therefore, putting away lying, "Let each one of you **speak** truth with his neighbor," for we are members of one another.

Eph 4:26　　"Be **angry**, and do not **sin**": do not let the sun **go** down on your wrath,

Eph 4:27　　Nor **give** place to the devil.

Eph 4:28   Let him who stole **steal** no longer, but rather **let** him **labor**, working with his hands what is good, that he may have something to give him who has need.

Eph 4:29   Let no corrupt word **proceed** out of your mouth, but what is good for necessary edification, that it may impart grace to the hearers.

Eph 4:30   And do not **grieve** the Holy Spirit of God, by whom you were sealed for the day of redemption.

Eph 4:31   Let all bitterness, wrath, anger, clamor, and evil speaking be put **away** from you, with all malice.

Eph 4:32   And **be** kind to one another, tenderhearted, forgiving one another, even as God in Messiah forgave you.

Eph 5:1   Therefore **be** imitators of God as dear children …

Eph 5:2   And **walk** in love, as Messiah also has loved us and given Himself for us, an offering and a sacrifice to God for a sweet smelling aroma.

Eph 5:3   But fornication and all uncleanness or covetousness, let it not even **be named** among you, as is fitting for saints.

Eph 5:6   Let no one **deceive** you with empty words, for because of these things the wrath of God comes upon the sons of disobedience.

Eph 5:7   Therefore do not **be** partakers with them.

Eph 5:8   For you were once darkness, but now you are light in the Lord. **Walk** as children of light.

Eph 5:11   And have no **fellowship** with the unfruitful works of darkness, but rather expose them.

Appendix

Eph 5:14   Therefore He says: "**Awake**, you who sleep, **arise** from the dead, and Messiah will give you light.

Eph 5:15   **See** then that you walk circumspectly, not as fools but as wise.

Eph 5:17   Therefore do not **be** unwise, but understand what the will of the Lord is.

Eph 5:18   And do not **be drunk** with wine, in which is dissipation; but **be filled** with the Spirit

Eph 5:22   Wives, **submit** to your own husbands, as to the Lord.

Eph 5:25   Husbands, **love** your wives, just as Messiah also loved the church and gave Himself for her.

Eph 5:33   Nevertheless let each one of you in particular so **love** his own wife as himself, and let the wife see that she respects her husband.

Eph 6:1   Children, **obey** your parents in the Lord, for this is right.

Eph 6:2   "**Honor** your father and mother," which is the first commandment with promise.

Eph 6:4   And you, fathers, do not **provoke** your children to wrath, but **bring** them up in the training and admonition of the Lord.

Eph 6:5   Bondservants, be **obedient** to those who are your masters according to the flesh...

Eph 6:9   And you masters, **do** the same things to them, giving up threatening...

Eph 6:10   Finally my brethren, be **strong** in the Lord and in the power of His might.

Eph 6:11 **Put** on the whole armor of God, that you may be able to stand against the wiles of the devil.

Eph 6:13 Therefore take **up** the whole armor of God, that you may be able to withstand in the evil day, and having done all to stand.

Eph 6:14 **Stand** therefore, having girded your waist with truth, having put on the breastplate of righteousness.

Eph 6:17 And **take** the helmet of salvation, and the sword of the Spirit, which is the word of God.

Philippians

Phil 2:2 **Fulfill** my joy by being like-minded, having the same love, being of one accord, or one mind.

Phil 2:4 Let each of you **look** out not only for his own interests, but also for the interests of others.

Phil 2:5 Let this **mind** be in you which was also in Messiah Yeshua.

Phil 2:12 Therefore, my beloved, as you have always obeyed, not as in my presence only, but now much more in my absence, **work** out your own salvation with fear and trembling;

Phil 2:14 **Do** all things without complaining and disputing.

Phil 2:18 For the same reason you also be **glad** and **rejoice** with me.

Phil 2:29 **Receive** him therefore in the Lord with all gladness, and hold such men in esteem;

Phil 3:1 Finally, my brethren, **rejoice** in the Lord.

Phil 3:2 **Beware** of dogs, **beware** of evil workers, **beware** of the mutilation!

Appendix

Phil 3:17 Brethren, join in following my example, and **note** those who walk, as you have us for a pattern.

Phil 4:1 Therefore, my beloved and longed-for brethren. my joy and crown, so **stand** fast in the Lord, beloved.

Phil 4:3 And I urge you also, true companion, **help** those women who labored with me in the gospel...

Phil 4:4 **Rejoice** in the Lord always. Again I will say **rejoice**!

Phil 4:5 Let your gentleness be **known** to all men. The Lord is at hand.

Phil 4:6 Be **anxious** for nothing, but in everything by prayer and supplication, with thanksgiving, let your requests be made known to God;

Phil 4:8 Finally, brethren... if there is anything praiseworthy **meditate** on these things.

Phil 4:9 The things which you learned and received and heard and saw in me, these **do**, and the God of peace will be with you.

Phil 4:21 **Greet** every saint in Messiah Yeshua.

Colossians

Col 2:6 As you therefore have received Messiah Yeshua the Lord, so **walk** in Him,

Col 2:8 Beware lest anyone **cheat** you through philosophy and empty deceit...

Col 2:16 So let no one **judge** you in food or in drink...

Col 2:18 Let no one **cheat** you of your reward...

Col 3:1   If then you were raised with Messiah, **seek** those things which are above, where Messiah is, sitting at the right hand of God.

Col 3:2   Set your **mind** on things above, not on things on the earth.

Col 3:5   Therefore put to **death** your members which are on the earth: fornication, uncleanness, passion, evil desire, and covetousness, which is idolatry.

Col 3:8   But now you yourselves are to **put** off all these: anger, wrath, malice, blasphemy, filthy language out of your mouth.

Col 3:9   Do not **lie** to one another, since you have put off the old man with his deeds…

Col 3:12   Therefore, as the elect of God, holy and beloved, **put** on tender mercies, kindness, humility, meekness, longsuffering

Col 3:15   And let the peace of God **rule** in your hearts, to which also you were called in one body; and **be** thankful.

Col 3:16   Let the word of Messiah **dwell** in you richly in all wisdom…

Col 3:18   Wives, **submit** to your own husbands, as is fitting in the Lord.

Col 3:19   Husbands, **love** your wives and do not be **bitter** toward them.

Col 3:20   Children, **obey** your parents in all things, for this is well pleasing to the Lord.

Col 3:21   Fathers, do not **provoke** your children, lest they become discouraged.

Appendix

Col 3:22 Bondservants, **obey** in all things your masters according to the flesh ...

Col 3:23 And whatever you do, **do** it heartily, as to the Lord and not to men.

Col 3:24 Knowing that from the Lord you will receive the reward of the inheritance; for you **serve** the Lord Messiah.

Col 4:1 Master, **give** your bondservants what is just and fair, knowing that you also have a Master in heaven.

Col 4:2 **Continue** earnestly in prayer, being vigilant in it with thanksgiving

Col 4:5 **Walk** in wisdom toward those who are outside, redeeming the time.

Col 4:10 ... Mark the cousin of Barnabas (about whom you received instructions: if he comes to you, **welcome** him),

Col 4:15 **Greet** the brethren who are in Laodicea, and Nymphas and the church that is in his house.

Col 4:16 Now when this epistle is read among you, **see** that it is read also in the church of Laodicea...

Col 4:17 And **say** to Archippus, "**Take** heed to the ministry which you have received in the Lord, that you may fulfill it."

Col 4:18 **Remember** my chains. Grace **be** with you.

1 Thessalonians

1 Thess 4:18 Therefore **comfort** one another with these words.

1 Thess 5:11 Therefore **comfort** each other and edify one another, just as you also are doing.

1 Thess 5:13 Be at **peace** among yourselves.

Appendix

1 Thess 5:14   Now we exhort you, brethren, **warn** those who are unruly, **comfort** the fainthearted, **uphold** the weak, be **patient** with all.

1 Thess 5:15   **See** that no one renders evil for evil to anyone, but always **pursue** what is good both for yourselves and for all.

1 Thess 5:16   **Rejoice** always.

1 Thess 5:17   **Pray** without ceasing.

1 Thess 5:18   In everything **give** thanks; for this is the will of God in Messiah Yeshua for you.

1 Thess 5:19   Do not **quench** the Spirit.

1 Thess 5:20   Do not **despise** prophecies.

1 Thess 5:21   **Test** all things; **hold** fast what is good.

1 Thess 5:22   **Abstain** from every form of evil.

1 Thess 5:25   Brethren, **pray** for us.

1 Thess 5:26   **Greet** all the brethren with a holy kiss.

2 Thessalonians

2 Thess 2:15   Therefore, brethren, **stand** fast and **hold** the traditions which you were taught, whether by word or our epistle.

2 Thess 3:1   Finally, brethren, **pray** for us, that the word of the Lord may run swiftly and be glorified, just as it is with you

2 Thess 3:10   For even when we were with you, we commanded you this: If anyone will not work, neither shall he **eat**.

2 Thess 3:14   And if anyone does not obey our word in this epistle, **note** that person and do not **keep** company with him, that he may be ashamed.

Appendix

2 Thess 3:15   Yet do not **count** him as an enemy, but **admonish** him as a brother.

1 Timothy

1 Tim 2:11   Let a woman **learn** in silence with all submission.

1 Tim 3:10   But let these also first be **tested**; then let them **serve** as deacons, being found blameless.

1 Tim 3:12   Let deacons **be** the husbands of one wife, ruling their children and their own houses well.

1 Tim 4:7   But **reject** profane and old wives' fables, and **exercise** yourself toward godliness.

1 Tim 4:11   These things **command** and **teach**.

1 Tim 4:12   Let no one **despise** your youth, but **be** an example to the believers in word, in conduct, in love, in spirit, in faith, in purity.

1 Tim 4:13   Till I come, **give** attention to reading, to exhortation, to doctrine.

1 Tim 4:14   Do not **neglect** the gift that is in you, which was given to you by prophecy with the laying on of the hands of the eldership.

1 Tim 4:15   **Meditate** on these things; **give** yourself entirely to them, that your progress may be evident to all.

1 Tim 4:16   **Take** heed to yourself and to the doctrine. **Continue** in them for in doing this you will save both yourself and those who hear you.

1 Tim 5:1   Do not rebuke an older man, but **exhort** him as a father, younger men as brothers

Appendix

1 Tim 5:3   **Honor** widows who are really widows.

1 Tim 5:4   But if any widow has children or grandchildren, **let** them first **learn** to show piety at home and to repay their parent

1 Tim 5:7   And these things **command**, that they may be blameless.

1 Tim 5:9   Do not **let** a widow under 60 years old be **taken** into the number, and not unless she has been the wife of one man.

1 Tim 5:11   But **refuse** the younger widows; for when they have begun to grow wanton against Messiah, they desire to marry.

1 Tim 5:16   If any believing man or woman has widows, let them **relieve** them, and do not let the church be **burdened**, that it may relieve those who are really widows.

1 Tim 5:17   Let the elders who rule well be **counted** worthy of double honor, especially those who labor in the word and doctrine.

1 Tim 5:19   Do not **receive** an accusation against an elder except from two or three witnesses.

1 Tim 5:20   Those who are sinning **rebuke** in the presence of all, that the rest also may fear.

1 Tim 5:22   Do not lay hands **on** anyone hastily, nor **share** in other people's sins; **keep** yourself pure.

1 Tim 5:23   No longer **drink** only water, but **use** a little wine for your stomach's sake and your frequent infirmities.

Appendix

1 Tim 6:1   Let as many bondservants as are under the yoke **count** their own masters worthy of all honor, so that the name of God and His doctrine may not be blasphemed.

1 Tim 6:2   And those who have believing masters, let them not **despise** because they are brethren, but rather **serve** them because those who are benefited are believers and beloved. **Teach** and **exhort** these things.

1 Tim 6:5   Useless wranglings of men of corrupt minds and destitute of the truth, who suppose that godliness is a means of gain. From such **withdraw** yourself.

1 Tim 6:11   But you, O man of God, **flee** these things and **pursue** righteousness, godliness, faith, love, patience, gentleness.

1 Tim 6:12   **Fight** the good fight of faith, lay **hold** on eternal life, to which you were also called …

1 Tim 6:17   **Command** those who are rich in this present age not to be haughty, nor to trust in uncertain riches but in the living God, who gives us richly all things to enjoy.

1 Tim 6:20   O Timothy! **Guard** what was committed to your trust, avoiding the profane and idle babblings and contradictions of what is falsely called knowledge.

2 Timothy

2 Tim 1:8   Therefore do not be ashamed of the testimony of our Lord, nor of me His prisoner, but **share** with me in the sufferings for the gospel according to the power of God.

2 Tim 1:13   **Hold** fast the pattern of sound words which you have heard from me, in faith and love which are in Messiah Yeshua.

Appendix

2 Tim 1:14   That good thing which was committed to you, **keep** by the Holy Spirit who dwells in us.

2 Tim 2:1   You therefore, my son, be **strong** in the grace that is in Messiah Yeshua.

2 Tim 2:2   And the things that you have heard from me among many witnesses, **commit** these to faithful men who will be able to teach others also.

2 Tim 2:3   You therefore must **endure** hardship as a good soldier of Yeshua Messiah.

2 Tim 2:7   **Consider** what I say, and may the Lord give you understanding in all things.

2 Tim 2:8   **Remember** that Yeshua Messiah, of the seed of David, was raised from the dead according to the gospel.

2 Tim 2:14   **Remind** them of these things, charging them before the Lord not to strive about words to no profit, to the ruin of the hearers.

2 Tim 2:15   Be **diligent** to present yourself approved to God, a worker who does not need to be ashamed, rightly divining the word of truth.

2 Tim 2:16   But **shun** profane and idle babblings, for they will increase to more ungodliness.

2 Tim 2:19   Nevertheless the solid foundation of God stands, having this seal: "The Lord knows those who are His," and, "Let everyone who names the name of Messiah **depart** from iniquity.

2 Tim 2:22   **Flee** also youthful lust; but **pursue** righteousness, faith, love, peace with those who call on the Lord out of a pure heart.

Appendix

2 Tim 2:23 But **avoid** foolish and ignorant disputes, knowing that they generate strife.

2 Tim 3:1 But **know** this, that in the last days perilous times will come.

2 Tim 3:5 Having a form of godliness but denying its power. And from such people **turn** away!

2 Tim 3:14 But you must **continue** in the things which you have learned and been assured of, knowing from whom you have learned them.

2 Tim 4:2 **Preach** the word! Be **ready** in season and out of season. **Convince**, **rebuke**, **exhort**, with all longsuffering and teaching.

2 Tim 4:5 But you be **watchful** in all things, **endure** afflictions, **do** the work of an evangelist, **fulfill** your ministry.

2 Tim 4:9 Be **diligent** to come to me quickly.

2 Tim 4:11 **Get** Mark and **bring** him with you, for he is useful to me for ministry.

2 Tim 4:15 You also must **beware** of him, for he has greatly resisted our words.

2 Tim 4:19 **Greet** Prisca and Aquila, and the household of Onesiphorus.

2 Tim 4:21 **Do** your utmost to come before winter.

Titus

Titus 1:13 Therefore **rebuke** them sharply, that they may be sound in the faith.

Titus 2:1 But as for you, **speak** the things which are proper for sound doctrine.

Titus 2:6 Likewise, **exhort** the young men to be sober minded.

Titus 2:15 **Speak** these things, **exhort**, and **rebuke** with all authority. Let no one **despise** you.

Titus 3:1 **Remind** them to be subject to rulers and authorities, to obey, to be ready for every good work.

Titus 3:9 But **avoid** foolish disputes, genealogies, contentions, and striving about the law; for they are unprofitable and useless.

Titus 3:10 **Reject** a divisive man after the first and second admonition.

Titus 3:14 And let our people also **learn** to maintain good works, to meet urgent needs, that they may not be unfruitful.

Titus 3:15 **Greet** those who love us in the faith. Grace be with you all.

Philemon

Phil 12 I am sending him back. You therefore **receive** him, that is, my own heart.

Phil 17 If then you count me as a partner, **receive** him as you would me.

Phil 18 But if he has wronged you or owes anything, put that on my **account**.

Phil 20 Yes, brother, let me have joy from you in the Lord; **refresh** my heart in the Lord.

Phil 22 But, meanwhile, also **prepare** a guest room for me, for I trust that through your prayers I shall be granted to you.

Appendix

Hebrews

Heb 1:6   But when He again brings the firstborn into the world, He says: "Let all the angels of God **worship** Him."

Heb 1:13   But to which of the angels has He ever said: "**Sit** at My right hand, till I make Your enemies Your footstool"?

Heb 3:1   Therefore, holy brethren, partakers of the heavenly calling, **consider** the Apostle and High Priest of our confession.

Heb 3:12   **Beware**, brethren, lest there be in any of you an evil heart of unbelief in departing from the living God.

Heb 3:13   But **exhort** one another daily, while it is called "today," lest any of you be hardened through the deceitfulness of sin.

Heb 6:10   For God is not unjust to forget your work and labor of live which you have **shown** to ward His name, in that you have ministered to the saints, and do minister.

Heb 7:4   Now **consider** how great this man was, to whom even the patriarch Abraham gave a tenth of the spoils.

Heb 8:5   **See** that you make all things according to the pattern shown you on the mountain.

Heb 8:8   Because finding fault with them, He says: **Behold**, the days are coming, say the Lord, when I will make a new covenant with the house of Israel and with the house of Judah.

Heb 8:11   None of them shall teach his neighbor, and none his brother, saying, **Know** the Lord, for all shall know Me, from the least of them to the greatest of them.

Heb 10:7   "Then I said, **Behold**, I have come (in the volume of the book it is written of Me) to do Your will, O God.

Heb 10:9 Then He said, "**Behold**, I have come to do Your will, O God.

Heb 10:32 But **recall** the former days in which, after you were illuminated, you endured a great struggle with sufferings

Heb 12:3 For **consider** Him who endured such hostility from sinners against Himself, lest you become weary and discouraged in your souls.

Heb 12:5 My son, do not **despise** the chastening of the Lord, nor be discouraged when you are rebuked by Him.

Heb 12:12 Therefore **strengthen** the hands which hang down, and the feeble knees

Heb 12:13 And **make** straight paths for your feet, so that what is lame may not be dislocated, but rather be healed.

Heb 12:14 **Pursue** peace with all people, and holiness, without which no one will see the Lord.

Heb 12:25 **See** that you do not refuse Him who speaks.

Heb 13:1 Let brotherly love **continue**.

Heb 13:2 **Do** not forget to entertain strangers, for by so doing some have unwittingly entertained angels.

Heb 13:3 **Remember** the prisoners as if chained with them, those who are mistreated, since you yourselves are in the body also.

Heb 13:7 **Remember** those who rule over you, who have spoken the word of God to you, whose faith **follow**, considering the outcome of their conduct.

Heb 13:9 Do not be **carried** about with various and strange doctrines.

Heb 13:16 But do not **forget** to do good and to share, for with such sacrifices God is well pleased.

Heb 13:17 **Obey** those who rule over you, and be **submissive**, for they watch out for your souls, as those who must give account. Let them do so with joy and now with grief, for that would be unprofitable for you.

Heb 13:18 **Pray** for us; for we are confident that we have a good conscience, in all things desiring to live honorably.

Heb 13:22 And I appeal to you, brethren, **bear** with the word of exhortation, for I have written to you in few words.

Heb 13:23 **Know** that our brother Timothy has been set free, with whom I shall see you if he comes shortly.

Heb 13:24 **Greet** all those who rule over you, and all the saints.

James

James 1:2 My brethren, **count** it all joy when you fall into various trials.

James 1:4 But let patience **have** its perfect work, that you may be perfect and complete, lacking nothing.

James 1:5 If any of you lacks wisdom, let him **ask** of God, who gives to all liberally and without reproach, and it will be given to him.

James 1:6 But let him **ask** in faith, with no doubting, for he who doubts is like a wave of the sea driven and tossed by the wind.

James 1:7 For let not that man **suppose** that he will receive anything from the Lord.

James 1:9 Let the lowly brother **glory** in his exaltation.

James 1:13 Let no one **say** when he is tempted, "I am tempted by God"; for God cannot be tempted by evil, nor does He Himself tempt anyone.

James 1:16 Do not be **deceived**, my beloved brethren.

James 1:19 So then, my beloved brethren, let every man **be** swift to hear, slow to speak, slow to wrath.

James 1:21 Therefore lay aside all filthiness and overflow of wickedness, and **receive** with meekness the implanted word, which is able to save your souls.

James 1:22 But **be** doers of the word, and not hearers only, deceiving yourselves.

James 2:1 My brethren, do not **hold** the faith of our Lord Yeshua Messiah, the Lord of Glory, with partiality.

James 2:3 And you pay attention to the one wearing the fine clothes and say to him, "You **sit** here in a good place," and say to the poor man, "You **stand** there," or, "**sit** here at my footstool."

James 2:5 **Listen**, my beloved brethren: Has God not chosen the poor of this world to be in faith and heirs of the kingdom which He promised to those who love Him?

James 2:12 So **speak** and so **do** as those who will be judged by the law of liberty.

James 2:16 And one of you says to them, "**Depart** in peace, be **warmed** and **filled**," but you do not give them the things which are needed for the body, what does it profit?

James 2:18 **Show** me your faith without your works, and I will show you my faith by my works.

Appendix

James 3:1   My brethren, let not many of you **become** teachers, knowing that we shall receive a stricter judgment.

James 3:3   **Indeed**, we put bit in horses' mouths that they may obey us, and we turn their whole body.

James 3:4   **Look** also at ships: although they are so large and are driven by fierce winds, they are turned by a very small rudder wherever the pilot desires.

James 3:5   **See** how great a forest a little fire kindles!

James 3:13   Let him **show** by good conduct that his words are done in the meekness of wisdom.

James 3:14   But if you have bitter envying and self-seeking in your hearts, do not **boast** and **lie** against the truth.

James 4:7   Therefore **submit** to God. **Resist** the devil and he will flee from you.

James 4:8   **Draw** near to God and He will draw near to you. **Cleanse** your hands, you sinners; and **purify** your hearts, you double minded.

James 4:9   **Lament** and **mourn** and **weep**! Let your laughter be **turned** to mourning and your joy to gloom.

James 4:10   **Humble** yourselves in the sight of the Lord, and He will lift you up.

James 4:11   Do not **speak** evil of one another, brethren …

James 4:13   **Come** now, you who say, "Today or tomorrow we will go to such and such a city, spend a year there, buy and sell, and make a profit."

James 5:1   **Come** now, you rich, weep and howl for your miseries that are coming upon you!

James 5:7 Therefore be **patient**, brethren, until the coming of the Lord. See how the farmer waits for the precious fruit of the earth, waiting patiently for it until it receives the early and latter rain.

James 5:8 You also **be patient**. **Establish** your hearts, for the coming of the Lord is at hand.

James 5:9 Do not **grumble** against one another, brethren, lest you be condemned. **Behold**, the Judge stands at the door!

James 5:10 My brethren, **take** the prophets, who spoke in the name of the Lord, as an example of suffering and patience.

James 5:11 **Indeed** we count them blessed who endure.

James 5:12 But above all, my brethren, do not **swear**, either by heaven or by earth or with any other oath. But let your "Yes" **be** "Yes," and your "no," "no," lest you fall into judgment.

James 5:13 Is anyone among you suffering? Let him **pray**. Is anyone cheerful? Let him **sing** psalms.

James 5:14 Is anyone among you sick? **Let** him **call** for the elders of the church, and let them **pray** over him, anointing him with oil in the name of the Lord.

James 5:16 **Confess** your trespasses to one another, and **pray** for one another, that you may be healed.

James 5:20 Let him **know** that he who turns a sinner from the error of his way will save a soul from death and cover a multitude of sins.

1 Peter

1 Peter 1:13 Therefore gird up the loins of your mind, be sober, and rest your **hope** fully upon the grace that is to be brought to you at the revelation of Yeshua Messiah.

Appendix

1 Peter 1:15   But as He who called you is holy, you also **be** holy in all your conduct.

1 Peter 1:16   Because it is written, "**Be** holy, for I am holy."

1 Peter 1:17   … **conduct** yourselves throughout the time of your stay here in fear.

1 Peter 1:22   … **love** one another fervently with a pure heart.

1 Peter 2:2   As newborn babes, **desire** the pure milk of the word, that you may grow thereby.

1 Peter 2:6   "**Behold**, I lay in Zion a chief cornerstone, elect, precious, and he who believes on Him will by no means be put to shame."

1 Peter 2:13   Therefore **submit** yourselves to every ordinance of man for the Lord's sake, whether to the king as supreme.

1 Peter 2:17   **Honor** all people. **Love** the brotherhood. **Fear** God. **Honor** the king.

1 Peter 3:3   Do not let your adornment **be** merely outward, arranging the hair, wearing gold, or putting on fine apparel.

1 Peter 3:10   For he who would love life and see good days, let him **refrain** his tongue from evil, and his lips from speaking deceit.

1 Peter 3:11   Let him **turn** away from evil and **do** good; Let him **seek** peace and **pursue** it.

1 Peter 3:14   "And do not be **afraid** of their threats, nor be troubled."

1 Peter 3:15   But **sanctify** the Lord God in your hearts, and always be ready to give a defense to everyone who asks you a reason for the hope that is in you, with meekness and fear.

1 Peter 4:1   Therefore, since Messiah suffered for us in the flesh, **arm** yourselves also with the same mind, for he who has suffered in the flesh has ceased from sin,

1 Peter 4:7   But the end of all things is at hand; therefore be **serious** and **watchful** in your prayers.

1 Peter 4:12 Beloved, do not **think** it strange concerning the fiery trial which is to try you, as though some strange thing happened to you.

1 Peter 4:13 But **rejoice** to the extent that you partake of Messiah's sufferings, that when His glory is revealed, you may also be glad with exceeding joy.

1 Peter 4:15 But let none of you **suffer** as a murderer, a thief, an evildoer, or as a busybody in other people's matters.

1 Peter 4:16 Yet if anyone suffers as a Christian, let him not be **ashamed**, but let him **glorify** God in this matter.

1 Peter 4:19 Therefore let those who suffer according to the will of God **commit** their souls to Him in doing good, as to a faithful Creator.

1 Peter 5:2   **Shepherd** the flock of God which is among you, serving as overseers, not by compulsion but willingly, not for dishonest gain but eagerly.

1 Peter 5:5   Likewise you younger people, **submit** yourselves to your elders. Yes, all of you be submissive to one another, and be **clothed** with humility …

1 Peter 5:6   Therefore **humble** yourselves under the mighty hand of God, that He may exalt you in due time.

1 Peter 5:8   Be **sober**, be **vigilant**; because your adversary the devil walks about like a roaring lion, seeking whom he may devour.

1 Peter 5:9   **Resist** him, steadfast in the faith, knowing that the same sufferings are experienced by your brotherhood in the world.

1 Peter 5:14   **Greet** one another with a kiss of love.

2 Peter

2 Peter 1:5   But also for this very reason, giving all diligence, **add** to your faith virtue, to virtue knowledge …

2 Peter 1:10   Therefore, brethren, be even more **diligent** to make your call and election sure, for if you do these things you will never stumble.

2 Peter 3:8   But, beloved, do not **forget** this one thing, that with the Lord one day is as a thousand years, and a thousand years as one day.

2 Peter 3:14   Therefore, beloved, looking forward to these things, be **diligent** to be found by Him in peace, without spot and blameless

2 Peter 3:15   And **consider** that the longsuffering of our Lord is salvation…

2 Peter 3:17   You therefore, beloved, since you know this beforehand, **beware** lest you also fall from your own steadfastness, being led away with the error of the wicked.

2 Peter 3:18   But **grow** in the grace and knowledge of our Lord and Saviour Yeshua Messiah.

1 John

1 John 2:15   Do not **love** the world or the things in the world.

1 John 2:24   Therefore let that **abide** in you which you heard from the beginning.

1 John 2:27   But the anointing which you have received from Him abides in you, and you do not need that anyone teach you; but as the same anointing teaches you concerning all things, and is true, and is not a lie, and just as it has taught you, you will **abide** in Him.

1 John 2:28   And now, little children, **abide** in Him, that when He appears, we may have confidence and not be ashamed before Him at His coming.

1 John 3:1   **Behold** what manner of love the Father has bestowed on us, that we should be called children of God!

1 John 3:7   Little children, let no one **deceive** you.

1 John 3:13   Do not **marvel**, my brethren, if the world hates you.

1 John 4:1   Beloved, do not believe every spirit, but **test** the spirits, whether they are of God; because many false prophets have gone out into the world.

1 John 4:2   By this you **know** the Spirit of God: Every spirit that confesses that Yeshua Messiah has come in the flesh is of God,

1 John 5:21   Little children, **keep** yourselves from idols.

2 John

2 John 8   **Look** to yourselves, that we do not lose those things we worked for, but that we may receive a full reward.

2 John 10   If anyone comes to you and does not bring this doctrine, do not **receive** him into your house nor **greet** him.

3 John

3 John 11   Beloved, do not **imitate** what is evil, but what is good.

Jude

Jude 14   Now Enoch, the seventh from Adam, prophesied about these men also, saying, **Behold**, the Lord comes with ten thousands of His saints.

Jude 17   But you, beloved, **remember** the words were spoken before by the apostles of our Lord Yeshua Messiah.

Jude 21   **Keep** yourselves in the love of God, looking for the mercy of our Lord Yeshua Messiah unto eternal life.

Jude 22   And on some have **compassion**, making a distinction.

Jude 23   But others **save** with fear, pulling them out of the fire, hating even the garment defiled by the flesh.

Revelation

Rev 1:7   **Behold**, He is coming with clouds, and every eye will see Him, even they who pierced Him.

Rev 1:11   "What you see, **write** in a look and **send** it to the seven churches which are in Asia …

Rev 1:17   But He laid His right hand on me, saying to me, "Do not **be** afraid; I am the First and the Last."

Rev 1:18   I am He who lives, and was dead, and **behold**, I am alive forevermore.

Rev 1:19   **Write** the things which you have seen, and the things which are, and the things which will take place after this.

Rev 2:1   To the angel of the church of Ephesus **write**, 'These things says He who holds the seven stars in His right hand, who walks in the midst of the seven golden lampstands.

Appendix

Rev 2:5 **Remember** therefore from where you have fallen; **repent** and **do** the first works, or else I will come to you quickly and remove your lampstand from its place unless you repent.

Rev 2:7 He who has an ear, let him **hear** what the Spirit says to the churches.

Rev 2:8 And to the angel of the church of Smyrna **write**, 'These things says the First and the Last, who was dead, and came to life.

Rev 2:10 Do not **fear** any of those things which you are about to suffer. **Indeed**, the devil is about to throw some of you int prison, that you may be tested, and you will have tribulation 10 days. Be faithful until death, and I will give you the crown of life.

Rev 2:11 He who has an ear, let him **hear** what the Spirit says to the churches.

Rev 2:12 And to the angel of the church in Pergamos **write**, 'These things says He who has the sharp two-edged sword.'

Rev 2:16 **Repent**, or else I will come to you quickly and will fight against them with the sword of My mouth.

Rev 2:17 He who has an ear, let him **hear** what the Spirit says to the churches.

Rev 2:18 And to the angel of the church in Thyatira **write**, 'These things says the Son of God, who has eyes like a flame of fire, and His feet like fine brass.'

Rev 2:22 **Indeed** I will cast her into a sickbed, and those who commit adultery with her into great tribulation, unless they repent of their deeds.

Rev 2:25 But hold **fast** what you have till I come.

Rev 2:29   He who has an ear, let him **hear** what the Spirit says to the churches.

Rev 3:1   And to the angel of the church in Sardis **write**, 'These things says He who has the seven Spirits of God and the seven stars ...

Rev 3:2   **Be** watchful, and **strengthen** the things which remain, that are ready to die, for I have not found your works perfect before God.

Rev 3:3   **Remember** therefore how you have received and heard; **hold** fast and **repent**.

Rev 3:6   He who has an ear, let him **hear** what the Spirit says to the churches.

Rev 3:7   And to the angel of the church in Philadelphia **write**, 'These things say He who is holy ...

Rev 3:8   **See**, I have set before you an open door, and no one can shut it ...

Rev 3:9   **Indeed** I will make those of the synagogue of Satan, who say they are Jews and are not, but lie, **indeed** I will make them come and worship before your feet, and to know that I have loved you.

Rev 3:11   **Behold**, I am coming quickly! Hold **fast** what you have, that no one may take your crown.

Rev 3:13   He who has an ear, let him **hear** what the Spirit says to the churches.

Rev 3:14   And to the angel of the church of Laodiceans **write**, 'These things says the Amen, the Faithful and True Witness, the Beginning of the creation of God.'

Rev 3:18   I counsel you to buy from Me gold refined in the fire, that you may be rich; and white garments, that you may be clothed, that the shame of your nakedness may not be revealed; and **anoint** your eyes with eye salve, that you may see.

Rev 3:19   As many as I love, I rebuke and chasten. Therefore be **zealous** and **repent**.

Rev 3:20   **Behold**, I stand at the door and knock.

Rev 3:22   "He who has an ear, let him **hear** what the Spirit says to the churches."

Total verses: 497   **Total imperative commands: 627**

ENDNOTES

1 Arnold G. Fruchtenbaum, *Israelology: The Missing Link in Systematic Theology* (San Antonio, TX: Ariel Ministries, 1994), 570.

2 Fruchtenbaum, *Israelology*, 588.

3 The old name for the covenant was the Palestinian Covenant, but current use of that name makes the reference unclear, because of the Palestinian issue in Israel with the West Bank territory. Today the term *Palestinian Covenant* refers to a call for the eradication of the state of Israel. Thus, I use the name the "Land Covenant" to avoid confusion.

4 The term *Gospel* means good news. The Good News is the death, burial, and resurrection of Jesus Christ. We receive the "Gospel" as we put our faith and trust in the finished work of Jesus Christ on the cross of Calvary. We are saved thereby; thereby absolutely no works can be done on our part to merit anything of God.

5 Charles C. Ryrie, "The End of the Law," *Bibliotheca Sacra* 124, no. 495 (July 1967): 240 (emphasis added).

6 Arnold G. Fruchtenbaum, *The Law of Moses and the Law of Messiah* (Manuscript #6) (San Antonio, TX: Ariel Ministries, 2005), 8.

7 Charles C. Ryrie, "The End of the Law," *Bibliotheca Sacra* 124, no. 495 (July 1967): 242.

8 Arnold G. Fruchtenbaum, *The Eight Covenants of the Bible* (Manuscript #21) (San Antonio, TX: Ariel Ministries, n.d.).

9 Renald Showers, *There Really Is a Difference: A Comparison of Covenant and Dispensational Theology* (Bellmawr, NJ: Friends of Israel Gospel Ministry, 1990).

10 John B. Metzger, *Israel's Only Hope: The New Covenant* (Keller, TX: JHouse Publishing, 2015).

11 Arnold G. Fruchtenbaum, *Faith Alone: The Condition of Our Salvation* (San Antonio, TX: Ariel Ministries, 201). This investigation of the Book of Galatians is highly recommended.

Endnotes

12   Geoffrey W. Bromiley, *The International Standard Bible Encyclopedia* (Grand Rapids, MI: Eerdmans, 1988), 2:163.

13   Arnold G. Fruchtenbaum, *The Sabbath* (San Antonio, TX: Ariel Ministries Press, 2012), 22–24.

14   Ken Ham, *The Lie* (Green Forest, AR: Master Books, 2006), 80.

15   All nine of these purposes come from Arnold G. Fruchtenbaum, *Israelology: The Missing Link in Systematic Theology* (San Antonio, TX: Ariel Ministries Press, 1994), 590–93.

16   Arnold G. Fruchtenbaum, *The Eight Covenants of the Bible* Manuscript #21) (San Antonio, TX: Ariel Ministries Press), 18–19.

17   Walter C. Kaiser, "God's Promise Plan and His Gracious Law," *Journal of the Evangelical Theological Society* 33, no. 3 (September, 1990): 293.

18   Dr. Fruchtenbaum has dedicated a whole book to the issue of the Sabbath. Arnold G. Fruchtenbaum, *The Sabbath* (San Antonio, TX: Ariel Ministries Press, 2012).

19   Arnold G. Fruchtenbaum, *The Eight Covenants of the Bible*, manuscript #21 (San Antonio, TX: Ariel Ministries), 19–20.

20   Richard N. Longenecker, *Paul: Apostle of Liberty* (Grand Rapids, MI: Eerdmans, 2015), 128–29.

21   For a fuller treatment on the teaching of the law being rendered inoperative, see Arnold G. Fruchtenbaum, *Israelology: The Missing Link in Systematic Theology* (San Antonio, TX: Ariel Ministries Press, 1994), 643–49.

22   Fruchtenbaum, *Israelology*, 873 74.

23   Richard N. Longenecker, *Paul: Apostle of Liberty* (Grand Rapids, MI: Eerdmans, 2015), 132–34.

24   Wayne G. Strickland, "The Inauguration of the Law of Christ with the Gospel of Christ: A Dispensational View," in Greg L. Bahnsen et al., *Five Views on Law and Gospel* (Grand Rapids, MI: Zondervan, 1996), 277.

25   Strickland, 277 (emphasis added).

26   In Greg L. Bahnsen et al., *Five Views on Law and Gospel* (Grand Rapids, MI: Zondervan, 1996), 310.

27   Steven Ger, *The Book of Hebrews: Christ Is Greater* (Chattanooga, TN: AMG, 2009), 127.

28   William D. Mounce, *Mounce's Complete Expository Dictionary of Old and New Testament Words* (Grand Rapids, MI: Zondervan, 2006), 445.

29   Kenneth S. Wuest, *Wuest's Word Studies in the Greek New Testament: Hebrews* (Grand Rapids, MI: Eerdmans, 1966), 149.

30   Raphael Patai, *The Messiah Texts: Jewish Legends of Three Thousand Years* (Detroit, MI: Wayne State University Press, 1979), 247.

31   Rabbi Itzhak Shapira, *The Return of the Kosher Pig* (Clarksville, MD: Lederer Messianic Publications, 2013), 70–74, 76, 93–94, 138–40, 146, 158. See the key phrase "Contradicts the principles of Maimonides."

32   Ger, *The Book of Hebrews*, 136.

33   Richard N. Longenecker, *Word Biblical Commentary: Galatians* (WBC 41) (Dallas, TX: Word Books, 1990), 146 (emphasis added); Richard N. Longenecker, "The Pedagogical Nature of the Law in Galatians 3:19:4–7," *Journal of the Evangelical Theological Society* 25 (1) (1982): 53.

34   A. Blake White, *The Law of Christ: A Theological Proposal* (Frederick, MD: New Covenant Media, 2010), 60 61.

35   Kenneth S. Wuest, *Wuest's Word Studies in the Greek New Testament: Galatians* (Grand Rapids, MI: Eerdmans, 1966), 110.

36   Strickland, "The Inauguration of the Law of Christ," 244–45.

37   G. Abbott-Smith, *A Manual Greek Lexicon of the New Testament* (Edinburgh, Scotland: T & T Clark, 1960), 333.

38   W. E. Vine, *Vine's Expository Dictionary of Old and New Testament Words* (Old Tappan, NJ: Fleming H. Revell, 1981), 2:264.

39   Doug Friedman, "The Mosaic Law: A New Perspective on an Old Problem," *Ariel Ministries Magazine* 21 (Winter 2016), 8–11. I would encourage every Torah-observant believer to investigate Friedman's study.

40   Mal Couch, *The New Covenant Blessings for the Church* (Clifton, TX: Scofield Ministries, 2010).

41   Arnold G. Fruchtenbaum, *Israelology: The Missing Link in Systematic Theology* (San Antonio, TX: Ariel Ministries Press, 1994), 590–93.

Endnotes

42   Andrew Murray, *Messianic Good News: The New Covenant: A Ministration of the Spirit*, vol. 62 (Wading River, NY: Messianic Good News, 2012), 4. These are two excerpts from Murray's book "The Two Covenants" taken from chapter 7 of that book. It was first published by J. Nisbet in London, 1899.

43   Murray, *Messianic Good News*, 5.

44   Murray, *Messianic Good News*, 6.

45   D. Thomas Lancaster, *The Holy Epistle to the Galatians* (Marshfield, MO: First Fruits of Zion, 2014), 110.

46   Arnold G. Fruchtenbaum, *Yeshua: The Life of Messiah from a Messianic Jewish Perspective*, vol. 3, paragraphs 110 and 114 (San Antonio, TX: Ariel Ministries Press, 2017), 76, 105–106.

47   Kenneth S. Wuest, *Wuest's Word Studies in the Greek New Testament: Galatians* (Grand Rapids, MI: Eerdmans, 1966), 1:36–1:37.

48   Wuest, 1:40.

49   Fruchtenbaum, *Israelology*, 650.

50   John B. Metzger, *Israel's Only Hope: The New Covenant* (Keller, TX: JHouse Publishing, 2015).

51   Itzhak Shapira, *The Return of the Kosher Pig* (Clarksville, MD: Lederer Messianic Publications, 2013).

52   *Talmud*: A body of Jewish civil, ceremonial, and religious law. It was the work of the Pharisees and involved three stages: the Sophim, the Tannim, and the Gemara. The time period was from after Ezra the Scribe through about 600 AD.

53   *Midrash*: An ancient commentary on part of the Hebrew Scriptures from the second century AD. Its purpose was seeking the answers to religious question from the Torah.

54   *Targum*: An Aramaic translation or paraphrase of the Hebrew Bible in the first century BC through the first century AD.

55   *Zohar*: A foundational work in the literature of Jewish mystical thought known as Kabbalah. It first appeared in Spain in the 13th century by Shimon bar Yochai (Rashbi).

56   Sages: The title *rabbi* was borne by the sages of ancient Israel.

57   Rashi: Shlomo Yitzchaki, a French Ashkenazi rabbi living from 1040 to 1105. He is very respected in rabbinic Judaism.

58   Rambam or Maimonides: Rabbi Moses ben Maimon, born in Cordoba, Spain, in 1135 and died in Fustat, Egypt, in 1204. He was a Sephardic Jewish philosopher and is the author of the 13 principles which are the true and valid principles or framework of the Jewish faith even today.

59   Shapira, *Kosher Pig*, 138.

60   Nosson Scherman & Meir Zlotowitz, *The Stone Edition: The Chumash—The ArtScroll Series* (Brooklyn, NY: Mesorah Publications, 2004), xix–xx.

61   Shapira, *Kosher Pig*, 139.

62   Shapira, 161.

63   Shapira, 86. *Yalkut* stands for Rabbi Shimon Ashkenazi.

64   Shapira, 98.

65   Shapira, 162.

66   Shapira, 162 63.

67   Shapira, 165.

68   Shapira, 185.

69   Shapira, 186.

70   Shapira, 193.

71   Shapira, 194.

72   Shapira, 195.

73   George Robinson, *Essential Judaism: A Complete Guide to Beliefs, Customs, and Rituals* (New York: Pocket Books, 2000), 265.

74   Jacob Neusner & William Scott Green, *Dictionary of Judaism in the Biblical Period* (Peabody, MA: Hendrickson Publishers, 1996), 637, 641.

75   Robert Wilkin, "What Is Free Grace Theology?" Grace Evangelical Society blog post Sept-Oct 2014. https://faithalone.org/grace-in-focus-articles/what-is-free-grace-theology/

76   Wilkin, at 27.

77   Dwight L. Moody, *Sovereign Grace* (Chicago, IL: Fleming H. Revell, 1891), 46–56.

78   Personal communications with Gary Hedrick of CJF Ministries.

79   Law of Liberty: There is a fourth verse that I did not include in this book, but that needs to understood in the light of the Law of Messiah and that is the Law of Liberty that James references in his book in 1:25 and 2:12, also see Gal 5:13.

80   In-Gyu Hong, *The Law in Galatians* (Sheffield, UK: Sheffield Academic Press, 1993), 173.

81   Kenneth S. Wuest, *Wuest's Word Studies in the Greek New Testament: Galatians* (Grand Rapids, MI: Eerdmans, 1966), 37.

82   Cherem: An example of Cherem curse in the Hebrew Scriptures was the city of Jericho which was under the cherem curse (Josh 6:17–19, 26; I Kgs 16:34), see Joshua 6–8.

83   Arnold G. Fruchtenbaum, *Faith Alone: The Condition of Our Salvation* (San Antonio, TX: Ariel Ministries Press, 2014), 13.

84   Fruchtenbaum, 13.

85   Wuest, *Galatians*, 35.

86   Dave Olander, of Tyndale Bible College and Seminary, personal communication with author.

87   Edgar H. Andrews, *Free in Christ: The Message of Galatians* (Durham, UK: Evangelical Press, 1996), 279–310.

88   Andrews, 280.

89   Andrews, 280.

90   Andrews, 286.

91   Andrews, 286.

92   Andrews, 281.

93   Andrews, 283.

94   Richard N. Longenecker, *Word Biblical Commentary: Galatians* (WBC 41) (Dallas, TX: Word Books, 1990), 242–43.

95   Longenecker, *WBC* 41, 241.

96   Longenecker, *WBC* 41, 240.

97   Ben Witherington III, *Grace in Galatia: A Commentary on Paul's Letter to the Galatians* (Grand Rapids, MI: Eerdmans, 1998), 393.

98   See Andrews, 294 96.

99   See Andrews, 293.

100   Witherington III, *Grace in Galatia*, 393.

101   Witherington III, *Grace in Galatia*, 394, quoting J. D. G. Dunn, Galatians, 299–300.

102   Andrews, 289.

103   Andrews, 298.

104   Andrews, 290.

105   Andrews, 298.

106   Longenecker, *WBC* 41, 259.

107   Andrews, 300.

108   Andrews, 305.

109   Andrews, 306.

110   David H. Stern, *Jewish New Testament Commentary* (Clarksville, MD: Jewish Messianic Publishers, 1992).

111   Stern, *Jewish New Testament Commentary*, 566.

112   Stern, *Jewish New Testament Commentary*, 569.

113   Stern, *Jewish New Testament Commentary*, 567.

114   Jot, Tittle: *Jot* is the smallest letter in the Hebrew alphabet, called a yod (y). *Tittle* is a diacritical mark, specifically the small tail on a Hebrew letter that distinguishes it from another Hebrew letter. For example, the Hebrew letters "bet" (b), "kaf" (k), "dalet" (d), and "reysh" (r) are distinguished by the tail on the bet.

115   Stern, *Jewish New Testament Commentary*, 569.

116   Arnold G. Fruchtenbaum, *Israelology: The Missing Link in Systematic Theology* (San Antonio, TX: Ariel Ministries Press, 1993), 873–74.

117   Stern, *Jewish New Testament Commentary*, 567.

118 Stern, *Jewish New Testament Commentary*, 570.

119 Arnold G. Fruchtenbaum, *The Twelve–Minor Prophets* (transcription of Fruchtenbaum's teaching from Zechariah 8 at Camp Shoshanah, _____, 20__).

120 Stern, *Jewish New Testament Commentary*, 570.

121 D. Thomas Lancaster, *The Holy Epistle to the Galatians* (Marshfield, MO: First Fruits of Zion, 2014), 21–33.

122 Arnold G. Fruchtenbaum, *Yeshua: The Life of Messiah from a Messianic Jewish Perspective*, vol. 3 (San Antonio, TX: Ariel Ministries Press, 2017), 75–76, 306–310.

123 Arnold G. Fruchtenbaum, *Yeshua: The Life of Messiah from a Messianic Jewish Perspective*, vol. 2 (San Antonio, TX: Ariel Ministries Press, 2016), 2:628.

124 Gerald F. Hawthorne and Ralph P. Martin, *Dictionary of Paul and His Letters* (Downers Grove, IL: InterVarsity Press, 1993), 544.

125 Glenn F. Yeckley, *The Ten Commandments* [tract], n.d.

126 Kenneth S. Wuest, *Wuest's Word Studies in the Greek New Testament: Galatians* (Grand Rapids, MI: Eerdmans, 1966), 165.

127 John Witmer & Mal Couch, *The Books of Galatians & Ephesians* (Chattanooga, TN: AMG Publishers, 2009), 91; Warren W. Wiersbe, *Be Free: Galatians* (Colorado Springs, CO: David C. Cook, 1975), 142.

128 Wuest, *Wuest's Word Studies: Galatians*, 165.

129 Wuest, *Wuest's Word Studies: Galatians*, 27.

130 A. Blake White, *The Law of Christ: A Theological Proposal* (Frederick, MD: New Covenant Media, 2010), 87.

131 Timothy George, *The New American Commentary: Galatians* (Nashville, TN: Broadman & Holman, 1994), 30:416.

132 Charles C. Ryrie, "The End of the Law," *Bibliotheca Sacra* 124, no. 495 (July 1967): 243.

133 White, *The Law of Christ*, 88–89.

134 Both quotes are from White, *The Law of Christ*, 88–89.

135 Thomas L. Constables, *Notes on Galatians*, www.SonicLight.com, 86.

136   Robert N. Wilkin, *The Grace New Testament Commentary* (Denton, TX: Grace Evangelical Society, 2010), 2:852 53.

137   Femi Adeyemi, "The New Covenant Law and the Law of Christ," *Bibliotheca Sacra* 163, no. 652 (October December 2006), 449.

138   Dave Olander of Tyndale Bible College and Seminary, personal communication with author.

139   Steven Ger, http://www.Ariel.org/qna.htm#!prettyPhoto?127/ Steven Ger is the Director of Sojourner Ministries.

140   Stanley N. Gundry, *Five Views on Law and Gospel* (Grand Rapids, MI: Zondervan, 1999), 343. The statement was made by Douglas Moo.

141   White, *The Law of Christ*, 83. This is a synopsis of Richard N. Longenecker's book *Paul: Apostle of Liberty* (Grand Rapids, MI: Eerdmans, 2015), 191.

142   Arnold G. Fruchtenbaum, personal correspondence with the author.

143   Merriam-Webster's Collegiate Dictionary, 11th ed. (Springfield, MA: Merriam-Webster, 2008), 38.

144   R. C. H. Lenski, *The Interpretation of 1 & 2 Corinthians* (Minneapolis, MN: Augsburg, 1961), 1049.

145   White, *The Law of Christ*, 113.

146   Andrews, *Free in Christ*, 309.

147   Gunther Bornkamm, *Paul* (New York: Harper & Row, 1971), 158.

148   Ryrie, "The End of the Law," 246.

149   Ryrie, "The End of the Law," 246.

150   Gordon D. Fee, *God's Empowering Presence: The Holy Spirit in the Letters of Paul* (Grand Rapids, MI: Baker Book House, 2009), 463–64.

151   Ronald F. Youngblood, *Nelson's New Illustrated Bible Dictionary: Corinth* (Nashville, TN: Thomas Nelson, 1995), 297–300.

152   Paul Benware, *Survey of the New Testament* (Chicago, IL: Moody Press, 1990), 192.

153   Archibald Robertson & Alfred Plummer, *The International Critical Commentary: 1 Corinthians* (Edinburgh, Scotland: T & T Clark, 1991), 191; Leon Morris, *Tyndale New Testament Commentaries: 1 Corinthians* (London, UK: Tyndale Press, 1971), 138.

Endnotes

154   Dwight L. Hunt, *The Grace New Testament Commentary: 1 Corinthians* (Denton, TX: Grace Evangelical Society, 2010), 2:740.

155   Charles Hodge, *Commentary on the First Epistle to the Corinthians* (Grand Rapids, MI: Eerdmans, n.d), 165.

156   The street of the righteous Gentiles is in Jerusalem at Yad Vashem (the Holocaust Memorial in Jerusalem). It honors Gentiles who, prompted by their conscience, chose to rescue Jewish people during the dark days of the Holocaust at the risk of losing their own lives (and some of them did). Many of you have read Corrie ten Boom's book *The Hiding Place*; ten Boom who was a righteous Gentile and also a true believer in Messiah Yeshua as her Savior.

157   Femi Adeyemi, "The New Covenant Law and the Law of Christ," *Bibliotheca Sacra* 163, no. 652 (October December 2006), 443–44.

158   Charles C. Ryrie, "The End of the Law," *Bibliotheca Sacra* 124, no. 495 (July 1967): 240.

159   Ryrie, "The End of the Law," 246.

160   James Burtchaell, "A Theology of Faith and Works: The Epistle to the Galatians: A Catholic View," *Interpretation* 17 (1963), 45.

161   Robert N. Wilkin, *The Grace New Testament Commentary: 1 Corinthians* (Denton, TX: Grace Evangelical Society, 2010), 2:740.

162   John MacArthur, *The MacArthur New Testament Commentary: 1 Corinthians* (Chicago, IL: Moody Press, 1984), 213.

163   **Depravity**: Man cannot merit anything before a holy God, because man has had sin imputed to him from Adam which all of history will unquestionably bear out.

164   **Justification** means being declared righteous by God, because of Messiah's finished work on the cross, and our acceptance of the Messiah as our personal savior (Romans 3:24–28; 5:8–10).

165   **Grace**: the means by which God is able to save humanity (all that is involved in salvation), when man puts his faith and trust in Messiah alone, and His finished work of redemption (Ephesians 2:8; Romans 3:24; Titus 2:11–15).

166   **Redemption**: the act whereby God redeems us based on Messiah's finished work on the cross, with the price being His blood (1 Peter 1:18–19; Revelation 5:9; Romans 3:24).

167 **Propitiation**: the work of Messiah that satisfies all the claims of divine holiness, righteousness, and justice, so that God is free to act on behalf of sinners (Romans 3:25; 1 John 2:2; 4:10).

168 **Blood**: the blood of the sinless Lamb of God who became my sacrifice for my sin and also the foundation for the New Covenant and the Law of Messiah.

169 **Sanctification**: literally, the point of salvation where we are set apart unto holiness. This involves my position in Messiah as well as my daily walk (1 Corinthians 11:2; Ephesians 4:1).

170 **Reconciled**: indicates that I as a sinner, an enemy of God, was accepted back by (reconciled with) God because of the finished work of Messiah on the cross of Calvary (2 Corinthians 5:17 -21).

171 **Imputation**: assignment to a person; to reckon over to one, or a setting down to one's account (Romans 5:12, 17 19).

172 **Glorification**: means that we will be like Messiah when we see him face to face. We will have a body as His, and our redemption is completed (Philippians 3:21; 1 Corinthians 15:42 57).

173 Wayne G. Strickland, "The Inauguration of the Law of Christ with the Gospel of Christ: A Dispensational View," in Greg L. Bahnsen et al., *Five Views on Law and Gospel* (Grand Rapids, MI: Zondervan, 1996), 265.

174 Roger Liebi, *The Messiah Temple* (Dusseldorf, Germany: Christlicher Medien Vertrieb, 2012), 179.

175 John MacArthur, *The MacArthur New Testament Commentary: Romans 1–8* (Chicago, IL: Moody Press, 1991), 399.

176 John Murray, *The New International Commentary on the New Testament: The Epistle to the Romans* (Grand Rapids, MI: Eerdmans, 1968), 274, 276.

177 Herman A. Hoyt, *The First Christian Theology: Studies in Romans* (Winona Lake, IN: BMH Books, 1977), 87.

178 Thomas R. Schreiner, *Baker Exegetical Commentary on the New Testament: Romans* (Grand Rapids, MI: Baker Book House, 1998), 398.

179 Robert H. Mounce, *The New American Commentary: Romans* (Nashville, TN: Broadman & Holman, 1995), 174 75.

180 Douglas J. Moo, *The NIV Application Commentary: Romans* (Grand Rapids, MI: Zondervan, 2000), 249.

181 Lewis Sperry Chafer, *Systematic Theology* (Grand Rapids, MI: Kregel, 1993), 6:274–275.

182 Moo, *NIV Application Commentary: Romans*, 248.

183 William S. Plumer, *Commentary on Romans* (Grand Rapids, MI: Kregel, 1993), 370.

184 James M. Stifler, T*he Epistle to the Romans: A Commentary Logical and Historical* (Chicago, IL: Moody Press, 1960), 135.

185 William Sanday and Arthur C. Headlam, *A Critical and Exegetical Commentary: The Epistle to the Romans* (Edinburgh, Scotland: T & T Clark, 1955), 189.

186 John R. W. Stott, *The Message of Romans* (Downers Grove, IL: InterVarsity Press, 1994), 218.

187 Steven J. Cole, "Lesson 85: How the Holy Spirit Works (John 16:12–15)," *Bible.org*, March 8, 2015, https://bible.org/seriespage/lesson-85-how-holy-spirit-works-john-1612-15.

188 Chafer, *Systematic Theology*, 6:272.

189 Rene A. Lopez, *The Grace New Testament Commentary* (Denton, TX: Grace Evangelical Society, 2010), 2:662.

190 Sanford C. Mills, *A Hebrew Christian Looks at Romans* (Grand Rapids, MI: Dunham, 1969), 238.

191 Mills, *A Hebrew Christian Looks at Romans*, 235.

192 Mills, *A Hebrew Christian*, 237.

193 Moo, *The NIV Application Commentary: Romans*, 249.

194 Moo, *The NIV Application Commentary: Romans*, 248.

195 Moo, *The NIV Application Commentary: Romans*, 249.

196 Mills, *A Hebrew Christian*, 236.

197 Mills, *A Hebrew Christian*, 237 38.

198 Arnold G. Fruchtenbaum, *The Eight Covenants of the Bible* (Manuscript #21) (San Antonio, TX: Ariel Ministries Press, n.d.); Mottel Baleston, *The Eight Covenants* [DVD] (San Antonio, TX: Ariel Ministries Press, 2008).

199   Arnold G. Fruchtenbaum, *The Dispensations of God* (Manuscript #41) (San Antonio, TX: Ariel Ministries Press, n.d.); Charles C. Ryrie, *Dispensationalism Today* (Chicago, IL: Moody Press, 1965); Renald E. Showers, *There Really Is a Difference: A Comparison of Covenant and Dispensational Theology* (Bellmawr, NJ: Friends of Israel Gospel Ministry, 1990); Mottel Baleston, *The Plan of the Ages: Dispensationalism* [DVD] (San Antonio, TX: Ariel Ministries Press, 2008).

200   Ray Summers, *Essential of New Testament Greek* (Nashville, TN: Broadman Press, 1950), 12, 35.

201   Summers, *Essentials of New Testament Greek*, 113.

202   Arnold G. Fruchtenbaum, *Thirty-Three Things: A Study of Positional Truth*, manuscript #110. (San Antonio, TX: Ariel Ministries Press, n.d.).

203   A. Blake White, *The Law of Christ: A Theological Proposal* (Frederick, MD: New Covenant Media, 2010), 2, 41–47. I am indebted to him for bringing this to my attention.

204   White, *The Law of Christ*, 44.

205   White, *The Law of Christ*, 44.

206   David Filbeck uses this as the title of his book, *Yes, God of the Gentiles, Too: The Missionary Message of the Old Testament* (Wheaton, IL: Billy Graham Center, 1994). Although I do not agree with all of Filbeck's contentions, his book is still worth reading.

207   Kenneth S. Wuest, *The New Testament: An Expanded Translation* (Grand Rapids, MI: Eerdmans, 1961), 566.

208   Tremper Longman III & David E. Garland, *The Expositor's Bible Commentary: Romans Galatians* (Grand Rapids, MI: Zondervan, 2008), 11:339.

209   Merriam-Webster Collegiate Dictionary: 11th Edition (Springfield, MA: Merriam-Webster, Incorporated, 2003), 17.

210   Charles C. Ryrie, *The Holy Spirit* (Chicago, IL: Moody Press, 1997); R. A. Torrey, *The Holy Spirit* (New York: Fleming Revell, 1927); Arnold G. Fruchtenbaum, *The Ministries of the Holy Spirit*, Manuscript #66 (San Antonio, TX: Ariel Ministries Press, n.d.); John Walvoord, *The Holy Spirit* (Grand Rapids, MI: Zondervan, 1991).

211   Arnold G. Fruchtenbaum, *The Eight Covenants of the Bible* (manuscript #21) (San Antonio, TX: Ariel Ministries Press, n.d.), 29.

212 W. E. Vine, *Vine's Expository Dictionary of Old and New Testament Words* (Old Tappan, NJ: Fleming H. Revell, 1981), 2:150.

213 Arnold G. Fruchtenbaum, *The Ten Facets of Our Salvation* (Manuscript #103) (San Antonio, TX: Ariel Ministries Press, n.d.; Robert N. Wilkin, *The Ten Most Misunderstood Words in the Bible* (Denton, TX: Grace Evangelical Society, 2012), 107–26.

214 Arnold G. Fruchtenbaum, *The Gifts of the Holy Spirit* (Manuscript #71) (San Antonio, TX: Ariel Ministries Press, n.d.).

215 John B. Metzger, *Discovering the Mystery of the Unity of God* (San Antonio, TX: Ariel Ministries Press, 2010), 341–54.

216 Justin Peters, *Clouds Without Water: A Biblical Critique of the Word of Faith Movement, Exposing the False Prosperity Gospel* (Sandy Point, ID: Justin Peters Ministries), www.JustinPeters.org.

217 See Dennis M. Rokser, *Salvation in Three Time Zones; Past, Present, Future* (Duluth, MN: Grace Gospel Press, 2013), 10.

218 Paul N. Benware, *The Believer's Payday* (Chattanooga, TN: AMG, 2002), 9–10.

219 Lewis Sperry Chafer, *Systematic Theology, Vol. 4: Ecclesiology-Eschatology* (Dallas, TX: Dallas Seminary Press, 1948), 406.

220 Per Benware, *The Believer's Payday*, 2–6.

BIBLIOGRAPHY

Abbott-Smith, G. *A Manual Greek Lexicon of the New Testament*. Edinburgh, Scotland: T & T Clark, 1960.

Adeyemi, Femi. "The New Covenant Law and the Law of Christ." *Bibliotheca Sacra* 163, no. 652 (October December 2006), 438–52.

Andrews, Edgar H. *Free in Christ: The Message of Galatians*. Durham, UK: Evangelical Press, 1996.

Greg L. Bahnsen, et al. *Five Views on Law and Gospel*. Grand Rapids, MI: Zondervan, 1996.

Baleston, Mottel. *The Eight Covenants* [DVD]. San Antonio, TX: Ariel Ministries Press, 2008.

———. *The Plan of the Ages: Dispensationalism* [DVD]. San Antonio, TX: Ariel Ministries Press, 2008.

Benware, Paul. *Survey of the New Testament*. Chicago, IL: Moody Press, 1990.

———. *The Believer's Payday*. Chattanooga, TN: AMG, 2002.

Bornkamm, Gunther. *Paul*. New York: Harper & Row, 1971.

Bromiley, Geoffrey W. *The International Standard Bible Encyclopedia*. Grand Rapids, MI: Eerdmans, 1988.

Burtchaell, James. "A Theology of Faith and Works: The Epistle to the Galatians: A Catholic View," *Interpretation* 17 (1963), 39–47.

Chafer, Lewis Sperry. *Systematic Theology, Vol. 4: Ecclesiology-Eschatology*. Dallas, TX: Dallas Seminary Press, 1948.

———. *Systematic Theology*, vol. 6. Grand Rapids, MI: Kregel Publications, 1993.

Cole, Steven J. "Lesson 85: How the Holy Spirit Works (John 16:12 15)," *Bible.org*, March 8, 2015. https://bible.org/seriespage/lesson-85-how-holy-spirit-works-john-1612-15.

Constables, Thomas L. *Notes on Galatians*. www.SonicLight.com.

Couch, Mal. *The New Covenant Blessings for the Church*. Clifton, TX: Scofield Ministries, 2010.

Fee, Gordon D. *God's Empowering Presence: The Holy Spirit in the Letters of Paul*. Grand Rapids, MI: Baker Book House, 2009.

Filbeck, David. *Yes, God of the Gentiles Too: The Missionary Message of the Old Testament*. Wheaton, IL: Billy Graham Center, 1994.

Friedman, Doug. "The Mosaic Law: A New Perspective on an Old Problem," *Ariel Ministries Magazine* 21 (Winter 2016): 8–11.

Fruchtenbaum, Arnold G. *Israelology: The Missing Link in Systematic Theology*. San Antonio, TX: Ariel Ministries Press, 1994.

———. *The Law of Moses and the Law of Messiah* (manuscript #6). San Antonio, TX: Ariel Ministries Press, 2005.

———. *The Sabbath*. San Antonio, TX: Ariel Ministries Press, 2012.

———. *Faith Alone: The Condition of Our Salvation.* San Antonio, TX: Ariel Ministries Press, 2014.

———. *Yeshua: The Life of Messiah from a Messianic Jewish Perspective.* Vol. 2. San Antonio, TX: Ariel Ministries Press, 2016.

———. *Yeshua: The Life of Messiah from a Messianic Jewish Perspective.* Vol. 3. San Antonio, TX: Ariel Ministries Press, 2017.

———. *The Dispensations of God* (manuscript #41). San Antonio, TX: Ariel Ministries Press, n.d.

———. *The Twelve—Minor Prophets.* Transcripts from Camp Shoshanah presentation, n.d..

———. *The Eight Covenants of the Bible* (Manuscript #21). San Antonio, TX: Ariel Ministries Press, n.d.

———. *The Gifts of the Holy Spirit* (Manuscript #71). San Antonio, TX: Ariel Ministries Press, n.d.

———. *The Ministries of the Holy Spirit* (Manuscript #66). San Antonio, TX: Ariel Ministries Press, n.d.

———. *The Ten Facets of Our Salvation* (Manuscript #103). San Antonio, TX: Ariel Ministries Press, n.d.

———. *Thirty-Three Things: A Study of Positional Truth* (Manuscript #110). San Antonio, TX: Ariel Ministries Press, n.d.

George, Timothy. *The New American Commentary: Galatians.* Nashville, TN: Broadman & Holman, 1994.

Ger, Steven. T*he Book of Hebrews: Christ Is Greater*. Chattanooga, TN: AMG, 2009.

Gundry, Stanley N. *Five Views on Law and Gospel.* Grand Rapids, MI: Zondervan, 1999.

Ham, Ken. *The Lie.* Green Forest, AR: Master Books, 2006.

Hawthorne, Gerald F., & Ralph P. Martin. *Dictionary of Paul and His Letters.* Downers Grove, IL: InterVarsity Press, 1993.

Hodge, Charles. *Commentary on the First Epistle to the Corinthians.* Grand Rapids, MI: Eerdmans, n.d.

Hong, In-Gyu. *The Law in Galatians.* Sheffield, England: Sheffield Academic Press, 1993.

Hoyt, Herman A. *The First Christian Theology: Studies in Romans.* Winona Lake, IN: BMH Books, 1997.

Hunt, Dwight L. *The Grace New Testament Commentary: 1 Corinthians.* Denton, TX: Grace Evangelical Society, 2010.

Kaiser, Walter C. "God's Promise Plan and His Gracious Law." *Journal of the Evangelical Theological Society* 33, no. 3 (September 1990): 289–302.

Lancaster, D. Thomas. *The Holy Epistle to the Galatians.* Marshfield, MO: First Fruits of Zion, 2014.

Lenski, R. C. H. *The Interpretation of 1 & 2 Corinthians.* Minneapolis, MN: Augsburg, 1961.

Liebi, Roger. *The Messiah Temple.* Dusseldorf, Germany: Christlicher Medien Vertrieb, 2012.

Longenecker, Richard N. "The Pedagogical Nature of the Law in Galatians 3:19:4-7," *Journal of the Evangelical Theological Society* 25, no. 1 (1982): 53–61.

———. *Word Biblical Commentary: Galatians* (WBC 41). Dallas, TX: Word Books, 1990.

———. *Paul: Apostle of Liberty*. Grand Rapids, MI: Eerdmans, 2015.

Longman III, Tremper, & David E. Garland. *The Expositor's Bible Commentary: Romans–Galatians*. Grand Rapids, MI: Zondervan, 2008.

Lopez, Rene A. T*he Grace New Testament Commentary*. Denton, TX: Grace Evangelical Society, 2010.

MacArthur, John. *The MacArthur New Testament Commentary: 1 Corinthians*. Chicago, IL: Moody Press, 1984.

———. *The MacArthur New Testament Commentary: Romans 1–8*. Chicago, IL: Moody Press, 1991.

Merriam-Webster's Collegiate Dictionary, 11th ed. Springfield, MA: Merriam-Webster, 2008.

Metzger, John B. *Discovering the Mystery of the Unity of God*. San Antonio, TX: Ariel Ministries Press, 2010.

———. *Israel's Only Hope: The New Covenant*. Keller, TX: JHouse Publishing, 2015.

Mills, Sanford C. *A Hebrew Christian Looks at Romans*. Grand Rapids, MI: Dunham, 1969.

Moo, Douglas J. *The NIV Application Commentary: Romans*. Grand Rapids, MI: Zondervan, 2000.

Moody, Dwight L. *Sovereign Grace: Its Source, Its Nature, and Its Effects*. Chicago, IL: Fleming H. Revell, 1891.

Morris, Leon. Tyndale *New Testament Commentaries: 1 Corinthians* (London, UK: Tyndale Press, 1971.

———. The Pillar New Testament Commentary: The Epistle to the Romans. Grand Rapids, MI: Eerdmans, 1988.

Mounce, Robert H. *The New American Commentary: Romans*. Nashville, TN: Broadman & Holman, 1995.

Mounce, William D. *Mounce's Complete Expository Dictionary of Old and New Testament Words*. Grand Rapids, MI: Zondervan, 2006.

Murray, Andrew. *The Two Covenants*. London, England: J. Nisbet, 1899.

———. *Messianic Good News: The New Covenant: A Ministration of the Spirit,* vol. 62 (Wading River, NY: Messianic Good News, 2012).

Murray, John. *The New International Commentary on the New Testament: The Epistle to the Romans*. Grand Rapids, MI: Eerdmans, 1968.

Neusner, Jacob, & William Scott Green. *Dictionary of Judaism in the Biblical Period*. Peabody, MA: Hendrickson Publishers, 1996).

Patai, Raphael. *The Messiah Texts: Jewish Legends of Three Thousand Years*. Detroit, MI: Wayne State University Press, 1979.

Peters, Justin. *Clouds Without Water: A Biblical Critique of the Word of Faith Movement: Exposing the False Prosperity Gospel* [DVD]. Sandy Point, ID: Justin Peters Ministries [various editions].

Plumer, William S. *Commentary on Romans*. Grand Rapids, MI: Kregel, 1993.

Robertson, Archibald, & Alfred Plummer. *The International Critical Commentary: 1 Corinthians*. Edinburgh, Scotland: T & T Clark, 1991.

Robinson, George. *Essential Judaism: A Complete Guide to Beliefs, Customs, and Rituals.* New York: Pocket Books, 2000.

Rokser, Dennis M. *Salvation in Three Time Zones: Past, Present, Future.* Duluth, MN: Grace Gospel Press, 2013.

Ryrie, Charles C. *Dispensationalism Today.* Chicago, IL: Moody Press, 1965.

———. "The End of the Law," *Bibliotheca Sacra* 124, no. 495 (July 1967), 239–47.

———. *The Holy Spirit.* Chicago, IL: Moody Press, 1997.

Sanday, William, & Arthur C. Headlam. *A Critical and Exegetical Commentary: The Epistle to the Romans.* Edinburgh, Scotland: T & T Clark, 1955.

Scherman, Nosson, & Meir Zlotowitz. *The Stone Edition: The Chumash—The ArtScroll Series.* Brooklyn, NY: Mesorah Publications, 2004.

Schreiner, Thomas R. Baker Exegetical *Commentary on the New Testament: Romans.* Grand Rapids, MI: Baker Book House, 1998.

Shapira, Itzhak. *The Return of the Kosher Pig.* Clarksville, MD: Lederer Messianic Publications, 2013.

Showers, Renald. *There Really Is a Difference: A Comparison of Covenant and Dispensational Theology.* Bellmawr, NJ: Friends of Israel Gospel Ministry, 1990.

Stern, David H. *Jewish New Testament Commentary.* Clarksville, MD: Jewish Messianic Publications, 1992.

Stifler, James M. *The Epistle to the Romans: A Commentary Logical and Historical.* Chicago, IL: Moody Press, 1960.

Stott, John R. *The Message of Romans*. Downers Grove, IL: InterVarsity Press, 1994.

Strickland, Wayne G. "The Inauguration of the Law of Christ with the Gospel of Christ: A Dispensational View," in Greg L. Bahnsen et al., *Five Views on Law and Gospel*, 229–318. Grand Rapids, MI: Zondervan, 1996.

Summers, Ray. *Essentials of New Testament Greek*. Nashville, TN: Broadman Press, 1950.

Torrey, R. A. *The Holy Spirit*. New York: Fleming Revell, 1927.

Vine, W. E. *Vine's Expository Dictionary of Old and New Testament Words*. Old Tappan, NJ: Fleming H. Revell, 1981.

Walvoord, John. *The Holy Spirit*. Grand Rapids, MI: Zondervan, 1991.

White, A. Blake. *The Law of Christ: A Theological Proposal*. Frederick, MD: New Covenant Media, 2010.

Wiersbe, Warren W. *Be Free: Galatians*. Colorado Springs, CO: David C. Cook, 1975.

Wilkin, Robert, N. *The Grace New Testament* Commentary: 1 Corinthians. Denton, TX: Grace Evangelical Society, 2010.

———. *The Ten Most Misunderstood Words in the Bible*. Denton, TX: Grace Evangelical Society, 2012.

———. "What Is Free Grace Theology?" Grace Evangelical Society blog post, September October 2014. https://faithalone.org/grace-in-focus-articles/what-is-free-grace-theology/.

Witherington III, Ben. *Grace in Galatia: A Commentary on Paul's Letter to the Galatians*. Grand Rapids, MI: Eerdmans, 1998.

Witmer, John, & Mal Couch. *The Books of Galatians & Ephesians.* Chattanooga, TN: AMG Publishers, 2009.

Wuest, Kenneth S. *The New Testament: An Expanded Translation.* Grand Rapids, MI: Eerdmans, 1961.

———. *Wuest's Word Studies in the Greek New Testament. Vol. 1: Galatians.* Grand Rapids, MI: Eerdmans, 1966.

———. *Wuest's Word Studies in the Greek New Testament. Vol. 2: Hebrews.* Grand Rapids, MI: Eerdmans, 1966.

Yeckley, Glenn, F. *The Ten Commandments* [tract]. Duncansville, PA: n.d. (Available from P.O. Box 515, Duncansville, PA 16635).

Youngblood, Ronald F. *Nelson's New Illustrated Bible Dictionary: Corinth.* Nashville, TN: Thomas Nelson, 1995.

Other Titles by John Metzger

ariel.org

Other Titles from Grace Acres Press

Available at GraceAcresPress.com
or wherever books are sold.

Growing Your Faith One Page at a Time

Resources for Cultivating Joy
Small Group—Sunday School—Personal Study

Grace Acres Press
GraceAcresPress.com
303-681-9995

www.ingramcontent.com/pod-product-compliance
Lightning Source LLC
Chambersburg PA
CBHW070043080526
44586CB00013B/900